Principles of
SAN Design

by **Josh Judd**

Second Edition

Copyright © 2005 – 2007
Brocade® Communications Systems, Inc.

Brocade Bookshelf ™
Series designed by Josh Judd

Principles of SAN Design
Written by Josh Judd
Edited by Daniel Krueger, Kent Hanson, and Josh Judd
Reviewed by the Brocade Marketing and Engineering teams
Second Edition cover designed by Brocade Marketing

Printing History
"Advance Edition" printed in June 2005
"First Edition" first printed in August 2005,
    with revisions in September 2005 and July 2006
"Second Edition" first printed in August 2007

ISBN 0-7414-2824-5

Published by:

PUBLISHING.COM

1094 New Dehaven St.
West Conshohocken, PA 19428
info@InfinityPublishing.com
www.InfinityPublishing.com
www.BuyBooksOnTheWeb.com
Toll-free: (877) BUY-BOOK
Local Phone: (610) 941-9999
Fax: (610) 941-9959

Legal Information

Brocade Corporate Headquarters
San Jose, CA USA
T: (408) 333 8000
info@brocade.com

Brocade European and Latin American Headquarters
Geneva, Switzerland
T: +41 22 799 56 40
emea-info@brocade.com

Brocade Asia Pacific Headquarters
Singapore
T: +65 6538 4700
apac-info@brocade.com

Acknowledgements

Special thanks are due to Mike Klayko and Tom Buiocchi for executive-level support.

In a few areas, concepts were adapted from slides and whitepapers prepared by Brocade Education Services and/or Brocade Marketing. Several Brocade sources were used for cross-checking references and stock-verbiage, such as a number of Brocade or classic-McData whitepapers, glossies, and solutions documents.

Jed Bleess, Jim Heuser, Lisa Guess, Steve Wynne, and Martin Skagen provided feedback on graphics. Martin Skagen and Simon Gordon provided content for the appendix. AJ Casamento provided historical information. Material was adapted from a Brocade-branded whitepaper written by Tom Clark and others.

This book would not have been possible without reviews from Thomas Carroll, Derek Granath, Martin Skagen, Todd Einck, Michael O'Connor, Mike Schmitt, Mario Blandini, Kent Hansen, Robert Snively, and Sue Wilson.

Finally, the authors would like to acknowledge the hard and often thankless work of all of the Brocade Engineering teams, without whom there would be little point in writing a book about SAN design.

About the Author

Josh Judd is a Principal Engineer at Brocade reporting to Technical Marketing. People ask what that means. Basically, it's "Senior Nerd." Besides writing, he provides support for strategic roadmap activities, new product requirements, and works with SEs, OEMs, and end-users worldwide.

At various times, he has been responsible for selecting, installing, deploying, and administering systems such as NetWare, Windows, and UNIX. There is a largish pile of certifications and a computer science degree with highest honors sitting... somewhere... maybe in a storage space? Anyway, he could probably find these things if they ever became relevant. He has at least some level of experience designing, deploying, and managing networks from every major vendor, from local to global. He has been responsible for IT architecture starting from a scratch environment and growing to the multi-national level. Somewhere in there he even acquired a bit of storage expertise.

When he first went to work for Brocade a bit over ten years ago, he was the company's senior IT technical contributor, responsible for the network, server, and desktop infrastructure. He was the first person at Brocade to hold the title "Senior SAN Architect," which means that he was one of the first full-time FC SAN designers in the world.

Josh currently lives in California, but he also travels a lot. He's editing this blurb on the train from Paris to London, for example. Go Chunnel.

About the Book

What does this book contain?

This book provides general information about storage area networks (SANs), as well as material specific to the Brocade family of products. It can be considered a reference work on the subject at large as well as being useful for customers deploying Brocade solutions. As the title implies, the focus is on general principles of SAN design, from which specific configurations may be derived by the reader, rather than simply listing case studies or examples.

Most of the book is presented in a tutorial format, and can be read linearly. However, Brocade has found that most readers are looking for both tutorial and reference material. Therefore this book is divided into different sections, each of which is focused at a different kind of reader, or the same reader on different days.

The first section contains an overview of SAN technology, a discussion of basic Fibre Channel concepts, and an introduction to Information Lifecycle Management and Utility Computing. Each chapter in this section has a flow, and it is intended to be read front-to-back, like a novel. An effort has been made to discuss products covering the range of SAN deployments, to provide a reader already in the IT field with the background to become a SAN designer.

The second section provides practical information about using Brocade products in SANs. The subjects covered include advice on network design, implementation, and management, though the primary focus is on design. It is a collection of best-practices and guidelines, and can be used either as a reference section or read as a tutorial. As before, the focus is on material that does not change much from release to release, instead of on more transient topics.

The final section has appendices with a FAQ, standards information, product architectural details, information about specific Brocade hardware and software products, and a glossary. It is exclusively intended for use as reference.

Each section has a focus, but each section also contains material pertinent to every other section. There are therefore many cross-references between sections, for users who want to "drill down" on a particular topic. Each section has many diagrams, tables, and footnotes to provide more extensive detail than could fit well into the main flow of the text.

What is new in this edition?

This is the second generally available version of *Principles of SAN Design*. Some sections were improved substantially, and bear only structural resemblance to the original. In addition to improved readability, a number of changes to technical content were made. For example, this edition:

- Added content related to McData-classic products
- Added content specific to new Brocade SAN products
- Incorporated feedback from readers and Brocade reviewers
- Added minor additional content to each chapter
- Adjusted the formatting of the book to contain the additional content within approximately the same page count

Who should read this book?

Some of the readers who should enjoy this book include:

- Anybody interested in taking the BCSD examination
- IT personnel responsible for or intending to deploy SANs
- Systems Engineers who design and deploy SANs

- OEM personnel involved in selling or supporting SANs
- Analysts who need an in-depth understanding of SANs
- Network Engineers wishing to expand their skills

What is a "BCSD" and how is one obtained?

BCSD stands for Brocade Certified SAN Designer. The holder of a BCSD must have an understanding of process of designing and implementing end-to-end SAN solutions.

From the point of view of an employee working in the storage industry, the BCSD certification provides a number of advantages. Passing the test entitles the certification holder to use the BCSD logo on their business cards and marketing materials, claim the achievement on their resume, receive discounts on Brocade Education Services classes, and gain access to the knowledge-base through Brocade Connect. The certification has wide industry recognition, giving the holder an advantage in today's competitive job market. In fact, many Brocade partners require the BCSD and/or BCFP certifications as a prerequisite for employments. To learn more about obtaining this certification, contact Brocade Education Services on the web at:

http://www.brocade.com/education_services

Where can more information be found?

There are a number of books available with introductory material on SANs such as *Practical Storage Area Networking* by Dan Pollack. *Multiprotocol Routing for SANs* by Josh Judd is a good reference for users generally familiar with SANs, who need more background on FC-FC routing, iSCSI, or FCIP. For readers interested in the emerging File Area Network (FAN) technology, the book *Introducing File Area Networks* by Josh Judd is recommended.

Information about this and other books can be found at **http://www.brocade.com/bookshelf.** Users of

Brocade products should consider joining Brocade Connect at **http://www.brocade.com/connect.** This provides access to forums, documentation, and scripts. There is a similar online community designed for Brocade partners and OEMs: **http://partner.brocade.com**.

How can errors or omissions be reported?

Feedback should be sent to **bookshelf@brocade.com**. Please include the name of the book, the edition, the publication date, and if applicable the page number and paragraph to which each comment applies. It will not always be possible to reply to such e-mails, but they will be reviewed prior to publication of the next edition.

Contents

Table of Contents (High Level)

Table of Contents (Detailed)

Table of Figures

Table of Tables

Section One

SAN Design Overview

Section Topics

- Review of SAN Basics
- Business-Oriented SAN Solutions
- Utility Computing Model
- Information Lifecycle Management
- General SAN Design Considerations

1: SAN Basics

This chapter covers the basics upon which the remainder of the book is built. This includes a discussion of what Storage Area Networks (SANs) are, why they are beneficial, and some of the protocols and products that can be used to build them. Given that most SAN design students are familiar with these concepts, this chapter just provides an overview.

Storage Area Networks

SANs are networks primarily intended to provide connectivity - usually block-level - between hosts and storage devices such as disks, RAID arrays, and tape libraries. If a network meets that definition, it is a SAN, and this could theoretically apply to a broad range of technologies including virtually all traditional network protocols such as IP/Ethernet. As a practical matter, however, SANs must meet additional requirements to be usable in the real world.

Networking protocols such as IP were designed for applications that are tolerant of packet loss, errors, and performance bottlenecks, so IP was designed with the assumption that these characteristics were acceptable. SANs, in contrast, simply *cannot* lose data, corrupt data, or run slowly for long periods of time. Applications and operating systems may be tolerant of data loss in the *LAN*, but these same applications were designed with the assumption that their *storage* would be fast and reliable. (Try pulling the LAN cable out of a Windows XP server for a few minutes and see what happens. Now try pulling out the C: drive...) This means that, as a practical matter, a SAN must be extremely high performance, and have top-tier reliability characteristics.

This book discusses many things related to SAN technology as a whole, independent of protocol. However, it *focuses* on SANs built using Fibre Channel (FC) because this is by far the most widely-deployed SAN protocol. This is in large part because Fibre Channel was designed from the ground up to meet SAN performance and reliability requirements.

With that said, it would be more accurate to define "SAN" this way:

SANs are fast, highly-reliable networks primarily intended to provide block-level connectivity between hosts and storage devices such as disks, RAID arrays, and tape libraries, most often consisting of Fibre Channel switches, routers, bridges, hosts, and storage devices.

Fibre Channel SANs are *primarily* used for host–to–storage traffic, but they do not need to carry host–to–storage traffic *exclusively*. In many cases, a SAN will also enable host–to–host and/or storage–to–storage connectivity.

For example, a SAN might be constructed primarily to allow hosts to reach storage using SCSI over Fibre Channel. (The SCSI over FC mapping is known simply as "Fibre Channel Protocol," or *FCP*.) However, the same infrastructure could allow storage devices to reach each other directly for serverless backups or volume replication. In addition, hosts could reach each other using Internet Protocol[1] over Fibre Channel (IP/FC). Hosts may use a low-latency protocol such as FC-VI for DMA inter-process communication between cluster nodes.

----

[1] IP is the standard communication method for the Internet, and IP/Ethernet is the de-facto standard for *data* network communications within enterprise IT environments. However, IP/Ethernet is almost never used for *storage* networks. That said, it is practical to use IP/FC in addition to FCP on a SAN, because in this case, the characteristics of IP are not used to *carry* storage traffic; IP packets simply co–exist on the wire with storage traffic, rather than transporting that traffic.

point of view of each host, so that the SCSI protocol layer can work exactly the same way for SAN as it does for DAS.

When today's most popular applications, operating systems, and drivers were originally written, the only thing between a host and its disk was – at most – a few meters of SCSI cabling with no other devices between. With this architecture, there was little chance of losing data, or of data flows becoming "slow" anywhere along the link. It could be assumed that such issues would never occur, so developers tended not to write robust error checking and correction mechanisms: SCSI drivers are unforgiving of network problems. They make up for this by being fast and able to use inexpensive hardware, but there are noticeable top-level impacts if error conditions or performance bottlenecks *do* occur. For example, frame loss and/or performance impairment will cause most tape drives to abort backups, or at best to go into a degraded "start/stop" mode. The way to avoid this and similar issues is to use switches and routers designed to meet SAN reliability and performance requirements.

The Fibre Channel standards were written this way, and all platforms shipped by Brocade were designed with this in mind: it cannot be assumed that nodes in a SAN will handle errors well, so – in short – there had better not be any errors. Whatever technology is used for SAN infrastructure it is critical to use the best infrastructure available in its class to ensure reliable and deterministic application behavior. This means zero frame loss in normal operation, no chance of out of order delivery, fair balancing of traffic on ports with contention, and never, ever allowing head of line blocking.

More information about designing for appropriate performance characteristics can be found in "Chapter 8: Performance Planning" starting on page 185.

HBAs and NICs

Fibre Channel Host Bus Adapters (HBAs) and their drivers provide the interface between a Fibre Channel fabric and a host OS. Modern HBAs operate at either 2Gbit or 4Gbit, and have substantial hardware acceleration to allow hosts to achieve these speeds without using up the CPU cycles which are needed for running applications.[6] Brocade offers the most cost-effective and robust HBA solution on the market for attaching Linux and Windows hosts to Brocade FC SANs.

iSCSI solutions use Network Interface Cards (NICs) instead of HBAs. While it is possible to deploy special-purpose accelerated iSCSI HBAs, as a practical matter this erodes the value proposition of iSCSI. An iSCSI HBA typically costs as much as a Fibre Channel HBA to purchase, but will run less than half as fast at best, and generally more along the lines of 75% slower. The value proposition of iSCSI is based on a trade-off between performance, maturity, and reliability vs. cost, so in the rare cases where iSCSI is used in production environments at all, it is almost always done using software drivers running on general-purpose Gigabit Ethernet NICs.

That said, Brocade and other vendors do offer hardware accelerated iSCSI NICs, as well as FC–iSCSI gateways. These can make sense for some deployments.

JBODs and SBODs

In many respects, the JBOD ("Just a Bunch of Disks") is the simplest kind of storage that can be attached to a SAN. As the name implies, there is not much to a JBOD other than,

---

[6] As a rule of thumb, it takes 1GHz of CPU to generate 1Gbit of application data. Without a hardware accelerated network interface, it takes about twice as much CPU for a given network speed, since the CPU is also responsible for protocol headers in addition to generating the application layer of the stream. This can be an expensive proposition, since it means that literally half of the performance on the host is dedicated to protocol overhead instead of being used to make its application(s) run faster. In order to ensure high performance on applications, it is therefore necessary to make sure that the SAN interface has hardware acceleration. Realistically, this caveat only applies to iSCSI at the time of this writing, since Fiber Channel HBAs all use hardware acceleration today.

Volume Managers and Virtualizers

Volume Management (VM) software and virtualizers have quite a bit in common with RAID arrays. A RAID array takes many physical disks and abstracts them: it presents LUNs that have independent characteristics from their underlying disks. Each LUN can be bigger or smaller than a physical disk. Each can be faster or slower, more or less reliable. The RAID controller allows a storage administrator to make trade offs between cost, availability, and performance. (See "RAID Arrays" on page 16.) RAID arrays are the preferred method for handling most volume management tasks, since they have high performance and reliability. Some issues related to using RAIDs for volume management include high cost, low flexibility, lack of open systems architecture, and inability to handle scenarios related to multi-array mirroring and replication.

Volume Management software usually runs on hosts instead of RAID controllers, but it provides similar functions. A volume manager takes the disk set visible to the host and abstracts it. This may be useful to provide RAID-like functionality for non-RAID systems like JBODs, or to provide a layer of abstraction above RAID systems for mirroring, replicating, or migrating data between arrays. Host-based VM solutions typically cost less than hardware RAID arrays, are better at handling multi-vendor storage environments, and are, overall, more flexible. They generally also provide a multipathing layer. However, they perform poorly, and are *very* hard to manage in large-scale installations.

Recently, another solution has started to appear: storage network-based virtualizers. Virtualization has been part of the data center lexicon since the 1960s, when mainframes were designed to "share" resources between independent programs. Virtual memory, virtual tape devices, and logical volume managers are all widely used examples of products that present a "virtual" view of a set of physical resources. Today, "storage virtualization" is often used as a catch phrase to describe many different sets of capabilities of managed storage systems.

Brocade defines storage virtualization in terms of the services it enables. Some examples of these services are:

- Volume Management – This capability enables volumes to be dynamically moved or resized, and to be more efficiently provisioned.

- Data Migration – The transparent movement of the data on storage volumes between heterogeneous devices. This capability enables applications to continue operating while their data moves between storage devices.

- Data Replication – Similar to data migration, this is the creation and continuous updating of independent copies of critical data.

- Backup Enhancement – Data can be restored to any point in time by using virtualization techniques to create a log of all changes made to a particular volume and then applying the changes to a previously created copy.

Because they sit between hosts and storage, virtualizers can handle can handle RAID-to-RAID operations such as mirroring, replication, and migration. Some virtualizers (such as the Brocade 7600 and FA-18 blade) are hardware-based and can handle full performance loads which would not be possible with host-based solutions.

The future of volume management seems to be a combination of all three approaches. Host-based software is the best approach for multipathing. RAID arrays will continue to be used to provide high-performance protected LUNs. And the network will be used to migrate data, provide array-to-array operations such as migration and mirroring, to facilitate boot-over-SAN processes, and to manage volume mappings for advanced Information Lifecycle Management (ILM) and Utility Computing (UC) solutions.

reliability. The shortcomings of IP in these respects are well known in the industry, and were a major driver behind the creation of Fibre Channel and other SAN-optimized technologies in the first place. It is not acceptable to "hit refresh" on a mission-critical database if the network drops data, and so SAN infrastructure needs to be many orders of magnitude more reliable than IP networks.

Note that it is *possible* to use IP for SAN infrastructure, and indeed Brocade offers multiple IP SAN solutions. (Such as FCIP and iSCSI, which are discussed later.) The important point is that these solutions are not appropriate for all or even most applications, and since Brocade offers SAN-optimized technologies such as FC, users should consider IP SAN offerings – even from Brocade – as a last resort.

iSCSI

iSCSI is a slowly emerging protocol for transporting SCSI across IP networks. This is similar in concept to the FC-4 mapping already provided by FCP for Fibre Channel.

Since Brocade has both FC and iSCSI products, the company has no bias between them. However, there are differences between iSCSI and FC which users need to be aware of before making a choice.

For example, iSCSI packets have more protocol overhead than FC frames. FC was designed from the ground up to be an efficient transport for storage. Ethernet, IP, TCP, and IPSec were not. In order to initiate an iSCSI "conversation" with a target, a host must construct a header chain such as the one in Figure 10.

Granted, some iSCSI packets may have shorter header chains than the one depicted, but other iSCSI packets will have even longer chains. In contrast, Fibre Channel frames all use the same short header. Figure 11 (page 42) shows how the iSCSI header chain combines with the standard Ethernet packet size to magnify the inefficiency vs. FC.

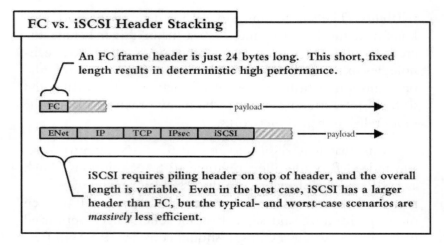

Figure 10 - iSCSI and FC Header Comparison

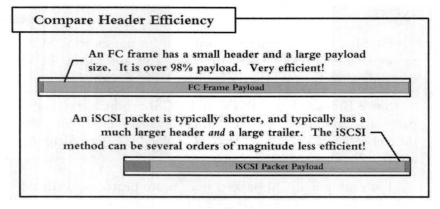

Figure 11 - iSCSI vs. FC Header Efficiency

Unless the iSCSI network is constructed entirely out of expensive high-end switches and routers, the end-to-end conversation between iSCSI endpoints will need to use the lowest common denominator packet size (MTU). The only workaround for this problem is to use jumbo Ethernet packets. Indeed, all iSCSI vendors recommend this, and always use jumbo packets and Enterprise-class switches to generate marketing performance statistics. In fact, the inherent inefficiencies of iSCSI are so severe that industry commentators

Realistically, iFCP never had any application except for IP distance extension, where "expensive and slow" was already assumed. This made it a direct competitor with FCIP (below). Prior to the invention of the FC-FC Routing Service, iFCP proponents could claim one advantage over FCIP: It could isolate edge fabrics from WAN instabilities. This argument can no longer be used.

iFCP was ratified as a standard, but it never caught on. Only one vendor shipped an iFCP solution. That vendor was acquired, and iFCP technology is no longer on the roadmap. Therefore the viability of iFCP is doubtful at best: it seems likely that the protocol will go away completely in the near future.

FCIP

Fibre Channel over Internet Protocol (FCIP) is a mechanism for connecting Fibre Channel E_Ports using IP infrastructure. It is *possible* to configure FCIP links in a point-to-point manner without intermediate IP network equipment between them. In this case, the physical topology looks much as if the tunnels were Fibre Channel ISLs. However, such a design could be built more economically and with better performance by using native Fibre Channel links, so real world FCIP deployments use IP switches and/or routers between FCIP gateways, as in Figure 13.[32]

In this example, two sites are connected across an IP WAN. Each site has a Fibre Channel director (e.g. Brocade 24000 or 48000) and an FCIP gateway (e.g. Brocade 7500 or

---

[32] There are a few real-world use cases for point-to-point FCIP links. If a customer has a DWDM chassis with Gigabit Ethernet cards in it, they may want to connect FCIP ports to the chassis instead of native FC. However, it takes many FCIP links (more than two) to equal the performance of one native FC link, and even then it will not be possible to support many SAN usage cases. The DWDM chassis will require many GE ports, using many frequencies, and connecting to many external FCIP gateway ports, all of which tends to add more cost than simply adding a native FC card to the DWDM chassis.

FR4-18i blade). The gateway is connected to an optional LAN switch, which is connected to an IP WAN router. Once the solution is configured, a host at one site will be able to access storage at the other site as if the switches were directly connected via an FC ISL and there were no intermediate IP network.

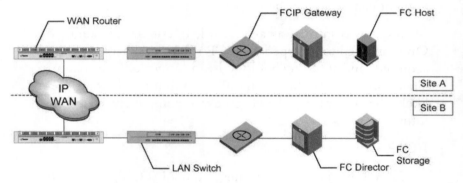

Figure 13 – FCIP Physical Topology Example

FCIP is the industry-accepted protocol of choice for extending SANs across distance when IP networks are available but more reliable and higher performance technologies such as ATM, SONET/SDH, dark fiber, and WDM are *not* available. Like most SAN infrastructure vendors, Brocade sells an FCIP product, and also partners with third-party vendors to offer a wider range of FCIP solutions. However, FCIP is inherently less reliable and lower performance than other SAN extension technologies, so it is not appropriate for many usage cases. It should not be considered a panacea for SAN distance extension. The book *Multiprotocol Routing for SANs* has more information about FCIP in general and Brocade FCIP solutions in particular.

2: SAN Solutions

This chapter provides an overview of a few of the more popular solutions for which SANs have been used. Keep in mind while reading this material that only a sample of possible SAN solutions are presented, and that a strategic investment in network infrastructure tends to result in new use cases becoming self-evident. Even if a SAN is deployed for one specific application, it is common for other applications to migrate to the SAN once connectivity is in place.

Storage Consolidation

Storage consolidation is the process of combining many scattered storage resources into fewer centralized resources. This approach provides ongoing manageability benefits as well as direct cost savings. The primary "hard" benefit of storage consolidation comes through more efficient utilization of storage assets: in consolidated environments there is less unused disk space overall and fewer arrays to buy and manage. Storage consolidation also allows administrators to work more efficiently.

In DAS[33] environments, each host would need to have its own storage. This could be internal or external, but it could not be shared with other hosts, or located far away from the host, as shown in Figure 14.

---

[33] Directly Attached Storage

Direct Attached Storage (DAS)

Directly attached storage devices were most often located inside a host enclosure. This required a case large enough to accommodate devices needed at deployment *and* in the future.

Host Enclosure

SCSI Bus

Disk
Disk
Disk
Disk

Host Enclosure

SCSI Bus

Disk
Disk
Disk
Disk

External disk enclosures could be used, which helped with future-proofing somewhat. However, there were still limitations. They could not be located far away, could not be shared, and could not support large numbers of devices. Worst of all, it would require downtime to add or change an enclosure.

Figure 14 - DAS Architecture - Before Storage Consolidation

Because of the potential – or, really, the inevitability – of unplanned increases in storage demand, each storage device in a DAS environment needed to have substantial unused space (a.k.a. "white space") to allow for growth. It is not usually acceptable to take application downtime frequently, which is required in DAS environments since new storage arrays cannot be added "live" to a DAS solution. Figure 15 shows how multiple DAS subsystems would each have their own individual white space areas, with different levels of utilization.

Figure 15 - White Space Utilization in a DAS Environment

In this diagram, each host has its own dedicated storage subsystem illustrated by a partially filled cylinder. The level of the fill indicates the level of utilization of the subsystem. Note that the overall unused space − the average of all hosts − is about equal to the total used space. This example shows an average 50% utilization of storage assets, which means that half of the storage investment in this DAS environment shown in the figure would be classified as a non-earning asset: white space simply sits on the data center floor, drinking power and cooling budget, and depreciating. [34]

The reason that white space in DAS environments tended to be high was that there was no way for a host in need of storage to get at excess free space located on storage attached to a different host, and therefore each host needed its own dedicated pool of white space to be sized according to its projected worst-case need. Most hosts would never actually *use* that space, but it had to be there to prevent downtime for occasions when it *was* needed. In addition, storage devices could not be purchased with any arbitrary degree of granularity. If an IT organization standardized on buying 100GByte hard drives, and a particular application only needed 1GByte, the host running that application would have 99% white space. If another nearby host needed 101GBytes, it would need two drives: the two systems would have 300GBytes of storage and only 102GBytes used between them: nearly $2/3^{rds}$ white space overall.

When using a SAN, however, the major portion of white space can be kept in a central pool, since any host can access any storage device to get at free space when it is needed. If the two hosts from the previous example were SAN attached, then the host needing 101GBytes could have gotten the extra

---

[34] 50% utilization might seem to be an unrealistically high percentage of white space. However, the "Storage Report" by Merrill Lynch and McKinsey stated in 2001 that up to 70% of the storage in a typical data center was white space: costing money, but not providing any benefit to the organization. In contrast, the same report estimated 80% to 90% utilization in SANs: "For large customers, this results in effectively cutting storage subsystem costs by 40-66%." This provides a clear, immediate, and substantial return on investment.

storage from the first host's largely unused disk. The two hosts together would need a third less storage, and would have better than $2/3^{rds}$ utilization instead of $2/3^{rds}$ white space. In a SAN, whichever host suddenly has a need for storage can get more out of the central pool on the fly. Some white space is still needed, but utilization is at a much higher rate, which means less money spent on non-earning assets. Figure 16 shows the six-host environment from Figure 15, but migrated from DAS to SAN.

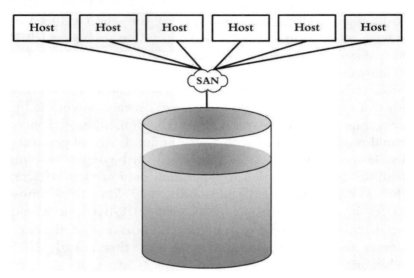

Figure 16 – White Space when DAS is Migrated to SAN

Not only does the SAN version have higher utilization and therefore lower cost, but it also consolidates storage subsystems into fewer devices. (Six individual small disk subsystems become one large array in this example.) This means lower power consumption, lower load on the data center cooling infrastructure, simplified support contracts, more efficient depreciation cycles, and more efficient use of administrator time since there are fewer devices to manage.

Of course, it is not always possible or even desirable to collapse *all* storage into *one* subsystem as shown in the figure. Particularly in enterprise environments, there may still be

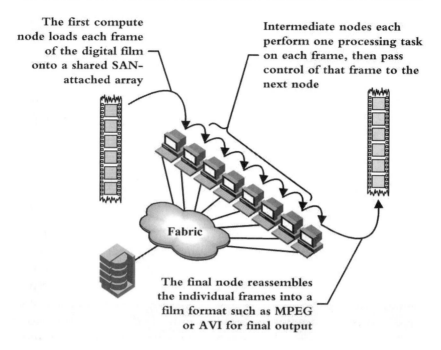

The first compute node loads each frame of the digital film onto a shared SAN-attached array

Intermediate nodes each perform one processing task on each frame, then pass control of that frame to the next node

Fabric

The final node reassembles the individual frames into a film format such as MPEG or AVI for final output

Figure 19 – Pipeline System for Film Processing

Eight nodes are used in this example to divide the load for an image processing application. This shows a pipeline approach: each node performs one stage of the processing before passing control to the next node. For example, the first node might take an uncompressed digital video format and turn it into a set of individual uncompressed bitmap image files and associated sound files. The next node might apply a filter to the images to reduce film grain, or balance color. Another node might eliminate background noise in a sound file, or key out a green screen. While each movie frame in this example is handled sequentially by different compute nodes, the overall film is processed in a parallel manner.

Techniques like this might be used when performing a series of CPU intensive operations on each frame of a digital video for a commercial, or a movie, or a television show, but the approach can also be used for applications such as data mining, scientific research, or business decision support. In many cases, solutions in this category use proprietary load balancing mechanisms.

Just as in the case of HA clusters, parallel computing clusters can benefit from disk consolidation. Of course, disks and RAID arrays are not the only kinds of storage that can be consolidated: it is possible to achieve large and recurring savings by consolidating tape devices as well.

Tape Consolidation / LAN-free Backup

Systems administrators have long understood the value of centralizing resources. In the context of disks, centralization enabled better utilization and simplified management. For backups, having tape drives dedicated to each host was inefficient in terms of tape media utilization, administrative time spent rotating media every day, recurring off-site media storage costs, equipment depreciation, and downtime for applications associated with upgrading backup hardware and software. Naturally, administrators looked for ways to move data to a central location for backups. The only way to do this in the early 1990s was to use the LAN, as in Figure 20.

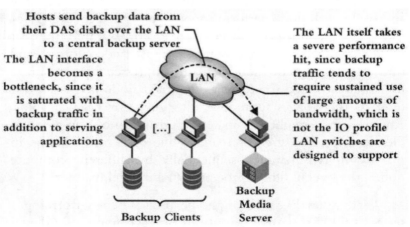

Figure 20 - Backing Up Data via the LAN

Unfortunately, this approach provided minimal administrative benefits while causing noticeable performance problems in most environments. While this did solve the consolidation problem to some extent, it created performance issues for the backups themselves, for the production applications which the backup clients were intended to serve, and for the overall LAN. IP networks were not reliable enough for backups: packet loss would often cause backups to crash mid-way through, and many if not most backup applications could not gracefully resume an interrupted operation. IP LANs were not able to support continuous full-speed load from many simultaneous sources: both IP switch design and standard network architecture methods involved high levels of over-subscription, which was ideal for the bursty traffic patterns common on LANs, but ill-suited at best for a backup set that would run at full speed for hours at a stretch. In short, this approach did not optimally solve the backup problem, and indeed it created many new issues.

Despite the shortcomings, LAN-based backups became popular for a time, but then several trends combined to make this approach unsupportable in most enterprises. The volume of data to be backed up grew exponentially, thus increasing the bandwidth required to perform backups and the time required to saturate the LAN, while at the same time the performance demands on the LAN for serving *other* applications also grew at a steady rate. Since TCP/IP stacks are CPU and RAM intensive, running backups over that network stack also robbed hosts of memory and processing power sorely needed to meet those increasing application performance requirements. Finally, it was not possible to run native block-level operations between the hosts being backed up and the central backup server, so both the hosts and the server needed to run a proprietary protocol on top of TCP/IP that locked users into proprietary solutions and created further network and host performance problems.

In addition, backup windows – the time during which a backup set must be completed – continued to shrink as the growing globalization of businesses dictated 7x24[35] operation of most services. With the competing performance requirements of backups and production applications both escalating faster than LANs could be upgraded, it was inevitable that the LAN-based backup approach would result in *longer* backup windows, rather than shorter ones.

Creating a physically separate IP/Ethernet LAN dedicated for backups solved some of these problems. Indeed, this was one of the first wide-scale appearances of dedicated storage networks. However, both Ethernet and IP were still unreliable by storage standards, with packet loss causing backup sets to crash, and CPU-intensive IP stacks were still competing with production applications for resources. To make matters worse, many Ethernet vendors – not understanding storage requirements – recommended using VLANs to separate backup traffic from LAN traffic instead of a physically separate network. This did nothing to address the shortcomings of LAN-based backups, since the same inadequate physical NIC interfaces and LAN switch interconnects were still being used for both kinds of traffic. And since applications using this method could not operate at the block level, performance and flexibility was still limited further by the need to run a proprietary upper level backup protocol on the host's CPU.

The final solution was to move backup traffic off of the IP LAN and onto an FC SAN. Figure 21 shows how the example from Figure 20 would look after backup traffic was moved to the FC SAN. This approach solved the issues inherent with LAN-based storage IO. While physically dedicated backup LANs were arguably storage networks, the first *real* solution came with the advent of Fibre Channel. Unlike either IP or Ethernet, FC guarantees on-time in-order packet delivery with negligible error rates, so backup applications do not fail or need to be restarted due to packet loss. In

---

[35] Seven by twenty-four refers to environments that must be online seven days a week, twenty-four hours a day.

addition, the FC protocol is designed from the ground up to be light weight, so it uses minimal resources on hosts. Most of the remaining resource requirements are offloaded onto the hardware of the FC Host Bus Adapter (HBA) cards. Finally, FC could run ten times faster than the "fast" Ethernet technology prevalent in LANs at the time, and with the CPU freed up from needing to process protocol overhead, many hosts could actually use this much bandwidth.[36]

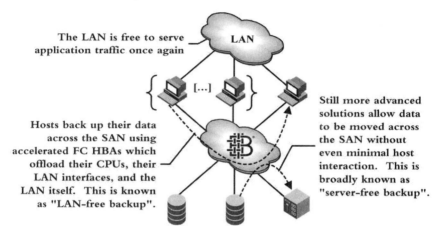

The LAN is free to serve application traffic once again

Hosts back up their data across the SAN using accelerated FC HBAs which offload their CPUs, their LAN interfaces, and the LAN itself. This is known as "LAN-free backup".

Still more advanced solutions allow data to be moved across the SAN without even minimal host interaction. This is broadly known as "server-free backup".

Figure 21 - LAN-free Backups

In fact, the benefits of changing from IP/Ethernet to Fibre Channel were so compelling that some companies began to deploy SANs purely to improve application performance.

---

[36] Ethernet soon caught up in terms of basic line rate by taking the lower Fibre Channel layers (FC-0 and FC-1) and tacking on the higher-level Ethernet layers (802.2 LLC and 802.3 CSMA/CD). This became known as "Gigabit Ethernet." (GE) However, FC almost immediately doubled its speed to 2Gbit, while GE remained at 1Gbit, and FC has already doubled again. Hosts with GE adapters had to spend so much CPU time processing protocol overhead that they could not even saturate 1Gbit networks, whereas FC had HBA hardware accelerators, allowing applications to run faster. At this point, a few host and storage vendors are able to exceed 2Gbit slightly, so the FC industry introduced a 4Gbit interface for roughly the same cost per port as 2Gbit. Brocade also ships a 10Gbit blade for directors (used for long distance) and has 8Gbit products on the horizon.

Performance Enhancement

Fibre Channel is not the only technology used for creating storage networks, but it is the most popular by a wide margin, and performance is one part of the reason. At the time of this writing, almost all FC devices shipping are 2Gbit, although 4Gbit devices are now beginning to ship. Since Fibre Channel HBAs offload operations from the CPU, many hosts can actually take advantage of these speeds, unlike IP/Ethernet solutions. But this does beg the question of why a customer would need to optimize their storage subsystem performance.

In some cases, the need is clear. Perhaps a backup operation cannot be completed within the allowable window. Perhaps an On-Line Transaction Processing (OLTP) database is not keeping up with demand. Perhaps compute server applications are running slowly. Whatever the specific business problem, if there is a storage- or CPU-related performance bottleneck in a DAS environment, moving to a Fibre Channel SAN may be the answer.

In some cases, however, it may be desirable to seek higher performance even if there are no specific problems. Perhaps there are no apparent performance issues *yet*, but there are expected to be in the future as utilization increases. Perhaps applications are running slowly, but the cause is unknown. Perhaps application performance is simply so important to a business that no risk of performance reduction can be accepted. In any of these or dozens of similar cases, a SAN might be installed proactively.

Some cases where Fibre Channel performance and reliability can be particularly useful are synchronous mirroring, asynchronous data replication, and backup / restore systems. These may require large amounts of bandwidth for extended periods of time. In addition, they often need to span distances that DAS cannot support.

3

3: UC and ILM

Utility Computing (UC) and Information Lifecycle Management (ILM) are increasingly important for SAN designers. However, they are not specific products, technologies, or solutions. Because of this, it is common for industry commentators to refer to them as broad concepts, using phrases such as "the UC and ILM industry trends" rather than trying to pin down exactly what the terms mean. While it is true that UC and ILM are both industry trends, stating it that way does not necessarily help a designer understand what either term means, or how it may affect their environment.

UC and ILM are sets of processes. They can be enabled by specific top-level data-center architectures, and overall design and management philosophies. In fact, certain architectures and philosophies aid UC and ILM so much that they can be called by that name, as in "Our data center has an ILM architecture."

Of course, they can also both be enabled by specific products and technologies, and both are definitely enabled by SANs. In turn, ILM and UC can facilitate specific SAN solutions such as those discussed in the previous chapter. This chapter will help SAN designers understand more specifically what ILM and UC are, and how they related to SAN and overall data center architecture. It discusses the benefits that UC and ILM provide, the remaining challenges that must be overcome to realize their full potential, the current "state of the art" of enabling technology, and the ways in which SANs inherently benefit UC and ILM solutions.

UC and ILM Classifications

Before delving into UC and ILM in detail, it is important to understand that they are not all or nothing propositions. This section discusses some of the ways that ILM and UC relate to each other, and how they can both be classified based on the degree of implementation.

These two trends are very different in execution and in result, but have much in common as well. For example, they have similar business cases to show a Return on Investment (ROI): both result in more efficient utilization of hardware and human resources. Also, they can each be broken down into similar recommended implementation timelines, are enabled by underlying network infrastructure in similar ways, and can have varying degrees of automation.

This last point is the key to understanding what is really meant by the use of either term. Remember, UC and ILM are processes. Processes can be applied broadly or narrowly, and can be implemented manually or automatically. At the highest level, an ILM or UC environment may be classified using a square from each column of Table 1.

Table 1 – UC and ILM Environment Classification

Process Automation Level	Overall Solution Scope
Manual ("paper") process	Prototype (test lab)
Semi-automated process	Limited production rollout
Fully-automated process	Enterprise-wide rollout

The first column defines how much automation has been done to the processes. An ILM or UC environment may have little or no automation at all: the processes may simply be written down on paper, and implemented by an IT team. In fact, this is the most common approach today. Increasingly, vendors are producing tools that automate some tasks, which means that "semi-automated" environments are beginning to appear. However, almost no environments are fourth layer, the SAN, to reach their final destination in the fifth layer: the storage device which actually has their data. Data is returned to the user following the same path: it crosses the SAN, is processed by the application, crosses the front-end network, and finally arrives at the client system.

In addition to the five layers in the UC architecture, UC solutions need policies and procedures for deciding where an application needs to be at any point in time, and a solution for moving it between physical compute nodes as needs change. The solution can be purely manual, or partially automated, or completely automatic. If the solution has any automation, there must also be a set of management tools.

This illustrates why the SAN is critical to the UC architecture. Without a SAN, only one compute node would be able to reach any given piece of data, so clients would be locked in to a specific path to that data. They would not be able to scale or change their compute resources independently from their storage resources. With the SAN, compute nodes may be assigned to serve data based on many different criteria, such as how much CPU is required to run the application serving the data, or availability characteristics, or whatever the UC policy of the site dictates.

Whatever technical approach is used to implement UC in a data center, it is likely that the rollout will progress through something similar to the following phases:

1. Assess the environment to determine UC needs
2. Decide on policies for compute resource movement
3. Select enabling technologies to automate movement
4. Create specific processes for movement using enablers
5. Implement UC data center architecture (Figure 24)
6. Implement UC-specific enabling technologies
7. Transition applications and resources onto UC system

Benefits of Utility Computing

The preceding section illustrated how a UC architecture might look, and mentioned a few of the benefits of UC at a high level. However, the benefits of utility computing to a modern organization can go far beyond merely optimizing CPU utilization. In principle, UC can be *extraordinarily* compelling, which is why so many organizations are moving towards this model.

Moving to a UC management model allows systems administrators to decouple hardware and software management tasks to an unprecedented degree. There are many reasons why a systems administrator might want to move an application between servers besides CPU resources.

For example, some IT organizations lease equipment. The hardware platform running an application might be coming off lease, but the application might still be needed. Traditionally, dealing with this problem would require setting up a new server, installing the application, testing it, scheduling downtime for the service, moving the data, verifying the data, and then releasing the new server to production. This process could take a considerable amount of time and involve substantial business impacts and risks. In a Utility Computing data center, the systems administrator could theoretically move the same application with the touch of a button. This is possible because the application binaries, OS images, and user data all exist on SAN-attached storage. No *data* actually needs to be moved at all; just the *application* needs to migrate.

When used in this way, UC enables an Application Resource Management (ARM) strategy. ARM can be thought of as a subset of Utility Computing. The need for 7x24 applications has been skyrocketing in most organizations, which inevitably results in a proliferation of equipment, and increases in the operating expense of the environment. In addition to hardware cost, equipment proliferation exponentially increases the complexity of managing the environment:

deploying, configuring, changing, and monitoring large numbers of these "application containers" is very complex. ARM enabling technologies allow more efficient application management, by optimizing:

- How long it takes to deploy, provision, and test a new application, or application container.
- How application resources can be monitored and managed consistently across a large data center.
- How compute power can be matched to changing application requirements.
- How long it takes to recover from a failure.

This strategy becomes even more important in data centers which are moving towards a bladed server architecture. In these environments, optimizing CPU resources may not be a paramount concern, but the purpose of implementing a bladed environment can be ease of management. (I.e. the ROI is achieved through reduced per-application administration staff cost and other increased operational efficiencies.) Administrators want to be able to boot up any blade with any "personality" from a centralized management console so that any blade can take over any application as needed. By using this approach, hardware upgrade processes are also facilitated, as are replacements of failed hardware components.

UC helps with high availability architectures, and business continuity strategies. If an entire data center fails, the same software and processes used to implement UC e.g. to improve management efficiency can be used to implement a disaster recovery strategy. If it is possible to easily move an application between hosts within a data center, the solution is on the way towards being able to move them between data centers located outside of each other's "threat radii".

Challenges to Implementing Utility Computing

The concept of utility computing is simple: make all hardware resources transparently available on demand to all applications and users. At the most abstract level, the process of implementing it is also simple: define policies which can be used for allocating compute resources (i.e. deciding which compute nodes will run any given application), and define and implement procedures based on those policies for actually moving applications between nodes as needed.

However, as a practical matter, UC is much simpler in concept than it is in execution.

Think back to the electric power grid analogy. From the perspective of a person plugging a refrigerator into a wall outlet, a power grid is fairly simple. Plug in the appliance, turn it on, and wait while your food gets cold. Production, delivery, and billing for power will be automatic, and transparent to the person plugging in the appliance.

On the other hand, from the perspective of an engineer designing a hydroelectric dam, or an operator managing the distribution system between the dam and the end user, or an accountant setting up and maintaining the billing system, electric power is rather more complex. Anyone familiar with the "rolling blackouts" that happened periodically in California in 2001, or the "Great Northeast Power Blackout of 2003" could understand what happens when the real complexity of the electric power grid makes itself apparent to end users of the system.

In practice, the ultimate extension of the UC vision requires software and probably hardware which is complicated for vendors to design, build, and test. In order for UC to function as well as an electric power grid, it will take an equivalent effort on the part of the companies bringing forward UC enabling technologies.

An automated UC system must be able to move applications around at need, which requires that it integrate seamlessly with them, since each application has different startup and shutdown requirements and behaviors. When an application or OS image is moved, the system must be aware of and able to account for hardware dependencies. It must allow the managers of the UC system to define policies, providing controls to allow tasks such as defining which application gets priority access in the event of contention, and how users are charged for resources they use up. It must integrate with the front-end network to manage getting network traffic correctly routed to moving applications. It must handle connecting via the SAN to boot OS images on compute nodes and mount their data partitions.

These are all challenges to the community of software and hardware companies currently trying to realize the UC vision. Depending on what approach is used, software in the UC data center of the future might need to be installed on each host, and probably on network switches and routers as well. This means maintaining compatibility with all hardware, application software, and OS versions over time across multiple vendors. And in order to realize benefits from UC, the management software for all of this must have world-class usability and reliability.

Assuming that all of the requirements of an "ultimate" UC solution were available, it would still be challenging for end-users to implement. Systems might need to have new software installed. Administrators could need to be retrained. Network monitoring packages could need to be adapted. It might take quite some time to roll out a comprehensive solution even after all pieces are available.

Utility Computing State of the Art

The challenges are so daunting that the "ultimate" data center abstraction potential of UC is not available yet from any vendor. However, as will be seen in the next section, certain useful pieces of the solution *are* available today, as is the network infrastructure necessary to "plumb" an IT environment to take advantage of more and more UC applications as they become available.

Today, many vendors have what they characterize as utility computing solutions, although these are marketed under many different names. In fact, they *are* UC solutions, but they are not feature-complete, end-to-end solutions. They *are* beneficial, but it does mean that customers must be able to sift through vendor hype to find out what really exists and is practical to implement today, vs. what vendors plan to implement in the future.

For example, many manufactures are now shipping bladed servers. Customers can buy rack-mountable chassis which provides power, cooling, and some network infra-structure. These resources are made available to a number of "hosts" which are installed in the chassis as blades. This means that each host requires less cabling, takes up less rack space, power, and cooling, and usually optimizes LAN and SAN deployments as well since FC and Ethernet switches can be integrated into the chassis.

For Utility Computing, a blade server chassis must also support one or more management interfaces to control which blades are running what applications and OS images. Many chassis have this feature, which is definitely a UC function that simplifies administration. Next, blade server chassis now offer integrated Brocade Fibre Channel fabrics, which pro-vides the back-end network required for UC with a substantially lower deployment and management cost struc-ture. They also do this for front-end networks. Both of these reduce wiring headaches, rack footprint for networking gear, and overall deployment and ongoing management costs.

Implementing a blade server chasses is therefore definitely related to Utility Computing and definitely has near-term benefits, even thought it does *not* solve all of the problems that UC is eventually expected to address. For example, put-ting in a single blade server chassis right now will not make an entire data center into an abstracted UC environment, or allow applications to transparently and automatically move around. It will not allow ultimately fine granularity of re-

able but still relevant to the business, it might be moved onto lower-tier RAID arrays or JBODs. Towards the end of its useful life, it could be migrated onto tapes for long-term archiving. There must be software to manage data movement between storage tiers, and to ensure that compute nodes access their data on the correct storage device.

 Side Note

ILM is a hot buzz-word now, but it is important to remember that the overall concept is not new. Indeed, all IT environments already implement some form of ILM today. If you have ever deleted temporary files on a PC, you have used an ILM process. You assessed your environment to determine that temp files were no longer of value after a certain point, located the valueless files, and deleted them to recover disk space. Moving old, inactive files off of disk and onto a CD-R, or archiving them onto tapes would also be an ILM process that most IT professionals have used at some point in their careers. ILM in a large data center is not fundamentally different than these existing processes; it is just more complex and comprehensive.

In addition to the layers in the network architecture, ILM solutions need policies and procedures for deciding where data needs to be at any given point in its lifecycle, and some kind of technical solution for moving it between physical storage devices as its properties change. The technical solution can be purely manual, or partially automated, or completely automatic. If the solution has any degree of automation, there must also be a set of management tools.

This shows why the SAN is critical to ILM solutions. Without a SAN, each compute node would be able to reach any given piece of data only as long as it was directly connected to the correct storage array. This would severely limit the options for adjusting the location of data based on its value. With the SAN, applications on compute nodes may have their data locations assigned to any available storage device based on many different criteria, such as how much storage capacity is free on any given device, or availability characteristics such as RAID protection, or whatever the ILM policy of the site dictates.

Regardless of which technical enablers are used to implement ILM, it is likely that the rollout will be performed using something like the following process:

1. Assess the environment to determine ILM needs
2. Decide on policies for data movement
3. Select enabling technologies to automate movement
4. Create specific processes for movement using enablers
5. Implement ILM data center architecture (Figure 26)
6. Implement enabling technologies
7. Transition data sets onto ILM system

Benefits of ILM

The introduction showed at a high level how ILM can save money by optimizing which kind of storage device data is stored on based on properties such as its overall business value. More expensive storage devices may have performance, reliability, and availability properties needed for high-value data, while less business–relevant data could be stored on more cost-effective devices. ILM processes and tools can allow an organization to match storage device properties and cost to the requirements for any piece of data.

For example, when the files were being created to generate this book, they were critical to the project. If a failure occurred in the system on which the files were stored, it could cause a delay in the publication process. Due to the critical nature of the data at that stage of its life, care was taken to ensure that it was stored in multiple locations, with several versions kept of each file, all on highly available storage systems that were backed up daily. Once the book was published, the source files became less critical. All of the old versions of each file were deleted, as were the extra copies of the final versions. Only one copy of the final version was kept, and this was moved to lower-tier storage systems. Of course, additional copies still exist on archived tapes, in case the online copy becomes corrupted.

However, the benefits of ILM do not stop there. Lowering the cost of storage devices is only one of many reasons why IT departments need to move data between storage devices. ILM enabling technology inherently must provide a policy-driven mechanism for moving data around, so it will also facilitate other requirements for mirroring, replication, and data migration.

For example, many IT departments lease storage assets. Whenever a storage device comes off lease its data must be transferred to a new array. If a company has abstracted its storage layer as part of deploying a SAN virtualization ILM solution, then moving the data between arrays can be handled using the same technology and processes. Even if storage devices are owned and not leased, eventually they will run out of room and/or become obsolete. The ability of an ILM enabling technology to move data will help equally no matter what the reason for retiring a storage device. Users can look forward to data migration enabling technologies from Brocade and its partners in the very near future.

Similarly, ILM solutions can generally replicate data between arrays, and so ILM technology can potentially be used for business continuance solutions. In fact, there are so many reasons for data to move around that many large-scale storage administrators have implemented SANs largely in order to handle these tasks. Installing SAN-based data movers is simply a logical extension of this trend, in addition to being enabling for general-purpose ILM solutions in the future.

Challenges to Implementing ILM

It should be increasingly apparent that ILM and UC have quite a bit in common in their concepts and architecture. They also have quite a bit in common where implementation challenges are concerned. The ILM concept is simple:

make all storage resources transparently available on demand to all compute nodes, and provide policies and mechanism for ensuring that all data "lives" on the "right" kind of storage device. At the most abstract level, the process of implementing it is also simple: define policies which can be used for allocating storage resources (i.e. deciding which storage device will store any given piece of data), and define and implement procedures based on those policies for actually moving data between storage devices as needed.

As in the case of UC, the concept of ILM is much simpler than its real-world implementation.

An automated ILM system must be able to move data around as needed. Therefore an "ultimate" ILM solution will need to solve the problem of how to move a data set from one storage device to another online, without being disruptive to the host(s) accessing it. It is one thing to occasionally schedule downtime for an application when an array comes off lease, but if data migrations are happening constantly – potentially at the level of individual files on a minute by minute basis – then even the most forgiving of users will require the process to be transparent.

An ILM solution must be able copy data to a new location while it is actively changing, verify that the new copy is correct, and then release the old copy from active service. To do this without disrupting the application users means that special behaviors will need to be in place either on the application server, or in the SAN. Specifically, something between the application and the storage devices must be able to move the data, and still present the underlying device the same way to the application as if nothing changed.

Doing this i on the server means managing a large number of hardware and software dependencies, and going through an expensive and disruptive rollout process. As a result, the industry as a whole has moved to a SAN-based approach: in the ultimate ILM data center, the SAN itself will perform all required data movement and redirection tasks.

In addition, an ILM solution must allow the managers to define the policies which specify when to move data sets, and to where they should be moved. This may seem trivial, but to succeed an ILM system must be easy to use, reliable, and robust in its feature set. This kind of software development is harder than most consumers would expect: yet another challenge for the community of software and hardware companies currently trying to realize the ILM vision.

Even when all of the requirements of an "ultimate" ILM solution are available, the rollout would still have challenges. Even with SAN-based virtualization, the initial rollout of ILM might be at least somewhat disruptive. Administrators would need to be retrained, network monitoring packages would need to be adapted, and so on.

ILM State of the Art

The "ultimate" abstraction potential of ILM is yet not available, but certain pieces *are* available today. For example, it is possible to deploy the network infrastructure for the ILM architecture, allowing managers to prepare the data center to take advantage of more and more ILM solutions as they become available. Besides the application to ILM, this architecture provides many other benefits, and is a good *general* data center enhancement as well as an ILM enabler. In addition, there are a number of *specific* ILM enabling products on the market today.

For example, it is possible to argue that any technology which enables data movement is an ILM enabler. Host-based software mirroring applications can be used to attach a new storage device to a mirror set, synchronize it, verify the new copy, and detach the original copy. This is certainly a valid method for migrating data, and is – at least, relatively speaking – non-disruptive to the users of the system.

However, it does not in and of itself "solve" ILM. A feature-complete ILM system would be able to do this automatically based on user-set policies. It would ideally be able to do so without host OS and hardware dependencies. And host-based mirroring solutions rely on the main CPU of the system to do the data movement, which can slow down applications during the movement process.

Similarly, array-based replication software is available from most vendors. However, when an administrator copies data using this software, there are often features which prevent arrays from different vendors from working well together. Even if it works at all, migration cannot be done from the array without disruption, unless all hosts are running special software — which has the same problems as host-based mirroring. Finally, ILM solutions are inherently intended to have many tiers of storage, some of which must be very low cost. Ultra low cost storage cannot typically run enterprise-class array-based replication software.

Host- and array-based solutions will always have a place in the data center, but they are architecturally wrong for driving an "ultimate" ILM solution. For that, a SAN-based solution is required. SAN virtualization components and applications are now becoming available to end users, allowing at least some level of SAN-based ILM automation.

In the near term, these devices will accelerate and simplify administration of data migration tasks. These devices also solve some of the inherent problems associated with deploying a complete ILM solution, since they can prevent the need to install special software on each host. SAN-based virtualizers do not provide *all* of the pieces of the eventual ILM puzzle, but they have both near-term and long-term benefits, and should be strongly considered by any customers interested in ILM solutions.

SANs: The Intersection of UC and ILM

The final visions of ILM and UC are not yet broadly available, and may not be for some time, but there are useful pieces available for both of them. In order to take advantage of existing UC solutions and to prepare for future advances as they become available, it is necessary for any compute node platform to have access to the data set for any application or service it might be required to run. For a compute node to benefit from an ILM solution, it must have simultaneous access to storage devices on each tier, and the ability to move data between them transparently. For either to work properly, network connectivity is needed. Specifically, SANs are required to allow data and compute mobility. This means that SANs sit at the *intersection* of these two important trends, as shown in Figure 27.

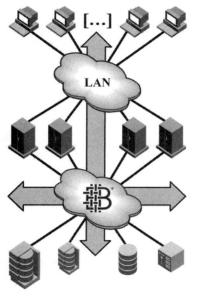

The SAN is the intersection of the ILM and UC architectures:

- UC: Applications can be moved between compute nodes as needed.

- ILM: Data can be moved between storage devices as needed.

- SAN: Any compute node can reach data on any storage resource, based on where the data for its current application resides at any point in time. The SAN therefore supports both data and compute mobility for ILM and UC.

Figure 27 – The SAN as the Intersection of UC and ILM

The IT industry is moving towards a model in which data mobility and compute-power flexibility are both required to stay competitive. As previously demonstrated, SANs are required to achieve this mobility, so making a strategic investment in SAN infrastructure enables both approaches.

ILM and UC Phased Implementation Plan

To enable ILM and UC with SANs, a phased approach to implementation is recommended.

The first step is assessment. Determine what problems need to be solved or enhancements need to be provided by the ILM and/or UC solutions. It may help to conduct an audit of the existing IT environment to analyze what resources already exist and how they are being used today. Then look at how things could operate more efficiently with enhanced storage and/or compute mobility.

When trying to estimate what an implementation plan might look like, or what it might cost, pay special attention to the existing network infrastructure. Is a SAN already in place? If so, does it architecturally provide for any-to-any connectivity across all storage tiers and to all compute nodes? Does it have appropriate HA characteristics? Will each network handle the increased throughput that ILM and UC solutions are likely to generate? (These concepts will be covered in greater detail later in the book.)

If a SAN is in place, consider expanding it to include any stranded servers. If many small SANs are in place, consider consolidating them using FC Routers with LSANs. Finally, consider upgrading to faster network devices, such as 2Gbit or 4Gbit switches and routers which support trunking.

After the assessment is complete, the team will need to come up with a set of policies that define what data (ILM) and applications (UC) will be moved around, where they will go, and under what circumstances this should happen. At this stage, do not worry about the technical method that will be used perform the movement. Instead, focus on the business needs which drive the movement. For example, you might write a report with a statement such as this:

Our business is spending far too much money on new enterprise-class storage arrays. According to the recent survey, 50% or more of the data stored on our existing enterprise-class arrays is accessed rarely if ever, and does not require enterprise-class performance or HA characteristics. We need to be able to move this lower-priority data onto lower-cost storage devices as its business value changes. This must be accomplished without simply transferring hardware cost to increased administrative cost, so an automated solution is called for. If an automated ILM solution is deployed, it could save our business $x per month in recurring administrative costs and $y per year on capital expenditures for storage arrays.

Notice that this is phrased in terms of what can be improved about the current storage management methodology, but begins and ends with the positive monetary impact to the business of putting the solution in place. "Chapter 5: Project Planning" (starting on page 119) has more examples of how to gather business requirements, and ways to phrase them when including them in a SAN rollout project plan.

By the end of that process, you will have determined *what* should moved (data or compute resources), *why* the movement should occur (money, compliance, etc.), *where* the data or compute resources should move to and from (the nodes involved), and *when* to do the movement. If you have all of that, you have defined your business–oriented ILM and/or UC policies.

The next step is to decide on a phased approach to enabling automatic execution of these policies. The top-level structure of this plan would consist of short-, medium-, and long-term project milestones, with costs and benefits called out for each stage of the plan. For example, you might decide to roll out an ILM solution in the following manner:

Phase I: Deploy top-level network architecture and manually implement ILM processes for a limited number of nodes. The nodes included will be only business-critical servers. Data movement will consist of nightly backups across the DR network. While this process will still be largely manual, it will comply with regulations that require our business to increase the protection of its data.

Phase II: Expand the number of controlled nodes, add replication tasks, and implement limited automation. Nodes controlled will be business–critical systems and nodes for which downtime costs $x per hour or more. Backups and data replication tasks across the DR network will be automated, which will ensure compliance and save on administrative costs. This model may also support manual movement between tiered storage devices.

Phase III: Cover remaining data center nodes, increase process automation, and increase the types of movement supported. Include automatic migration between cost–driven storage tiers to reduce capital expenditures. This will save on enterprise–class storage.

Selecting Enabling Applications

As shown above, you might decide that the first logical step in the implementation is to deploy the top-level network architecture, and to try manually running the processes on a limited number of hosts for a month or two. This will allow you to be certain that the processes are correctly defined before putting any kind of automation in place. In this case, you would put the SAN in place, and enough technical pieces to perform the movement yourself.

For example, you might need to deploy – at minimum – HBAs, switches, routers, and software to facilitate booting over the SAN, if you wanted to roll out a UC solution. When it came time to move an application to a new node, if the hardware architecture was different on the new platform, you might manually perform configuration modifications on the network-based boot image to account for hardware dependencies. Even if you are executing the processes manually such as this, it is still a UC solution; it might simply be in the upper row of Table 1 (p68) instead of the lower row.

At some point, however, users will want to improve their processes by automating them and including more and more nodes. This is the time during which you would deploy a host- or SAN-based "boot configuration controller" or a similar enabling technology. Even if you do not intend to deploy something such as this right away, it is best to select an overall approach at the front-end of the process, to be sure that your overall SAN design will work well when it is time for the final solution to be deployed. Evaluate the *strategies* being proposed by different vendors, and decide which will likely benefit your business the most in the long term.

Design a SAN Connectivity Model

Eventually, you would probably want the entire data center to be controlled by this process. While it would be premature to design the solution that way at the start of the deployment, you should at least think about how your SAN can scale to this level. Generally, this means selecting best-in-class infrastructure providers, high-performance 4Gbit Fibre Channel switches within each fabric, and a hierarchical routed architecture (LSANs) spanning fabrics that can scale out as your deployment matures. Important things to look for in a network architecture are:

1. Can all servers potentially reach all storage devices? Even if locality is used, you should allow for the effects of *operational entropy*, which is the principle that any solution will need to adapt to changing requirements. The only way to be sure that future contingencies are covered is to allow for any-to-any connectivity. In large scale environments, it may be impossible or at least undesirable to connect all devices to one large fabric, but new technologies such as FC routers running LSANs can be used to solve the problem.

2. Will the *port-count* of the solution scale to include all nodes in the data center? The value of any network increases exponentially as the number of nodes increases,

and you should expect a high-value ILM or UC solution to grow rapidly.

3. Will the network *performance* scale to support all anticipated data movement needs? E.g. what will happen if all servers need to reboot simultaneously, or when recovering from a large-scale failure, or when migrating multiple arrays simultaneously?

If the network design provides for all of those factors, it will be well-positioned to take advantage of any ILM or UC solutions which become available in the future, as well as getting near-term benefits. See "Chapter 5: Project Planning" and the following chapters in that section starting on page 119 for more information about building fully-connected, highly-scalable, high-performance SANs.

4: Design Overview

This chapter will familiarize readers with some of the major considerations involved in SAN design. It discusses some of the choices that a designer must make, and provides a few factors to think about when making these choices. Since many of the subtopics in this chapter are very complex, many of them have entire chapters dedicated to them later in this book. In these cases, this chapter will provide a brief overview of the design consideration, and refer the reader to the appropriate subsequent chapter for further information.

As with most IT infrastructure categories, designing SANs involves balancing requirements against each other, and achieving a compromise when requirements conflict. For example, there is an inherent conflict between the requirement to deploy a network for low cost, and the requirement to deploy a network with best-in-class performance and availability characteristics. Because of this, SAN design is often about making tradeoffs. There are discussions throughout this chapter about how designers have resolved various conflicts, and why they made those decisions.

The intent of this book is not to lay down immutable *laws* of SAN design. Since every network has slightly different requirements, there are no absolute rules about the "right" way balancing requirements which can cover all possible scenarios. The intent is to show the reader areas that will need thought in a SAN design, and to provide recommendations based on industry-accepted guidelines and best practices.

The first topics cover some of the areas which apply to any SAN design, regardless of variables such as protocol, distance, topology, or performance. These factors have such ubiquitous applicability that it is important to keep them in mind when making all subsequent evaluations. After that, the chapter goes into considerations, such as long distance technologies and trading off cost vs. performance requirements.

Compatibility

The first thing to consider when designing a SAN is the compatibility of each piece of infrastructure equipment with the rest of the infrastructure, and with each host or storage device which may interact with it. If devices are incompatible, then the network will not function, so any further considerations are simply irrelevant.

When devices are compatible with each other, it means that they are capable of being connected to each other, either directly or across a network. It means that they can "talk." This can apply equally to hardware and software.

For example, it is necessary for an HBA driver to be compatible with the operating system in its host. If the driver only works with Windows, and the host is running Solaris, they are incompatible. This is not an example of a piece of *hardware* being compatible (or not) with a piece of software, but rather of two software packages being incompatible with each other. Similarly, the HBA hardware must be compatible the hardware in the host: a PCI HBA cannot be installed in a host that only has free SBUS slots.

Like all new protocols, when Fibre Channel was first conceived in the mid 1990s, it had compatibility challenges ranging from the frame format level all they way up to the application layers. Considerable effort was expended to resolve these challenges by Brocade and other companies throughout the industry. While challenges remain at some levels, the result was, overall, successful: most Fibre Channel products are compatible with each other at almost all layers. The remaining challenges are all related to upper layer services. For example, some multipathing drivers may be supported only with certain storage devices, or may need to use certain HBA and RAID controller firmware levels.

The good news for SAN designers is that the FC community has solved many compatibility challenges and is actively working on the remaining areas. The bad news is that some other SAN technologies such as iSCSI are not so far along. Before choosing a SAN technology, look at the overall maturity of the technology. Ask questions such as, "How many years has the protocol been used in large-scale mission-critical environments?" Or, "How many millions of ports are in *production use* today?" Ask about compatibility with other vendors at *all* layers; not just the frame or packet level, but also between storage services, applications on hosts, and storage arrays. Ask about end-to-end vendor support.

In the context of a SAN, compatibility applies to all hardware and software components end to end, from the application to the final storage location. For example, it is possible for an HBA to be compatible with a storage device and the switch hardware in-between, but still not be compatible with a feature of the SAN such as proprietary VSAN tags. Areas to evaluate for compatibility include:

- Protocol (frame formats)
- Do all devices in the chain use the same protocols?
- E.g. do all devices follow the FC standard frame format? If the FC header is not standard, there is no chance of interoperability between devices.
- Do they all use the standard frames in the same *way*? Even if the correct frames are being sent between two devices, the vendors still need to have worked together to insure a consistent *interpretation* of the standards. This caveat applies to each of the following services discussions as well.

- Node to switch (services, protocols)
- Will the node (host or storage) be able to attach successfully to the fabric? This requires that it follow certain protocols defined in the standards, and that implementation details must also be compatible.
- The node must interact correctly with all fabric services and processes, most notably including fabric login (FLOGI) and the name server (SNS).
- How will the node behave in failure cases? Evaluate all components in the chain: cables, media, switch, even the entire fabric. Look at each component and decide how the node will behave if that component fails completely, or what will happen if it becomes unstable. (Unstable components can often be much worse than failed components.)[41]
- Node to node (applications, services, protocols)
- The major challenge to SAN interoperability today is at the application layer. Will the multipathing driver on the host work with the RAID controller firmware? Will the HBA driver be able to talk to the JBOD and the tape library at the same time?[42]
- Switch to switch or router (services, protocols)
- SAN switches have compatibility challenges that just do not apply in other kinds of networking. Building a SAN switch is like building an Ethernet L3 switch

---

[41] When Brocade tests a node, it is subjected to rigorous testing to ensure proper handling of even the most obscure of failure modes. This process is known as an "OEM qualification." The standard for passing a qual is set high because the consequences of a failure in a SAN are also high.

[42] It is important to understand that this is the major remaining challenge for SAN interoperability when evaluating vendor marketing hype about emerging technologies. Some vendors claim that iSCSI will solve all compatibility issues because it is "just IP." The remaining compatibility issues for SANs are not at the frame layer, so changing from FC to IP will not help with compatibility in any way. Indeed, the industry as a whole has not yet begun to address the application layer challenges of iSCSI interoperability, so deploying iSCSI today will create considerably more interoperability issues than an equivalent FC network.

that also runs services like DNS, DHCP, WINS, NIS, LDAP, and so on. Furthermore, all services need to cluster across all switches, and self-configure in the majority of cases. Other network technologies have fundamentally different requirements, and so are not architected in this manner.

- All non-VSAN FC switches today use compatible frame formats, but protocols also define details such as *when* to send specific frames, and how long to wait for a response.[43] To connect switches from different vendors, it is vital to ensure that upper layer services such as the name server, FSPF, and zoning have all been explicitly certified by *all parties involved in support* to interoperate in the configuration being deployed.

- Even when multi-vendor networks seem to work, it is possible for a firmware upgrade on either side to make a subtle change that could affect compatibility.

Without end-to-end compatibility at all layers, it is not possible for a solution to work *at all*. Even if a solution has end-to-end compatibility at the transport layer, an incompatibility at the multipathing driver layer could still prevent it from being a viable option. Brocade has vastly more experience in this area than any other vendor, so a network built using Brocade switches and routers is more likely to have compatibility than any other approach. However, using Brocade alone cannot guarantee end to end compatibility between nodes: it is still necessary to evaluate whether or not a particular host will work together with a particular storage array, and so on.

---

[43] For example, it turns out that there are subtle differences in timing of frames that can make or break a solution. If one device expects a response in two seconds, and the other device believes that it has four seconds to respond, communication will be unreliable at best.

Side Note

Implementation details matter as much as standards.

For example, one particular microchip used in many 1Gbit FC HBAs worked well in general, and was FC standards-compliant. However, it had originally been designed for point-to-point applications, and had a characteristic that could degrade its performance in a fabric if it was connected to a switch that had been designed according to the most popular interpretation of the standards documents.

Because Brocade was involved in the industry "from the ground floor," the Brocade ASIC engineering team knew about that characteristic, and added an ASIC hardware assist mode to compensate. Whenever a Brocade switch detected that an HBA was using that chip, it could use the appropriate interpretation of the standards when communicating with it. Whenever the switch was talking to any other kind of HBA, the more popular interpretation could be used. This allowed Brocade to maximize performance with all first- and second-generation HBAs.

In contrast, vendors new to the industry lacked this intelligence, and were unable to communicate well if at all with installed-base HBAs. Even to this day, most other vendors are not even minimally qualified with these widely-deployed, installed-base chipsets. This is just one more example of the advantages a SAN designer may get from using Brocade products.

Network Topologies

There are a number of different definitions for "SAN topology" depending on context. For example, it can refer to the type of port on a Fibre Channel switch, as in, "Port #1 is using a *loop* topology, since it is in FL_Port mode." However, in the context of SAN design, it is most common for topology to refer to the geometrical arrangement of switches, routers, and other networking infrastructure elements which form the storage network.

When a network diagram is created, the infrastructure equipment can be seen to form geometrical shapes. Topologies are named based on the shapes that they create.

There are literally an infinite number of possible topologies, and the robust architecture of fabric services does allow arbitrarily complex fabrics to be built. Fortunately, in the majority of real-world cases, it is possible to use simple solutions. This means that few topologies are typically used as the basis for SANs, and these are combined or varied to fit the needs of specific deployments. These topologies are popular because they yield networks with superior scalability, performance, availability, and manageability. In fact, the choice of topology has such a profound impact on the properties of a SAN that many designers consider it to be the single most important decision point in the design process.

The most common topologies for SANs include:

- Cascade
- Ring
- Mesh
- Core / Edge (CE)

More information on this topic can be found in "Chapter 6: Topology Planning" starting on page 141.

Reliability, Availability, and Serviceability

These three topics are often collectively referred to as RAS. While each RAS component is substantially different from the others, they each have an effect on the overall functionality of a product, network, or solution. SAN designers must keep RAS in mind when selecting components and when choosing a top-level network architecture.

Reliability

Reliability is a measure of how much time a component is statistically expected to be working vs. how much time it is expected to require service for failures. Hardware and software components both have reliability characteristics. If fact, so do networks, and overall solutions.

One way to look at reliability is that it is a measure of how often service personnel need to "touch" a system. A "reliability event" occurs any time service is needed, even if the component is still online for the duration of the service. For example, take a SAN switch that has redundant hot swappable power supplies. If one fails, the switch will remain online during the replacement, but a reliability event will still have occurred.

SAN designers must consider reliability when selecting system components for two reasons:

1. Higher reliability means lower ongoing support cost. Each time a component fails, a support action must take place. There may be hardware replacement costs, support personnel costs, and opportunity costs since personnel repairing a system are not working on other – probably more strategic – activities.
2. In some cases, low component reliability can translate into system-wide downtime. In other words, a reliability event can become an availability event, as will be shown in the next section.

The most common measurements of reliability are Mean Time Between Failures and Mean Time To Repair. (MTBF and MTTR.) Respectively, these refer to how often a component is expected to fail, and how long it generally takes to fix the component when a failure occurs. SAN designers should look for components with high MTBF and low MTTR.[44]

---

[44] In addition to the *time* to repair a component, it is also critical to look at the *procedure* for the repair. For example, on SAN vendor sells a "director" with active components on the backplane. The procedure to repair a failed backplane requires

There are quite a few things that can effect MTBF and MTTR values.

For example, the overall maturity of a product plays a role in MTBF. No matter how much diligence a company puts into designing hardware and software, it is inevitable that some flaws will still be present in the product when it is shipped. It takes time in the field for these issues to be found and fixed. (This is why many network managers refuse to install any OS version or hardware platform until it has at least one patch released.) Comparing the amount of production experience a company has in a particular market segment is a good way of estimating how reliable their products will be. For example, many SAN designers select Brocade infrastructure because Brocade has been shipping SAN switches into mission-critical production environments for about a decade. No other vendor can match this. This means that both hardware and software maturity are expected to be *much* higher with Brocade than with competitors' products, and real-world observations of reliability bear this out.

Another factor is component integration. It is axiomatic that systems with fewer parts tend to have fewer failures. Directors in particular have many sub-components on each blade. One way to get a feeling for the expected reliability of a product is to look at the hardware design and count parts. Brocade has spent a great deal of time and effort consolidating sub-components throughout all product lines in order to increase reliability. To see the effect of this effort, take a Brocade 48000 blade or Brocade 4100 motherboard. Set it down next to any similar product from any competitor. It will be immediately obvious which will fail more often. The primary switching logic on a 16-port Brocade 48000 blade has been squeezed down onto a single microchip! It is hard to achieve much greater integration that that.

---

taking the entire director apart. It really doesn't matter how long that takes; that operation is simply unacceptable in a director-class product.

☑ Side Note

Frame format compatibility was brought up as a consideration early in this chapter. It is almost not worth mentioning. There have been few frame header incompatibilities in Fibre Channel since the protocol was ratified in the 1990s. There are, unfortunately, two reasons to bring it up:

(1) While FC has matured well beyond this point, IP SAN technologies still have issues at this level. Only one vendor ever shipped iFCP, which is incompatible with everything else, and iSCSI devices may use any of twenty different drafts of the standard.

(2) One newcomer to the SAN arena introduced a feature (VSANs) that violates the FC frame header format, and is not compatible with any existing FC nodes, switches, or routers. The vendor in question requires that its users turn VSAN tags off on all ports attached to 3rd party devices – including hosts and storage. In general, the solution to the level of incompatibility created by VSAN tags is just what that vendor recommends: the problem is solved by not using the incompatible feature. Aside from that vendor, however, frame level incompatibility is simply a non-issue in the FC industry, so for the most part it is appropriate to concentrate on higher layers.

The effects of component integration on reliability are generally intuitive, but the effects of maturity and integration on total system reliability can sometimes also have counterintuitive effects. For example, the Brocade SilkWorm 3800 had hot swappable power supplies, whereas the SilkWorm 3850 power supplies could not be replaced. Intuitively, most people think that this means that the 3800 would have better RAS characteristics overall. However, hot swappable power supplies increase the component count and complexity of the 3800 *motherboard* radically, and the motherboard is a nonredundant component. The simpler and more tightly integrated design of the 3850 increased motherboard reliability to such an extent that the entire switch – including both of the two power supplies – had a better MTBF than the 3800 motherboard alone. It was more likely to need to take a 3800 down for maintenance on its motherboard than to take a 3850 down for maintenance on its motherboard *or* power supplies. The lesson is that a SAN designer should look at the *overall* MTBF of components when trying to evaluate the RAS characteristics of a product.

Availability

Availability of a system is a measure of how much time it is able to perform its higher-level functions, such as serving applications to end users. As with reliability, both hardware and software play a role. However, availability is not *necessarily* impacted by failures in components.

For example, assume that the system being analyzed is a host. Most SAN-attached hosts have redundant interfaces connected to the SAN with multipathing software to handle failures gracefully. (See "Multipathing Software" on page 22, and the sections following "Redundant Fabrics" on pages 251 through 260.) If one of the HBAs has an SFP failure, the system has experienced a reliability event, since the SFP will need to be "touched" by service personnel. More SFPs implies more frequent SFP failures. However, the system and its application are still available during an SFP failure: the host can still access data through the other HBA and serve its applications. At some point, someone will need to replace the SFP, but even this will not cause downtime if the HBA is designed correctly.

Application availability is usually considered to be the most important consideration in SAN design overall. Problems with availability have an impact at the end-user level, rather than being contained within IT or other systems management organizations. In the previous example, the SFP failure caused a reliability event which required service personnel to replace the part, but the application stayed online. If a non-redundant component failed – such as the host operating system or motherboard – then an availability event would have occurred which would require service involvement *and* application downtime. Given a choice between more frequent reliability events vs. more frequent availability events, most designers chose the former.

This is important because often the measures instituted to *in*crease availability also *de*crease reliability. If each system had only one HBA, then statistically there would be fewer service events: all things being equal, fewer components in a system implies less frequent failures, because there are fewer things which can fail. However, when a reliability event *did* occur, it would *also* cause an availability event.

The most common measure for this system characteristic is "nines of availability." As in, "this application has five nines of availability." It also may be abbreviated to simply "nines," as in, "this is a five–nines app." This measure refers to the *percentage* of *time* that a system is available. "Five nines" means that a system is available 99.999% of the time or more. To put it another way, it means that the system is <u>un</u>available no more than about 0.0001% of the time, which comes to about five minutes each year.

In order to achieve five nines of availability for a SAN-attached application, SAN designers implement physically isolated A/B redundant fabrics. With this strategy, an entire fabric can fail without causing an application availability event. Because availability tends to be more important, fully redundant designs are the industry best-practice.

Availability considerations are discussed in more detail in "Chapter 9: Availability Planning" starting on page 239.

Serviceability

Serviceability is a measure of how easy it is for service personnel to perform their jobs with respect to a particular product or system. This is largely a subjective measurement. As with the previous two RAS metrics, serviceability can include hardware, software, solutions, and even the overall network architecture.

This is an important consideration for SAN designers for two reasons:

1. Products with better serviceability tend to cost less to manage on an ongoing basis. For example, if a product is hard to use, more money will need to be spent on training, or on outside consultants.
2. Serviceability can affect uptime. Products that can be serviced faster can recover from outages faster. Also, more complex products are more likely subject to human administrator errors.

MTTR can be viewed as a serviceability metric as well as playing a role in reliability. If a component fails, how long will it take service personnel to fix it? The smaller the number for MTTR, the faster service was performed. This implies better serviceability.

However, this is not the most important aspect of serviceability, and most other aspects cannot be described by well-defined metrics. For example, many products have built-in diagnostic tools. Simply counting the number of tools would not provide a useful metric, since each tool might have or lack features that affect how easily a system can be serviced.

Many designers use feature checklists to compare products, listing the functions of the tools and weighting the ones that are the most important. E.g. "ping" might be a frequently used function, and therefore be worth "2" whereas "crash dump" might not be used often – we hope – and have a weight of "1". When two products are being compared, the features of each are mapped against this checklist. Bonus points may be awarded based on "more mature implementation" of a feature, or "more complete implementation."

In fact, maturity and completeness of implementation are usually more important to real-world serviceability than quantity of features. Having a large number of broken management features will be less helpful than having relatively few features which work properly. While no vendor has a perfect score on maturity or completeness, Brocade does outscore all competitors in these areas by a wide margin.

Unfortunately, doing a thorough evaluation of serviceability as part of the approach to component selection requires substantial effort on the part of the designer. Since serviceability is rarely the top concern when making a product selection, the time is usually better spent elsewhere. As a result, many SAN designers will use a simpler approach of listing e.g. just the top ten serviceability features on a checklist (e.g. no active components on chassis backplane) and scoring vendors based on how long they have been in the industry, and then using other criteria to make component selection decisions.

Performance

There are several areas to consider when thinking about SAN performance, including protocols, link rates, congestion, blocking, and latency. Trade-offs often need to be made between these and other performance considerations vs. cost.

For example, extending a SAN via any IP gateway product from Brocade or any other vendor will almost always underperform native FC extension, or FC over DWDM, or FC over SONET/SDH. It is simply not possible for a 1Gbit Ethernet link carrying high-overhead IP SAN traffic to perform on-par with 4Gbit FC links carrying protocol-efficient Fibre Channel frames. While the Brocade FCIP solution outperforms any competitive product from any vendor in real-world traffic conditions, even that platform cannot process large IP packets as efficiently as it could process streamlined FC frames. (See "SAN Protocols" on page 27 for a discussion of the differences between these approaches.) However, IP SAN solutions will also usually cost the least to implement, so the SAN designer must balance the performance and reliabil-

ity of FC against the sometimes-lower cost of IP. Most designers lean towards more reliable and faster solutions, since
they also tend to be simpler to implement, easier to troubleshoot, and capable of supporting future growth, but it is
something that must be evaluated on a case-by-case basis.

The bottom line is that the designer should keep performance in mind when evaluating any candidate SAN
design. Be sure to make decisions that can support the performance requirements of the initial deployment, *and* all
anticipated future increases in performance demand. Network
performance requirements tend to increase rather than decrease over time, and so all SAN protocol and topology
choices should be able to accommodate a wide range of performance scenarios.

SAN performance is discussed in more detail in "Chapter
8: Performance Planning" starting on page 185.

Scalability

Scalability can mean quite a few different things in the
context of storage networking. For example, it can be a
measure of how much data a particular RAID enclosure ac-
commodates. (As in, "*This* RAID array is more scalable than
that one because the cabinet is larger and therefore it can accept more disks.")

However, in the context of SAN infrastructure design, it
usually refers to how many ports a network model can support without needing to be fundamentally restructured. (As
in, "*This* network design is more scalable than *that* one because in this design each switch is larger and therefore the
network can accept more total ports for a given number of
domains.")

In theory, a single FC fabric could scale to over 16 million devices. This would be more than enough to meet the
projected demands of even the most aggressive customers. In

practice, however, it is not possible to achieve that size in a fabric. There are many factors which cause this, including limitations of fabric services, SAN management software, support matrices, and SAN management processes. (See also "Fabric vs. SAN vs. Meta SAN" on page 34.)

The bottom line is that SANs should be designed to scale to the largest size they could be expected to need to grow to in a reasonable time frame, rather than merely using the requirements at the time of implementation as a target. This prevents the SAN from being "painted into a corner" and needing to be fundamentally restructured after entering production. Because of this, SAN designers must consider scalability carefully when deciding on a top-level architecture.

More information on this topic can be found in "Chapter 7: Scalability Planning" starting on page 167.

Total Solution Cost

IT departments no longer have unlimited budgets, so it is necessary for SANs to be implemented in a cost-effective manner. The job of the SAN designer should be to consider the total cost of a solution, rather than looking only at a limited subset of the cost.

For example, some approaches to SAN design save on hardware cost, but offset that savings with an even larger increase in cost to the business from downtime. Using non-HA design strategies is an example of this. Before deploying a non-redundant SAN solution to save on cost, be sure to consider the long-term impact of downtime to the attached systems. Consider what the cost would be if a non-redundant SAN was used to support a disaster recovery solution, and failed during the disaster... thus preventing a restoration of business services. Even one incident like this in a large-scale operation would more than cover the entire cost of deploying several redundant SANs.

Similarly, it is sometimes possible to save money in the short term by using lower performing technologies. The hidden costs of this include lower productivity for personnel using SAN-attached systems, more frequent upgrades to the SAN infrastructure, and the potential of "painting the SAN into a corner" when it comes time to deploy next-generation solutions such as ILM and UC (p67), which inherently have higher performance requirements.

In most cases, SAN designers have found that cutting corners on infrastructure to save short-term cost tends to radically increase the total cost of ownership of the SAN. Even when cost is a key requirement for the design team, the key takeaway is to look at the *whole* picture of SAN cost, not just at any one aspect of it. Keep this in mind when evaluating network topologies and top-level HA architectures.

Distance Extension

In the wake of recent global events, corporations and government agencies alike have been focusing on disaster recovery and business continuance solutions. In some cases, this is driven by fiduciary duty to investors. In others, it is mandated by regulations. In addition, companies are increasingly looking at mergers or acquisitions and datacenter consolidation, which demands site-to-site data migration solutions. These trends tend to require connecting FC SANs at different sites separated by long distances.

The preferred approaches for this are based on higher performance and reliability technologies such as dark fiber, *x*WDMs, or SONET/SDH gateways. However, there are cases where these solutions are either unavailable or prohibitively expensive. If a high performance IP network with a high reliability service level agreement is available, an IP SAN approach can be considered.

More information on this topic can be found in "Chapter 11: Distance Planning" starting on page 275.

Implementation and Beyond

Once the SAN design is complete, in many cases, the job of the designer will be done. In most large-scale environments, the jobs of designer, implementer, and manager will be distinct. However, there are areas in which the designer can either facilitate or hinder subsequent tasks. SAN designers should therefore consider how the SAN will be installed and then managed on a day-to-day basis. Day-to-day management tasks generally include monitoring the health of the network, and performing adds, moves, and changes to the SAN itself and to the attached hosts and storage devices.

The scope of the "SAN implementation and management challenge" is radically different in small SANs vs. large ones.

In small deployments, SANs built with Brocade components rarely require day-to-day management at all because of Brocade's high product maturity and focus on plug-and-play functionality. In fact, Brocade periodically surveys user sites, and has found that a very large percentage of switches found in small deployments do not even have their management IP addresses configured at all; the switches simply take care of themselves without any intervention. At most, users in these environments need to understand the WEBTOOLS zoning interface, which is simple and intuitive.

In a large organization, however, installation and manageability are more complex issues. This is where the designer can affect the short- and long-term ease of use of the SAN.

For example, it tends to be more difficult to manage a SAN consisting of a single extremely large fabric, compared to managing a SAN consisting of two redundantly-configured fabrics. (p251) Intuitively, some designers might think that managing a single fabric would be easier, because changes such as zoning modifications would only need to be performed once. However, modern SAN management tools like

the Brocade Fabric Manager allow multiple fabrics to be controlled from a single point.

Additionally, having two physically separate fabrics allows
changes such as firmware upgrades to be applied one fabric at
a time, thus greatly reducing the risk associated with modifications to the environment.[45] Dividing the SAN into two
fabrics reduces the single-fabric size by 50%, which tends to
increase the reliability and response times of management
tools, and improves scalability at the management layer.[46]

In a large enough environment, the top-level SAN architecture selection also has an impact on manageability even if
"A/B" fabrics are used. If a designer selects a single *pair* of
large fabrics, for example, managing the potential downtime
caused by ongoing changes can be prohibitively difficult. If
the designer uses many smaller and unconnected fabrics, the
lack of data–plane connectivity can be just as challenging.
This is one reason for the explosive growth in the market for
the LSAN feature on the Brocade AP7420, 7500, and FR4-
18i blade: the LSAN architecture allows data–plane connec-

---

[45] This is one area where VSAN switches fall short. If you have one fully-
connected network and use VSAN software to segment it into "A/B" VSANs, as
recommended by the lone VSAN vendor, then a change to firmware affects all
VSANs simultaneously. Similarly, a denial of service attack which "took down" a
chassis would affect all VSANs at the same time. The bottom line is that the
VSAN vendor simply does not understand the HA requirements SAN design yet,
which is not surprising given that they have no experience in this category of
networking. Of course, Brocade does offer products which *can* support this model.
A designer could use hardware zoning instead of separate fabrics, or could use the
two domains of a SilkWorm director in this way, but these strategies are never
recommended.

[46] This is *yet another* area where VSAN switches fall short. All VSANs run their
fabric services on the same CP within a director. Scalability is a function of the
number of domains and ports being served in a SAN by a given set of compute
resources. If you have one flat fabric with x domains and y ports running on a CP,
you have a certain scalability function. If you have the same basic design, but use
VSANs to partition it, you will have at least 2x domains, and you will still have y
total ports, still being serviced by the same hardware. In other words, VSANs will
actually have *reduced* the scalability of the network…

tivity without creating one large, flat management region. (p255)

The designer is also likely to have input into the zoning strategy. By using a naming scheme that has short but meaningful identifiers for zone and alias names, the job of a subsequent SAN manager will be greatly simplified. (Zoning is discussed in "Chapter 10: Security Planning" starting on page 263.)

It is also possible to affect manageability when selecting SAN components. The designer may choose mature products from established vendors, or "bleeding edge" technologies from vendors new to the industry. Each approach has advantages.

New players in a market tend to deliver a larger quantity features, but not to fully implement or even test them, so their overall manageability strategy tends to be broad, but not deep. New players have even been known to give their equipment away for free, which reduces acquisition cost.

Vendors with mature technology tend to be more conservative about releasing new features, since they must protect their production installed base and new features tend to involve risk. However, these vendors tend to have more robust and stable implementations of the features which they do sell, since they have had more time to complete their code. Mature vendors are far less likely to give their equipment away, but it is almost always the case that the data served by the SAN is vastly more valuable than the SAN itself, and equipment cost must be taken in that context.

The SAN designer has substantial influence on which criteria to prioritize: quantity of management features, or quality. It often comes down to a choice between long-term cost due to management headaches, bugs, and lost data, vs. short term cost for non-free equipment.

Finally, the designer typically has influence on the selection of management packages. Using the Brocade Fabric Manager tool will simplify tasks associated with coordinating day-to-day management of multiple fabrics. Using Brocade SAN Health and SAN Health Professional will vastly simplify proactive management, since it automatically checks the SAN against evolving best-practices and has automated "housekeeping" features such as looking for unused zones.

More information on this topic can be found in "Chapter 12: Implementation Planning" starting on page 303.

Section Two

SAN Design Planning

Section Topics

- SAN Design Theory and Practice
- Installation and Configuration Tips
- Ongoing Management Tips

5: Project Planning

Any SAN deployment project can be broken down into discrete phases. First, requirements are gathered to determine what the SAN is supposed to accomplish. Second, the SAN is designed. Then equipment is purchased. The new equipment is deployed in a pre-production environment which is then tested. Next, the SAN is rolled into production. Finally, it enters a maintenance phase. Eventually, pieces of the SAN will become obsolete, and may be removed from service altogether or reallocated to lower-tier functions.

This set of phases is referred to as the overall "lifecycle" of a SAN. It will also apply to a project if a designer is adding to, removing from, or changing things about an existing SAN. Whatever the nature of the project, it will have to go through those steps. Perhaps the most important, though, are the first two: the requirements gathering and design phases. This is when most of the decision-making takes place, and is the part of the lifecycle which is the focus of this chapter.

In order to execute any of the subsequent phases properly, these first phases must be on target. If business requirements are ill considered, or if the design is badly conceived, then even a flawless execution on subsequent phases will be ineffective at meeting business objectives.

To ensure that the design is appropriate, use a structured project planning process for these steps. The process might be based on existing formalized IT department policies and procedures, or might be something that applies just to the SAN rollout. One way or another, there needs to be a process which results in the creation of a solid project plan before buying any equipment. Developing the plan requires research and analysis. This chapter discusses how to construct an effective SAN planning process, showing what data to collect, how to interpret it, and providing some tips on how to use this data to cost-justify the project.

Overview of the SAN Planning Process

There are many effective ways to approach SAN planning. As long as the end result is an effective design that meets all business objectives, then the planning process is a success. The remainder of this chapter uses one possible planning method as an example, but this should not be construed as precluding other approaches. The example SAN planning process is intended mainly for enterprise-class deployments, and may be more involved than smaller-scale deployments require. It is divided into five phases:

Phase I: Gathering Requirements
Phase II: Developing Technical Specifications
Phase III: Estimating Project Cost
Phase IV: ROI or TCO Analysis (if needed)
Phase V: Detailed SAN Design and Rollout Plan

In the first phase, the SAN designer will interview everybody who has a stake in the project. This may include systems, storage, and network administrators, IT managers, application owners, key end users, and functional owners of business processes related to systems attached to the SAN.

The second phase consists of analyzing the data collected in Phase I, and determining – at least in broad terms – what technology will need to be used to meet the business requirements. It is not yet necessary to decide exactly which port on which switch will be used to connect a given host, but the designer should analyze and decide on things such as how many ports are required in total, and what the high-level network topology will look like.

That data will be used in Phase III to create a list of required parts and equipment. Once a designer knows what software packages will be used, and how many cables, media, HBAs, switch ports, routers, and gateways will be needed, it will be possible to estimate the cost of deployment. There may be room for error in that estimate, but it should be possible to get fairly close.

Once a reasonably accurate cost estimate is available, it can be used to calculate whether or not the SAN project makes business sense. In most cases, the Return on Investment (ROI) analysis will be very simple. "The disaster recovery SAN will cost $x to deploy. Our company has a regulatory requirement to implement a disaster recovery solution to do business in Europe. If we fail to do so, the penalty to our business will be in excess of 100,000 times the project cost in lost profit, since we will be forced to shut down our operations." In cases this clear-cut, spending a great deal of time on an ROI analysis would be silly, but in other cases the analysis will take more work. A very simple calculation is provided in this chapter; a more comprehensive approach is discussed in "Appendix A: Basic Reference". It is also possible to perform a "Total Cost of Ownership" (TCO) analysis to make the case for a SAN. This kind of analysis tends to make the case *very* strongly, since it more accurately reflects the savings achieved through management simplification. It is generally accepted in the industry that SANs yield more than a 50% improvement on data management TCO. However, performing a TCO analysis is much more difficult than calculating ROI, and is beyond the scope of this work.

Either way, once the project is justified, the designer will create a more detailed design document and plan for deploying it. This can be very specific, including a zoning and port-attachment plan, specific steps for installing, testing, and releasing the SAN to production, and a more detailed set of topology diagrams showing how everything is supposed to be connected.

Maintaining a SAN Project Plan

Throughout the planning process, it is necessary to document the collected data, the interpretations of the data, the equipment needed and its associated costs, and the design that emerges from the process. In most respects, this set of documentation *is* the project plan. It is used by the SAN project manager to get the SAN in place on time and within budget. Many IT departments already have forms and processes in place for building project plans. If so, these can be adapted to the SAN project. If not, simply record all activities discussed in the remainder of this chapter, maintaining them both electronically and in print form.

When the SAN project plan is complete, the project manager will have enough information to buy all required equipment, and stage its deployment. Assigning and scheduling resources to meet the project budget, milestones and goals should be easy, and justifiable to the IT department chain of command.

For projects which involve growing or changing an existing SAN, consider using Brocade SAN Health to produce an initial documentation set.

Determining the Players

Before gathering customer requirements, identify the implementation team members, the key decision makers, and eventual customers of the SAN.

Identify the SAN Project Manager and Designer

The SAN Project Manager has the responsibility of coordinating the entire SAN effort and usually has the SAN project plan as a deliverable. The designer has responsibility for translating business needs into technical requirements, and turning those into a detailed design. The manager's coordination effort includes holding regular meetings, creating action items and driving the decision making process to resolve them. Many times, it also involves getting the right personnel to communicate with each other, and keeping everyone informed of the plan and progress.

In some cases, the manager will also be the SAN designer and therefore responsible for technical deliverables as well. In other cases, it will be the manager to whom the SAN designer reports. At other times, the manager will be a peer of the designer, with overall responsibility for the success of the project being shared.

Identify the Technical Team

Small SANs can be put in place by a single person, but if the SAN consists of more than one switch, generally the team will have multiple members. It is important to engage these people during the design phase if possible. This will ensure that any technical considerations they might have are addressed, to minimize implementation timeframe surprises. It will usually also help for them to feel engaged in the process, so that they feel ownership of the eventual success of the project. Depending on the intended job(s) that the SAN will perform, and the scale of the deployment, in large environments, the technical team will consist of one or more members covering each of the following areas:

- SAN Administrators
- Systems Administrators
- Storage Administrators
- IP Network Administrators
- Database Administrators
- Application Specialists

Identify the Decision Makers

There are generally three groups of decision makers involved in a SAN rollout: the people who are responsible for signing off on the expenditure, the people who are responsible for deploying and/or managing the SAN, and the people who will actually use the applications running on the SAN-attached servers. Just as in the case of the technical team, it is always a good idea to engage these people early in the project. If they understand the business value of the SAN, and have the opportunity to give input about its design, they are more likely to support a smooth approval process. Key decision makers in large environments often include:

- CEO, CTO, CIO, or CFO
- Accounting Personnel
- Purchasing Personnel
- IT VPs, Directors, and/or Managers
- Technical Team Members
- Senior Business Application Users
- Business Process Owners

Identify the Customers of the SAN

"SAN customers" could be defined as anyone using any system connected to the SAN in any way. With that definition, if the SAN supported a web server cluster, then any client accessing the cluster from the Internet could be considered a customer of the SAN. It is beneficial to know this during the design phase, so that you will know the scope of the customers served by the SAN. This can affect decisions about SAN design. A cluster providing web hosting for a popular Internet site will generally have more sensitivity to downtime and higher performance requirements than a departmental SAN serving a workgroup inside a small business.

However, that broad of a definition is not always useful, since the real question at *this* point is who should be involved in the design process. It will be more efficient to include only those users who have a strong professional interest in, or also have decision making authority related to the project. In practice, this usually means only including a few "power users" to represent the customers in the design phase.

Gathering Requirements

Organizations no longer have the luxury of implementing technology for its own sake. "SANs are cool therefore we should build one" is unlikely to get the job done. Even though SANs are indeed cool – and Brocade SANs in particular are *very* cool – most IT departments will need a more specific reason to invest the time and money on the project. If business requirements for a SAN do *not* exist, the IT dollars will likely be spent on other technologies such as FAN software. In addition to ensuring that the project gets funded, gathering requirements is also critical to establishing the objectives of the SAN, which ensures that the eventual design will be appropriate. Information gathered in this phase should be as complete and accurate as possible.

Each individual identified in the previous section may be considered a "stakeholder" in the SAN project. The next step is to interview them to determine what they feel the SAN should provide, and how it should work overall. The stakeholders should be interviewed in person, if possible, or at least by telephone. They should be asked about any current issues which need to be resolved, and what they believe to be their requirements for the SAN. It is usually desirable to interview one person at a time, synthesize the data collected from them, and then hold at least one "roundtable" meeting where all stakeholders present to review the requirements before proceeding to the next phase.

Determine the Business Problems

The set of business problem statements in a SAN project plan show *why* the SAN is needed from the point of view of the overall business. I.e., in a for-profit organization, these statements answer the question, "How does the SAN make more money for our business?" If the organization is not for-profit, these statements answer a similar question: "How does the SAN help us better achieve our mission?" These statements will be created by interviewing the stakeholders identified in previous steps.

In each interview, try to determine all of the business problems which each stakeholder believes need to be addressed by the SAN, in order to ensure that it solves as many of them as possible. Also make sure to ask about future requirements as well as current needs. It is generally accepted that SANs should be designed according to *projected* requirements three or more years out.

It is important to avoid having preconceptions about a particular technical implementation strategy while doing this. Do not ask a stakeholder, "Does the SAN need to have a core/edge architecture?" since that does not relate to a business need. Ask the stakeholders about technology only when it is related directly to business objectives. For example, in some situations, you might ask a technical team member, "How fast does the backup have to complete?" That would be a legitimate question to ask a systems administrator; because they might have a backup window that constrains the amount of time they are allowed to complete the operation, determined by business needs such as the hours of operation of an assembly line. On the other hand, "How fast should each ISL run" would not be appropriate, since it does not relate directly to a business need. The speed of an ISL is not necessarily correlated to the speed at which a backup can complete.[47] It may take multiple interviews and discussions to correctly identify each business issue, since many stakeholders

---

[47] Another way to look at that is to compare 4Gbit and 10Gbit ISLs. If a user is asked about ISL link speed, and says that each ISL has to run at 10Gbit, this is likely based on their desire to move a specific amount of data in a specific amount of time, rather than a real need to have 10Gbit ISLs. They may not be aware that 4Gbit links can be trunked together to form evenly balanced 32Gbit pipes: much faster than 10Gbit technology. It is also possible to balance up to eight of those using Dynamic Path Selection, forming a balanced 256Gbit path. By stating that the links must be 10Gbit, the users would actually be precluding a faster, less expensive, and more highly-available solution. If the designer had asked how much data needed to be moved in what timeframe, they would be able to apply any technical solution to meet the real business requirements.

will be unable or unwilling to separate technical implementation from business needs in their minds.

In most cases, a business need driving the creation of a SAN can be phrased in one or two sentences, containing a problem statement. Some examples of business problems for which SANs are an appropriate solution include:

- "Backups are taking too long to complete. We need to reduce the time by 50%."
- "We are spending too much money on storage, and the storage we already have is underutilized. We need to be able to use the storage we already have instead of buying more arrays."
- "We are spending too much money on administering storage. We need to have more data managed by fewer personnel."
- "We have regulatory requirements that make HA and business continuance solutions mandatory."
- "We've had too much downtime lately. Uptime must be 24 x 7 and backups must not impact users."

Determine the Business Requirements

Business requirements are subtly different from business problems. A problem shows what issue must be solved; a requirement shows – at least partially – what the solution must look like. Business problem statements such as those shown above generally translate directly into business-oriented SAN requirements. For example, this problem statement was made in the previous section:

We are spending too much money on storage, and the storage we already have is underutilized. We need to be able to use the storage we already have instead of buying more arrays.

This problem statement could translate directly into a SAN business requirement such as this:

The SAN must allow more hosts to reach any given storage array, so that utilization can be improved. This must allow us to attain an x% increase in storage utilization efficiency to reduce expenditures on new arrays.

Phrasing the problem this way shows how the SAN relates to business objectives. One way to include this in the SAN project plan would be to show the business problem first, followed by the business requirements. For example, the SAN project manager might write the following entry into the project plan after interviewing a stakeholder named Joe who made statements such as those above:

Notes from interview with Joe

According to Joe, we are spending too much money on storage, and the storage we already have is underutilized. In some cases, we have 80% free space on a storage array, and yet need to buy another array because the systems which need space cannot access the storage arrays which have space available. He says that we need to be able to use the storage space we already have instead of buying more arrays. Therefore the SAN must allow more hosts to reach any given storage array, so that utilization can be improved. He was not sure about the exact amount of money we're spending on arrays today, so I will have to do further research on that. As a starting point, I'm guessing that in order to be meaningful to our business, the SAN must allow us to attain an 80% or greater increase in storage utilization efficiency to reduce expenditures on new arrays. I therefore conclude based on this interview that a probable business requirement for the SAN is as follows:

Requirement*: Provide an 80% or greater increase in the utilization of our storage assets to save $x on new array purchases over a period of y years.*

Some common business requirements include:

- The SAN must allow the business to continue to operate during times of catastrophe, such as a fire, flood, hurricane, or earthquake.

- The SAN must reduce our overall IT storage management personnel costs by $x per month over a period of y years.
- The SAN must allow full backups to complete in no more than x hours, and must allow all systems to remain online during the backup process in order to save $y by increasing manufacturing line productivity.

Notice that one of the statements above is not very specific. The first of the three statements does not say *how long* the business is allowed to be interrupted in a disaster, or *how much money* is lost per time period of inactivity. By "continue to operate", does the statement mean that there cannot be even one second of interruption? Or one minute? Or one day? How much money is involved if the interruption time period goal is not met? One dollar per day? One million dollars per hour? Will somebody *die* if the system is down? (This is quite possible with military or other government installations, or medical facilities.) Each answer can lead to radically different technical approaches and radically different allowable cost structures for the SAN. Be sure to gather *specific* business requirements, with each requirement statement specifying *what* needs to happen, *when* it needs to happen, and *how much money or mission impact* is involved if the requirement is not met.

Determine the Technical Requirements

Once the business requirements of the SAN project have been identified, focus on translating those into technical requirements. This will include gathering information about technology already known to apply to the project – such as the applications and existing devices which will be connected to the SAN - and forming high-level conclusions about the new technology which must be deployed – such as the number of switch ports for devices to be initially attached and the expected rate of growth in port count.

Identify Existing Equipment and Components

Make a survey of the devices already in place which will be connected to the SAN. It is usually a good idea to keep an open mind about which pre-existing devices need to be kept vs. which devices might be candidates for upgrading. Often, older hardware can be upgraded at little or no cost, because new hardware has dramatically reduced support costs. (I.e. often the cost of supporting existing hardware is greater than the cost of replacing it as part of the SAN rollout. Just keep an open mind for this possibility.)

If the SAN project is a modification of an existing SAN, use the Brocade SAN Health tool to make a survey of the existing devices. Switch hardware types and firmware levels are particularly important in this case.

Also include questions about existing equipment when interviewing any technical team members. Ask if there is any documentation for existing devices covering things such as host names, application names and versions, and hardware installed. Ask if any new equipment or software has already been selected and/or purchased.

Once you have a high-level list of the equipment and components, assess each piece in more detail to minimize the chance of having any surprises during installation. The following questions are examples of details that the SAN project manager should have:

- What hardware (hosts, HBAs, storage, switches, routers, bridges) is currently installed?
- How is the hardware (hosts, HBAs, storage, switches, etc.) currently being utilized?
- What firmware is installed on each component?
- What software is installed on each component?
- Are there any known compatibility issues between any of these devices?

- Which devices will need to access each other, vs. simply being attached to the same fabric(s)? (This affects the design of the zoning configuration.)
- Where is the hardware located and how is it physically and logically accessed?
- What are the dimensions of each of the components and are they rack mounted?

Identify All Business Critical Applications

During the interview process make sure to identify all business- or mission-critical applications and how they are used. Find out what happens to the operation if these systems are down. Anything considered critical should be dual-attached to *physically* separate fabrics in order to be in line with industry best-practices for HA SAN design. Using a single director chassis and dividing it in half via zoning, Virtual Fabrics, Administrative Domains, FC routing, VSANs, or any similar technology *does not produce an HA solution*.

Assessment of Data center Facilities

The facilities need to be assessed to find out if there are limitations on the space, power, cooling, or physical access which would need to be factored into the SAN design. Required upgrades or modifications should be accounted for in the project budget and schedule. Alternately, if upgrades or modifications to the facilities are impractical, then this can constrain the SAN design: the equipment used in the design might have to work within the limits of the facilities. Brocade directors lead the industry in power and cooling efficiency, but even these systems still need resources.

The assessment of the facilities should include the following information:

- The name of the person with authority over and responsibility for the facility
- Is the following infrastructure sufficient for the SAN?
  - o   AC Power

- Number of available circuits
- Available rated draw on each circuit
- Voltage and connector types
- UPS protection
  - Cooling
    - Total capacity
    - Airflow to SAN equipment
  - Network cabling
    - Both optical and copper infrastructure
    - For optical cables, note the connector type (e.g. SC, ST, LC), diameter (e.g. 9, 50, 62.5 micron), and "mode" (e.g. SMF, MMF)
    - Also consider testing for cable reliability and DB loss, especially if connections will traverse multiple patch bays or run for long distances.
  - Available rack space
    - Is the space is in a 4-post cabinet or 2-post "telco" rack?
    - Note contiguous blocks of space, not just total space
  - Elevator capabilities, if not on ground floor
  - Lift(s) available, if installing directors into racks

Develop Broad Technical Specifications

Now that the business requirements have been documented, and the specifications of any pre-existing technical constraints have been listed, the next phase is to create a working document of technical specifications of your SAN. In other words, to map business requirements onto existing SAN technologies which address them.

It is important to note that the following material relies on concepts which may not yet have been thoroughly introduced in previous chapters. For example, a top-level high-availability SAN architecture might need to be selected in this phase, but how to evaluate different availability options is not discussed in detail until a later chapter. Similarly, this section calls upon the designer to estimate performance requirements, the process for which is not discussed until much later in the book. In this chapter, the intention is to communicate the overall process, and then fill in the details throughout the remainder of the work.

Throughout this process, it is important to keep the future of the SAN in mind. Again, it is a generally accepted best practice to design SANs according to *projected* requirements, looking three to five years out.

The first step in developing technical specifications is to identify the physical locations of the *data centers* in which SAN-attached equipment will reside. For example, if the SAN is to provide a disaster recovery solution, it is likely that some components will reside in a primary data center and others will reside at a recovery site. Within a campus, equipment may be spread across different buildings. This will dictate the highest level of the SAN design: the endpoints of the MAN/WAN topology. Often, designers create multiple architectural diagrams for their project, and they usually start with the highest level diagram: how different geographical areas of the SAN relate to each other.

Next, identify the mechanisms available for connecting these locations together. If existing networking infrastructure is in place and the SAN is expected to use it, document its characteristics. This can include available bandwidth, latency, packet loss rates, uptime, etc. In many such cases, it will be necessary to come back to this stage and reevaluate whether or not the SAN really needs to use a pre-existing network if it turns out that the characteristics of said network are insufficient for the needs of the SAN. If a network is *not* already in place, or if the existing network is not going to be able to support the SAN, then list the options which are available in the area. More information about this process is available in "Chapter 11: Distance Planning" starting on page 275.

Next, estimate how much bandwidth will be required to traverse each intra-site link. This estimate will be refined later, but for now base it in the data collected earlier such as how long a backup across the SAN is allowed to take. Compare all of the characteristics of a pre-existing network, or a proposed candidate network against the throughput and availability requirements of the SAN. Be sure that these characteristics are appropriate for the SAN, since many WANs and MANs are not sufficiently fast or reliable for storage traffic, especially IP networks. Since most networks tend to increase their loading over time, make sure that the evaluation takes into account both increasing SAN utilization and any other network applications which use or are intended to use the same infrastructure.

These steps should allow the SAN project manager to work with the SAN designer to complete a top-level architectural diagram of the SAN, showing any campus, metro, or wide area connections. It should include the locations, the distanced between them, the required performance between each site, and information about the networks which could connect them. This yields a "10,000 foot view" of the SAN.

After that is complete, decide on the overall high-availability model for the SAN. If the SAN is expected to have high enough uptime to support mission-critical applications, and/or is expected to grow to a large scale, then a redundant fabric approach is always recommended. This has been the industry-wide best-practice for many years. It is possible to implement a single SAN with "highly available" directors and partition them into separate fabrics, but the chassis itself will still be a single point of failure. (Look at it this way: if a fire suppression system like a sprinkler goes off above a single chassis, it will fail as a unit no matter how robust its software architecture might be.) This is discussed in "Chapter 9: Availability Planning" starting on page 239.

Note down how many device ports (hosts and storage) will be located at each site. The design will need to allocate switch ports for all of these devices. Be sure to include all *ports*, not just *devices*. Any given device can have one, two, or many ports connected to the SAN. Also be sure to specify to which of the redundant fabrics the ports are connected, and to note down any expectations the device port may have about the availability characteristics of the switch port on the other end of the cable. Devices with high availability expectations should generally be connected to directors such as the Brocade 24000 or 48000, whereas lower-tier devices might be connected to either over-subscribed blades on directors or to switches such as the Brocade 200e, 4100, 4900, or 5000. This should give the designer a list of how many and what kind of device ports each fabric will need.

Then add to this the number of additional devices which are expected to be added to the SAN within a reasonable timeframe. "Reasonable" can vary from one month to several years. It depends on how often the environment can withstand major changes, and how much data is available to make projections. If the SAN must remain stable for a long time, then it is advisable to pre-allocate ports for future devices, in order to minimize the effort of deploying them. If the data for making projections is limited, it is best to assume a high growth rate in the design, to avoid running out of scalability down the road.

In addition to ports for current and future host and storage devices, the SAN may need ports for ISLs or IFLs. For SANs measured in the 100s or 1000s of ports, the rule of thumb is to allocate about 10% to 15% of ports for these links in "typical" customer environments. If the SAN will rely heavily on traffic locality,[48] then fewer links may be needed. Generally speaking, this should never be fewer than two links per switch, so that resilient topologies can be supported. If lo-

---

[48] Locality is the practice of connecting storage "close" to their hosts. This increases performance and reliability, since that traffic will not need to traverse many if any network links. However, using locality does take planning effort.

cality is *not* employed, or if the SAN requires particularly high performance, then more links may be needed. In some customer environments, up to 50% of ports are use for ISLs. Other customers have zero ISLs. Whatever seems most appropriate, add this to the required port count.

At this point, the designer should have enough information to come up with a slightly more detailed preliminary sketch of the SAN. It would show the sites involved, the connections between sites, the overall number of ports needed at each site, the availability and performance requirements of those ports, and – usually – a breakdown of those ports into multiple fabrics (A/B) for high availability.

If any of the fabrics are "large" – such as a thousand ports or more – or are expected to become so, then the designer should consider breaking the design up into smaller fabrics interconnected via routers using LSANs. This should also be considered if any wide or metropolitan area links are involved, or if different administrators are responsible for different areas of the SAN, or if any ISLs will be mapped over unreliable IP networks. Modify the preliminary sketch to account for connecting the individual fabrics together with FC routers if this is desired.[49]

Estimate Project Cost

Once the technical specifications of the SAN have been documented, the next step is to estimate the cost of the SAN project. While it is true that the SAN diagram is still preliminary, it should now be possible to create a list of all parts needed to build the SAN with a reasonable degree of confidence. This should include cables, media, switches, routers, HBAs, racks, patch panels, wide area connections, gateways, projected electric power consumption, and so on. Also in-

---

[49] Other sections of this book talk about the use of LSANs and the router. For more in-depth discussions, see *Multiprotocol Routing for SANs* by Josh Judd.

clude any consulting or professional services personnel needed during the rollout. This list can be used to request quotes from vendors, which in turn can be used to estimate the cost for the deployment.

Project Justification (ROI or TCO)

The design team should now have an idea about the cost of the project and the benefits it will provide. To determine whether or not the SAN makes financial sense, subtract the costs from the benefits. Make sure to include something for both "hard" and "soft" benefits, to accurately represent the value of the SAN. Several methods for doing this calculation are well established in the industry. The two most popular are known as "Return on Investment" (ROI) and "Total Cost of Ownership" (TCO) analysis.

In most cases, the ROI or TCO analysis does not need to be detailed or exhaustive. Most often, IT department personnel simply need to show management that the SAN will produce a real benefit, since the IT industry as a whole has accepted the SAN model of datacenter design. Look at it this way: how much justification is required prior to deciding to install a LAN? In the early days of networking, quite a lot. Today, however, it is simply accepted that IT departments need one or more LANs, and doing an ROI or TCO project to prove that a LAN is needed simply does not occur to people. SANs have now moved into a similar realm.

Because SANs are now generally accepted as a basic datacenter networking requirement, the justification analysis may often be presented verbally, or as a hand-written calculation on a piece of scratch paper. In most cases, if more analysis is required, it will generally take the form of justifying *which* SAN to implement, rather than justifying why to implement a SAN at all. If the SAN justification analysis needs to be more detailed, there are structured ways of approaching it. One method is discussed in the section entitled "Return on

Investment Calculation" starting on page 394 within the "Appendix A: Basic Reference" chapter.

Detailed SAN Design and Rollout Plan

Once the project is approved and equipment has been ordered, the SAN designer and project manager should create a more detailed design, and a step-by-step plan for rolling it out into production.

The design should cover exactly where each switch is to be located, how it is to be configured, what zoning policy will be used, which switch or router ports will be connected to each other, and connections to nodes such as hosts and storage devices. It is also beneficial to specify how the SAN is expected to grow. If certain ports or chassis blade slots are reserved for future use as ISLs, specifying that in the initial design document will save a great deal of time and trouble later on. Also consider how each piece of the SAN will be managed. Brocade has a number of switch and router management tools. For example, in most routed environments, Brocade Fabric Manager is always recommended. In any environment, Brocade SAN Health should always be used as an ongoing proactive monitoring and auditing tool. At the time of this writing, it is available for free on the Brocade website.

Most large-scale organizations already have a formalized "release to production", "change control", or "change management" process. If so, the SAN rollout plan will be mapped onto that process. In any case, most network rollout plans generally have something like the following structure:

1. Stage the SAN in a pre-production environment and test it prior to rollout.
2. Once functionality has been verified, move the SAN to production. Depending on the project, this could simply mean changing a DNS entry, or it could involve a planned application outage. The goal should be to minimize risk and application downtime as much as

possible. Remember that rule #1 in IT is "Don't break any production applications." Also keep in mind rule #2, which is: "See Rule #1." List all steps involved in the rollout, any risks associated with those steps, and a fallback plan in case one or more of the risks is realized.

3. During the rollout, verify all major functionality again. Be prepared to use a fallback plan if functionality is compromised and the issues cannot immediately be corrected.

4. After deployment, monitor the SAN regularly using SAN Health and other proactive troubleshooting tools to ensure that it is performing correctly. Also monitor help desk calls related to SAN-attached applications to determine if users are still able to work effectively.

The first step in the process above talked about pre-production staging. This may or may not be a requirement, depending on the scale of the project and the criticality of the affected applications. Many large-scale operations will maintain a separate test environment for some of their applications, but smaller scale operations might not be able to afford this. For example, a bank might have a set of servers running the back-end database for their world-wide ATM (Bankomat) network. Making changes directly to these servers would involve unacceptable risk to their operations. They would maintain a completely separate group of servers for pre-production database testing: a single change-related problem would cost the bank massively more than the cost of the pre-production staging environment, so justifying the expense would not pose a problem. Those servers will often be connected to a permanent pre-production SAN, which mirrors the production environment in most respects. Using Brocade routers, they can move data from production into the test SAN via LSANs, so that their pre-production servers are using the latest data, then back into production efficiently after changes have been tested. If this is the case, the SAN project plan would call for deployment in the test environment, followed by testing, followed by production rollout.

Using a conservative change control approach such as the one outlined above is not a SAN-specific requirement. Using this kind of rollout strategy is the best practice for any new IT installation, if it can affect existing production applications. Smaller scale projects or projects involving only net new applications can use a simpler release process, and larger scale projects involving mission-critical applications would tend to use a more involved process.

6: Topology Planning

Every network design has a topology. In this context, "topology" refers to the arrangement of switches, routers, and other pieces of network equipment. When diagramming a network, these elements will form various geometric patterns, which are generally recognizable, and will largely define the major properties of the network. Factors in a SAN fabric or Meta SAN such as performance, availability, and scalability can be affected by topology more than anything else. It is therefore critical for a designer to understand what topology options are available, and how each will affect the SAN.

The robust nature of the Brocade Fabric Operating System allows SAN designers to create fabrics with arbitrarily complex topologies, provided that vendor support limits such as scalability and hop counts are observed. However, just because it is *possible* to do something complex does not mean that it is *advisable* to do so. Use Occam's Razor[50] when configuring networks: if you can make a network smaller in radius and simpler in design, it is usually best to do so.

To keep things simple, most designers use a limited number of topologies, with the most common being the storage-centric, cascade, ring, mesh, and core/edge (CE). Almost all SAN design problems can be solved using one of these to-

---

[50] William of Occam was a medieval European philosopher who said something which amounted to, "all other things being equal, the simplest solution is usually the best." Which means that if your network diagram looks like a bowl of spaghetti, it's time to go back to the drawing board...

pologies, and/or combining them in various ways. For example, it is possible to take four CE networks and connect their cores together in a mesh. This is a hybrid of the CE and mesh designs, and is very useful for disaster recovery solutions.

This chapter discusses the first three topologies briefly, defining the topology and describing its characteristics. After this, the remainder of the chapter – and indeed the remainder of the book – focuses almost exclusively on CE designs and their variations, since these are by far the most popular designs for larger networks.

Storage-Centric Design

This approach isn't exactly a "network topology" in quite the same way as the following options. The idea with storage-centric design is that only multi-port storage arrays will be used, and the storage network will consist of directors or switches attached to these ports, but *not* to each other. That is, there will be no ISLs or IFLs in the design. The RAID controller can "steer" LUNs to whichever fabric needs it by moving it between ports, so any host can reach any LUN.

This design strategy has some advantages. It tends to be reliable, fast, and simple. However, it isn't scalable or flexible. For example, if it becomes necessary to attach a 2-port RAID array or a JBOD at some point, then this networking model stops working. Similarly, if it is necessary to scale past the number of ports on one array, the strategy breaks down. It also is not possible to have hosts on those fabrics directly access centralized disaster recovery or tape SANs; hosts will require three or more HBAs to connect to these services.

That is not to say that there is anything "wrong" with this approach. Like everything else in network engineering, there are simply trade-offs to consider. If this approach is used, consider connecting the fabrics together with routers, to handle off-fabric connectivity needs.

Cascade Topology

Cascaded networks consist of a group of switches connected in a row. Each switch in the middle of the line is connected to the switches on either side, and the switches on the endpoints are connected to only one inside switch. It is possible to use one or many ISLs between adjacent switches. Figure 28 shows two examples of cascaded networks.

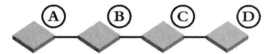

Four-Switch Cascade

Six-Switch Cascade

Figure 28 - Cascade Topology

This design is not scalable, not high performance, and not highly reliable. Scaling the SAN requires adding more switches to either end, which increases the end-to-end hop count and the potential for performance-limiting latency and congestion. In other words, the overall network performance *decreases* as the number of devices and switches attached to the network *increases*. This is the exact opposite of the desired situation: designers would want performance to increase.

It is possible to mitigate this by adding ISLs between existing switches whenever new switches are added. For example, if the A → D network at the top were to be scaled into the A → F network below, perhaps the designer would add ISLs between A and B, B and C, and C and D when the E and F switches were added to the fabric.

Of course, adding interior ISLs whenever a switch is added to the exterior of the chain is cost prohibitive, and limits the scalability of the solution, so as a practical matter this is never done, so cascaded networks inevitably have reducing performance as they grow.

Look again at Figure 28. In the SAN at the top of the figure, there might be a "conversation" between the A and D switches. This would use the ISLs AB, BC, and CD. If the E and F switches were added to the end of the chain, there might suddenly be conversations between B and E, and C and F. Note that none of these three conversations use either the same starting point or endpoint, so they *should* be unrelated. However, the B–E conversation uses two of the same ISLs at the preexisting A–D conversation: both flow over BC and CD. Similarly, the C–F conversation uses CD and DE, thus overlapping with both of the others. In a cascaded network, seemingly unrelated conversations tend to contend for the same limited network bandwidth.

In addition, the failure of a switch in the middle will cause the network to segment: it is a single point of failure. If the "D" switch or CD ISL failed, it would interrupt all three conversations, not just the A–D flow. Adding more interior ISLs will not mitigate this problem.

Because of these undesirable characteristics, designers should not generally use cascaded designs if performance, availability, or scalability are factors. However, the cascade is the most basic topology. It is easy and inexpensive to deploy. As a result, cascaded topologies can be appropriate for very, very small fabrics. Ideally, cascades should be limited to two-switch networks. With these networks, the issues mentioned above simply do not apply, since a two-switch design is a "degenerate case" of the cascade topology. They may also be used when most or all traffic is localized (p209) within each switch, and the ISLs are for management and/or low-priority / occasional use applications.

Ring Topology

Rings are like cascaded networks, except that the end-points are connected together. Figure 29 shows a six-switch ring topology SAN.

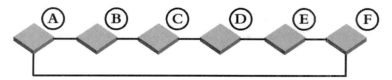

Six-Switch Ring

Figure 29 - Ring Topology

Rings have an important advantage over cascades in that they offer an alternate path. If a switch or link in a ring fails, traffic will flow around the ring in the other direction. Devices on A would normally go through F to get to a device on switch E. If switch F failed, the traffic would go through switches C, B, and D.[51] Recall the previous example in which all three conversations in the cascade network failed when switch D went down. In a ring, two of those conversations would have been able to continue by using an alternate path.

In addition to being more available, rings improve performance. In Fibre Channel networks running FSPF, traffic should always flow between switches in a ring using the shortest available path. For example, a device on switch A talking to a device on switch F would use ISL AF, instead of going the other direction through switches B through E. A cascaded network would not have that link and therefore could not choose the shorter path, so rings have lower hop counts than cascades on average. While rings are better than cascades in some ways, most of the same issues apply to both topologies. For example, installing an additional switch in-

---

[51] Rings become cascades when broken in this way.

creases the hop count in a ring, thus lowering performance and reliability.

In fact, in some ways rings are worse than cascades. With rings, the installation of a new switch is disruptive: part of the ring must be broken temporarily to insert a new switch. In order for a seventh switch to be installed in the Figure 29 network and still maintain its ring topology, one of the ISLs would need to be disconnected, and all IO using that path would be adversely affected for the duration. For example, if the switch were installed on the far side of F, then the AF ISL would need to be disconnected temporarily, disrupting any traffic which was using that path.

Like cascaded networks, rings are appropriate for small designs with high locality. Beyond four domains or so, a different topology will likely be a better choice. They are also appropriate for some MAN/WAN applications, where the topology of a preexisting MAN/WAN dictates the topology of the SAN being carried over it.

Side Note

Ring topology networks gained popularity early in the evolution of data networking. Protocols such as ARCNet, FIDDI, and Token Ring all had ring characteristics built into them. However, a number of inherent limitations were discovered to apply to rings, and even these ring-centric protocols were adapted to support star topologies. (The star topology was the basis for Core/Edge networks.)

Mesh Topology

Mesh topologies involve the connection of every switch to every other switch using at least one ISLs per connection path.[52] Figure 30 shows a six-switch mesh. Mesh designs solve many of the problems associated with rings and cascades. Every switch is just one hop away, so adding more switches will not increase hop count. Installing a new switch is non-disruptive, since it does not need to be installed between two already-connected switches. Not only are there alternate paths, unlike a cascade, there are in fact *many* of them, so mesh designs are highly resilient.

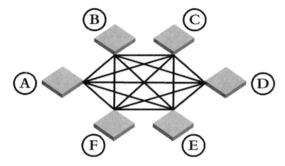

Six-Switch Mesh

Figure 30 - Mesh Topology

However, there are several very important disadvantages to this approach.

- Cost. Even in relatively small meshed networks, the ratio of ISLs to usable ports is unfavorable. As the total network size increases, the available ports per switch will decrease.

- Scalability. Meshed networks simply do not scale, because of the principle outlined in point #1. Every switch added takes up a port on every other switch. This creates an exponential ISL consumption prob-

---

[52] Actually, this is the definition of a full mesh topology. It is also possible to use a variation called a "partial mesh" in which some of the ISLs are left out. However, partial mesh designs result in extremely odd and counter-intuitive performance and scalability characteristics, and are therefore rarely recommended.

lem. Two switches in a mesh will require two ports in total for the ISL. Three switches require six ports. Four switches take twelve ports. Five switches require twenty ports. And so on. Meshes become *very* uneconomical *very* quickly, and they actually become mathematically untenable when the switch count reaches half of the per-switch port count. E.g. the largest mesh that can be created out of 16-port switches is eight domains. Beyond that, the total free port count actually *reduces* as switches are added.

- Performance. Even though each switch may have half of its ports used as ISLs, there is only one path available between any two domains. To get from switch A to switch B in the figure, only ISL AB is usable. If five devices on switch A need to reach devices on switch B, the other four links out of switch A will never be used.[53] It would be possible to add more ISLs between switches A and B, but this has even worse scalability, and if the other ISLs are never used, it begs the question of why they are present in any case. In order for the ISLs in a mesh to be utilized, traffic needs to be multipoint in nature and perfectly evenly distributed. This last requirement is not a typical case for SANs.

Because of these characteristics, full mesh networks are not viable beyond about four domains in a fabric. Still, if each domain is a 384-port director, it is possible for a full mesh to create a fairly large fabric. They are also popular in small MAN/WAN designs, where each *site* is a point on the mesh. It is common to have a hybrid network with CE designs within each site, and a mesh or ring design interconnecting the sites. This is viable when there are just a few sites; larger

---

[53] Unless ISL AB fails. In that case, all four remaining paths out of switch A become equal cost paths to B and the load would be shared across them. It is ironic and counter-intuitive that a link failure in a mesh can actually *increase* performance... which is related to the reason why partial meshes are not used.

MAN/WAN networks tend to use partial mesh or CE variations.

Core/Edge Topology

The core-to-edge topology, also known as "CE", is an evolution of the well-established "star" topology popular in data networks. Figure 31 and Figure 32 show resilient (p249) CE Fibre Channel fabrics. Switches in the lower tier of the fabrics are "core switches," and those interconnected by the core switches are "edge switches." In Figure 31, the edge switches are A through D, and the core switches are E and F.

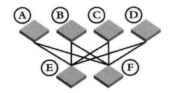

Figure 31 – CE Topology

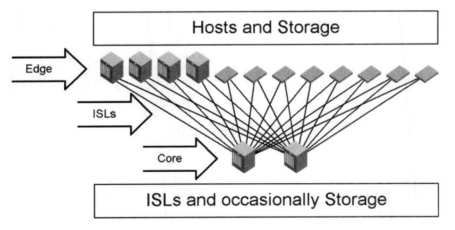

Figure 32 – Simple Resilient Core/Edge Fabric

CE designs have dominated the SAN architecture space for many reasons. Networks built using this approach are:

- Well tested, since most large fabrics in production and in Brocade test labs take one Core/Edge form or another. This is true of most SAN testing facilities.

- Well balanced, since the symmetrical design takes full advantage of load sharing and redundancy. Traffic between edges can be balanced across all cores.

- Deterministic. Performance between any two edge switches will not impact flows between any other two edge switches. For example, a conversation between A and B in Figure 31 will never use the same ISLs as a conversation between C and D.

- Economical, having options to support differing cost-to-performance ratios. Users who want more performance for any given edge switch can add core-to-edge ISLs on that switch alone, without adding cost anywhere else in the SAN.

- Easy to adapt and modify over time, since each core is duplicated and edge switches are interchangeable.

- Simple to understand, document, troubleshoot, and understand. Unlike a partial mesh, characteristics of a CE design are intuitive to most people.

- Easy to scale without downtime by adding more edge switches to free ports on the cores, or by migrating to higher port-count core switches one at a time.

While other topologies are still used in smaller SANs, virtually all large-scale deployments now use CE variations.

CE Fabric Performance Optimization

One difference between a CE fabric and a traditional "star" is that CE networks tend to have two or more core switches to enhance redundancy and performance, whereas stars tend to have one switch or hub in the center. In an Ethernet network, multiple switches at the center of a star would usually act in an active/passive relationship using Spanning Tree Protocol (STP). STP does not offer any performance benefits at all, and may take several minuets to reconverge around failures, so redundant core elements do not offer compelling advantages.

Side Note

All topologies have "degenerate cases" in which they become other topologies. For example, a two-switch full mesh is also a two-switch cascade and a two-switch ring. A three switch full mesh is a three-switch ring, and a triangle. A four-switch ring with a broken ISL is a four-switch cascade. If a switch fails in a four-switch ring, it becomes a three-switch cascade. And virtually any topology at all can be described as some form of partial mesh.

Topology classifications are one useful tool for determining how a network might behave, but they cannot be viewed with too much purity. When reading the remainder of this work, look at some of the diagrams and see how various networks contain multiple topologies, or could become other topologies in failure cases.

Fabrics, on the other hand, use FSPF (p415). This allows active/active load sharing (p220; p384; p415) of equal-cost paths. All paths from any edge switch to any other edge switch are equal-cost: exactly two hops away. This means that the fabric can make full use of all ISLs, instead of having mostly unused links as in the full mesh case. FSPF also offers extremely fast convergence around failures.

Because of this, CE networks built using Brocade platforms tend to "take care of themselves" from a performance standpoint. However, in high-performance environments where best-possible performance is mission-critical, additional tuning may be desirable. Optimization for such corner-case deployments can be accomplished in several ways, which are discussed in detail in "Chapter 8: Performance Planning" starting on page 185.

Briefly, there are two commonly used options for performance optimization based on node attachment strategies:

The best approach from a performance standpoint is to localize "hot" connections within edge switches. This ensures that most traffic will not even need to cross any ISLs.

The second approach is to *tier* host and storage connections. This ensures that traffic will have the best chance of being evenly balanced across all available ISLs. While tiering does not perform as well as using locality, it is easier to deploy, visualize, and manage.

Many customers take a blended approach: tiering the majority of connections, but localizing mission-critical hosts.

CE Topology Scalability

In a "formulaic" resilient CE fabric, two or more core switches interconnect many edge switches. Free ports on core switches are generally reserved strictly for ISLs and IFLs to allow maximum scalability, and nodes are usually attached to edge switches. Ports to which nodes are attached are therefore referred to as "edge ports," or "user ports" to distinguish them from ports used for ISLs/IFLs.

Figure 33 shows how scalability is affected by node placement in a CE fabric. In both halves of the diagram, the SAN is constructed using 16-port switches. In both, there is a ~7:1 ratio of hosts to storage. Both use a 7:1 ISL oversubscription ratio.[54] The difference is that in the left-hand pane, storage is connected to the edge, whereas it is connected to the core in the right-hand pane. The edge-attached version can architecturally support 224 total devices before the core switches run out of ports for ISLs.[55] The core-attached ver-

---

[54] These could be any value, as long as the *same* value is used in both versions for the sake of the comparison. E.g. if you change the ISL over-subscription to 3:1 for both examples, you get different results, but the same *relative* effect. Similarly, changing the size of switches in the design changes the resulting scalability, but devices placement affects the total number in the same way.

[55] 16 edges with 12 free ports each yields a 96-port fabric. At a 7:1 fan-out ratio, this is 12 storage and 84 hosts.

sion can only support 24 storage nodes before the limit is reached, with a total SAN port-count limitation of 80 ports.[56]

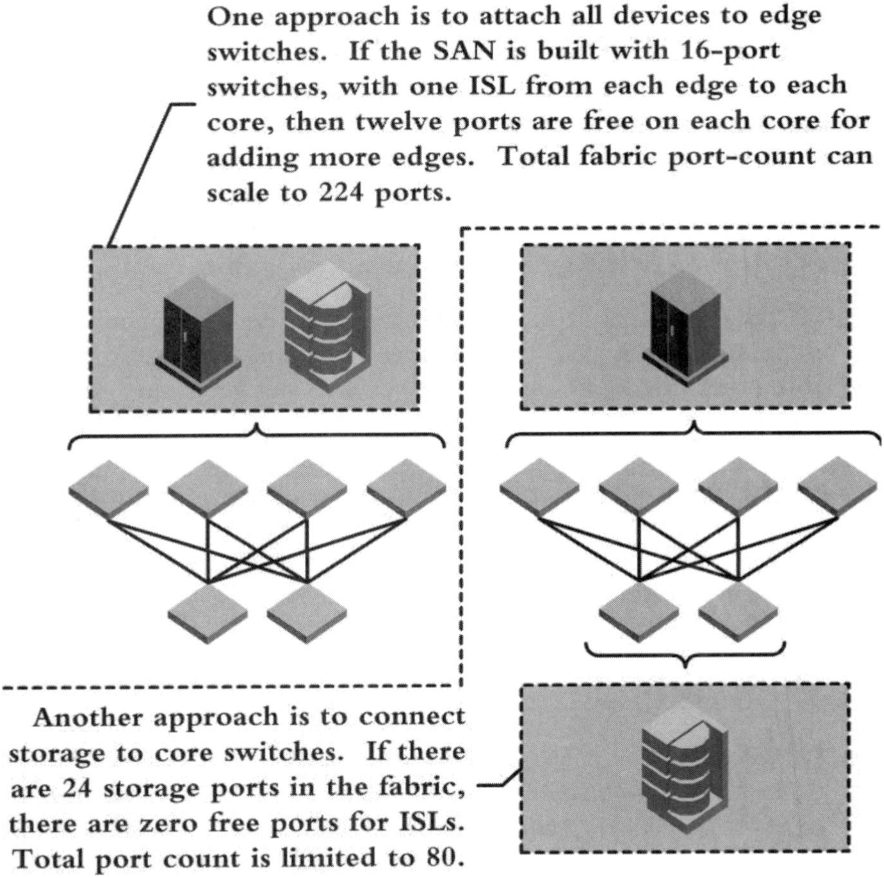

One approach is to attach all devices to edge switches. If the SAN is built with 16–port switches, with one ISL from each edge to each core, then twelve ports are free on each core for adding more edges. Total fabric port-count can scale to 224 ports.

Another approach is to connect storage to core switches. If there are 24 storage ports in the fabric, there are zero free ports for ISLs. Total port count is limited to 80.

Figure 33 - Scalability as a Function of Device Placement

This illustrates the reason that core-attachment limits scalability. A core port with a storage device attached to it adds one node to the total scalability of the solution. A core port with an ISL attached to it adds an entire *switch* to the scalabil-

---

[56] With 11 edge switches, there are 66 user ports on the edge for hosts and 10 user ports on the core for storage. 66:10 is as close to 7:1 as this design can get.

ity of the SAN. With a storage port attached to the core, the same port only adds one *device* to the scalability of the SAN. The larger the edge switch and the higher the ISL over-subscription ratio, the greater this effect.

If core attachment is desired, there is an effective way to support it. Nodes may be connected to the core if it consists of high-port-count directors such as the Brocade 24000 and 48000. In this case, the architectural impact to the topology will not be a major limiting factor on scalability: fabric services scalability will generally come into play first.

Before deciding on this strategy, evaluate performance as well as scalability. If hosts stripe IO evenly across storage ports, and these are distributed evenly between the cores, *and/or* there is only one core switch, then performance will generally be better with *core*-attached storage. If hosts do *not* evenly balance IO (typical case) and/or there is more than one core switch, performance will likely be better with *edge*-attached storage. When in doubt, connect all nodes to edge switches and use core switches just for ISLs/IFLs.

 Side Note

The Brocade 200e, 4100, 4900, 5000, 7500, 7600, and 48000 all have a feature that substantially improves load balancing in CE networks: Dynamic Path Selection. (p220; p384) Frame-based trunking operates only between ports connecting one ASIC directly to another, so it cannot balance traffic between different core switches. DPS, in contrast, can operate between ports on different ASICs: balancing between cores is done by hardware.

CE Topology Hybrid Designs

It is possible to vary the CE formula in many ways.

For example, it is possible to combine switches with different port counts and HA characteristics in many ways. Some designers use high-port-count directors as core switches with low-port-count edges for fan-out. Other designers choose to deploy directors at the edge as well, while still other designers use only low-port-count switches.

It is also possible do vary the HA characteristics of the fabric. Many SAN designers deploy completely redundant fabrics (p251) with dual-homed hosts and storage devices each attached to at least two isolated networks. Some designers feel that this supplies sufficient redundancy, and that using redundant cores within each fabric is not needed. In this case, each fabric might have only one core switch, as shown in Figure 34. This is a single point of failure for the fabric, but even if one entire fabric fails, all applications will still have access to their storage through the other fabric.

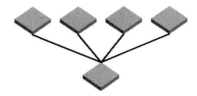

Figure 34 - Non-Resilient CE Fabric

Note that this is not considered to be the "best practice" for HA SAN design. It is a compromise some designers will take to lower cost at the expense of increasing risk. As discussed in "Chapter 9: Availability Planning", whenever a large number of hosts need to fail over simultaneously, there is a greater chance of a problem occurring.

Some designers hedge their bets by using resilient designs for "A" fabrics, but not for "B" fabrics. This is better than using two non-resilient designs, especially if multipathing drivers are configured to prefer the "A" path. Similarly, if locality is high and/or differing requirements exist for HA on different nodes, designers may not use a CE design for the "B" fabric at all. Figure 35 (page 156) shows how this might look.

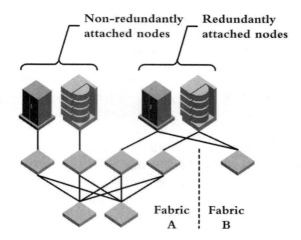

Figure 35 - Asymmetrical Redundant "A/B" Fabrics

In this example, some devices require HA access to the SAN, and others do not. All devices are connected to a scalable CE fabric, "Fabric A". The redundant connections from the devices *with* an HA requirement go to a physically separate "B" fabric. Because there are fewer HA devices than non-HA, the "B" fabric does not need to be as large as the "A" fabric, so the "B" fabric consists of a single switch.

Another way to approach this would have been to create two equally-sized CE fabrics, with the non-redundantly-connected devices spread out between them. In fact, this is the more typical approach, and results in a higher overall level of SAN scalability. This is shown in Figure 36 (page 157).

The bottom line is that there are many ways to vary a CE topology, while still maintaining the fundamental properties with respect to scalability, performance, reliability, and so on. SAN designers interested in large-scale deployments generally start with a CE design, and then modify it as needed to meet the specific needs of their deployment.

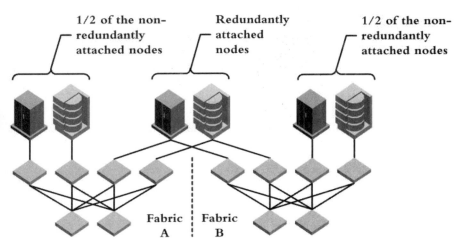

Figure 36 - Redundant Fabrics with HA and non-HA Systems

Core/Edge Meta SANs

As shown in the previous subsection, the CE topology offers compelling advantages for SANs composed of Fibre Channel fabrics. Variations on this approach would also apply to iSCSI SANs, though limitations on Ethernet protocols might limit the benefits. All of the advantages apply when using the FC-to-FC router (FCR) feature of the Brocade AP7420, 7500, or FR4-18i blade to create Meta SANs[57] with LSANs spanning between those fabrics. As a result, routed Meta SANs are also generally based on a CE topology.

Figure 37 has a generic block diagram of a CE fabric, while Figure 38 has a similar diagram of a CE Meta SAN. Note that the edge fabric blocks in the second diagram could contain any reasonable fabric design, including CE fabrics. That is, a CE Meta SAN may contain *n* CE or other fabrics.

---

[57] See "Fabric vs. SAN vs. Meta SAN" on page 34 for a general discussion of the category of network.

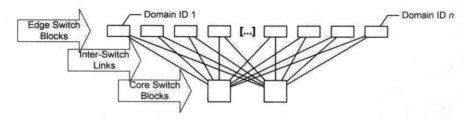

Figure 37 - Generic CE Fabric Block Diagram

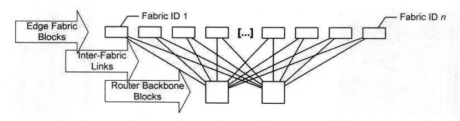

Figure 38 - Generic CE Meta SAN Block Diagram

Figure 38 could optionally contain *n* copies of Figure 37. This is illustrated in Figure 39.

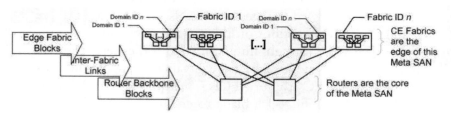

Figure 39 - Generic CE Meta SAN with CE Edge Fabrics

In general, any topology that can be used in a fabric can be used in a Meta SAN. More information about Meta SAN design can be found in the book *Multiprotocol Routing for SANs*, a member of the *SAN Administrator's Bookshelf* series.

Embedded Switch Topologies

Brocade offers a number of switching platforms which are built or installed directly into bladed server chassis or storage platforms. (See "Embedded Platforms" starting on page 344 for current platforms, and also page 367 for embedded plat–

158

forms which are no longer in the active selling phase of their lifecycle.)

The general architecture of a SAN with embedded switches inside bladed server chassis can look quite a bit like any other SAN architecture. Figure 40 shows how the top-level design might be depicted.

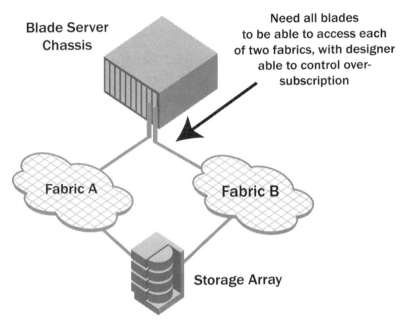

Figure 40 - Top-Level Embedded Switch Architecture

In this design, each blade server chassis has two embedded switches. Each switch connects to a separate fabric for redundancy. Each server blade has an embedded dual-port HBA controller connecting to each embedded switch via traces across the chassis backplane. In this way, each server blade can access storage on each fabric, just as if it were a dual-HBA host connected to a pair of edge switches, each in a different fabric.

In some cases, particularly in small to medium sized businesses, the end user of such a product may not even know that they have a switch at all. For example, if a customer has a blade chassis which contains an embedded switch, they might connect the switch ports directly to storage devices. In that case, the "Fabric A" and "B" clouds from the figure would be fully integrated inside the blade server chassis. If the customer were using LUN masking on the storage side, there may never be any reason for them to manage the switches directly. In such cases, it is possible that the end user might not even set the switch management IP addresses.

However, when using these products in enterprise SANs, it is necessary to recognize that they are switches, and design and manage the fabrics accordingly. For medium sized fabrics – with, say, a dozen or fewer domains, including embedded switches – it might just be a matter of treating them as if they were edge switches in a simple CE design. That is, the ports on the embedded switches could be used as ISLs connecting to one or more core switches.

If the environment is larger than that, or might grow to become larger in the future, then using embedded switches in this way can create a scalability problem. For instance, if the fabric is expected to eventually support 100 blade server chassis, each with 10 blades, this might appear to be a modest 1,000 name server entries for hosts plus a few more entries for the storage devices – certainly supportable. But it also means that the fabric would have more than 100 switch domains – which can be a management challenge at best, even if it were supported in theory.

Figure 41 shows how a blade server chassis with two embedded switches traditionally connects to a pair of external fabrics. In this illustration, each embedded switch forms one or more ISLs to its fabric via E_Port connections. The switch participates fully in the fabric services of its fabric, just as any other switch, and so it has the full scalability impact of a switch domain.

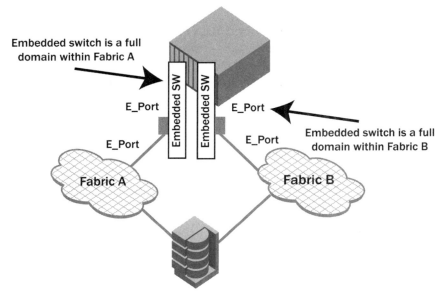

Figure 41 – E_Port Connection from Embedded Switches

At first look, it might seem that using an optical pass-through module would eliminate the domains, but in reality it does not solve this problem; it simply changes from one scalability issue to another since the HBAs which were passed through still have to be connected to switches. Those switches simply move outside the chassis, thus taking up more rack space, power, cooling, and cabling resources. In fact, it creates additional problems, since cable management with optical pass-through devices is vastly more complex.

There are two options for handling this situation in an architecturally-valid manner: (1) Break the design up into multiple fabrics, optionally using FC routers to interconnect them, or (2) use the Brocade Access Gateway product to make the embedded switches in blade server chassis appear as individual hosts *instead* of appearing as switch domains.

In some cases, depending on required connectivity, the routed approach may work quite well. However, if any-host-to-any-storage-port connectivity is required which crosses the fabric boundaries, then the router approach may not provide the intended scalability benefits. This is because the router would need to "project" all of the edge fabrics with blade server embedded switches into a single centralized storage fabric. In fact, the routed solution might actually be *less* scalable in this situation, because the routers themselves would start to have scalability problems associated with the number of edge fabrics, in addition to the scalability problem in the centralized storage fabric. Routers are an extremely good solution for scalability and fault isolation, but *only where some degree of fabric-level traffic localization can be used.* In the case of embedded switches, this is often not achievable.

Fortunately, Brocade has a product to address this scenario. Access Gateway was introduced with Fabric OS 5.2.1b. It leverages NPIV (N_Port Id Virtualization) to hide the embedded switches from the fabric, while still allowing easy SAN connectivity for the host blades.

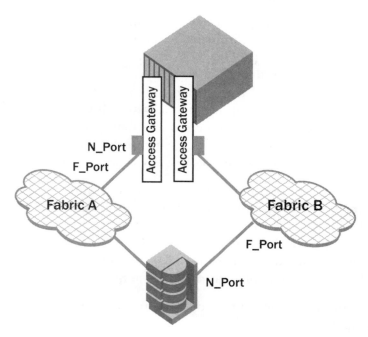

Figure 42 – NPIV Connection from Embedded Switches

Figure 41 and Figure 42 look quite a bit alike. The only difference is that Figure 42 uses F_Ports instead of E_Ports. Indeed, the deployment model for Access Gateway can look virtually identical to the simple CE design discussed earlier in this chapter. That is, the designer would connect each Access Gateway "switch" directly to the core of the fabric, just as if the Access Gateway were an edge switch in a CE network.

The key difference is that the Access Gateway does not attach via E_Ports, and does not provide fabric services. Instead, the fabric switch to which each Access Gateway is connected provides services, while the Access Gateway attaches to the switch using what *appears* to be an HBA connection. Service requests from the embedded HBAs (such as Name Server inquiries) are passes through from the Access Gateway to the fabric switch. As a result, there is no need for the full set of switch-to-switch fabric protocols to operate between the Access Gateway and the fabric. The NPIV connection is shown in more detail in Figure 43.

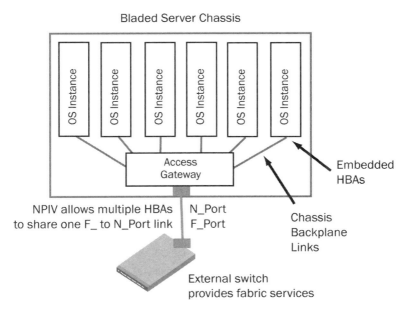

Figure 43 – NPIV Detail

This architecture allows the deployment of many additional servers without requiring a domain and the associated fabric rebuild traffic that is prevalent when switches are powered on, added to, or removed from a fabric. In other words, it provides all of the required connectivity, without running the services which typically cause scalability limitations. In addition to providing scalability benefits, this also eliminates most of the switch-to-switch compatibility challenges which have historically prevented intermix between FC switches from different vendors.

This feature is simple to use, and does not require much effort from the SAN designer. The only major caveat is that, at the time of this writing, the Access Gateway feature itself is only supported on platforms powered by the "Goldeneye" ASIC (p430) such as the 4Gbit embedded products and the Brocade 200e switch.

Of course, an Access Gateway platform can *connect to* other switches powered by different ASICs. For example, a Brocade 200e can act as an Access Gateway and connect to a Brocade 48000 director or classic McData platform which is acting as a fabric switch, but the reverse is not true. It is simply necessary to make sure that the Access Gateway feature is running on a Goldeneye platform and that the fabric switch to which it is connected is running a code version which supports NPIV.

Access Gateway is also discussed on page 376.

Distance Extension Topologies

Perhaps the most common variation with CE fabrics is related to multi-site networks extended over a long distance. There may be one or more CE networks at each of several sites, and these may need connectivity between them e.g. for disaster recovery. It is common in this case to interconnect the cores in a full mesh, partial mesh, or ring, depending on the number of sites, the WAN topology, and the inter-site performance requirements. See Figure 44.

This example shows two sites connected across an un-specified distance. Each site has a pair of CE fabrics, in an "A/B" redundant relationship. Both core switches in the "A" CE network at site 1 are connected to both core switches in the "A" network at site 2. These networks would form a single fabric unless isolated using FC-to-FC routers. (Which has now become the preferred mechanism for connecting sites together over distance.) Either way, the resulting network would be considered a CE variation, and the performance characteristics *within* each site would be as expected of a pure CE network.

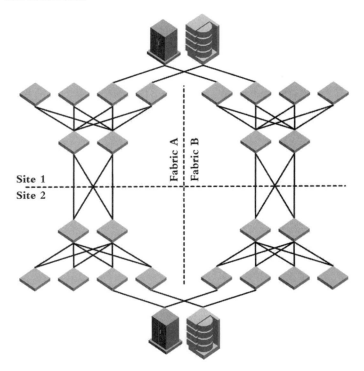

Figure 44 – Inter-Site Extension of CE Fabrics

The most reliable and highest performance technology which can handle inter-site the links is native Fibre

Channel. In this case, the links would simply be very long FC ISLs. In order to guarantee full performance on such links, Brocade has created a product called "Extended Fabrics" (p390) which allows optimal buffer-to-buffer credit management on those links. With Brocade routers, the Extended Fabrics license key is generally included in the base price, and it is also often bundled with other Brocade switches from many vendors.

More information on this topic can be found in "Chapter 11: Distance Planning" starting on page 275.

7

7: Scalability Planning

There are generally two ways to think about SAN infrastructure scalability: considering things which affect scalability <u>limits</u>, and considering things which affect scalability <u>requirements</u>. It is generally best to focus on the latter first to determine what the SAN needs, and then look into limits when trying to decide how best to meet those needs.

Scalability Axioms

Before discussing the details of how to determine scalability requirements and what factors influence SAN scalability, this section briefly lists the most important principles a SAN designer can use when trying to build large-scale solutions.

Design Large Solutions with Large Elements

It is much easier to design a 3,000 port fabric using ten 384-port directors than using 50 64-port switches or 100 32-port switches. Networks do not need to be in the multithousand port range to benefit from using large elements. The rule of thumb is that if your fabric will have hundreds of ports or more in a single location, it will be easier to design, deploy, and manage it using directors instead of switches. It will probably also be less expensive, due to the savings on software licenses, ISL cables, E_Port SFP media, power, cooling, rack space, and so on. In fact, if you compare a 300-port design with 10x 32-port switches to a collapsed design using a single Brocade 48000, the total cost of ownership savings is generally immense.

Locality is Your Friend

If you can figure out how to localize (p209) IO to some extent, you will be able to reduce the number of required ISLs, and may be able to break up your design into smaller "manageable units" of separate fabrics. Trying to design for and then maintain 100% locality is usually a *lot* more trouble than it is worth, but localizing IO for just the most business-critical applications tends to be relatively easy, and tends to provide most of the benefits.

Data-Plane Connectivity is Not Always Helpful

Designers will sometimes connect ISLs between unrelated fabric segments for "manageability" reasons. The theory is that this allows easier zoning operations, and some management applications can "see" the entire fabric through a connection to any given switch. If you find yourself putting ISLs between switches purely for management reasons, and do not anticipate these links ever being used for IO, then it is likely that the SAN will be better off without the ISLs. Consider using management applications which were designed to manage multiple fabrics such as Brocade Fabric Manager and SAN Health. That is, solve management problems using management tools, rather than using data-plane solutions to management-plane problems.

Routers Tend to be Useful

If there is substantial locality within a fabric, but there is some need for connectivity to other fabrics, then connecting the fabrics together with FC routers will probably be a good idea. Routers allow selective data-plane connectivity, without merging fabric services. For instance, if a primary datacenter has 1,000 nodes, and 10 of them need connectivity to a DR site, then connecting the sites via routers will be more scalable than merging the fabrics would be. Note that routers can provide this benefit only if there is fabric-level locality. If every host in one fabric needs access to every storage device in another fabric, then routers will be rather less helpful.

Embedded Switches Should Use Access Gateway

When you design a large fabric, you should use generally large elements such as the Brocade 48000 director. However, when you use bladed server chassis, it is generally best to use embedded switches rather than optical pass-through modules. Unfortunately, if you connect a large number of embedded switch platforms into a fabric, the domain count can get out of control very quickly. The solution is to use Brocade Access Gateway (p158 and p376) which allows embedded switches to connect to a fabric as HBAs instead of as switches.

Determining Scalability Requirements

There are four areas on which the SAN designer should focus when determining the scalability requirements: connectivity model, port count for hosts and storage devices, port count for links, and geographical considerations.

Requirements for Connectivity

In some cases, it may be necessary for every port in the network to reach every other port all the time. This is often the case in IP networks. Some designers chose to apply this model to SANs as well. However, in the vast majority of SANs, real connectivity requirements are more limited. If a few constraints are allowed on connectivity, high degrees of scalability can be much simpler to achieve.

For example, take an environment with 10,000 dual-attached hosts and 5,000 storage ports. On the surface, it might seem like this requires a connectivity model with 25,000 ports, which would not be practical. However, there are a number of ways to limit the connectivity requirement without giving up functionality. Dividing the SAN into redundant A/B SANs cuts the per-fabric scalability requirement in half, and increases availability as well. It will not be possible for a port connected to the "B" fabric to reach an "A" fabric port, but this is not actually a requirement: if a storage device has both "A" and "B" attachments, a host can reach data stored on it via either path. Still, 12,500 ports is beyond even the most aggressive single-fabric scalability limits, so further analysis is required.

It is rarely necessary for every host to access every other host in a SAN. In fact, it is rarely necessary for *any* host to access *any other* host in a SAN, since the focus is generally on host-to-storage connections. Even the most aggressive SAN connectivity requirements usually boil down to "any host to any storage LUN" rather than "any port to any port". This can help with scalability in several ways.

For example, if the storage devices are enterprise-class RAID arrays with e.g. 20 ports each, these could be spread out across many different fabrics. Instead of 2x 12,500 port fabrics, with 10 ports connected from each storage array, the designer could chose to build 20 fabrics with 1,250 ports each, with one port connected from each array. In this case, there would be 10 "A" fabrics and 10 "B" fabrics, each of which fell within the realm of achievable port count. If some traffic needs to cross between the different "A" or "B" fabrics, then additional connectivity could be provided using routers and LSANs to create "A" and "B" Meta SANs.

The bottom line is that, to maximize the scalability of a very large SAN, it is best to break it down into smaller fabrics. Use an A/B redundant model first, then split off other fabrics by function, geographical location, administrative groups, or by spreading storage ports as in the example.

Host and Storage Device Port Count

How many free ports are needed for devices when the SAN first enters production? It should be easy to answer this question during the interview process. How will this requirement change over time? This might be more complex to determine, but it is equally important. The geometry of the SAN should scale to support the maximum number of devices which could reasonably be expected to need to enter the connectivity model in the future, not just at the point of roll-out. Else, it will be necessary to fundamentally restructure the SAN later... which is not fun during production.

Be aggressive when calculating the potential SAN attachment rate, since it will be much easier to implement fewer ports than were planned for than it will be to re-architect the SAN to support more. Be sure to account for *ports* rather than just *devices*, since most SAN-attached hosts and storage arrays have two or more ports. Then create a top-level SAN architecture based on the *eventual* port-count requirements, and scale it backwards to the *initial* requirements.

ISL and IFL Port Count

Even if the initial SAN deployment has only one switch in it, the odds are that it will grow past the number of ports on that switch and will require ISLs or IFLs. It is then necessary to consider how many ISLs are needed. There are two parts to that question:

- How many switches, routers, and gateways are being connected, and in what topology? This geometry will dictate a minimum number of links.
- What are the performance requirements of each of those connections? This may require having multiple parallel links between network elements.

As with host and storage port count, it is necessary to meet requirements both for today and for the future. What are the initial connectivity and performance requirements for inter-switch and inter-fabric links? Ports need to be allocated for these links. How will this increase over time? As the host and storage port count increases, generally the number of switches will increase as well. In addition, performance requirements tend to increase over time, which may require adding parallel links.

It is best to be aggressive in assumptions about performance requirements, since an under-utilized link has no end-user impact, but a slow network will be noticed. If ILM or UC are on the agenda, SAN performance requirements might skyrocket. Fortunately, the Brocade 4Gbit switches are the highest performing SAN products in the industry, and can scale from 1Gbit to 256Gbits on a single network path.

The best approach is to reserve some ports for extra ISLs or IFLs if it seems likely that the SAN might need more performance or device port-count scalability over time. Estimate the number of extra ISL and IFL ports to reserve based on how many switches are expected to be needed, how much performance is expected to need to grow, and whether or not links need to be reserved for specific future projects, such as disaster recovery connections, or integration with other fabrics. Again, just as with host and storage port counts, it is best to design a top-level SAN architecture for the eventual aggressive target design, and then work backwards to the initial deployment.

Geographical Considerations

What are the geographical characteristics of the solution? Networks which span distances – even at the campus network level – usually require additional switches and/or routers. This is because it is almost always desirable to co-locate switches with the devices they will interconnect.

For example, take a customer with six hosts and two storage ports, with half located in each of two different data centers within a campus. This might seem like a perfect job for a SilkWorm 3250 8-port switch, or a Brocade 200e with an 8-port license. However, there are issues with that approach.

First of all, it would leave zero ports available for expansion: if the customer wanted to add one more host, it would require a fundamental restructuring of their SAN. Granted, this is mitigated in the case of the 200e, which could have it's port count doubled with a software license upgrade.

More importantly, it would require that the switch be physically located in a different data center from half of its devices. With short distances like this example, it might be possible to run optical cables directly from the three remote hosts and the remote storage port, and connect them to the switch that way. This would require four cable runs between the data centers. (Eight fibers.) In many cases, four optical cable runs would cost as much as or even more than the switch itself.

It would also be possible to install a second SilkWorm 3850, so that each data center had its own switch. Connecting the data centers would then require just one cable run for an ISL. In addition to simplifying the campus networking problem, this would also solve the free-port scalability issue: there would be three free ports one each of the switches to add future devices and/or ISLs.

Most geographically extended SANs have rather more need for extra switches than this example. If the SAN is designed to solve a disaster recovery problem, the inter-site links might easily be a hundred kilometers long. Running each host and storage connection over that distance would be completely impractical. The bottom line is that it is almost always desired or required to have separate groups of switches at each separate host or storage device location. Therefore the SAN designer should analyze each site separately from a scalability standpoint.

Maximizing Scalability

Once a designer knows how a SAN will need to scale initially and over time, the task is to design an architecture which will support all current and future requirements. To do that effectively, it helps to understand what places limits on SAN scalability, and how to get around those limitations without sacrificing needed functionality.

The limitations can be classified into five categories: manageability, fault containment, vendor support matrices, storage networking services, and the protocol itself.

Protocol Characteristics

Fortunately, the Brocade implementation has such high architectural limits that it is not worth considering them. The addressing limitations would allow millions of devices in a fabric. However, other vendors have made more limiting choices, so it is worth spending a moment on the topic.

Each FC fabric has a three-byte address space. The first byte is used to represent the domain of a switch in the fabric. The next byte represents a port on that switch. The final byte represents a particular device hanging off of the switch port, which is needed if the port is attached to an FC-AL hub or to a loop device such as a JBOD.

If all of those addresses were available, that would yield a potential of 16.7 million addressable devices. (256^3) The FC fabric standards reserve some addresses for fabric services, such as the name server, and others are inaccessible because of limitations on the FC-AL protocol, but the standards still provide for over 7.7 million usable addresses. (239 domains times 256 ports times 127 FC-AL addresses.)

It has never been possible to construct a stable FC-AL loop with more than twenty or so devices. Using this number, fabric address space scalability would be "limited" to 1.2 million devices. Using no loop device address space at all, the address space still supports over 60,000 ports.

This is still a "large" number. No customer has ever requested a fabric with anything close to that scalability requirement.[58] Therefore the real-world address limits of the FC protocol are not a constraint for Brocade fabrics.

---

[58] Although one Brocade customer has a design intended to scale to 600,000 ports, and another is targeting over 100,000 ports… both using in multi-fabric designs.

However, not all vendors implement the address space properly. One other vendor was historically incapable of addressing more than 31 domains. If each switch had 256 free ports, this would still be a fairly high number: over 7,000 ports per fabric. While this is a tenth of Brocade's theoretical capability, it is probably sufficient.

As a practical matter, address space *should not* be the limiting factor for SAN scalability, with any vendor. It is *theoretically* possible to construct a Brocade fabric with over a million devices, but in the real world, other limiting factors would come into play long before that size was reached.

The bottom line is that, with Brocade fabrics, there are no practical address space scalability limitations. Designers should be aware of such limits when considering equipment from other vendors, and be aware of the differences between theoretical and practical use of the address space.

Manageability Scalability

First, a designer creates a diagram of a SAN. Then, the SAN is built by an implementation team. At that point, the job is done. Right? Wrong. The fabric still has to be managed on an ongoing basis. The process of fabric management can itself become a scalability limit.

In some ways, the scalability of manageability can be related to technology. All software has scalability limits, unless it is being run on compute platforms with an unlimited amount of RAM and CPU cycles, which is impossible. SAN management software is no exception. The scalability limit of a management application might be quite high, but it will exist at some level.

However, it can also be related to human factors, or process definitions. If many different applications are connected to the same fabric, then many different groups of users and IT administrators might need to be involved in change control processes for that fabric. Scheduling the time to add a switch, or change a firmware version might become difficult. In many environments, even changes which can be made in a totally non-disruptive manner still need to go through a change control process simply to manage risk, and coordinating this kind of activity with many people is always harder than coordinating with just a few. The larger the fabric, the more people may need to sign off on a change.

Whether the cause is human, process, or technological, any organization will run into scalability challenges related to manageability. The SAN designer should therefore consider how the final solution will be managed, and how the people, processes, and technology related to this will scale.

Fault Containment

Any single entity is a single point of failure. This includes networks and network services software. This principle is not specific to SANs; it is generally true of any system of any complexity. SAN designers interested in availability should therefore assume that a single fabric can fail as a unit, in much the same way that a single Ethernet segment can fail when subjected to a broadcast storm.

Continuing that analogy, the networking industry as a whole realized years ago that Ethernet segments had a practical scalability limited related to fault isolation. Even if it was *possible* to create a single Ethernet segment with thousands of devices, it was not a *good idea* to do so. Inevitably, no matter how diligent the network engineering and management teams had been, eventually something unanticipated would go wrong, and take down the segment.

To address this issue, network designers began to limit the size of any given segment to limit the scope of any problems which might come up. The industry as a whole eventually settled on a preferred Ethernet segment size of no more than one class C IP subnet, or about 250 devices at the most. Of course, this also caused a problem: they needed more connectivity than this could provide, since organizations had more than 250 computers.

To strike a balance between providing connectivity and limiting the scope of faults, engineers created a hierarchical networking model based on routers. This approach is now available for storage networks as well, by connecting fabrics together via FC routers such as the Brocade 7500.

Vendor Support Matrices

There is often a difference between what actually works from a technical standpoint, and what a vendor has qualified for support. Brocade may have tested and declared support for a certain number of ports in a fabric with a particular release of the Fabric Operating System, but not all Brocade OEMs will support that immediately. It is important to understand the technology that Brocade has created, *and* the relationship with the support provider. Obtain an up-to-date version of the provider's support matrix before finalizing a design, and check the design against its scalability metrics.

It is critical to discuss any areas in which the design might fall outside of the supported configuration matrix with engineers from the support provider. The designer should try to understand (a) *why* the configuration is outside the matrix, and (b) whether or not the provider will agree to support it anyway. In many cases, the desired configuration may not be one that the support provider has explicitly tested, and therefore might not be on their list, but it might still be a *reasonable derivative* of a tested configuration. If so, they might be willing to sign off on supporting it anyway. When implementing a SAN which falls outside the vendor support matrix, be sure to get the statement of support in writing, if for no other reason than to be sure that all parties involved have a consistent understanding of what will be covered.

Storage Networking Services

The major limiting factor for SAN scalability is *not* related to the lower layers in the protocol stack, or any of the other criteria discussed above. As shown previously under "Protocol Characteristics" (p174), the Fibre Channel addressing scheme used in the frame format scales far beyond any size fabric which has even been proposed. So do the lower layers, such as cables and media. Even scalability limits for management processes are comparatively solvable problems: they can generally be addressed by written policies and procedures, and − in extreme cases − by breaking up management of the SAN into multiple administrative regions.

The most limiting technical factor turns out to be the design of the services which support SAN-specific functions. These can be fabric services in a Fibre Channel solution, or the analogous services in an iSCSI network. The scalability challenge is the same either way.

For a SAN switch engineering standpoint, services are the most complex piece of the design and testing process. The design complexity related to these services stems from the fact that each of the many services is dependant on the correct function of each of the others. [59]

Brocade Zoning, for example, includes a switch-to-switch zone transfer protocol and a method for programming zones into hardware at each port. This poses some technical scalability limitations related to how large a zoning table can be, but this does not relate directly to how many ports could be in the fabric, and so it might seem that the design of the zoning service itself was not a scalability consideration.

However, the zoning daemons on each switch also need to "talk" to the NS daemons to coordinate hardware access control with discovery. It would not be a good idea to have the NS "tell" a node about any nodes to which it did not

---

[59] This is not protocol-specific. Service interdependency is caused by the relationships between the functions of the services, not the low-level protocol upon which the services happens to run. iSCSI services behave the same way.

have access via zoning,[60] which would happen if the services did not coordinate their activities. The NS daemons *do* have scalability limitations related to the number of ports in a fabric, because each switch has finite RAM and CPU resources. More importantly, the NS service has a *timing* challenge: it must be able to respond in a timely manner even when all devices in a fabric log into the name server at the same time. And the speed of response of the NS processes can be limited by the response speed of the zoning processes. This means that the zoning processes *can* have an effect on fabric scalability, through their interaction with other services.

In fact, interactions like the one above cause service scalability to be a non-linear function. In other words, the load placed on the CPU of a switch increases exponentially as more ports and domains are added to a fabric. It is important to understand this, because it prevents linear increases in CPU speed from producing linear improvements in fabric scalability. Doubling the CPU speed may only provide a 0.01% improvement in fabric scalability.

Of course, it is not necessary for a SAN designer to understand exactly how fabric service processes are implemented, and how they interact. The point is that, in order to scale a fabric, it is necessary for a *switch vendor* to spend a considerable amount of time and effort tuning the internal behaviors of the switch processes running each service, *and* their relationships with every other service. If all devices in a fabric simultaneously query the fabric name server – which does happen periodically – the NS processes must be able to respond in a timely manner, which means that they must coordinate efficiently with the zoning processes, and, in fact, with most of the other SAN services as well. As the size of a

---

[60] Aside from potentially creating security issues, this would cause most hosts to attempt to access all devices on the fabric, which would be denied by zoning. This would generally cause each host to go into a loop of continually and futilely retrying access, taking up CPU cycles on both the host and the switches.

fabric increases, the complexity of process interactions increases non-linearly: doubling the size of a fabric can create considerably more than double the CPU load on each switch, depending on how services are designed, and a SAN designer should therefore be wary of any vendor who claims that a faster CPU will make up for their inexperience at tuning fabric services processes.

Fortunately, Brocade learned these lessons over the course of more than a decade of shipping FC switches into mission-critical production environments, and so Brocade products are the undisputed leader in real-world scalability support. SAN designers do not need to understand how to engineer a set of storage services, but do need to understand what issues exist when selecting SAN equipment because, while Brocade has taken the time to design its switches in a scaleable manner, not all other vendors have done so.

To take a case in point: The failure to understand this scalability relationship caused other players in the SAN industry grief in recent years. One vendor tried to solve scalability problems by dividing each network into different "VSAN" regions, each running different services instances. Unfortunately, all of these services were still running *on the same CPUs*. In other words, for a given overall network size, the segmented design had the same CPU load as if it were one flat fabric. Adding more switches in a new VSAN had as much scalability impact as adding more switches in a single-VSAN network. Indeed, VSANs could add *more* processing load for a given number of ports, since each switch would present one or more separate domains for each VSAN. The result of this was that the vendor in question actually reduced scalability because they did not understand how SAN services worked. Brocade offers an analogous feature (Virtual Fabrics) but does not position it as a scalability panacea. Rather, Brocade positions this as a manageability enhancement.

For scalability, the Brocade LSAN approach will isolate services onto CPUs on physically separate switches, so adding additional fabrics to a network does not have the same scalability impact. Each time a fabric is added to the SAN, it brings its own CPU resources. The routed "Meta SAN" architecture prevents services on different fabrics from interacting with each other directly, so Meta SANs do not have non-linear scalability issues. (See "Fabric vs. SAN vs. Meta SAN" on page 34.)

So far, the LSAN solution is the only approach any vendor has delivered which solves the inherent scalability difficulties of services in a storage network. It is analogous to the solution provided by IP routers to the Ethernet segment scalability problem in some ways, but is optimized for the more stringent performance and reliability requirements of storage networks. SAN designers can therefore solve the services challenge for extremely large-scale design problems using this approach, whereas other solutions simply move services scalability issues around, or even compound them.

Interestingly enough, while it is possible to draw a loose analogy between FC fabric and Ethernet subnet scalability, there is no analogous *service* scalability problem in IP networks. Vendors who have experience creating large-scale Ethernet solutions with IP routers have no relevant information about creating scalable SANs, which may explain why the "VSAN vendor" made this mistake. In order to create an analogous problem for an IP Layer 3 VLAN switch, the switch itself would need to be running DNS, DHCP, WINS, NIS+, NTP, LDAP, iSNS, RADIUS, and many other networking services *in addition* to running protocols like STP, RIP, and OSPF. No IP vendor has even attempted a design this ambitious, but FC SAN switch vendors like Brocade have been doing so for over a decade. It does make FC fabric switches harder to design and build, but results in products which are much easier for users to deploy and manage.

The solution to services scalability is simple. The SAN designer should first select equipment with a highly scalable services architecture. This means using vendors with a long track record of SAN services development. The next step is to make sure that the redundant design is separated into physically separate "A/B" fabrics. (Services interact with each other within a fabric to create a scalability challenge, but do not cross the "air gap" between physically separate A/B fabrics.) Then, the designer should create a network architecture for each half ("A" and "B") which supports scaling in a hierarchical manner, using FC routers to scope service interactions. If the network uses bladed server chassis, the Access Gateway feature should be used. (See page 158 and page 376.) With this multi-pronged approach, it should be possible to create storage networks with port-counts which would have been inconceivable only a few years ago.

Scalable Topologies

In order to maximize SAN scalability, it is helpful to select a topological strategy which is conducive to large scale deployments. Theoretically, one could build a 100,000 port partial mesh topology fabric. However, as a practical matter this would (a) not work, (b) not be supported even if it did work, (c) be too complex to troubleshoot even it if were supported, and (d) would have totally un-understandable performance characteristics. In short, it would not be advisable even if it were possible.

The best strategy for highly scalable SANs it to first break down the design problem into smaller chunks. Often, these are referred to as "manageable units". This can be done by functional area, or application grouping, or geography, or whatever makes the most sense in the particular environment. The key criteria is that each unit should require relatively little connectivity to the other units. That is, locality within a unit should be very high.

If no connectivity is required between units at all − such as in the case of A / B redundant fabrics − then it is possible to configure these units as totally independent SANs. If some connectivity is required between hosts in one unit and storage LUNs in another unit, then it might be possible to use a storage-centric strategy (p142) or use a routed design. Routed designs are quite popular in DR or BC deployments. In the case of separated backup fabrics, most often the connectivity is provided by routers or by hosts with an extra HBA. That is, the backup servers can connect to each relevant "disk" fabric plus the "tape" fabric via different adapters.

This process should result in a top-level architecture with some number of fabrics, and a defined inter-fabric communication method. Once the top-level design is complete, each fabric can be designed with a low-radius architecture such as a collapsed director design, or a core/edge topology.

8: Performance Planning

It is always a good idea to put thought into performance when designing a SAN, even if the applications running on it are not considered especially performance-critical.

To some extent, the need for performance planning is a general principal applicable to all kinds of network engineering, but it is a particularly strong requirement in storage networks. It is important that even lower-tier storage networks have high performance and reliability in order to work *at all*, which is one of many reasons why Fibre Channel is the dominant SAN transport.

Low performance and reliability are often acceptable for applications that networking technologies such as IP and Ethernet generally support. The upper-level protocols running on these networks were designed with the assumption that packet loss, congestion, delay, and out of order delivery would be not only possible, but commonplace. IP networking applications such as web browsers evolved for low-speed connections such as 9600 baud modems. Low reliability on an IP network does destabilize connections, but if the connection e.g. between a web client and a web server becomes unstable, the user is expected to simply "hit refresh" and try again. This is *not* an acceptable solution for SANs. (Picture "hitting refresh" on an ERP system when its storage LUNs go away unexpectedly...)

SANs support applications which evolved from dedicated SCSI buses, where such performance and reliability concerns are unheard of, and are often architecturally impossible. For example, if there is only one initiator on a SCSI bus, there cannot be congestion. Because SAN nodes assume top-tier reliability, if a SAN became sufficiently unstable or slow, it could result in data corruption, restoration from backups, or even require activating a disaster recovery plan. "Hitting refresh" on a mission-critical database server to make up for flaws in the underlying network architecture is not allowed.

This is not to imply that SANs are "scary" technology by any means. Fibre Channel SANs have proven to be reliable in mission-critical production environments for many, many years at the time of this writing. It simply means that performance should always be a consideration, even when applications *apparently* do not require it.

The remainder of this chapter discusses how to determine performance requirements, and some of the tools that a SAN designer can work with to meet them.

Overview of Performance Factors

This section discusses some of the most important factors that can affect performance in a SAN. It provides a brief definition of the factor, a discussion of how it can affect SAN performance, and ideas about how to prevent it from becoming a performance-limiting factor to applications.

Edge Devices

The single most common performance limiting factor in a SAN is not, strictly speaking, related to the SAN. It is the devices which are attached to the SAN. Designers should take the time to understand both the external *and* internal performance characteristics of devices attached to the SAN in order to ensure that they do not become bottlenecks.

For example, it may be possible to install a pair of 4Gbit Fibre Channel interfaces into an 800MHz PC. The interfaces will each be capable of driving 8Gbits (full duplex), so the host could theoretically drive 16Gbits across the SAN. However, an 800MHz PC will never be capable of producing even a noticeable fraction of this performance: its CPU simply cannot generate data at that rate. Limitations on RAM or bus speed can produce similar effects.

In fact, *most* hosts attached to a SAN at the time of this writing are not capable of generating traffic at the full Fibre Channel bandwidth rate of 4Gbits/sec., much less of saturating multiple FC interfaces. This does not imply that a designer should avoid 4Gbit FC HBAs. On the contrary, many designers rely on this fact, because it insures that a Fibre Channel SAN will never be the bottleneck for application performance.

Similarly, Fibre Channel disk, tape, and RAID interfaces are capable of delivering 1Gbit, 2Gbit, or 4Gbit streams, but in many cases, the devices *behind* those interfaces are not capable of these speeds. If a 2Gbit SAN interface is connected to a disk which can only deliver 200Mbits of data, then there will be a bottleneck, but not in the SAN itself.

With slower hosts, using 1Gbit or 2Gbit FC HBAs will usually provide the best performance at a reasonable price. It may be tempting to use software iSCSI on these hosts, but remember that the performance of the host is already CPU-constrained. Using a software iSCSI stack will often render such a host unusably slow and unstable.

Slower storage devices will benefit from upgrades – such as adding more RAM to the cache of a RAID controller – or the use of striping techniques. For example, it is possible to use host- or SAN-based volume managers to create a stripe across multiple slow disks in a JBOD. This improves performance in much the same way that a hardware-based RAID controller does so. The best solution, though, is simply to use faster storage nodes in the first place.

SAN Protocols

The next consideration related to performance is the selection of a SAN protocol. This is the first component of the
mechanism which carries traffic between edge devices. Assuming that there are no major bottlenecks within the edge
devices themselves, this is the next most likely factor which
can cause a problem.

Fibre Channel networks can be configured to meet any
performance requirement. This can range from the most basic
entry-level deployment all the way up to full-speed full-
duplex any-to-any connectivity for thousands of nodes in a
single fabric. The Brocade 5000 is a stellar example of a high
performance Fibre Channel switch: despite its small form factor (1U) and aggressive price point, the Brocade 5000 has an
internal cross-sectional bandwidth of 256Gbits: considerably
more performance than any SAN application requires today.

IP SAN protocols such as iSCSI are suitable for the low
performance environments, and may have an attractive cost-
point for use cases where performance is not a consideration.
A recent issue of a major networking magazine stated that
iSCSI required "the right hardware and software" to achieve
4Gbits of real performance on a 10Gbit Ethernet link. The
"right" hardware in this case is fairly expensive: certainly
much more expensive than 4Gbit FC. Some of the many
technical reasons for the large gap in iSCSI vs. FC performance are discussed further in the "SAN Protocols" section of
"Chapter 1: SAN Basics" starting on page 27. The main
thing for a SAN designer to keep in mind is that iSCSI loses
its cost advantages when it is engineered to support even a
noticeable fraction of FC performance.

The bottom line is that a SAN designer has to consider
the inherent performance characteristics of the protocol because all other considerations will be constrained by this
choice. If iSCSI is selected, there is a very limited selection of

line rate choices, and node performance will also be affected if software iSCSI stacks are used.

Of course, the protocol affects more than just performance. Other effects include maturity of the protocol itself, reliability, general market acceptance and penetration, and maturity of services and management applications available for that protocol. All of these considerations point to Fibre Channel implementations, which is why FC represents the vast majority of SAN deployments. However, price is also a consideration. If the SAN is not designed for high performance or reliability, it might be possible to implement an iSCSI network more cost effectively than by using Fibre Channel. The general rule of thumb is that iSCSI sometimes should be considered as a substitute for NAS protocols such as CIFS or NFS, whereas FC should be used in all other cases.

Link Speeds

Next, consider link speeds. Should the network run at 1Gbit, 2Gbit, 4Gbit, 8Gbit, 10Gbit, 16Gbit, 32Gbit, 256Gbit, or some other speed? In fact, this might more properly be called "path speeds", since Brocade switches support evenly balanced paths of up to 256Gbit using hardware-trunking methods, and on the same physical ports Brocade can support 1Gbit links. (This is also discussed in the appendix under "Link Speeds" starting on page 444.) No other SAN vendor can make a similar claim, however, and iSCSI implementations are incapable of using most of these options, so designers will need to consider link rates before purchasing any equipment which will connect to the SAN.

When evaluating link speeds, there are several things for a designer to keep in mind. The cost to performance ratio is probably the most obvious, but some designers may forget to consider the *total* cost of a connection. For example, 10Gbit interfaces may require single-mode fiber, whereas 4Gbit interfaces can use multi-mode fiber. (p311 and p312) Even if the cost per bit of data moved were the same between these speeds, the cost of the cables between the interfaces would not even be close. This is one reason why 4Gbit has taken off rapidly, while 10Gbit has lagged in adoption. However, in long distance applications, the same more-expensive media and cabling may be required for 4Gbit or 10Gbit, and in these cases 10Gbit might be the more advantageous because it would allow using fewer links for a given required performance metric. (See "10Gbit Blades and DR/BC Solutions" on page 296 for an example.)

Generally speaking, it is best to keep as many options open as possible. Even if the SAN will initially need only 1Gbit of performance, trends in the storage industry are moving sharply in the direction of higher and higher performance requirements. Certain industry trends such as ILM and UC (p67) are driving this acceleration, as is the general trend towards needing more and more data.

The best approach is therefore to select infrastructure which can scale with changing business requirements. For example, it is possible to use ports on a Brocade 48000 for 1Gbit links, and scale their performance to 4Gbit as needed without additional cost, and add even faster interfaces later if needed by purchasing new blades. If the infrastructure selected by the designer were more limited, it might require a forklift upgrade to increase performance. Brocade platforms have even higher speed capabilities today with trunking. As the environment continues to grow, and multiple switches are added to the network, Brocade ISL trunking and Dynamic Path Selection (DPS) can connect elements together with single-path performance as high as 256Gbit, again without adding cost beyond the original purchase price.

With less capable products, it might not only require swapping out all infrastructure to get this kind of performance, it might well require changing to an entirely different *kind* of SAN. For example, if the designer had initially installed iSCSI, then it might subsequently be necessary to upgrade to Fibre Channel for improved performance by "forklifting" out the entire iSCSI SAN. The best practice is therefore to select network components which have flexible performance capabilities, and can grow with the changing business needs of an organization.

Over-Subscription and Congestion

Over-subscription is a condition in which more devices *might* need to access a resource than that resource could fully support. This is similar to what happens when an airline sells more tickets for a flight than there are seats on the airplane. If all passengers show up on time, then the airline will have to bump passengers to a later flight and a few individual passengers will be delayed. However, if some passengers do not show up, or change their flights at the last minute, then everybody will get on the airplane without even knowing that the over-subscription[61] condition existed. Therefore it is *not* true that over-subscription of flights causes passenger delays. In and of itself, it does not. Over-subscription can *combine* with other factors to *contribute* to delays.

The same thing happens in a SAN when more than one host or storage device could potentially use a single ISL. The ISL is said to be over-subscribed, but that does not create a performance issue in and of itself. For example, what if two hosts share a link, and one of them only uses it at night, while the other only uses it during the day? Technically, they *could* both use the link at the same time, but as a practical matter, they do not behave that way.

When an over-subscribed link *is* used in that way, the over-subscription becomes congestion. Congestion is a condition in which devices are actually trying to use a path beyond its capacity, so some of the traffic destined for that path must be queued and transmitted after a delay. This can lower the effective bandwidth between endpoint devices. In

---

[61] Airlines usually call this an "over sold" condition, but the idea is the same.

most networks, congestion is not a disaster: it does not stop communication between endpoints entirely, it just slows it down somewhat for a period of time.

Over-subscription does not cause congestion, but it does create the potential for congestion. The link — or, rather, *path* — rate combines with the overall network design to either create or prevent the potential for congestion, but only the IO patterns of devices attached to the network can actually cause the congestion to appear.

 Side Note

An over-subscribed link is one on which multiple devices might *contend for bandwidth. Traditional data networks have been built with high levels of over-subscription for years. The Internet is the best-known example. A congested link is one on which multiple devices* actually do *contend for bandwidth. The key to managing bandwidth is estimating performance requirements and matching these to an appropriately designed SAN. If all of the applications attached to a switch put together are only capable of generating 4Gbits/sec. of traffic at peak, and there are two 4Gbit/sec. ISLs connecting that switch to the rest of the SAN, then congestion cannot occur on those links even though they are theoretically over-subscribed.*

SANs are generally not capable of supporting massive, Internet-like over-subscription ratios, but most real-world SANs have characteristics that allow them to function well with *somewhat* over-subscribed links. These characteristics include bursty traffic, shared resources, low peak usage by devices, locality, and devices that can use only a fraction of the available bandwidth. Most networks have all of these characteristics to some degree.

Moreover, organizations can realize cost savings by designing a SAN with over-subscription, so over-subscription is often engineered into a SAN to reduce cost. If 16-port edge switches are connected in a core/edge design, the SAN architect might use two ISLs per switch, and have fourteen devices sharing those links. This is less expensive than connecting just eight devices and using the other eight ports for ISLs.

SAN designers usually consider some potential for congestion to be acceptable, but also consider ways to mitigate the likelihood of congestion manifesting to any great extent. The degree to which designers pursue congestion-prevention depends on performance requirements of the SAN-attached applications. When performance service levels are critical and bandwidth requirements are high, lower over-subscription ratios or traffic localization are most often used. The most common approaches for dealing with congestion include:

Using locality – Connecting source and destination ports close together means that traffic between them will rarely if ever have to cross ISLs, which is usually where congestion would occur.

Using large switches – Directors like the Brocade 48000 have world-class internal performance and scalability. Up to 384 4Gbit devices could be connected to a single Brocade 48000. The typical case is that there will be, say, 10 or more hosts per storage interface, in which case connections to a 384-port 48000 can be arranged to prevent congestion. This also works when some degree of blade-level locality is employed. Alternately, "hot" devices can be connected to e.g. 16-port or 32-port blades to ensure higher performance.

Using faster links – 4Gbit FC ISLs have more bandwidth and therefore tend to congest less often than e.g. 1Gbit FC or Ethernet links. Upgrading to a faster line rate inherently reduces congestion. For particularly high performance DR or BC solutions in which the per-link cost is high, using 10Gbit links might be appropriate.

Using trunking to broaden links – Up to eight 4Gbit ISLs can be combined into a single 32Gbit trunk, and up to eight of those can be balanced using Dynamic Path Selection to form a 256Gbit path. There are no known applications to date which use more ISL bandwidth than this, so congestion is not a real concern where trunking is used.

Blocking (HoLB)

Blocking is related to queuing. In a poorly architected switch, router, or director, it is possible for the traffic between two devices to entirely prevent communication between another unrelated pair.

Blocking and congestion are often confused in the industry. A blocking condition may occur when two or more devices contend for a limited resource, just like congestion. Also like congestion, blocking causes a performance problem for one or more of those devices. However, the technical causes of blocking and congestion are completely unrelated, as are some of the effects.

Blocking is more properly called "Head of Line Blocking" (HoLB) and refers to a severe queuing problem, not merely to contention for bandwidth on a link. If a switch is poorly designed, a frame can get "stuck" at the front of a queue, thus blocking the frames behind it. This can happen even if the link itself has plenty of free bandwidth. Instead of *limiting* the performance of the other devices trying to use the link, blocking can actually *stop* other conversations in their tracks for an extended period of time.

Brocade does not ship products which are capable of exhibiting this misbehavior. Unfortunately, other SAN infrastructure vendors do so. Users should be wary of crossbar switches and hubs, as most of these are subject to HoLB. Some crossbar vendors claim that proprietary "virtual queuing" algorithms solve the problem, but independent tests have proven this to be untrue.

Loss and Error Rates

All networks have the potential to lose or corrupt individual pieces of data. When frame corruption happens in an

FC network – an exceedingly rare event – the FC switches will always detect it by using a CRC check, and drop the corrupted frame. From the point of view of a node using the SAN, loss and error rates are therefore functionally identical. Since applications evolved on essentially error and loss free storage subsystems – such as directly attached SCSI drives – it is *never* acceptable to have a noticeable loss rate.

With native Fibre Channel SANs, error and loss rates are very close to zero unless something is broken. Even a single lost frame should be investigated, if the loss occurred during normal network operations. (I.e. it is not unusual to drop frames during certain kinds of fabric reconfiguration, or when a link is initializing, but under normal conditions all frames should be delivered.)

Other protocols tend to have higher error and loss rates. SAN designers implementing long distance solutions over IP WANs should watch these statistics closely.

Latency and Delay

Another consideration is latency, which is – in the context of SAN switches – how long it takes a switch or router to process a frame and then forward it onwards. Once the frame starts going into one port of a Brocade switch, it normally also starts being sent out the destination port even before it has been fully received. This is known as "cut-through routing" and is the most efficient way to move frames theoretically possible. Other vendors do not use this method, and instead rely on some form of "store and forward" switching. This means that the frame has to be completely received before it will be processed, which results in significant delays in traffic delivery.

From the point of view of an application, switch latency is just one of many latency factors. The total amount of time it takes a frame to traverse from its source to its destination is referred to as the latency of the path. Path latency does have an impact, but an application is affected by the overall delay between when it decides to send IO to an HBA and when it gets a response back. This includes the latency of all switches in between the two points, and potentially latency within the storage device at the other end.

It can also include latency generated "artificially" by a switch vendor implementing certain congestion control mechanisms, which obscure high-latency switch or director designs by "pushing back" on a host or storage port. The net effect of this on the application is that, instead of waiting for frames to propagate through a slow fabric, the IO sits inside the host waiting for the fabric to accept the frames in the first place. In other words, it simply moves the latency from the fabric to the host, but does not in fact make the application run any faster.

Sometimes a frame is switched from source to destination within a single switch, and other times a frame must traverse one or more ISLs or IFLs between switches before it reaches its destination. The number of ISLs and IFLs crossed is known as the *hop count* between the devices. In the vast majority of cases, hop count has little or no impact on application performance. The latency associated with traversing one or more Brocade ISLs is vanishingly small compared to other data path delays. For example, the access time for a "fast" disk device is typically measured in milliseconds. Every hop in a Brocade fabric adds about two microseconds of latency, and may be as low as 700 nanoseconds. This means that in a large fabric designed with seven hops between two devices, the path latency could be up to fourteen microseconds, and still be multiple orders of magnitude faster than the disks being accessed across those links. For most IO profiles, hop-count latency is inconsequential in FC networks, from both a switch latency and optical latency standpoint.

As a result, path latency is not the real reason to keep hop counts low in a SAN design. A more pertinent reason to reduce hop count is over-subscription: the more ISLs a frame has to traverse, the more likely it is to cross a congested ISL.

In addition to causing a reduction in throughput, congestion will generally cause delay, since frames will need to be buffered by switch ports until the congested link is ready to transmit them. In other words, congested links go into store-and-forward mode but worse, since there may be a large number of frames ahead of any given frame. Reducing hop count reduces the number of opportunities each frame has to become congested, and therefore delayed. The best hop count for reducing congestion is, of course, zero, so use locality when possible if performance is a driving requirement.

Path latency *is* worth considering in relation to long distance connections. For native Fibre Channel links, the amount of time that a frame spends on the cable between two ports is negligible, since that aspect of the connection speed is only limited by the speed of light. The speed of light in optics amounts to approximately five microseconds per kilometer. For short connections, this is not observable at the application level. When using dark fiber or xWDM equipment to span distance, latencies may be observed in the link, but (a) they are still small compared to e.g. disk access times, and (b) there simply is not any way to get frames to go faster than light.

Brocade addresses the need to keep long distance performance as high as possible with the Brocade Extended Fabrics product. (p390) This product enables full-bandwidth performance across distances spanning up to 100s of kilometers, with even greater distances possible at lower speeds. Brocade also offers an FC FastWrite product to further optimize long distance connections. (p383) The bottom line is that Brocade FC SANs will always do as good a job as possible of getting data between sites.

However, IP SAN technologies work in a fundamentally different way. To extend a SAN across a long distance using FCIP, for example, delay is incurred while frames are encapsulated at one end and while the encapsulation is removed at the other end. Furthermore, the nature of IP WANs typically places a massive amount of latency in the connection between endpoints, which is several orders of magnitude worse than native FC performance in the best of cases. Therefore it is always advisable to consider latency when designing long distance SAN solutions.

Determining Performance Requirements

It is axiomatic that all networks and networking products have some kind of performance limit. Given that this is true, the question becomes how to ensure that these limits will not turn into *application*-level performance issues. The first step in this process is to determine what the application performance characteristics really are.

Top-Level Approaches to Determining Requirements

There are several schools of thought on how to find out what performance an application will require.

Some architects believe that a detailed understanding of the performance characteristics of all applications is needed before the design phase is complete. Often, they believe that this can only be accomplished through a detailed understanding of the application usage patterns, analysis of the internal architecture of the server platforms, and empirical testing.

There are advantages to this approach, since it is the most accurate way to estimate required performance before deployment. However, it does have disadvantages as well. It takes much more time and effort, and delays the benefits which drove the creation of the SAN in the first place.

Others believe that it is acceptable to simply make an educated guess, and then tune the network after implementation. Designers who favor this method may ask the administrators responsible for the applications in question about how much data per second on average is moved by the application, how much is moved at peak, when peaks usually occur, and what would happen if performance on the SAN were more limited than the application required at some point. People following this method typically use industry "rules of thumb" in combination with systems administrator interviews when provisioning ISLs. They might decide to start with a 7:1 ratio of host connections to ISLs, and then increase the ISL count as needed based on interview answers.

The designer will treat the numbers derived from interviews and rules of thumb as if they were established facts when provisioning ISLs and making other network infrastructure choices.

This is a much more efficient method of decision making, and will greatly accelerate a SAN deployment. The danger is that the SAN might end up being under-provisioned if the systems administrators were unaware of their applications' real behaviors. Knowing that their performance information is *not*, strictly speaking, factual, and is really educated guesswork, the designer will provide "wiggle room" to add ISLs or take other corrective action if needed once the SAN is running.

Other designers like to over-provision networks to avoid even the possibility of performance problems. This involves doing a limited evaluation of application performance requirements and making a conservative assumption about required performance on that basis. These designers tend to estimate how much ISL performance *might* be needed, and then increase the number of links beyond the amount of bandwidth for which the designer has identified a need.

This is not a "bad" or "lazy" technique: it simply recognizes that no engineer will ever have *all* information about future performance requirements when designing a network. Given that there will always be missing data, analyzing things in great detail may not yield any better answer, and will certainly take much more time and money. Adding additional performance into the design to account for "the needs that the designer did not know about" is simply being realistic. The only disadvantage of this approach is that it tends to move cost to the initial deployment in cases where cost for additional ISLs etc. could have been delayed and added later.

The three methods outlined above are the three top-level approaches most-often used to determine performance requirements: exhaustive analysis, educated guesswork, and deliberate over-provisioning. Whichever approach the designer favors, there are certain key points of information for which the designer will be looking. The primary two are bandwidth utilization and response time.

Bandwidth Utilization

Bandwidth utilization is characterized as a measure of how many units of data an application needs to move across the SAN per unit of time in a given time period. This correlates most closely with the SAN performance factors of link (or path) speed, over-subscription ratios, and congestion.

When evaluating the requirements of a host for bandwidth, it is important to understand both the relationship of data to time *units*, and to time *periods*. For example, an application might need to move 50 Gigabytes in one hour to perform a nightly backup within the allowable window. This amounts to a bandwidth utilization of about 100Mbits/sec.. That same application might need to move 50 Gigabytes in one minute during peak hours to perform data mining operations for a business decision support system. This amounts to well over 6Gbits/sec.. To support the backup requirement, a LAN interface running iSCSI might suffice. To support the data mining requirement, it may be necessary to install multiple 4Gbit FC HBAs and balance the load across them. SAN designers should provision for the anticipated bandwidth requirement which either exists at deployment time, or is anticipated to exist within the useful life of the application.

To design a SAN to support a given application's bandwidth requirements using the "exhaustive analysis" approach involves looking closely at each and every component – both hardware and software – between the application and its data.

Look at the internal characteristics of the host and storage device, the speeds of their SAN interfaces, the kinds of switches between them, and the structure of ISLs and IFLs in the fabric. When evaluating the ISL structure, look at all of the applications which may use each path, and add together all of their performance data to calculate the total potential load on the network. Ensure that the path will continue to support the required data rate even in the event of a link failure.

Of course, this can be a complex and time consuming process, which is why so many designers simply over-provision their networks or base their performance requirements on educated guesses. In this case, the designer would take an estimate of the application's bandwidth requirements, assume that the hosts and storage arrays will be able to support the requirements, and make additional assumptions based on rules of thumb about the requirements of the network ISL and IFL structures.

Response Time

The application requirement for response time relates to the gap between the time that an application sends a frame into the network, and the time that it receives its reply. This is most directly influenced by protocol selection, network latency and delay, error and loss rates, and edge device performance.

All applications have some degree of sensitivity to response time. Eventually, if a network has a long enough delay, and a host has not received a reply to an IO request, it will time out and retry the operation. Retries are never beneficial to application performance. Increasing timeout values on a host can reduce retry rates, but can have other impacts on performance that are just as bad. The best solution is always to use a protocol which has low delay times, close to zero loss and error rates, a network design with low or no congestion, and edge devices capable of responding to requests in a timely manner.

How fast the response is needed depends on the host operating system settings such as timeout values, HBA and storage controller timeout values, and the fundamental nature of the application itself. For example, synchronous applications tend to be extremely sensitive to response time. Asynchronous applications are less sensitive.

One thing to keep in mind is that it is *not* necessary to connect core switches to other cores, or edge switches to other edges in a CE fabric. This is a mistake often made by IP network designers new to storage networking. While it is *allowable* to connect edges or cores together that way, there is almost never any benefit, and doing so always adds cost. This is because traffic flow in both cases will either not use the horizontal ISLs at all, or will use them *instead* of the CE ISLs. In fact, it is possible for horizontal ISLs to *reduce* performance. This is much like the performance issue with full meshes. If an edge switch has one 4Gbit ISL to each of two core switches, there is a total of 8Gbits available from that switch to any other.   If one ISL is connected directly from that switch to another edge switch, there will only be 4Gbits available between them. Connecting the horizontal link reduces the hop count between the switches, but also decreases bandwidth. Since the horizontal 1-hop path is shorter than the 2-hop CE path, the 4Gbits of CE ISLs will never be used. Hop-count is a lower-priority performance consideration than bandwidth, so reducing hops by 50% will not make up for reducing bandwidth by the same factor.

ISL and IFL Provisioning

Provisioning of links in any network is a matter of matching network bandwidth to application-driven load. To put is simply, how many Inter-Switch Links or Inter-Fabric Links are required depends on how much traffic will be placed on them. This section deals with how to turn performance requirements into ISL and IFL structures.

To determine the number of ISLs or IFLs needed, several methods could be used. This subsection discusses three approaches: provisioning for peaks, for averages, or by using rules of thumb. Whatever approach is preferred, the SAN designer is attempting to decide how many links are required *per edge device*. The ratio of links to devices is generally referred to at the network's "over-subscription ratio".

When all ports operate at the same speed in a SAN, the link over-subscription ratio is the ratio of device input ports to the number of links over which the traffic could flow. In Figure 45, the over-subscription ratio on the switch to the far left is twelve device ports to four ISLs, which reduces algebraically to a ratio of three to one.

An over-subscription ratio is usually abbreviated when written out. The figure above represents a network with a "3:1 over-subscription ratio". There are twelve hosts connected to the upper left edge switch and four ISLs to the core. Thus, there are three hosts for each ISL. If all of these hosts tried to simultaneously use the ISLs at full speed in a sustained manner — even if the hosts were accessing different storage devices — each would receive only one third of the potential bandwidth available.

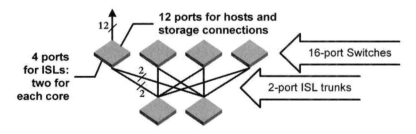

Figure 45 - ISL Over-Subscription Ratio of 3:1

The basic over-subscription formula is "ISL Over-Subscription = the Number of Nodes to the Number of ISLs", or $I_o = N_n : N_i$. This is generally reduced as a fraction so that N_i=1. (For example, 12:4 reduces to 3:1.)

Since SAN-attached devices can operate at different speeds, it is necessary to put some additional thought into calculating ISL over-subscription with variable speed hosts, storage, and ISLs. To calculate the ISL over-subscription ratio, average the speed of the input ports and divide this result by the speed of the output ports. If each host in Figure 45 had a 1Gbit HBA, and the ISLs all ran at 4Gbit, then the ISLs would actually be 3:4 *under*-subscribed, since 12x1Gbit of host-side input vs. 4x4Gbit of ISL-side bandwidth reduces that way. In this case, it would be common to leave the ratio written as above, or to reduce the value for N_n to "1" instead of N_i, e.g. writing it out as 1:1.3.

Different ratios are possible in CE networks by "tweaking" the number of ISLs configured. For example, if an edge switch in a CE network has sixteen ports, of which fourteen are used for devices and two for ISLs, then there are seven devices per ISL. That network would be said to have a seven-to-one over-subscription ratio, usually written as "7:1" for short. It is common to see ratios ranging from 1:1 to 63:1, depending on locality and performance needs.

The goal of the designer is to find an over-subscription ratio which provides enough bandwidth for all applications, so it might appear that the right thing to do would be to use a 1:1 over-subscription ratio for all SANs. If there is one ISL for every device, then it will never be possible for congestion to occur. However, provisioning that many links is expensive and limits scalability. Therefore the goal of the designer could more properly be stated as follows: provision only as many links as are needed to support application performance requirements, both at initial deployment and in the foreseeable future, but do not provision more than that.

The keys to finding the right ratio to use typically relate to understanding application capabilities and requirements, and looking at the over-subscription ratio of storage ports.

Any device that connects to a SAN with a 4Gbit interface is *theoretically* capable of achieving that rate, but in reality is probably capable of much lower performance. In this case, it is probably best to configure ISLs using rules of thumb. Specifically, by matching the ratio of ISLs to devices on an edge switch to the ratio of initiators to targets in a fabric. This approach is simple to understand and implement, and solves the vast majority of core/edge SAN design problems.

If a SAN is built to support a large number of devices which are truly capable of generating full-speed IO, then the principles of locality (p209) should be used if possible. If locality *is* used, then the ISL and IFL structures can support a very high degree of over-subscription no matter what the performance requirements might be. Once again, it is possible to use the ratio of hosts to storage as the ISL over-subscription ratio, which simplifies the design process significantly.

If localization not practical, and the SAN-attached devices are extremely fast, then the allowable over-subscription ratio will reduce as the required performance increases. In that case, further analysis is warranted to determine where the ratio should be set, using one of the following methods.

Provisioning for Peaks

In some cases, it is appropriate to provision the network for its worst-case, or *peak* utilization. This is generally the most expensive approach, but can be appropriate for environments in which the impact of a slow network is similar in scale to the impact of a down network. Real time applications such as satellite imagery download and analysis might qualify, for example, because if the network cannot keep up with incoming data, it will be lost. Similar situations can occur in large scale data mining operations, parallel supercomputer clusters, video editing workgroups, or television broadcast applications, to name just a few.

To determine the peak utilization for all of the IFLs going to/from a given fabric, find the total number of nodes on the fabric that may need to use those links at the same time, and add up their potential performance based on their interface types and any internal constraints. If historical performance data is available for those nodes, take the highest utilization level that has ever been observed from each and add them together. If not, add up the maximum speeds of their interfaces, less any known internal bottlenecks such as might be caused by a slow CPU or old-style PCI bus.

For example, an edge fabric may have 100 hosts and 15 storage ports. At any given time, most traffic may be localized within the fabric, but two of the storage ports will be mirrored across fabrics in a disaster tolerance solution, and two of the hosts will use ISLs for off-site backups. Assuming that real performance data were unavailable and that all ports were 2Gbit Fibre Channel, then peak usage for the inter-site ISLs would be assumed to be (2x storage ports + 2x hosts) x 2Gbit = 8Gbits/sec. of throughput. Four 2Gbit links would be required to handle this load, or two 4Gbit links could be configured.

For applications which warrant an even more conservative approach, a designer would allocate an additional "fudge factor" to handle short-notice requirements, link failures, and other unplanned events, as well as occasional imbalanced utilization of the links. It might be appropriate to configure six or even eight links to the remote fabric in this case.

The overall point of this method is to configure any given network path to accommodate the worst-case traffic pattern which might potentially be placed upon it.

Provisioning for Averages

In most environments, configuring links for peaks is not necessary, and only adds cost. Traffic flows do not often peak at the same time, do not do so for sustained periods even on those rare occasions, and there is no usually real business impact even if overlapping peaks were sustained for a short time. For this kind of environment, provisioning should be done based on projected *average* utilization.

In the previous example, it might be determined that on average the two mirrored storage ports are relatively inactive, using only an average of 0.5Gbits between them. Perhaps backup speeds are constrained by the tape drives, and can only sustain 1Gbit between the two hosts. Perhaps backups are done during off-peak hours, so they rarely intersect with high usage periods for the storage arrays. The average utilization would be something less than 1Gbit in this case.

This number has to be viewed through another filter, however. Backup traffic is sustained for the duration of the backups, so the bandwidth provisioned must not be less than the largest sustained application requires. It still would be possible in this case to sustain full performance on the solution using a single inter-site link, but in other cases this consideration could increase the provisioning.

The conservative approach in this example would be to configure two links for redundancy and future-proofing, but configuring up to eight as in the previously-discussed "peak" method would be needlessly excessive.

Provisioning Based on Rules of Thumb

In most cases, a designer will not know all of the usage cases for the network ahead of time. Even trying to figure this out is likely to waste time and money, and still not yield an accurate assessment. Once connectivity is in place, additional uses for it tend to present themselves. It may be possible to determine that a set of links need to have *at least* a certain capacity – for example using an average utilization method as above – but not so easy to say that they will need *no more than* a given amount short of 0% locality. However, configuring for 0% locality (i.e. assuming simultaneous peak usage of all links by every device in the fabric) is prohibitively expensive, and almost never accurate. It is more effective to use the average or even the minimum utilization as a baseline, and to provision above that level using rules of thumb.

One approach is to use the ratio of hosts to storage for the overall network. This is the method used for ISL provisioning in traditional core/edge fabrics, and is a good number because it is lower than the peak provisioning approach and is likely to be correct because hosts generally only "talk" to storage ports. While host to storage ratios vary, it seems to be most common for storage vendors to recommend ratios towards the lower end of the spectrum. The industry average seems to be in the 6:1 or 7:1 range for host to storage ratios, and for over-subscription of ISLs within a fabric.

However, the degree of localization related to edge fabrics within Meta SANs is likely to be much higher than switch-level locality within a fabric, so the provisioning of IFLs can be safely reduced still further in most cases. Reasonable IFL over-subscription ratios can be much higher than ISL ratios, even when specific performance data and LSAN configurations are unavailable.

The rule of thumb method for IFL provisioning can be stated this way:

1. First configure all known IFL utilization as a baseline.
2. Then add at least one additional IFL for redundancy and to support unanticipated needs.
3. In the absence of other traffic pattern knowledge, increase this number based on the ratio of initiators to targets in the Meta SAN modified by the anticipated localization percentage. If a Meta SAN has 1000 hosts and 100 storage ports, the ratio is 10:1. If an edge fabric

has 100 hosts, it would require 10 IFLs, reduced according to the level of fabric locality. If 90% of traffic is localized, then the fabric would only need 1 IFL added to the IFLs from rules 1 and 2.

To put it yet another way, IFL provisioning could be calculated according to the formula:

```
IFLs = ( known_traffic + 1 ) + ( fabric_hosts /
h:s_ratio ) * ( 1 - fabric_locality_percent ) )
```

Of course, this need not be followed as an axiomatic rule. If all storage in a Meta SAN is located on one fabric, and the hosts on another, then most of the IFLs must be configured going to the storage fabric. This is a *tiered* approach (p217), which is generally *not* recommended for routed Meta SANs.

It is important to remember that rules of thumb are *aids* to intelligent SAN designers, not *replacements* for them. If the designer knows of a reason to increase or decrease oversubscription, then sticking to the ratio of hosts to storage will not be productive.

Traffic Locality

The best possible performance in any network can be attained only through understanding its traffic patterns and optimizing a device connection strategy on this basis. If traffic patterns are well enough understood, it may be possible to optimize traffic by putting ports that communicate with each other – either most often or most critically – "close" together in the network. This concept is known as *locality*.

For example, in a CE network it may be possible to attach hosts and their primary storage ports to the same edge switch. This allows most IO to follow an efficient path, never leaving the switch, rather than traversing ISLs. Figure 46 shows one "conversation" in a CE fabric which has been localized, and one which has not.

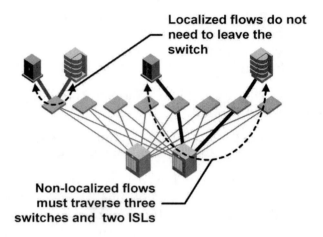

Figure 46 - Use of Locality

Although this technique has been used in data networks for decades, SANs are inherently better suited to this kind of analysis and design. For example, in most data networks, any-to-any patterns may occur and must be accounted for. On the other hand, in almost all SANs it is predictable that hosts will only communicate with storage ports – not other hosts – and that certain storage will be used most often.

It is possible to localize just a portion of the traffic in a SAN. In other words, both of the conversations depicted in the figure could occur within one fabric. In this case, traffic in the SAN would be said to be localized to some percentage. If all flows were localized, the SAN would have 100% locality. If none were localized, it would have 0% locality.

The vast majority of real-world storage networks are not so performance-sensitive that 100% locality is required or even necessarily desirable. Most designers only focus effort on localizing flows between mission-critical devices which are particularly performance sensitive.

However, in addition to improving performance, locality also improves RAS. If traffic patterns are localized to some extent, the impact on applications of network failures is more

210

limited in scope, so availability is improved. Locality also implies that there are fewer ISLs and therefore fewer total components in the network – reducing cost and improving reliability numbers like MTBF – and locality also facilitates service tasks such as troubleshooting, since there are fewer components to examine in a localized flow that is experiencing problems.

Locality can be designed into a network, and maintained rigorously for the lifetime of the SAN. Alternately, in many enterprise SANs, the percentage of locality used is a function of time. When a SAN is first deployed, it may be a migration from Direct Attached Storage (DAS). DAS inherently has 100% locality, so when moving from DAS to SAN it is possible to maintain much if not all of this localization initially. However, as the SAN matures, traffic patterns will likely move away from locality as nodes are added, moved, or decommissioned, or repurposed for new applications.

Bands of Locality

Locality is not an all-or-nothing technique. It may be that some locality occurs within an edge fabric in a Meta SAN[62], some within a switch in that fabric, and some within a blade or ASIC port group inside that switch. Locality therefore can be thought of as a set of bands moving outward from the traffic source port, as shown in Figure 47, with the highest RAS and performance being closer to the center and easier to create SAN designs being further out.

In general, the greater the performance and RAS requirements of an application, the greater the degree of locality that should be employed. The highest performance and RAS will occur when localization is done within a small port group on a single switch in a single fabric. However, designing for and maintaining such a high degree of locality is

---

[62] See "Fabric vs. SAN vs. Meta SAN" on page 34.

time consuming, tends to counter some of the benefits of networking, and in many cases is actually impossible to achieve. Therefore this degree of localization is generally reserved for connecting hosts to their primary storage arrays in mission-critical applications, or for cases where the SAN is used as a subsystem for a single massively high performance application like a parallel supercomputer, a data mining cluster, or for real time satellite imagery download and analysis.

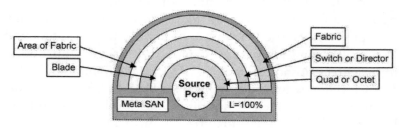

Figure 47 - Bands of Locality

In routed designs, locality can occur between edge fabrics co-located on a given router vs. fabrics that must be reached by crossing a backbone fabric. This may also occur between sites in a MAN or WAN. Locality within a Meta SAN itself will always add up to 100%. Each band below that level may have any portion of traffic localized.

If *all* traffic flows across ISLs and IFLs, then the lower bands will have 0% locality. If *no* traffic flows across these links, then the bands will add up to 100% locality. More often, the breakdown will be something like Table 2.

Table 2 - Utilization of Bands of Locality

Locality Band	Locality %	Running Total
ASIC	5%	5%
Blade	10%	15%
Switch/Director	40%	55%
Area of Fabric	25%	80%
Fabric	10%	90%
Area of BB	5%	95%
Meta SAN	5%	100%

The center column refers to the percentage of traffic localized at that level but not any level above or below. The right-hand column shows the traffic localized at that level *and* all previous levels. For example, if traffic flows between two ports on the same quad or octet, it is implied that it is also localized within the blade, director, area of fabric, fabric, area of backbone, and Meta SAN. Traffic localized within the blade but *not* within an octet is shown in the center column. Traffic localized within the blade *including* traffic localized within octets is shown in the right-hand column.

Localization closest to the source port (e.g. ASIC-level) tends to be a low percentage because it is difficult to design for and to maintain. Except in the most performance sensitive of applications, it is rarely worth the effort of pursuing localization at the port group or blade level. Localization at the switch level is easy to design for and yields a good return for the effort. If a fabric is complex, it is often possible to keep traffic within a thickly ISL-ed area, so only a relatively small percentage of traffic is truly any-to-any within a fabric.

In fact, there is so much "built in" localization at the edge fabric level within a Meta SAN that the traffic that must leave an edge fabric tends to be very small. Except in rare corner cases, locality is easy to achieve and provides strong benefits at the switch, fabric, and backbone area levels, so administrators do not actually *design* for it: it just *happens*. The locality distribution across bands most often has a shape somewhat like a bell curve, with the vast majority of traffic being localized before leaving a fabric. This fact should be kept in mind when provisioning IFLs.

Locality Within Switches

It is possible to localize traffic at different levels even within a single switch. It is not *necessary* to pursue this degree of performance optimization, and few customers go to the trouble of doing so to any great extent, but Brocade provides the capability for designers who need the absolute pinnacle of performance and availability. There are two different localization principles which apply at this level: localized switching within ASICs (p424) to improve performance, and localization within blades to limit interdependencies within directors.

All Brocade switches and directors[63] use extremely fast, custom-built central memory ASICs. Depending on which product is involved, there may be a single-stage central memory architecture inside a switch, or a multi-stage architecture. (p432) Multi-stage products have many switching ASICs which are interconnected on the back-end via channeled central memory links.

For example, the Brocade 48000 has eight slots for port blades, each of which may have one or more ASICs on it, depending on the features and port count of the blade. All vendors with large-scale products such as the Brocade 48000 have some variation on this architecture, in that no vendor has a single ASIC which can exist on more than one blade simultaneously. The typical approach is to place ASICs on port blades, and different ASICs on centralized "core" blades which interconnect the port blades. Brocade is different in that the multi-stage architecture used within its directors allows port blade ASICs to switch locally, without needing to cross the backplane to reach the core blades. Any port on a Brocade 48000 16-port blade can switch locally to any other port on that blade. The 32-port blade has two 16-port locality groups, and the 48-port blade has two 24-port groups.

With the SilkWorm 12000, it was possible to switch locally within a 4-port group, known as a *quad*. For example, if a host is placed on blade 1 port 1, and storage is located on blade 1 port 2, then they are in the same quad. Traffic between these devices did not need to cross backplane traces, and would therefore have optimal performance. On the other hand, engineering traffic patterns to keep IO within a 4-port

---

[63] Except for some products brought in through the acquisition of McData.

group is not practical on a large scale, so quad-level locality would only be used in rare cases. With the SilkWorm 3900 and 24000, the area in which locality could be employed was expanded to 8-port groups, or *octets*, which was somewhat easier to work with. Other switches, such as the Brocade 3250, 3850, and 4100, consist of single-stage designs, and so the entire switch can be considered "localized". It is relatively easy for many designers to localize the majority of traffic flows within a 32-port Brocade 5000 switch, or within a 24-port group on a 48-port Brocade 48000 blade.

Localization does improve performance, but it is necessary to put this in perspective. Crossing between localized ports as in the example above results in about 0.7µs or 0.8µs of delay. (That's 700 to 800 <u>nano</u>seconds, a.k.a. "fast.") Crossing the backplane of the Brocade 48000 in the *least* optimal manner results in 2.1µs to 2.4µs of delay. Typical access times for "fast" disk subsystems are many orders of magnitude slower than the "slow" switch traversal time. Because of this, most designers spend little time pursuing intra-switch locality when it is just a matter of optimizing latency.

However, there is another reason to consider intra-switch locality besides performance. When traffic is localized within a blade, it is less sensitive to failures of other blades. If a core blade fails, traffic will be redirected to the other blade, but some frames might be lost. This will not be a problem for modern SAN storage devices or HBAs, but it could cause a delay. Traffic patterns which had been localized would not be affected by this. This same effect applies to switch-level locality within a fabric, or at any other level: the more traffic is localized, the fewer dependencies exist which could interrupt the flow of traffic.

Again, this level of availability and performance engineering is not something that most designers will need to worry about, and most designers pursue locality only at the switch, director, or fabric levels. Think of intra-switch localization as a somewhat obscure tool in your toolkit: it is unlikely to be needed at any given time, but you might one day be very glad to have it if it *is* needed.

Locality and LSANs

As shown above, using locality within a single switch or director tends to be relatively low in value and require relatively high effort. Using locality at larger scales tends to have a better return for the design effort. The greatest effect is observed when traffic is localized at the fabric level within a Meta SAN. In other words, the conversation between an initiator and target which talk to each other frequently may be localized by placing the devices within the same fabric, even when there are multiple fabrics interconnected via routers. When locality is used at this level, SAN scalability is increased because of physical fabric services isolation (p177), and faults can be contained within a limited region.

In general, fabric locality within a Meta SAN tends to "take care of itself". The natural tendency of most designers is to connect devices which communicate frequently to the same fabric. Besides, most Meta SANs deployed to date have been formed by consolidating pre-existing "SAN island" fabrics, which previously had 100% locality at the fabric level. Before Brocade introduced the Fibre Channel Router feature and enabled Meta SAN creation, there was no way to get off of a SAN island, so there was absolutely guaranteed to be 100% locality to start with. Designers implementing Meta SANs in these environments would simply maintain some degree of localization after the router was introduced.

There is really only one factor that designers need to think about with respect to Meta SAN locality, which is the design of LSAN zones. An LSAN – or Logical Storage Area Network – is a zone which spans between fabrics in a Meta SAN. To the extent that LSAN zones are created, different fabrics in a Meta SAN begin to interact from a scalability standpoint. The interaction is limited, true, but it is best to keep fabrics separated except in cases where IO is required.

To ensure that this is the case, only create zones with the LSAN prefix when traffic actually does need to span between fabrics, i.e. when it is *not* localized.

Locality Moving Forward: UC and ILM

Next generation technologies and architectures related to Utility Computing and Information Lifecycle Management (p67) promise to provide many compelling benefits to SAN administrators and their customers. UC and ILM do, however, potentially have one drawback: both trends make localizing traffic impractical. The point of ILM and UC is to virtualize the server and storage infrastructure, so that the associations between applications, operating systems, and physical hardware can be altered dynamically at need. If this is the case, the physically locating a host port near its storage ports will not necessarily help, since that localization may go away whenever the ILM or UC policy dictates. This is discussed further in the next section, but the bottom line is that traffic localization is likely to reduce in popularity and effectiveness as ILM and UC proliferate, which will lead to wider deployment of tiered SANs.

Tiered CE SANs

"Tiering" is the practice of connecting hosts to one group (or *tier*) of switches, and storage to a different group. Dedicating certain switches for hosts vs. storage connections has manageability advantages, since it allows simplified capacity planning and tends to be more intuitive to look at on a diagram. Tiering is usually done to fabrics with a core/edge architecture. Either the storage tier will be located on the core switches (a two-tier model) or on a separate group of edge switches (a three-tier model). Figure 48 shows a CE fabric with devices connected using a two-tier approach. This is called a two-tier design because there is one tier for host connections, and one other tier for storage. The two tiers are directly connected together.

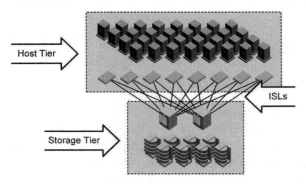

Figure 48 - Two-Tier CE Fabric

It is also possible to use a third tier of switches between the host and storage tiers. Figure 49 (page 218) shows this kind of three-tier design. Two-tier designs limit scalability, since they require attaching storage ports directly to core switches. (See "CE Topology Scalability" on page 152.) They can also have a negative performance impact in many cases, which is not the case with three-tier designs.

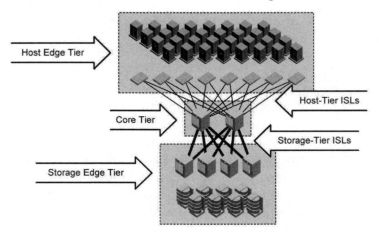

Figure 49 - Three-Tier CE Fabric

Look again at Figure 48. Notice that there are two storage-tier switches. If a storage device presents a LUN to just one of those switches, then each host will only be able to use one ISL to reach that LUN, even though there are two ISLs leaving every host-tier switch. If the same condition existed in the three-tier design depicted in Figure 49, each host would be able to use both ISLs, since they would both represent equal cost paths to the LUN. Brocade features such as DLS and DPS will balance IO between the ISLs (p220), ensuring better overall performance in the SAN. If IO is evenly balanced across all <u>LUNs</u> by the hosts themselves, then having the switches balance IO across <u>ISLs</u> is not needed, and the negative effect of two-tier designs is negligible. However, in most SANs, two-tier SANs tend to get "hot spots" with some ISLs over-burdened, and other ISLs completely unused, which is something designers should try to avoid.

There are manageability advantages to tiering, but designers should be aware that this practice is the exact opposite of locality from performance and RAS standpoints: it requires that every single frame traverse at least one ISL. From an ease of deployment and administration standpoint, tiered SANs are usually better, with three-tier designs being preferred over two-tier in almost all cases. Traditionally, from a performance standpoint, localization has always been the better option.

The exception to this performance analysis is that SANs using next generation technologies such as fabric-based data movers, virtualizers, or application platforms may not benefit from localization. Designers who intend to move towards a Utility Computing and/or Information Lifecycle Management automation architecture should consider tiered SANs for both management *and* performance reasons. This is because preferred implementations of next generation "application layer" SAN infrastructure products are expected to involve centralizing them in almost all cases. As long as that is the case, traffic will need to flow through the centralized device, even if the endpoints are localized on an edge switch. Figure 50 illustrates the typical traffic pattern expected in next generation SAN solutions.

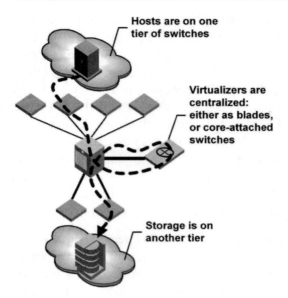

Figure 50 - Traffic Flow in Next Gen Fabric

In this example, traffic between all hosts and storage devices will flow through one or more virtualizers. These could be switches such as the Brocade 7600, or blades in a director such as the Brocade FA18, but either way they are likely to be centralized, if for no other reason than to control cost. Even if some storage ports were co-located onto the same edge switches as their hosts, traffic would still need to traverse the ISL structure to reach the virtualizer, so pursuing locality would not be effective.

Link Balancing

Even in over-provisioned networks, there may be "hot spots" of congestion, with some paths running at their limit while others are unused. This is similar to what happens in two-tier designs when hosts access LUNs in an unbalanced manner. In other words, the network may be a performance bottleneck even if it has sufficient raw bandwidth to deliver all flows without constraint. This happens when a network does not have the intelligence to balance load across all available paths. The unused paths may still be of some value for redundancy, but not for performance.

It may be surprising, but many network technologies have no link balancing capability at all. For example, Spanning Tree Protocol (STP is the standard used in most Ethernet networks) can only configure active/passive redundant paths.[64] Redundant links are not used for IO unless a failure occurs. Even then, it may take several *minutes* for STP to recalculate the topology and activate the standby link(s), and the network path will be down in the mean time. Users of storage networks, tend to be "dissatisfied" when a path is unavailable for even one or two seconds.

This is one of many reasons why IP/Ethernet was deemed fundamentally unsuitable for storage networking by *all* major vendors in the 1990s, which lead to the creation of more intelligent network protocols such as Fibre Channel. FC can handle rapid network convergence around failed links and balancing across different paths, and in fact FC supports several different options for doing this.

The available options are platform specific, since some of them require hardware support. All Brocade platforms support active source-port route balancing via FSPF. This is known as Dynamic Load Sharing (DLS). In addition to DLS, all currently-shipping Brocade fabric switches and directors support frame-level trunking between ASICs. The size of a trunk group may be four or eight links per trunk, depending on ASIC architecture. (See "Bloom and Bloom-II" on p427 and "Condor" on p428.) This is known as Advanced ISL Trunking. The most modern switches[65] and the Multiprotocol Router both support exchange-level trunking. This is known as Dynamic Path Selection (DPS). In switches with

---

[64] More advanced substitutes for STP now exist, but they are far from widely deployed. At the time of this writing, almost all Ethernet switches support STP.

[65] I.e. Condor-based platforms.

hardware support for the latter two forms of balancing, an optional license key may be required.

All three options can increase availability as well as performance. If multiple links are configured, a link failure will be dealt with automatically by the network, as opposed to causing a failover event on all hosts simultaneously. Performance may be degraded while the problem is fixed, but the overall network path will still be available. (The availability impact is even more apparent for hosts that do not use multipathing software.) A similar effect happens when *adding* a link: with frame-level trunking, links may be added dynamically without disrupting existing IO streams. Without an advanced link balancing mechanism, either the new link(s) would be unused, or IO would be disrupted.

Note that switches with trunking support can use all ports as trunks, or some as trunks and some as node attachment points. When used in the core of a network, switches often consist entirely of trunk groups. With edge switches, it is typical for 75% to 90% of ports to be used for nodes, with the remainder used as ISLs or trunks.

It is also important to note that the different balancing methods are not *exclusive* of each other. In switches with required hardware support, they can coexist effectively in any combination. For example, it is possible to use frame-level trunking to create multiple trunk groups, and either DLS or DPS at a higher level to balance traffic between those groups.

Dynamic Load Sharing: FSPF Route Balancing

All Fibre Channel fabrics support the FSPF[66] protocol. It is part of the base operating system as long as fabric and E_Port functions are present. FSPF calculates the topology of a fabric, and determines the path cost for any given endpoint.

---

[66] While originally authored by Brocade, FSFP is now a standards-mandated protocol for fabrics from all vendors. See "FSPF: Intra-Fabric Routing" on p415.

In many network topologies, such as the popular core/edge design (p149), there will be more than one equal-cost path between a source and any given destination edge switch. Which path to use can be controlled on a per-port basis from the source switch. By default, FSPF will attempt to spread connections from different ports across available paths at the source-port level. Brocade switches have an option that allows FSPF to reallocate routes whenever a fabric event occurs. This feature is called Dynamic Load Sharing (DLS) because it allows routes to be reset dynamically under conditions that can still guarantee in order delivery.

DLS does a "best effort" job of distributing IO by balancing source port routes. However, some ports may carry more traffic than others, and DLS cannot predict which routes will be "hot" when it sets them up, since they must be allocated before IO commences. In addition, traffic patterns tend to change over time, so no matter how routes were distributed initially, it would still be possible to have hot spots appear later, and changing the route allocation at runtime would cause out of order delivery.[67] Balancing the number of routes allocated to a given path is not the same as balancing IO streams, and so DLS does not do a perfectly even job of balancing traffic. This is why the feature is called load *sharing*, rather than load *balancing*.

The DLS feature is useful, and since it is free and works automatically, some form of it is used in virtually all Brocade multi-switch fabrics. However, DLS does not solve *all* performance problems, so there is a need for more evenly balanced methods. Such methods require hardware support, since path selection needs to be done on a frame-by-frame

---

[67] One Fibre Channel switch vendor attempted to use a similar method to change routes while IO was in flight. As they quickly discovered, this caused *massive* degrees of out of order delivery: something that violates FC standards and – as a more immediately practical concern – breaks many applications.

basis, and doing this in software would have a disastrous performance impact on the control plane.

Advanced Trunking: Frame-Level Load Balancing

Frame-Level Trunking Implementation

Trunking allows traffic to be balanced across ISLs while preserving in order delivery. Brocade supports two forms of trunking: frame-level and exchange-level. The frame-level method balances IO such that each successive frame may go down a different physical ISL, and the receiving switch ensures that frames are forwarded in their original order. Figure 51 shows a frame-level trunk between two SilkWorm 3850 switches. For this to work, there must be considerable intelligence in both the transmitting and receiving switches.

At the software level, switches must be able to detect that forming a trunk group is possible, program the group into hardware, display and manage the group of links as a single logical entity, and optimally manage low-level parameters such as buffer-to-buffer credits and virtual channels. Management software must represent the trunk group properly. This must be as user-transparent as possible.

At the hardware level, the switches on both sides of the trunk must be able to handle the division and reassembly of several multi-gigabit IO streams at wire speed, without dropping a single frame or delivering even one frame out of order. To add to the challenge, there are always differences in cable length between ISLs. Within a trunk group, this creates a *skew* in the time each link takes to deliver frames. This means that the receiving ASIC could receive frames out of order unless something is done to prevent it, and must be able to compensate for the skew to order the stream properly.[68]

---

[68] Other approaches to the de-skew problem exist, but affect performance. It is possible to tag each frame, but this would create the kind of frame-level standards violations and incompatibilities that caused a slew of issues for VSANs.

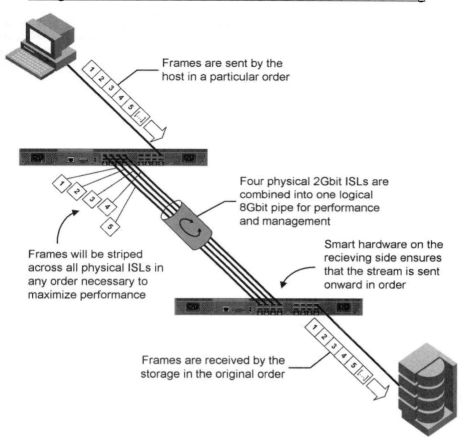

Frames are sent by the host in a particular order

Four physical 2Gbit ISLs are combined into one logical 8Gbit pipe for performance and management

Frames will be striped across all physical ISLs in any order necessary to maximize performance

Smart hardware on the recieving side ensures that the stream is sent onward in order

Frames are received by the storage in the original order

Figure 51 - Frame-Level Trunking Concept

There are limitations on the amount of skew than an ASIC can tolerate. These are high enough limits that they do not generally apply. The real-world applicability of the limitation is that it is not possible to e.g. configure one link in a trunk to go clockwise around a metro-area DWDM ring, and another link counterclockwise. As long as the differences in cable length are measured in meters, there will not be an issue, but if the differences are measured in tens of kilometers, a trunk group cannot form. Instead, the switch would create two separate ISLs, and use DLS or DPS to balance them.

Frame-Level Trunking Advantages

The main advantage to frame-level trunking is that it provides optimal performance: a trunk group using this method truly aggregates the bandwidth of its members. This feature also increases availability by allowing non-disruptive addition of members to a trunk group, and minimizing the impact of link failures.

Frame-Level Trunking Limitations

On Bloom-based platforms[69] multiple groups of from two to four 2Gbit links each can be combined into balanced pipes of from 4Gbit to 8Gbit each. Figure 52 shows a trunked configuration between two 3850 edge switches and two 24000 core switches, using two 2-port trunk groups each.

This would work in much the same way with other cores, such as the Brocade 4100, 4900, 5000, or 48000. This illustrates the primary limitation of frame-level trunking: it requires that all ports in a trunk must reside within an ASIC port-group on each end of the link. This is because it is the ASIC pairing that guarantees in order delivery, as shown previously in Figure 51.

On Bloom-based switches, port groups are built on contiguous 4-port groups called *quads*. On a SilkWorm 3250, for example, there are two quads: ports 0–3 and ports 4–7. On Condor-based[70] switches, trunking port groups are built on contiguous 8-port groups called *octets*.[71] In the Brocade 4100 switch, there are four octets: ports 0–7, 8–15, 16–23, and 24–31. Trying to form a frame-level trunk group outside of a port group will result in multiple independent ISLs forming, instead of a trunk.

---

[69] Such as the SilkWorm 3200, 3250, 3600, 3800, 3850, 3900, 12000, and 24000.

[70] Such as the SilkWorm 4100, 4900, 5000, and 48000.

[71] Octets have another meaning in the SilkWorm 3900 and 24000 related to local switching, not trunking. See "Traffic Locality" starting on p209.

On switches built using the Condor ASIC it is possible to configure multiple groups of up to eight 4Gbit links each. The effect is just like Figure 51, except that the performance per-trunk is quadrupled: instead of forming multiple 8Gbit pipes, Condor can create multiple 32Gbit pipes. (64Gbit full-duplex.) When connecting a Condor-based switch to a Bloom-based switch, a "lowest common denominator" approach is used, meaning that each trunk group will be limited to 4x 2Gbit instead of 8x 4Gbit.

While a frame-level trunk group will outperform DLS every time, using links only within port groups limits configuration options. The solution is to combine frame-level trunking with one of the other methods, as shown in Figure 52. This shows frame-level trunking operating within port groups, and DLS between trunks. Even though the ISLs are all within a trunk group on the edge switches, the four links could not form a trunk because they go to different port groups on different cores for resiliency.

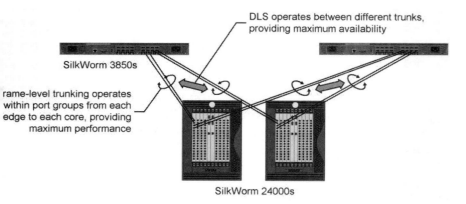

DLS operates between different trunks, providing maximum availability

SilkWorm 3850s

rame-level trunking operates within port groups from each edge to each core, providing maximum performance

SilkWorm 24000s

Figure 52 – Frame Trunking plus DLS

It is also possible to configure multiple trunks within a port group. For example, on the SilkWorm 3850, it is possible to configure one trunk on ports 12-13, and a separate trunk on ports 14-15. These could go to different core switches in a CE network, or different blades on a director.

When designing a SAN which spans long distances, it is important to select a technology that supports the required performance. It is therefore important to understand how frame-level trunking interacts with Extended Fabrics (p390).

Each ASIC has a certain number of buffer-to-buffer credits. On a Bloom-II switch, these are sufficient to operate all four ports in a quad in any mode over short distances.[72] Over longer distances, it is necessary to limit the functions of some of the ports. For example, Bloom-II can support a 4-port trunk at 25km, but at 50km only a 2-port trunk is supported, with the other two ports limited to node attachment.[73] At 100km, only one long distance port may be configured, which precludes trunking. It is possible to configure multiple 100km links on a Bloom-II switch: up to one per quad. However, since these cannot be in the same port group, it is necessary to use DLS to balance them, not trunking.

Switches using the Condor ASIC have more flexible support for trunking over distance. In Condor, buffers are shared across the entire chip, not limited by quads or octets. It is possible, for example, to configure up to 8-port x 4Gbit trunks at 50km (32Gbit trunk group) or 4-port x 4Gbit trunks at 100km (16Gbit trunk group). In some cases, it may be desirable to configure trunks using 2Gbit links. For example, the trunk group may cross a DWDM that does not have 4Gbit support. In this case, an 8-port by 2Gbit trunk can span up to 100km.

Dynamic Path Selection: Exchange-Level Trunking

Dynamic Path Selection (DPS) is a new trunking method available on all 4Gbit platforms. (See "Brocade ASICs" on

---

[72] "Short" being a relative term. This can be up to about 25km without performance degradation, and longer if full 2Gbit throughput per port is not required.

[73] For long distance trunking, minimum firmware versions may be required.

228

p424.) At the time of this writing, this means the Brocade 4100, 4900, and 200e (switches), Brocade 48000 (director), Brocade 7500 (router), and most of the currently-shipping embedded products.

Exchange-Level Trunking Implementation

The DPS method works by striping FC exchanges across equal-cost paths. An exchange identifier is placed by the sender into every FC frame header. In normal operation, the exchange ID remains consistent for the duration of a SCSI operation. When a DPS-enabled platform receives a frame, it takes all equal-cost routes and calculates the egress port from that set based on a formula using the sender's PID (SID), target's PID (DID), and exchange ID (OXID). The formula will select the same path for a given [SID, DID, OXID] set.

Effectively, DPS stripes IO at the SCSI level.[74] For a given "conversation" between a host and storage port, one SCSI command would go down the first path, and the next command would go down a different path. All frames within a given exchange would be delivered in order by virtue of going down the same network path. The potential exists for out of order delivery between *different* SCSI operations, but all devices tested to date are capable of handling this gracefully. Think of it this way: if two different hosts are writing to two different storage ports across the same network, in order delivery between the different hosts is not important. It only matters that in order delivery occur within the data stream sent by each host, not between the two different and unrelated streams.

This causes subtle differences in performance vs. frame-level trunking. These are discussed in detail in "Appendix A: Basic Reference" starting on page 384. The result is that ex-

---

[74] "Effectively" is an important word. This does happen *almost* all the time, but there are a small number of devices that do not map SCSI operations to OXIDs, and protocols such as FICON do not necessarily behave this way either.

change-level trunking outperforms all similar features from any vendor *except* for the Brocade frame-level trunking feature, and since DPS can be combined with frame-level trunking, it is possible to achieve both maximum performance and availability, as shown in the following subsection.

Exchange-Level Trunking Advantages

While performance might be slightly lower in some cases, there are also several advantages to the DPS method.

For one thing, DPS does not need to occur within ASIC port groups the way frame-level trunking must be configured. Much like DLS, DPS may be configured across different core switches in a CE network, or different blades in a director. However, unlike DLS, DPS actually balances traffic, rather than merely providing a best-effort by balancing source routes. Figure 53 shows an example of this between four Brocade 4100s in a Core/Edge arrangement.

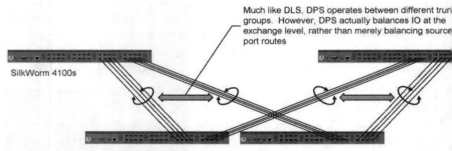

Much like DLS, DPS operates between different trunk groups. However, DPS actually balances IO at the exchange level, rather than merely balancing source port routes

SilkWorm 4100s

Frame-level trunks between SilkWorm 4100 switches can be up to eight links wide, with each link running at 4Gbit. This example shows four 4Gbit links trunked into a 16Gbit pipe between each edge and each of two cores. DPS balances the two trunks into a single 32Gbit path between edge switches.

Figure 53 - Frame Level Trunking plus DPS

Frame trunking cannot balance IO between different core switches, so DPS has an advantage in this case. In addition, DPS is not *exclusive* of frame-level trunking. It is possible to balance several groups of ports using the frame-level method, and then balance between the resulting trunk groups using the exchange-level method. This provides the optimal balance of performance (frame trunking is faster) and availability (DPS allows the flexibility to truly balance HA topologies). This is also shown in Figure 53.

Next, DPS can balance IO from an enabled platform to any other platform *even if the destination does not support the feature*. Path selection is made by the transmitting switch, and the receiver does not need to do anything to ensure in-order delivery. This allows backwards compatibility with installed base switches, and gives a performance benefit even if not all switches in a fabric are using the latest technology. Remember, path selection in a CE network is made by the edge switch, so if a Brocade 4100 is deployed in a CE network, even if the cores do not have DPS, users will have the benefit of the feature. Any traffic sent *from* a switch with the DPS feature will be balanced, regardless of whether or not the cores or the final destination edge switch support the feature. Traffic sent *from* edge switches without DPS would use DLS, whether sending to a DPS switch or not. (Figure 54)

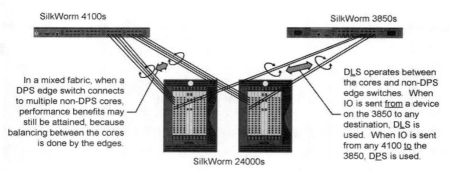

Figure 54 - DPS in a Mixed Fabric

Finally, DPS can balance IO across a long distance configuration not supported by frame-level trunking. (Figure 55.) For example, if there are two links configured between two sites which take substantially different paths, there may be too much skew to form a frame-level trunk. DPS would still be able to balance these links, since it does not rely on de-skew timers for in order delivery.

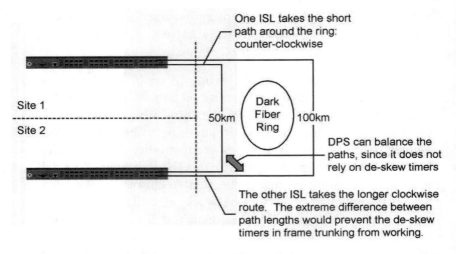

Figure 55 – DPS Balancing over a Large Fiber Ring

Exchange-Level vs. Frame-Level Balancing Performance

Advanced ISL Trunking operates at the frame level. DPS operates at the exchange level. In most FC fabrics, an exchange is equivalent to a SCSI operation. As noted previously in "Chapter 1: SAN Basics", an exchange may consist of a large number of frames, so frame-level trunking will "rebalance" more often than DPS.

The difference in granularity is usually not worth considering, but it can result in subtle performance differences between DPS and frame-level trunking. To understand why, it is necessary to understand how Fibre Channel nodes map SCSI data onto frames.

Fibre Channel frames may be of different sizes. They vary from about 60bytes up to about 2k bytes. SCSI block sizes can be much larger than 2k, so it may take more than one frame to carry the payload in a SCSI operation. These groups of frames are combined into FC exchanges.

For example, reading a SCSI block of 8k bytes might require many FC frames: one from the initiator to send the SCSI read command to the target, four 2k frames from the target to deliver the payload, and an acknowledgement form the initiator letting the target know that the data arrived intact. Typically, command frames are very small, so in this example there would be two small frames and four large ones. All known initiators will use the FC exchange ID to identify all frames in this group as belonging to the same SCSI operation. A subsequent SCSI operation might also consist of ten frames and might also have the same two endpoints, but it would use a different exchange ID for unique identification.

 Side Note

When reading this section, it is important to keep in mind that even the theoretical worst case performance for DPS is equal to or better than the best case performance of a SAN without such a feature.

For example, some other vendors only offer products with a version of DLS, which cannot outperform DPS in any usage case whatsoever. One such vendor attempted to make their DLS-like feature more dynamic, only to realize that this created massive out of order delivery and did not actually improve performance at all. Indeed, out of order delivery caused HBAs to entirely cease IO every time their "performance enhancing" feature was activated. Other competing products offer only a primitive form of DPS, and have no frame-level trunking feature at all. In other words, DPS will "merely" outperform Brocade competitors, but will not outperform Brocade frame-level trunks.

The take-away should not be that DPS is slow – it isn't – but rather that it is slower than the frame-level trunking feature.

The two reads would consist of two exchanges divided into a total of twenty frames. Switches using DPS would send the first ten frames down one path, and the second ten down a different path. If only one initiator/target pair were using the network to do only one SCSI operation at a time, then only one path would be used at a time. This is not even balancing of IO. Switches using frame-level trunking in contrast would stripe the frames evenly across all available paths in the trunk group, so utilization would be evenly spread out even with one "conversation."

This is not a *real* performance issue; it is simply an example to illustrate how the feature works. If only one initiator/target pair were using the network and they were only doing one SCSI operation at a time, then only one network path would be *needed* to maintain full performance.

It is more interesting to examine what happens when multiple flows are crossing the network at the same time. If two flows used the network, it is theoretically possible that they could be synchronized with each other in such a way as to map to the same path. If this happened for extended periods of time, it would be essentially as if no load balancing method were in place at all.

It is important to note that this is essentially a mental exercise. In real world applications, this kind of perfect synchronization would last a short time (sub-second) if it ever occurred at all, especially as the number of flows in the network increased beyond two.

This is called a *transient* performance effect, and does not generally affect throughput or application-level performance. What it *would* do is create slight irregularities in performance analysis graphs, such as might be created using SAN Health (p388) or Advanced Performance Monitoring (p390). The more traffic being carried by the network, the more load balancing will be needed, and at the same time the more even these graphs will become. That is, DPS becomes better at balancing load as the load to be balanced increases.

It is also worth noting that combining DPS with frame-level trunking tends to even out the performance graphs entirely. Even if the statistically rare sustained synchronization occurs between flows, they will be mapped to a frame-level trunk group instead of a single link. If this happens with e.g. two flows at a time, there is guaranteed to be enough bandwidth in even a 2-port frame-level trunk group to support their requirements. In order for the network to become a bottleneck, a large number of synchronizations would need to occur and be maintained for a long period of time, and they would all need to occur *in the same way*. This is statistically about as likely as being hit by a school bus while SCUBA diving.

The net result is that the performance differences between frame- and exchange-level trunking are theoretical rather than practical. In the highest performance networks, even the transient effects can be eliminated by combining trunking methods, and since there are major advantages to exchange-level trunking, purely theoretical performance differences are of little consequence. Again, since Brocade is the only vendor to offer both methods, users may select whichever approach they are most comfortable with.

Link Balancing Summary

All networks with more than one ISL can benefit from link balancing. The most effective high-performance / high-availability designs combine two forms of balancing: frame-level trunking for best performance, and DLS or DPS to balance multiple trunk groups for highest availability.

Even if a SAN does not require maximum performance right away, thought should be put into how trunking can be implemented later when needed. After all, it is axiomatic that network utilization will always grow to meet network capacity: no matter what bandwidth is initially configured, eventually more will be needed. For this reason, "Chapter 12: Implementation Planning" starting on p303 has more information related to designing SANs in a manner conducive to managed growth and change.

Performance Effects of BB Credits

Brocade switches handle BB credits in a manner transparent to the end user, and it is only necessary to think about them in relation to long distance native FC links. However, there are considerations associated with them that apply to short-distance connections; it is just that Brocade can will deal with these "auto-magically". This section discusses what some of those considerations are, and how Brocade deals with them. Most designers will never require this information in their jobs, but may still find it interesting.

Buffer Pooling

Traffic on SANs is typically "bursty," meaning that a fabric will carry short but demanding bursts of data. Because only a limited number of credits can be given to a device, these may get used up during long-duration bursts. If this happens, traffic must stop and wait for the receiving device to respond with an R_RDY if the length of a burst exceeds its available credit.

To address this issue, Brocade uses a buffer pooling mechanism in its ASICs. The buffer pool is a set of BB credits which are available on demand to any port on the ASIC which needs them on a first-come first-served basis. When an F-port or N-port is logged into the fabric, it is given a number of credits – typically 16 for most Brocade switches. When a device requests credits after the initial FLOGI/PLOGI process, a Brocade switch will start by using the buffer pool and then, once the pool is exhausted, it will utilize the original 16 buffer credits that were provided to the device.

The only caveat with this approach is that when using Fibre Channel test equipment such as traffic generators to measure "latency under load", the total pool (e.g. 64 credits) is immediately made available to the generator – as it would be to any real endpoint device – and once the pool is exhausted the remaining 16 credits are also provided. The traffic generator sends data into the switch, filling up the available buffers. Subsequently the buffer pool has to drain, which takes time. In this case the test equipment is actually measuring the depth of the buffer pool, and not switch latency:

apparent latency increases because e.g. 80 frames are in a queue and the frame at the end of the buffer queue will need to wait for all the others to be delivered before it will make it to the receive port. The fault in this case is not with the speed at which frames traverse the switch. It is simply that the switch is allowing frames to enter a buffer queue earlier rather than later... which is what such a queue is for.

If the test above were to be executed on a switch that had a small number of buffers, or did not have buffer pooling available, then few credits − perhaps 2 − would be given to the traffic generator. If only 2 buffers had to empty before the last frame was delivered, it would take less time than if 80 credits were provided. The lower buffer count switch would simply not allow the host to send frames into the switch at the same rate. The switch would in effect push back on the host, preventing it from sending data.

Here is the key point. The final delivery time of any given frame is at least as good with the pooling method as if the switch simply told the traffic generator to "hold off" on sending more frames... from an *application* point of view. If one were to measure the total time it took to complete the IO sequence, the switch with more buffering would perform at least as well as the switch with less buffering, provided that true latency (as opposed to latency under load) were more or less the same. The switch with fewer buffers would delay frames before they could even enter the switch by at least the same amount of time as − and usually more time than − the switch with pooling.

This can be demonstrated quite effectively. Buffer queues only back up when the egress port is unable to drain frames out at the same rate that the ingress port fills the queue. To ensure that this is the case, run the IO stream at just slightly under the theoretical maximum line rate. Perhaps the generator would be set for 99.9% of maximum speed. Brocade's ASICs demonstrate less than 2μs of latency in this case. Then try the test again at exactly 100% of line rate. This will cause the queue to back up, since the receiver will generally be just a hair out of sync with the transmitter, and the *apparent* latency will increase proportionally to the depth of the queue: switch vendors with small queues will show small amounts of additional latency; vendors with more buffers will show a larger difference. However, if the test measured the time it took to complete a given total IO sequence, such as copying 2GBytes of data, then the switch with larger buffer pool would perform as well or better than the buffer-poor switch.

Conclusion

Latency measurements can be misleading if the tests are conducted by parties who either have a vested interest in the outcome or simply do not understand Fibre Channel buffering mechanisms. Customers and partners should be aware of this, and should scrutinize test results to understand what has really been tested. Latency tests conducted under full load create congestion, and even a small amount of congestion causes buffer queues to back up. While this has no impact at all on real world end-to-end performance, it does cause latency tests to generate incorrect results. Therefore it is necessary to be highly critical of any test that claims to measure "latency under load" and does not give great detail on what steps were taken to prevent buffer depth from being measured instead of latency.

9: Availability Planning

"Availability" refers to the amount of time that a system or application is available for use. The focus of this chapter is on SAN availability from the point of view of *application* availability: it shows how each SAN component and the overall network design itself can contribute to or detract from the end user's application use experience. In this context, to the extent that individual component or element failures do *not* impact applications, these are referred to as "reliability" or "serviceability" events rather than "availability" events.

Overview of SAN HA Theory

In the context of storage network design, it is appropriate to consider the availability characteristics of each attached device, each SAN infrastructure component, and the network itself. This is because any system or application is only as available as the weakest link, so a SAN designer should examine all links when making an availability evaluation. To build a Highly Available (HA) SAN-attached computer system, it is not sufficient to have an HA cluster. It is necessary to account for availability throughout the entire system: dual HBAs, multipathing software, highly available and multi-ported storage subsystems, *and* clustering software are some of the components that may make up such a system.

However, the most operative consideration for most SAN designers is the availability of each SAN-attached *application*. From the point of view of end users of the application, it really does not matter if an individual part such as an SFP fails. They are interested in whether or not their application remains online. SAN designers should consider each component of the SAN, yes, but only in relation to how a failure in those components will affect application availability.

Single Points of Failure

The first principle of HA theory, for SANs or any other kind of system, is this: *"One of anything is not HA."*

This means that any component in a SAN is considered to be a single point of failure unless it is fully duplicated. This includes all hardware and software, up to and including the fabric itself. In order for a component to be considered highly available, it has to be duplicated, *and* the duplicate should not be tightly coupled — either at the hardware or software levels — to the component it is protecting. After all, whatever caused the primary component to fail could easily impact the duplicate as well, if they are too closely connected.

"Tightly coupled" includes both logical and physical relationships. For example, even a subsystem which has an HA architecture internally is still a single point of failure, because all components are physically located in the same place. Brocade directors have redundant power supplies, fans, CPUs, operating system images, switching components, and so on. Every active component in a Brocade director is duplicated, and software mechanisms are provided to ensure rapid failover between these components. Even if a major failure took down both a CPU and a switching blade simultaneously, the director could continue to forward frames without even a fraction of a second of downtime. And yet, if a sprinkler system went off overhead, the entire chassis could fail as a unit. If the data center fell down during an earthquake, or was destroyed in a tornado, then fans would not help.

Similarly, it is theoretically possible for a Denial of Service (DoS) attack to "take down" *any* system as a unit, even one as robust as a Brocade director. Of course, Brocade hardens its products against any kind of attack *that we know about*, but the nature of DoS attacks is that new categories of DoS threat are constantly being created. Indeed, a SAN administer – i.e. an administrator with duly granted authority to manage the system – can cause a DoS attack by making a sufficiently bad mistake at a command prompt. This is not a function of Brocade switches, or of FC fabrics; it is a reality of high availability theory throughout computer science. The only way to protect against this category of problems is to ensure that there is a robust "wall" between redundant components. This should be an "air gap" rather than a mere partitioning mechanism, since such mechanisms can also fail.

Following this train of thought to its furthest extreme, SAN designers may end up attaching HA clusters of servers to highly redundant components such as Brocade directors, in a reliable fabric design such as a resilient CE architecture, with a second resilient fabric for redundancy in case there is a fabric-wide problem with the first fabric, and replicating that entire setup in a second data center. After all, even a *site* is a single point of failure.

Of course, this approach is somewhat expensive. Not all customers have the budget for that much equipment, or the personnel to install and maintain it over time. The next logical thought is to see in which areas redundancy can be eliminated without compromising application availability – or at least without compromising it too much. Understanding which areas to eliminate to save on cost requires evaluating their relationships within the HA stack.

High Availability Stack

It is possible for components to be redundant in either horizontal or vertical relationships.

If a director has two power supplies, and can operate on just one, then the PS units have a horizontal redundant relationship to each other, because they are at the same "level" in the network. Similarly, if two directors are used, and a host has redundant HBA connections (p13; p22; p247) to them, or if two hosts form an HA cluster, then they have a horizontal relationship as well. This is illustrated in Figure 56.

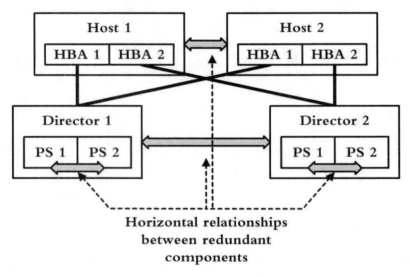

Figure 56 – Horizontal Redundant Relationships

Components in a SAN also have vertical relationships. The power supplies can be considered "below" the directors, which are "below" the host's HA clustering software. Vertical relationships are not *necessarily* relevant to HA, though. Having two power supplies in a horizontal relationship within one director implies an HA design strategy, but having one power supply and one director in a vertical relationship does not, because the components do not back each other up. Having redundant components positioned vertically above redundantly configured power supplies *does* relate to HA. Similarly, if redundant components at one level rely on a shared lower-level object, then a failure in the lower object can cause a simultaneous failure of the higher level objects.

Since there are two directors in a horizontally redundant relationship in this figure, an entire director can fail without causing downtime for either host or their applications. This *may* "trump" the need to have redundant power supplies within each director: a redundant power supply is intended to prevent a director from failing, but a director failing will not cause an application outage in this example.

In that case, why not save on equipment cost by removing the extra PS units from the design? To answer this, it is necessary to examine the HA stack in more detail. Figure 57 illustrates the HA scenario from Figure 56 as a stack.

This figure represents the HA stack from the example depicted in Figure 57.[75] If a UPS, power grid, or data center fails, the application most likely will be down. The power supplies (PS), fans, central processors (CP), and core cards of Brocade directors are all on the same "tier" of redundancy, so they are shown on a single line.

Component	HA?
Application	✅
Datacenter	❌
Server Clustering	✅
HBA	✅
Fabric	✅
Switch/Director	✅
PS	fan	CP	core	✅
UPS Protection	❌
Power Grid	❌

Figure 57 – HA Layers

To decide if redundancy is really needed at a given layer, evaluate what happens to upper layers if a failure occurs. For example, a lack of redundancy at the power grid level will impact both directors simultaneously, which will "take down" all higher layers regardless of their HA design.

---

[75] The example does not explicitly show redundant Uninterruptible Power Supplies (UPSs), power grids, or data centers, so the stack is assumed to be non-redundant at those levels.

Power supplies work a bit differently. When there is *not* redundancy at that level, but there *is* redundancy at the switch or director level, then it does *not* imply that the SAN has only one PS unit. There will be at least one different PS unit in each director, even if that layer is "non-redundant", simply because a director cannot work without one.

With that in mind, when there is a lack of redundancy at the PS level, a failure there will cause one and only one director to go down. If that happens in the Figure 56 example, the entire fabric will have failed. If *that* happens, the HBA attached to that fabric will fail. However, because there are redundant HBAs connected to separate fabrics, no layers above the HBA should be impacted. The failure will have been "caught" by the multipathing driver which supports the redundant HBAs. But what does that actually *mean*?

Generally speaking, it means that the application will sit idle for some number of seconds or even minutes while time-outs propagate up and down its driver stack, before the failover occurs. When it does switch to the alternate path, there is risk: a chance that something could go wrong, either due to a configuration error or a simultaneous failure of any component in the redundant fabric stack. In the best case, an administrative action is likely to be required to fix the SAN, *and* to switch the host back to the original fabric once the power supply has been replaced.

To make matters worse, in almost all SANs there will be more than one host connected to the failing director, which means that a single power supply failure will impact – to one extent or another – potentially hundreds of applications. This magnifies the impact of failover risk (e.g. multipathing configuration errors etc.) and the amount of effort needed to recover from the event.

Finally, the larger the scope of a failure, the more likely that a simultaneous failure will render some or all of the HA protection ineffective. If an SFP fails on a "Director 2" port attached to a storage array, and a simultaneous failure occurs on a "Director 1" power supply, then all applications relying on the storage array port will lose both paths to their data at the same time.

The bottom line is that the higher up the HA stack a problem gets before it is caught, the more complex the solution that finally catches the failure is likely to be, and the more likely that there will be an application impact even if the HA mechanism works perfectly. Server clustering and multipathing are more complex to design and implement than power supply redundancy. The higher up the stack an error propagates, the more risk there is that the redundancy mechanism will malfunction, and the more administrative effort will be required to remedy the problem even if all goes well. The net effect is that, if it is possible to "trap" a problem at the power supply level, then it is best to do, even if it could have been trapped at a higher level.

This leads to the second major principle of HA theory, which is: *"Always trap an error as low in the stack as possible."*

The reason designers use redundancy at multiple vertical layers (e.g. power supplies *and* fabrics) is that this method makes it vastly less likely that any given error will result in application downtime, *and* makes it much easier to recover from any problem at the lower levels in the stack. That is also why all Brocade directors ever shipped included redundant power supplies, fans, CPs, and, if applicable, cores.

Redundancy in SAN Design

Redundant network designs are always recommended for SAN deployments where downtime for the network could affect mission-critical systems. In addition, redundant designs are appropriate where large numbers of lower-tier systems are being served by the SAN. The rule of thumb is this: if the organization served by the SAN would be adversely affected if all devices attached to it suddenly stopped working, then the SAN should use a redundant network design. The greater the impact that would be caused by such an event, the greater the degree of redundancy which should be used.

This leads to the next major principle of SAN HA theory: *"Always match the redundancy model used to the criticality of the system(s) it protects."* The more important the system, the more robust the redundancy model should be.

There are four primary categories of availability in traditional SAN architecture. In order of increasing availability, they are:

Single non-resilient SAN fabric or Meta SAN

All switches are connected to form a single fabric, which contains at least one single point of failure. The "cascade" topology shown in Figure 28 (p143) is an example of this category of SAN. This is the least available approach.

Single resilient SAN fabric or Meta SAN

All switches are connected to form a single fabric, but there is no hardware-level single point of failure that could cause the fabric to segment. Topologies such as "ring", "mesh", and "core/edge" are usually examples of this (p145 - p149) and it is also discussed under "Resilient Fabrics" later in this chapter. This approach works well for protecting against most hardware failures, but failures at the fabric services level will still cause downtime for all attached systems, and so this is *not* considered an HA design method.

Redundant non-resilient SAN fabrics or Meta SANs

In a dual fabric non-resilient SAN, half of the switches are connected to form one fabric, and the other half form a separate fabric. (This is also often known as the "A/B redundancy model" since the fabrics or Meta SANs are usually labeled with those letters, though some designers refer to them as e.g. "red" and "blue" fabrics.) Within each fabric, at least one single point of failure exists. This design can be used in combination with dual-attached hosts and storage devices using multipathing drivers to keep an application running even if one entire fabric fails, or if a rolling upgrade is performed. An example of this type of SAN is shown under "Redundant Fabrics" starting on page 251. This design is considered HA, but slightly risky since a single minor failure can cause a large-scale multipathing failover event, as in the previous example.

Redundant resilient SAN fabrics and Meta SANs

For designers truly interested in availability, this is the "sweet spot" of SAN architecture. In a dual-fabric resilient SAN, half of the switches are connected to form an "A" fabric, and the other half form a separate "B" fabric, just as above, but this time neither fabric has a single point of failure that could cause it to segment. This design can be used in combination with dual-attached hosts and storage devices to keep an application running even if one entire fabric fails due to operator error, catastrophe, or quality issues. This is the only design approach recommended for critical high-availability environments. Another key benefit of this design is the ability to take part of the SAN down for upgrades or maintenance without affecting production operations on the remaining fabric(s). An example of this type of SAN is shown under "Redundant Fabrics" starting on page 251.

Dual-Homed Nodes and Multipathing

Dual-homed nodes, in the context of SANs, are host and storage devices which have multiple ports attached to the network. For hosts, this means multiple HBAs, as in the example from Figure 56 earlier in this chapter. For RAID arrays, this usually means two or more separate controller cards, with each usually has multiple ports.

When these ports are connected to separate switches in a resilient fabric, or, better yet, to separate fabrics in a redundant SAN, then it is possible for the dual-attached nodes to remain available for applications even when a major error occurs. With redundant fabrics, the error can take down an entire fabric without affecting an application.

However, in order for this to work, the nodes must all use multipathing software. Without multipathing software, redundant HBAs would each individually present the operating system with a view of their respective fabrics. If each HBA saw the same LUN, the operating system would see it as being two different storage devices. This could create major problems for an application accessing the LUN, up to and including data corruption. The job of the multipathing software is to sit between the HBA driver and the operating system, and cause the OS to present the application with a single instance of each LUN. The software also handles detection of failures through timeouts, and rapid switchover between the paths in the event of a failure.

SAN designers should take the time to understand how the timeout and switchover mechanisms in their multipathing solution work. Many multipathing drivers will allow the system administrator to "tune" them to accelerate or decelerate failovers. In general, it is best to leave the drivers at their default values unless there is a specific reason to change them. It is likely that the SAN designer will have a good idea about how quickly a failover should occur, and can give the system administrator a "heads up" if such tuning needs to be done. Accelerating retries or timeouts can improve performance when large-scale fabric failures occur, but accelerating them too much may cause failovers even when the SAN is healthy.

Some multipathing solutions take an active/standby approach. Just one HBA or controller port will handle all IO, unless there is a path failure. Other solutions take an active/active approach: IO is balanced between ports, usually on a SCSI operation or Fibre Channel exchange level similar to DPS (p220). SAN designers should keep two things in mind when evaluating multipathing solutions:

1. Active/active will perform better than active/standby in all normal operation cases. They will perform on par with each other in all failure cases.

2. Active/standby solutions will perform *consistently* whether there is a failure or not. When a failure occurs with active/active, users may perceive a reduction in application performance.

Which behavior is preferred depends on the nature of the applications being served by the SAN-attached hosts, and the perceptions of their users. If an applications benefits from receiving the best possible performance at any given point in time, then the active/active approach is better. This is the most typical case. However, if an application absolutely requires a *specific* performance level – no more and no less – then active/standby is the right approach. The provisioning of the active path *or* the standby path alone will need to fulfill 100% of the application's needs.

Another differentiator between multipathing solutions is whether they use an "open systems" approach, or if they are proprietary. In the former case, it will be possible to use one vendor's server platform with another vendor's storage array. The proprietary approach may have more features, and may be more reliable, since it will have been exhaustively tested in a specifically supported configuration. This makes it less likely to fail, and easier to fix if it does fail.

Whichever style of multipathing driver is used, the key take-away is this principle: *"Always use multipathing software to control redundant HBAs and storage connections in an HA SAN."*

Resilient Fabrics

According to the Encyclopedia Britannica,[76] "resilient" means, "tending to recover from or adjust easily to misfor-

---

[76] Encyclopedia Britannica 2004 Ultimate Reference Suite DVD.

tune or change." A resilient fabric "tends" to accommodate "misfortunes" such as ISL or individual switch failures without losing its integrity as a fabric, and can accommodate many kinds of "change" such as rolling core switch upgrades without downtime as well. In order to ensure that this is the case, the resilient fabric topology provides at least two routes between all switches that comprise the fabric, as in Figure 58.

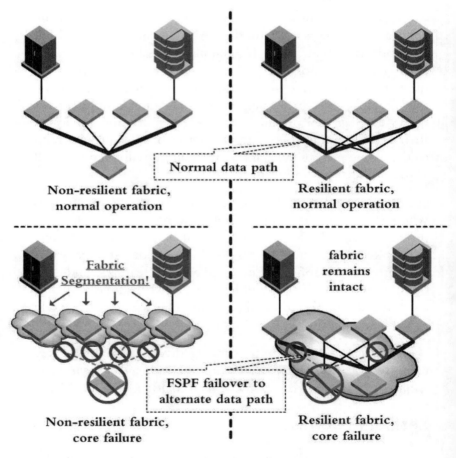

Figure 58 – Resilient vs. Non-Resilient Fabrics

The self-healing capability which allows the fabric to route around failures is provided by the Brocade-authored Fabric Shortest Path First (FSPF) protocol. While originally a

Brocade-only protocol, FSPF has been accepted by the standards bodies as the standard protocol for FC fabric routing, and is now implemented by all FC switch/router vendors.

It is also reasonable to consider a single Brocade director to be resilient. In the same way that the fabric in Figure 58 can withstand hardware failures and still remain operational, so, too, can a Brocade director continue to operate even when a blade fails. In fact, the internal architecture of a Brocade 48000 director is quite similar to a resilient fabric. Indeed, the rapid HA failover software and other similar mechanisms inside a director will outperform fabric-based mechanisms such as FSPF. (See Multistage Internal Architectures" on page 432 for more information.)

This does *not* mean that a resilient fabric or director *cannot* fail as a unit. There is no single point of failure in the *hardware* design of a resilient fabric or director, and the Brocade fabric services architecture is highly reliable as well. However, since all switches in a fabric and all blades in a director are "tightly coupled" together at both the data and control plane levels, it is theoretically possible for an entire resilient design to be impacted by events such as denial of service attacks, operator errors, severely malfunctioning nodes, or "physical" problems such as a malfunctioning fire-suppression system going off overhead. To protect against these kinds of problems, redundant fabrics are *always* recommended, preferably in combination with resiliency.

The applicable HA principle is this: *"HA SAN solutions should use resilient designs, but designers should still consider an entire resilient network to be a single point of failure."*

Redundant Fabrics

The encyclopedia[76(p249)] defines "redundant" as meaning, "serving as a duplicate for preventing failure of an entire system (as a spacecraft) upon failure of a single component." The "system" in this case is the overall SAN. Redundant fabrics are "components" of this system which "duplicate" each others' functions so that the failure of one fabric will not take down the entire SAN "system".

Resilient fabrics merely "tend" to "recover" from problems within a fabric, while redundant fabrics actually "prevent" the failure of an entire SAN. Resilient fabrics *are* reliable, yes. However, no single fabric can ever truly provide an HA solution. The fabric itself is subject to failures caused by disasters, operator errors, or software malfunctions.

To account for those kinds of errors, another level of availability must be used: the redundant "A/B" fabric SAN, also known as a "dual-fabric" SAN. In this architecture, there must be at least two completely physically separate fabrics – just as an HA cluster requires at least two completely physically separate servers. Duplicating components and providing switch-over (or fail-over) software is well established as the most effective way to provide high availability for server platforms. Similarly, multi-fabric architectures are the best way to achieve high availability in a SAN. In addition to enhancing availability, redundant fabrics enhance scalability: using dual-fabrics essentially doubles the maximum size of a SAN.

Without *physical* separation, the solution is not redundant; it is merely resilient, and is subject to the same failure modes that would impact a resilient fabric. Segmenting a director with partitioning, zoning, or "VSAN" software will *not* increase the availability of the SAN. Figure 59 (page 253) shows a properly architected HA solution, and an incorrectly designed single-point-of-failure SAN.

The failure of the VSAN director as a unit in the example can occur under many conditions. For example, all VSANs rely on the same underlying operating system image. A defect in immature code, or operator error during a firmware upgrade could render the entire chassis unrecoverably useless, and cause both paths to become simultaneously unavailable.

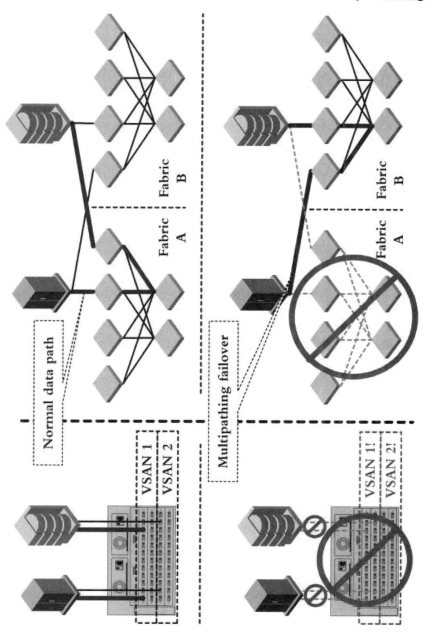

Figure 59 – Redundant Fabrics vs. Partitioning

This is not, in and of itself, and indictment of partitioning schemes like VSANs. Brocade has developed several such mechanisms, and is supportive of their use to solve many SAN administrator problems such as security, compatibility, and manageability. The Brocade mechanisms for partitioning including zoning, Virtual Fabrics, and multi-domain capabilities of some Brocade directors. For example, zoning partitions a fabric, which prevents different HBAs from interacting with each other. This prevents hackers in one host from gaining access to another via the SAN, prevents one HBA from inadvertently making a DoS attack against another, and allows separate management of disk subsystems on separate hosts. That is a useful capability, and indeed the use of zoning is considered to be a best-practice in SAN design. Partitioning mechanisms such as zoning and Virtual Fabrics have a place; it is just that their place *not* related to availability.

Using a fully redundant fabric, in contrast, makes it possible to have an entire fabric fail as a unit or to be taken offline for maintenance without causing downtime for the attached nodes. When describing availability characteristics, the concern is *path* availability. If a particular link fails, but the path to the data is still there, no downtime is experienced by the users of the applications running on the SAN. It is possible that a *performance* impact may occur, but this is a very small event compared to one or many crashed servers.

For redundant designs to work properly, the two or more fabrics must be used in conjunction with multiple HBAs, multiple RAID controllers, and multipathing software to be effective for those SAN devices that require the highest availability. Figure 59 (p253) illustrates the ability of redundant fabrics to withstand large-scale failures. It also illustrates the inability of any partitioning scheme to do so.

Note that the redundant fabric strategy is compatible with the resilient strategy. Indeed, the best designs use both approaches. In Figure 59, each fabric has a resilient design, in addition to being redundantly duplicated.

The principle for designers to take away from this is: *"HA SAN solutions should use fully redundant 'A/B' fabric designs, with each fabric preferably having a resilient design."*

Redundant Meta SAN Designs

The design methods preferred for Meta SANs are similar to those preferred for fabrics. Like fabrics, Meta SANs tend to be constructed in various core/edge topologies. Also like fabrics, Meta SANs tend to use resilient and/or redundant designs for high availability, which is the topic of this section.

Of course, there are many possible variations on the following techniques. It is possible that part of a Meta SAN will use one model, and another – perhaps less critical – section may use a different model. The bottom line is that the redundancy model should be tailored to the requirements of the business application, and should almost always be used end-to-end between the server running the application and all of its storage devices.

Resilient Meta SANs

The defining characteristic of a *resilient* SAN is that there is no single point of failure within the connectivity model. Each link has one or more alternates; each core switch is duplicated; each router has an alternate. It is possible to lose an edge switch, which would impact all nodes attached to it, but critical nodes are always connected to at least two edges.

In a resilient Meta SAN, each edge fabric that exports devices must have at least two routers providing paths to every other relevant edge fabric. Nodes generally are connected to A/B redundant fabrics within this model. Figure 60 shows an example of this style of deployment.

This is a highly reliable network design. It has the advantage of being able to route between A/B redundant fabrics, which can facilitate complex failover models, and is not possible without routers. It can also allow single-attached hosts to gain some degree of network-level multi-pathing when storage ports are redundantly attached to different fabrics in the Meta SAN. Finally, this can be useful when tape drives are single-attached to one or more backup fabrics, but hosts are dual-attached.

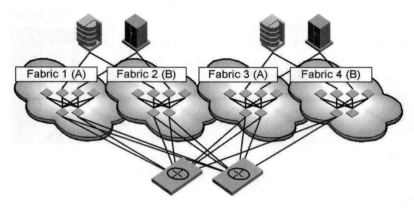

Figure 60 - Resilient Meta SAN

However, this is not a fully redundant solution. This is because catastrophic failures on the routers could – at least in theory – impact both the A and B edge fabrics simultaneously. High availability guidelines for mission-critical deployments require a fully redundant Meta SAN.

Redundant Meta SANs

Figure 61 (page 257) shows a fully redundant Meta SAN design. In a redundant *fabric*, there are two completely separate SAN fabrics. Similarly, in a redundant *Meta SAN*, there are two completely separate (A/B) Meta SANs. Critical hosts and storage arrays are dual attached, with at least one connection to each Meta SAN. This provides the greatest possible fault isolation. For example, it prevents a misbehaving HBA on one Meta SAN from being able to interfere with nodes on the other.

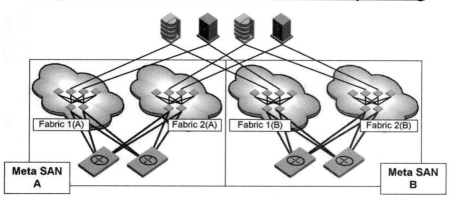

Figure 61 – Redundant Meta SANs

Parallel Redundant BB Fabric Meta SANs

When many routers need to be interconnected, either for scalability or for long distance support, they use a mechanism known as a "backbone fabric", or "BB fabric". In this kind of solution, the routers are connected together with E_Ports, and form a fabric via the usual switch-to-switch mechanisms. Upper-level routing software known as the "Fibre Channel Router Protocol" (FCRP) allows them to coordinate all Meta SAN activities automatically.

It is also possible for resiliently deployed routers to use separate backbones. This works much like the single backbone case, but has greater availability and scalability. An entire backbone fabric can fail without causing loss of connectivity across any LSANs, which eliminates certain failure modes. A redundant backbone design is shown in Figure 62. Note that each router can have many connections to its BB fabric for appropriate performance and reliability, but any given router can be attached to only *one* backbone fabric. It is not possible to cross-connect a single router to BB-1 and BB-2. Attempting to do so will either fail (segment) or merge the two backbones into one fabric, thus obviating their redundancy. Therefore deploying redundant backbones requires deploying multiple routers.

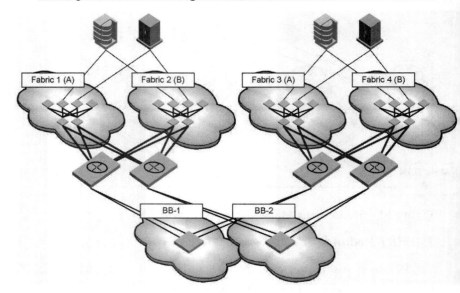

Figure 62 – Resilient Meta SAN with Redundant BB Fabrics

Redundant backbone fabric Meta SANs can be combined with the other redundancy models discussed in this chapter. For example, Figure 61 (p257) shows a degenerate case of this method combined with fully redundant Meta SANs. Figure 63 shows an expanded example of this.

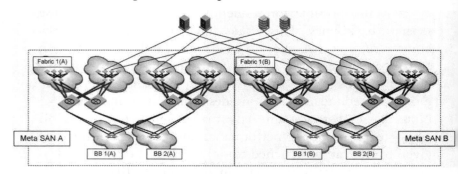

Figure 63 – Redundant Meta SAN + Redundant BBs

Finally, note that most distance extension usage cases use redundant backbone fabrics. In most FCIP deployments such as Figure 113 (p412), redundant backbone fabrics are tun–

neled through the IP network, even if this is not specifically called out in the diagram. This is an example of FC-FC Routing Service integration with the FCIP Tunneling Service, and is the best practice for redundant WAN deployments.

The principle to use when constructing highly available routed SANs is this: *"Always use the same availability model for a Meta SAN that would have been used in a similar large fabric."*

Fault Containment and LSANs

When pursuing the highest degree of scalability (1000s of ports per network), designs work better when many relatively small (100s of ports) fabrics are interconnected via Fibre Channel routers using LSANs. (See also "Maximizing Scalability" starting on page 173.) The mechanisms which cause that effect also allow the router to "scope" faults, preventing them from propagating between edge fabrics. This means that fewer devices will be impacted by a failure if one should occur. Indeed, they tend to prevent faults from developing in the first place, since smaller fabrics are inherently more stable than large fabrics.

This effect is particularly valuable where distance extension is involved. It is always recommended to use LSANs when building a long-distance solution, whether using native FC ISLs, the integrated FCIP gateway within the Brocade Brocade Multiprotocol Router, or third-party extension solutions. This prevents WAN instabilities from affecting fabrics at the WAN endpoints to the greatest extent possible. Only devices actually using the WAN will be impacted if it destabilizes. (Of course, that is unavoidable unless fully redundant WANs are used.)

In order for fault containment to work properly with Meta SANs, it is necessary to employ a degree of locality (p209) when building LSANs. Simply exporting all devices to all other fabrics will obviate many of the HA advantages *and* most of the scalability advantages of the router.

Designers building HA Meta SANs should follow this principle: *"Meta SANs should use locality to the greatest extent possible to maximize fault containment and scalability."*

Asymmetrical SANs

When deploying redundant SANs or Meta SANs, it is not always necessary to design them symmetrically. For example, when building a redundant fabric SAN, the "A" fabric could consist of a resiliently connected CE topology, while the second consists of an isolated switch. (See Figure 35 page 156.)

There are numerous variations on this theme. For example, a large-scale Meta SAN design might not be symmetrical. Perhaps Meta SAN A would be large and complex and have attachments from all nodes, while Meta SAN B would be small and only used for a few mission-critical nodes, similar to the example in Figure 35. Or perhaps the existence of two Meta SANs would lighten the resiliency requirements *within* each Meta SAN, much like a redundant but non-resilient fabric design. In this case, perhaps the second core switches would be removed from each edge fabric, or the second routers and the duplicated IFL connections could be dispensed with. Figure 64 shows such a variation.

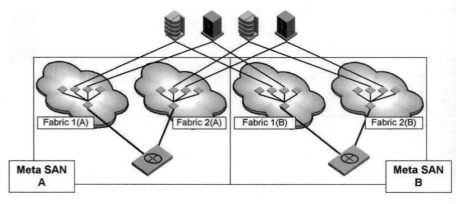

Figure 64 - Redundant Meta SANs – Variation

In general, it is best to design in redundancy at each level as long as budget constraints will allow. Just because redundant core switches within edge fabrics *could* be eliminated does not imply that they *should* be eliminated. Like many other things in network design, the decision about how much redundancy to build into each level of the network comes down to site-specific tradeoffs between price, performance, and RAS.

When cost is a primary concern, the principle to use is this: *"Sacrifice resiliency before sacrificing redundancy."* It is better to deploy two non-resilient "A/B" fabrics than one resilient fabric, as long as hosts and storage arrays are dual attached.

Device Attachment Strategies

If the SAN must be limited to a single resilient entity – be it a singe director, fabric, or Meta SAN – the highest availability will be had by following a few simple rules related to device connection points.

The best strategy is employ locality wherever possible. In a non-resilient SAN, a core switch failure could segment the fabric, but will generally *not* interrupt communications between localized devices. If locality is known, use it.

If traffic patterns make localization difficult or impossible – e.g. because they keep changing all the time – then the best strategy is to distribute devices in a certain way. When connecting them to a director such as the Brocade 48000, it is best to "stripe" hosts and storage connections horizontally across the blades. That way, if a port card fails, the fabric will not lose all storage or all hosts at the same time. Similarly, distribute host and storage connections across edge switches, so that no single switch failure will "take out" all hosts or storage ports in one shot.

10: Security Planning

Most organizations understand that the data served by their SAN is sensitive and must be secured properly to ensure confidentiality, integrity, and availability. A compromise in security could easily result in the loss of proprietary information, capital, or other negative impacts to core business resources. This chapter discusses some of the most common security considerations are for SANs, and some of the tools available for addressing them.

Security Overview

Since the introduction of Secure Fabric OS in 2001, Brocade has been a leader in SAN security. Based on several years of real-world experience deploying SANs of varying sizes and architectures, Secure Fabric OS was designed to meet the requirements of the most security-sensitive environments. Secure Fabric OS introduced the first Access Control Lists (ACLs) in the Fibre Channel industry and provided the first Fibre Channel authentication mechanism using PKI, which has since been replaced with the standards-based DH-CHAP.

Of course, SAN security models have continued to evolve since 2001. All of the features that were available in Secure Fabric OS have now been replaced with better and more flexible functionality in the base Fabric OS since version 5.3.0, which can be implemented by Brocade customers without adding supplemental licenses.

This book is not designed to substitute for product manuals, so it does not discuss specific commands or provide detailed configuration advice which would change from code release to code release. Rather, it provides information useful to a SAN designer which is based on general principles that do not change frequently. This chapter provides this kind of advice related to security.

The specific details of the security implementation for any given SAN are unique, since no two IT environments are quite the same, but many of the basic SAN security measures should be implemented on *all* SANs. These steps should be taken to provide some initial restrictions on accessing the SAN and to provide some control over change management. Some widely applicable SAN security considerations are:

- Physical Access
- Management Access
- Port Lockdown
- Zoning Policy

The remainder of this chapter discusses how to achieve security in those four areas at a high level.

Physical Security

Most computer security experts agree that, no matter what other security measures are in place, any high tech environment is *un*secure if it is not secured *physically*. For example, if an attacker can gain physical access to your SAN infrastructure, it may be possible for them to create a denial of service attack simply by pulling out a power cord or two. More sophisticated attacks can result in the attacker gaining access to the data stored on the SAN, and potentially being able to manipulate it.

This is not a text book on general datacenter security measures, and in any case, most modern environments already have a physical security policy in place for servers and storage devices. The rule of thumb is that SAN infrastructure which provides data-path access from hosts to storage should be physically protected to the same extent and using the same methods as the most highly secured device attached to the SAN. If one server attached to the SAN is located in an open, unsecured room, and another is located in a locked datacenter, then the infrastructure equipment should be in the locked datacenter. At very least, all switches through which the traffic from the high security devices will pass should be protected as if they were those same devices.

If it is necessary for some infrastructure to reside outside of a physically protected area, consider encrypting the data that traverses the unprotected infrastructure. For example, long distance links in remote access solutions should generally carry only encrypted data in case a hacker taps the line. However, it is not always enough to simply encrypt data on one end of the link and then decrypt it at the far end. For organizations with high-value data, is best to encrypt the data before it leaves the source host and leave it encrypted on the disk or tape at the far end: this protects the data both in flight and when it is at rest. There are a number of encrypted filesystem products available which solve this problem.

It is also very important to document the physical aspects of the network. The physical locations of all switches, routers, and cables should be recorded, and each component's location should be evaluated from a security standpoint. Be sure to include the physical aspects of all *management* network interfaces and workstations as well. Indeed, all aspects of SAN security – both physical and logical – should be documented in a formalized set of organization-wide storage security policies.

Management Network Security

If physical security of the data-path SAN infrastructure is the most important area to address, then security for the out-of-band management network is the second most important area. An attacker who can compromise the management interface may be able to defeat any of the other measures discussed later. It is therefore worth spending a bit of effort to protect the management network.

Just as with the rest of the SAN infrastructure, physically securing the management network is a good start. If a hacker can attach to the wire between the management workstation and the SAN, they have a much better chance of compromising the SAN – even if management traffic is encrypted. The best way to ensure that a hacker cannot attack a management interface is to secure it just as well as if it were a server or infrastructure component. Ideally, the LAN which serves as a management interface to the SAN should be physically isolated from the rest of the site LAN infrastructure. VLANs do *not* provide anything like the same level of security as physical separation, despite what some sales people would like customers to believe. If it is necessary to connect the rest of the site LAN infrastructure to the SAN management network at all, then the best practice is to protect that connection with a firewall.

Even when the management network is physically secure, however, it is also a best practice to provide logical security. All management software should use encryption when connecting to SAN equipment. For example, Brocade supports the secure shell (ssh) as an alternative to telnet.

Once a connection has been made to a management interface, of course a user should be challenged for a username and password. All Brocade switches and routers have a number of default account names and passwords when they leave the factory. Ideally, the passwords for all accounts should be changed prior to a switch or router entering production. Similarly, SMTP community strings should be changed or disabled. In fact, it is best to use different user IDs for different administrators, so it will be possible to remove accounts for administrators who leave the organization easily, and to track who is accessing which functions. Virtual Fabrics is a useful feature for environments in which a single physical SAN is broken up into multiple administrative domains: it allows considerable granularity for role-based access control. Passwords for management accounts should follow "strong password" best practices and should be changed frequently.

Port Lockdown Security

The next aspect of SAN security is the simplest to plan and to implement of all, and ironically it is also the most frequently overlooked. Port lockdown security involves persistently disabling ports to which devices are *not* attached, limiting which ports are allowed to become E_Ports, and locking device WWNs to specific ports. All currently shipping Brocade products support these functions as part of the base OS via CLI command and GUI options. For superior protection of hosts and switches, you can use DH-CHAP authentication to provide a strong authentication when adding new switches or hosts to an existing fabric. This is the strongest anti-WWN spoofing method available.

Device Access Security (Zoning)

The next step is to secure access between devices attached to the fabric. Zoning enables an administrator to partition fabrics, grouping devices which need to communicate, and providing best-in-class enforcement mechanisms to prevent devices from communicating when then are not zoned together. It is similar to VLANs[77] from the IP networking world, but allows superior configurability, and does not rely on proprietary and bandwidth-draining frame tagging mechanisms. Zones may overlap, and can support very simple or complex communication patterns. In fact, zoning can most properly be thought of as a combination of the best aspects of

---

[77] Brocade documentation in the 1990s called zones "virtual SANs" long before another vendor began misusing the term to refer to a proprietary feature.

VLAN techniques, coupled with more advanced security measures typically only found on enterprise-class firewalls.

Zoning may be used to set up barriers between different operating environments, to deploy logical fabric subsets by creating defined functional groups, or to create test environments and/or maintain areas that are separate within the fabric. If zoning is enabled on a fabric, any host or storage device is not permitted to participate in the fabric until it is has been explicitly included in at least one zone by the authorized fabric administrator(s).

Zoning is a fabric-wide resource, and zoning configurations are automatically distributed to every switch in the fabric. The configuration can be managed via telnet commands, the WEBTOOLS GUI interface, Fabric Manager, or via third-party SAN management applications using an API interface. Administrators may use each of these management interfaces standalone or in combination with each other. The fabric provides maximum redundancy and reliability, since each switch stores the zoning information locally and can distribute it to any switch added to the fabric.

Types of Zoning

The simplest kind of zoning is port-based zoning. This means defining membership in a zone base on physical ports on a switch. A port zoning entry could be translated something like, "Only allow devices on switch 1, port 1 to talk to devices on switch 3, port 2." In the early days of Fibre Channel, Brocade supported hardware enforcement of zoning only when port zoning was used, and so it came to be known as "hard zoning". These days, all modern switches support hardware enforcement on all forms of zoning, so this is now a misnomer.

WWN-based zoning is now generally the preferred alternative to port zoning. It provides the capability to restrict device access by specifying WWNs instead of port IDs. This is more flexible, since it allows nodes anywhere in a network to maintain the zones they are restricted to, and also supports loop devices such as JBODs. However, it does have one disadvantage: if a device needs to be replaced, its WWN might change, while the port address would stay the same. This means that replacing a device can take one extra management step when using WWN zoning. Of course, moving a device from one port to another will take one *less* management operation with WWN zoning, so this is generally not considered the overriding factor.

As mentioned briefly above, zoning is broadly classified into two types: hard and soft zoning. Soft zoning uses only switch operating system software to enforce zones – usually through selective information presented to end nodes through the fabric name server. Nodes in a fabric are informed about each other only through the names server, so if that service limits its responses to inquires based on zoning data, then as a practical matter devices will not access each other outside of the zoning policy. However, frames are not *barred* from being transmitted between nodes that are not in the same zone. This works fairly well, but does suffer if zones change, if hardware caches Name Server tables, or if a user needs to *guarantee* that no frames (intentional or accidental) are sent to devices outside of their zones.

While all modern Brocade switches use soft zoning, they all *also* use one form or another of hard zoning in all cases. Hard zoning uses specialized hardware within the ASICs in each switch to examine frames traversing the fabric. Generally speaking, enforcement is done by the final destination port. In other words, the ASIC hardware in the port that has the destination device physically attached to it will ensure that the frame should be allowed to pass through to the destination node before forwarding it. If it should not be allowed to pass, the frame will be dropped.

Zoning enforcement mechanisms are discussed in more technical detail stating on page 420.

Creating a Zoning Plan

While day to day management of zoning is typically handled by a SAN administrator, not a SAN designer, the designer should put thought into how devices will be zoned together, since this defines which "conversations" are allowed to take place. The designer should already have thought through traffic patterns when working on the design from a performance standpoint, so converting this data into a zoning plan should be straightforward.

Creativity is important in this area since there is no one "correct" zoning configuration for a given SAN configuration. The remainder of this section discusses one possible approach to zoning, but it is best to follow the zoning recommendations provided by the fabric support vendor, if any such recommendations have been provided.

First, create a list of all host and storage devices which need to be zoned. In most cases, a list of SAN-attached devices will already exist at this point. Depending on which tools the SAN designer is most familiar with, this could be a spreadsheet, ASCII text file, or any other reasonable format. Ideally, the list should at least include the name, physical location, WWN, port ID, and function of each device.

Next, evaluate the storage requirements for each host. Is the host already mapped to a specific storage device? If so, indicate that mapping in the list. If not, how much storage will be required, and of what type? Find the nearest storage port which can satisfy the host's needs, and allocate storage to the host from that array. Indicate in the list that the host will need access to that array. Be sure to consider any failover scenarios, multiple ports controlled by multipathing software, and access to backup servers and tapes.

After that, you should have a good idea of which host ports need access to which storage ports, and should have this written down.

It would be possible at that stage to create a broad zoning plan, which gave all of the required access and then some. For example, the designer could configure one zone which contained a storage port and all hosts which accessed it. While this would provide access from the hosts to their storage, it would also provide access between the hosts themselves: generally not either required or desired in a SAN. As a general rule, it works better to have one zone per device pair, and use many overlapping zones. An overlapping zone has the HBAs share one or more storage ports, but with the HBAs separate from each other. The rule of thumb for defining zones is that they should be a tightly scoped as possible, as long as this does not create an undue management burden. Ideally, the fabric would consist of many two-port or two-WWN zones, defining the communication between just one initiator and target pair. This is sometimes referred to as a point-to-point zone. When an initiator is configured to access more than one storage port, it should exist in multiple such zones, rather than putting many storage ports into one zone. This provides all required access, without providing any unintended access.

However, using point-to-point zones may be impractical in very large fabrics because it can require the creation of too many zones, and too many changes to the fabric configuration when devices need to be added or moved. Single-initiator zoning is a more popular method, because it balances the need to limit the scope of zones with the need to simplify management. In this form of zoning, one zone is created for each and every initiator in the fabric. That zone will contain just one initiator, plus *all* of the target ports to which it will communicate.

In addition to providing high security, this technique also provides the greatest benefit to fabric services optimization. Zoning optimizes fabric services, such as RSCN distribution and name server response, and limits unnecessary device discovery. Indeed, a proper zoning configuration is necessary for the functioning of large fabrics, even when security is not considered to be an issue, and the "point-to-point" ot "single-initiator" methods maximize the scalability and reliability benefits of zoning.

It is also appropriate for the designer to consider naming conventions. Ideally, a zone element names should be both as short and as meaningful as possible, to maximize scalability and manageability. Of course, these tend to be conflicting goals, so a designer should balance the requirements: make the names as short as possible without having them lose their meaningfulness.

Next, zones should usually consist only of device aliases, instead of the PIDs or WWNs of the devices. This allows a device to be defined in one place – the alias configuration – and used in multiple zones without redefinition. When a device fails, moves, or is upgraded, it may be necessary to change the alias, but this will automatically propagate to all zones which use that alias. Like zone names, device aliases should be short and meaningful: they should contain just enough information to uniquely identify the device at a glance when a SAN administrator looks at the zoning configuration, but not be any longer than necessary.

Also consider using switch zoning in combination with other methods such as HBA or storage controller LUN masking. Zoning offers many advantages, such as a single point of management, ASIC-enforced hard zoning, the ability to create virtual SANs, and RSCN scoping. However, node-based zoning also has advantages, and can add a "belt and suspenders" level of security to the SAN.

Enhanced Fabric Security (SFOS)

The continued growth of SANs in large-scale mission critical environments created the need for enhanced fabric-level security in addition to the security features present in the base operating system. The optionally-licensed Brocade Secure Fabric Operating System (SFOS) product was de-

signed to address such evolving customer security requirements by providing robust controls over the way in which
switches, routers, and devices are allowed to connect to a fabric, as well as further securing management channels. SFOS
features were first introduced in OS versions 2.6.1, 3.1, and
4.1 for Brocade switches.

As the SAN market continued to mature, it became clear
that some of the SFOS features were unnecessarily complex
and did not add as much value as previously thought, but that
other features were so useful that virtually all Brocade customers could benefit from them. The decision was made to
move SFOS features into the base operating system. The
functionality formerly provided by SFOS, and now offered in
the base OS, is divided into categories:

1. The Fabric Configuration Server (FCS) provides a cen-
    tralized way to manage fabric-wide security
    configurations and policies.
2. IP Filters adds additional layers of granularity when en-
    forcing which devices can access SAN switches by way
    of which applications. This feature has firewall-like
    properties and is used to control access to the IP man-
    agement interface.
3. Switch Connection Control (SCC) improves switch-
    to-switch authentication by allowing the use of digital
    certificates as well as locking down which ports can be-
    come E_Ports.
4. Device Connection Control (DCC) allows only spe-
    cific devices into the fabric (per their WWNs) from a
    specific port or group of ports.

These features can be efficiently managed via Fabric Manager, the WEBTOOLS interface, or the Fabric OS CLI.

11: Distance Planning

As noted in "Chapter 2: SAN Solutions" and "Chapter 4: Design Overview", the need for Disaster Recovery (DR) and Business Continuity (BC) solutions has been rapidly increasing in recent years. This has driven a rapid increase in the demand for high speed, high reliability block-level storage connectivity spanning sites. In addition to DR and BC, site-to-site SANs have economic drivers. Recent economic trends have caused IT departments to need to find ways to do more with fewer resources. Better utilization of enterprise-class storage systems has been a driving force behind SAN growth, and distance extension technologies allow these benefits to span sites. These same economic trends have caused some companies to look at mergers or acquisitions and datacenter consolidation, which has created demand for site-to-site data migration solutions.

FC storage networks which can span long distances are a natural fit for all of these deployments. When possible, the best practice is to use dark fiber, xWDMs, or SONET/SDH gateways. When these optiosn are unavailable or prohibitively expensive, FCIP can be used instead.

An exhaustive treatment of long distance network design could fill an entire book on its own. In fact, there are other books on the subject. Therefore this chapter is intended to provide a starting point for determining requirements for the solution, selecting the right technologies and products with which to build the SAN, and some tips on planning the topology of the WAN. It can be thought of as a collection of considerations for the designer, rather than a comprehensive cookbook for SAN extension solutions.

Determining Requirements

As with other network design problems, the first step if designing a long distance SAN is to figure out its requirements. In general, a designer needs to know:

- What distance will need to be supported by each link?

    o Some technologies are best suited to particular distance ranges. For example, native FC over dark fiber can only cover limited distances due to the limitations of the laser optics.[78]

    o Extending past these limits may be possible, and may even be recommended, but might require additional technologies such as repeaters.

    o FCIP may support longer distances, but delivers lower performance.

- How fast does the WAN need to be?

    o This includes both latency and throughput. While latency is generally a non-issue in native FC solutions, some other WAN technologies tend to produce enough latency to have a noticeable impact on application performance.

    o Also consider performance in failure modes. If redundant WAN paths are used, what will happen to applications if the primary path fails?

- How reliable and available does it need to be?

---

[78] The limitation for native FC extension used to be buffer-to-buffer credits, but FC buffering technology has now vastly outpaced advances in optics. Brocade switches and routers can support enough buffers to run full speed FC over hundreds of kilometers, but the optics generally support far less than 100km.

o Generally, long distance SANs are more tolerant of failures than SANs within a datacenter. However, this does not mean that failures are acceptable. What would happen to the solution if the WAN went down for a day or more?

o Reliability can impact performance. What is the expected packet loss / error rate on each link?

• Is it acceptable if a WAN problem destabilizes the end-point fabrics?

o In almost all cases, the answer is "no". If so, then it is best to use a reliable WAN technology and isolate it from the endpoints using routers.

o The more critical this requirement, the more weight should be placed on using transports such as native FC, *x*WDM, or SONET/SDH.

• What are the security requirements of the WAN?

o If the data traversing the WAN is sensitive, it should be encrypted. Ideally, it should be encrypted by the host, and should stay encrypted on the volumes at the far end.

o Is the WAN subject to management-plane attacks? Generally, this is true of IP SAN solutions, but it is theoretically possible with other technologies.

The remainder of this section discusses things to consider when evaluating specific long distance SAN design problems.

Overview of General Distance Considerations

• Availability of WAN resources: what kind of infrastructure is already available?

o If WAN resources are already in place, can the DR requirements be met with them? How will that impact the existing usage of the network?

o   In the 1990s, many organizations re-architected their backup solutions to get backup traffic off of the LAN, because LAN-based backups were preventing other applications from running. Combining DR traffic on a WAN with other applications can have a similar effect.

o   If the existing traffic is considered important, it would be better to deploy a separate DR WAN. If facilities for native FC solutions can be deployed, that is usually the best option. SONET/SDH is a good fallback position if native FC cannot be deployed, and FCIP should usually be considered a last resort.

- Budget vs. Value of Data: It will cost money to implement an effective solution.

  o   More effective solutions generally cost more. How does the cost compare to potential loss of data and application availability in a disaster?

  o   If a solution is less expensive to implement initially, will it be less expensive to maintain over time? FCIP may be cheaper to install if it uses existing IP infrastructure, but that can make it harder to manage and troubleshoot on an ongoing basis.

Overview of Data Migration Considerations

In most cases, when planning data migrations, the data being moved is not "live" at the time of its movement. Or, if it is live, it is being served by a local mirror copy while it is being replicated to a remote site. Because of this, data migrations tend to be tolerant of failures, performance issues, and errors compared to other SAN extension solutions. The main criteria to look at are usually how long the migration is allowed to take, and how well the production environment is insulated from the migration project. For narrower migration windows, native FC and similar upper-tier solutions are recommended based on performance criteria. If the migration is

278

allowed to take a long time, FCIP is usually acceptable. In either case, isolating the migration task from production using routers is recommended.

Overview of DR Considerations

For distance extension solutions intended to solve disaster recovery or business continuity problems, the following points should be considered during the planning process:

- Application critically: which applications and datasets require protection?

    o Critical application servers and storage arrays should be attached to "A/B" redundant fabrics, following industry best-practices.

    o The redundant fabrics at the primary site should be separated from the WAN and the recovery site via SAN routers, and only the volumes which are actually involved in the DR solution should be projected across the WAN via LSANs. This prevents a disaster at one site or in the WAN itself from destabilizing the fabrics at an unrelated site.

- Acceptable recovery time: the maximum time an application can be unavailable.

    o Decide the best mechanism for fast recovery in each scenario. If the data set at the primary location becomes corrupted, will you copy the data back over the WAN and restore the application at the primary site, or will you use a standby server at the recovery location?

    o For scenarios in which you need to copy data over the WAN, you will need to calculate how much time the copy is allowed to take. The performance of the infrastructure between sites will need to support this.

- Acceptable data loss: how much data can be generated at

the primary datacenter before it is copied to a remote site?

- o   In the event of a disaster or even small–scale failure at the primary datacenter, any data not copied to the remote site will be lost.

- o   This may dictate a synchronous vs. asynchronous solution. If the application cannot tolerate any data loss at all, synchronous solutions are needed. This in turn will dictate a high-performance intersite SAN transport, usually native Fibre Channel, xWDM, or FC over SONET/SDH.

- o   NOTE: Some SAN extension products use a "write acceleration" mechanism. This acknowledges the completion of writes to hosts at the primary site before the data has reached the far-end storage devices. Virtually all host- and storage-based replication software packages have this built in, which eliminates the need for it in network equipment. This reduces the potential for data corruption. Always use host- or storage-based write accelerators if the feature is needed.

- Location: the distance between datacenters should be great enough so that at least one site will survive any anticipated disasters. (Threat radius considerations.)

- o   The distance between sites may dictate technological options for the WAN. For example, if the sites are located halfway around the globe, FCIP or WAFS may be the only viable options. If they are located a few hundred kilometers apart, then native FC or xWDM will be a better choice.

- Testing: the business continuity strategy must be routinely tested, or it may not work when needed.

- o   Before implementation, decide what testing is needed, and how and when the tests will be carried out.

o It is also important to evaluate how testing will affect production operations. Fibre Channel routers using LSANs isolate testing at the recovery site from continuing operations at the production site.

FC Buffer-to-Buffer Credits

Some methods of extending fabrics – such as FCIP or SONET/SDH – use gateways that map Fibre Channel onto another protocol for transport between sites. While there are advantages to gateways, they can be expensive, complicated to manage, and tend to have undesirable performance characteristics when compared to native Fibre Channel.

It is also possible to extend Fibre Channel ISLs or IFLs over long distances. This is generally the easiest to manage and the highest performance. However, ensuring full performance on long distance ISLs requires that the SAN designer have an understanding of buffer-to-buffer credits. (BB credits.) For example, the inter-site ports connecting the core switches in Figure 44 (p165) might need to have more than the usual number of buffers to support full speed between sites 1 and 2, depending on the distance between the sites. This section discusses what BB credits are and how they relate to long distance.

While it is possible for any network to drop frames in certain failure modes, such as when a cable is cut, the Fibre Channel standards do not allow the network to drop frames in normal operation. In order to prevent that, no port is allowed to transmit frames unless the port to which it is directly communicating has the ability to receive them.

It is entirely possible that the receiving port will not be able to forward the frame immediately, in which case it will need to have a memory area reserved to hold the frame until it *can* be sent on its way. This memory area is called a buffer. All devices in a SAN have a limited number of buffers, and so they need a mechanism for telling other devices if they have *free* buffers before a frame is transmitted to them. In other words, the transmitter needs to know whether or not the receiver is in a position to accept a frame before it sends it. Flow control is used to ensure that every port in the chain between an initiator and target follow the "no frame dropping" rule.

There are many different ways to handle flow control in a network. Fibre Channel uses a mechanism called buffer-to-buffer credits. All Fibre Channel devices use BB credits, whether they are switches, routers, HBAs, or JBOD disks, or storage array controllers. The buffer credit mechanism ensures that no frames are sent unless the receiver has "OKed" it by releasing one or more buffer credits to the sender.

A buffer credit equals one frame regardless of frame size. Fibre Channel frames can vary from 60 bytes to 2148 bytes (~2k) in size. Since the majority of frames are 2k frames, devices such as HBAs and storage arrays negotiate to 2k frame sizes for payload. Research done by Brocade shows that 95% or more of all frames are 2k; lower frame sizes typically are not used for payload, but for various SCSI commands and FC class F traffic (Zoning updates, RSCNs, Name Server information etc). Therefore, as a practical matter, it is possible to think of a buffer credit as being a 2k memory area.

When device ports initially connect to a fabric, the receiving device tells the transmitter about the number of frame buffers it has available, and the transmitter tells the receiver how many it actually wants. When a node is negotiating BB credits with a switch, it will typically request anywhere from two to sixteen buffer credits. The switch will respond with the number of buffers it is able to dedicate to that port. The total number of buffers is "noted down" by the HBA. This is the number of "credits" it has to spend.

As frames are transmitted from a node to the switch, they are stored in memory on the switch[79] and the transmitting device "checks off" the credits it is using up. It stops transmitting if its available credit goes to zero. Meanwhile, the receiver will try to empty its buffers by forwarding the frames onward, and will notify the transmitter of any memory it manages to free up. In this way, BB credits are returned to the node as quickly as possible, and − if all is well in the fabric − it should be possible for the device to transmit continually at full line rate indefinitely. If there is a traffic congestion point − either in the fabric or within the receiving endpoint device − then eventually the buffer credits will run out, and the transmitting device will wait until the network path clears out enough to release at least one credit before sending any more data.

Buffer to buffer credits are generally handled transparently by Brocade FC switches, and in most cases, users do not even need to be aware of them. For example, local ports such as F-ports or FL-ports do not need many credits to maintain line speed. By default, Brocade 4Gbit products 'advertise' eight credits on F and FL-ports, which is more than enough to maintain line speed at 4Gbit within a large datacenter. No user interaction is required with this process.

However, when using Fibre Channel over long distance links (e.g. more than 500 meters), BB credits become very important. This is especially true when *very* long distances (10km to 500km) are required either over dark fiber, WDM, or SONET/SDH equipment. This is because frames take time to get from one end of an optical cable to the other.

---

[79] That is, frames are stored if the switch isn't able to immediately forward them. The typical case with Brocade switches is "cut-thru switching" which results in frame forwarding starting even before the entire frame has been received. In this case, the transmitting device would get its BB credit back rather quickly. FC switches from competitors which use antiquated "store and forward" technology are not able to release buffers as quickly, and therefore need many more credits for a given performance metric.

Granted, it is not a *long* time, since frames are moving at the speed of light, but with sufficiently long cables and sufficiently fast link speeds, there can be more than one frame in transit on the cable itself at a time. On a 120km 10Gbit link, for instance, there can be many hundreds of frames in flight at any given time. In this case, the transmitting switch need to be sure that the receiver has enough memory to receive *at least* as many frames as the link will ever be required to "hold" at a single instant, since it will not get a credit return on a frame right away. The SAN designer must ensure that there are enough credits to keep the ISLs "full".

The rule of thumb is that it takes one BB credit per kilometer of distance for full-speed 2Gbit operation. To sustain a full bandwidth over a distance of 30km, 30 buffer credits are required. Should only 15 credits be available, the bandwidth will simply drop, e.g. to 1Gbit. To put it another way, given a fixed number of BB credits, a link can go twice as far at 1Gbit as with 2Gbit. With 4Gbit links, twice as many buffers per kilometer are required as with 2Gbit links. The general "rule of thumb" formula for calculating required credits for a native FC link over distance is:

```
Credits = Kilometers * ( Gigabits / 2 )
```

Note that FC links will still *work* if insufficient buffers are available; they will just go slower. A 2Gbit link at 100 kilometers with only 75 buffer credits will come online, but the maximum performance would be limited to ~1.5Gbit.

It is important to understand that the number of frames in flight is equal to the number of buffer credits, i.e. if a 100km link needs to perform at maximum rate (in this case at 2Gbit) then 100 frames are required to do so. This example assumes that the frames used are 2k frames; to maintain line speed with 1k frames then twice the number of credits would be required. This might seem as a peculiar fact but it might help one to better understand buffer credits in Fibre Channel.

It is similarly important to note that if a given ISL runs 30km at 2Gbit/sec and 100 credits are assigned, then there is no performance improvement vs. if 30 credits were assigned. In other words, one cannot overdrive an ISL: 30 credits in the example above is enough to drive line speed, and assigning more credits will *not* get better performance. It is essentially never helpful to over-allocate credits.

LD Modes

Brocade offers several difference distance modes:

Table 3 - Long Distance Modes

Distance Mode	Distance	License Required?
L0 (local E-port)	<500 meters	No
LE	10km	No
L0.5	25km	Yes
L1	100km	Yes
L2	200km	Yes
LD	Auto Discovery	Yes
LS	Static Config.	Yes

The large number of modes could be confusing. However, there are a few easy rules to select the right mode.

All local or "normal" E-ports and EX-ports that are not used for distance are referred to as L0 in the distance scheme.

LE is used to support distance up to 10km and does not require a license. The 10km limit is not dependant on speed; if the ports negotiate to 4Gbit, more credits are automatically assigned to support 4Gbit at line speed.

L0.5, L1 and L2 were originally introduced to make it simpler for customers to configure long distance links. It has become apparent that these modes can be inflexible as they are completely static and the credits are automatically assigned to match the mode and speed. Just like the LE counterpart, credits are assigned based on the port speed to sustain the given length specified in the above table. It is expected that these modes will be converted to either LD or LS over time.

LD – dynamic distance discovery mode – is the most user-friendly mode. It automatically probes the link and via a sophisticated algorithm calculates the amount of credits required based on the distance and speed set for the link.

LS is a statically configured mode which was added to FOS 5.1. This is the most flexible mode for the more advanced user: it allows complete control for special requirements. For example, on a 110 km link running at 2Gbit where all the frames are 1k frames instead of the normal 2k frames. This means that twice the amount of credits is required--i.e. 220 buffer credits are required because the frame size is 1k instead of 2k.

MAN/WAN Speeds and Technologies

This section compares and contrasts some of the more popular approaches for SAN extension.

- **FC Over Dark Fiber**. In this case, native Fibre Channel traffic – usually running on E_Ports or EX_Ports – is carried over a dedicated optical connection between sites. If the dark fiber is leased, the owner does not provide services on the line.[80] This is left entirely to the customer. FC over dark fiber is highly reliable and high performance, as it minimizes equipment that could fail, does not require protocol conversions, and the bandwidth is never shared with non–SAN applications. This has the lowest

---

[80] This is how dark fibre got its name: there is no laser light coming out of the service provider's cable drop because – until the customer connects their equipment at the far end – there is nothing plugged into it that would generate light. Other services involve active equipment owned by the service provider and located at their facilities, which shine laser light down the pipe.

latency impact, and is practical to distances in the order of hundreds of kilometers[81] with Brocade routers and most 4Gbit switches due to their high per-port buffer credits.

- **FC Over xWDM**. Native Fibre Channel connections are made to a dense or coarse wave division multiplexer. (DWDM or CDWM are collectively referred to as *x*WDM.) The traffic is carried on a dedicated wavelength, but the fiber it is carried on between sites may have other services running on different wavelengths. This is equal in performance to dark fiber as it does not add latency beyond the speed of light or constrain throughput, and is nearly as reliable. (It is only *slightly* less reliable because the WDM device itself might fail.) Distances supported may be in excess of those supported by dark fiber if intermediate WDMs are used as repeaters. Note that the FC switches or routers on each end may need to support a large number of BB credits in some cases, unless the WDM itself does this.

- **FC Over SONET/SDH**. It is possible to carry Fibre Channel over Synchronous Optical Networks. (The analogous service is known as Synchronous Digital Hierarchy in Europe, Asia and other regions.) This may involve OC3, OC12, or even native FC services depending on the provider. Lower speeds such as E3/T3 may also be usable for connectivity at lower cost points. SONET/SDH adds minimal latency, can often support full FC bandwidth, is highly reliable, and can span arbitrarily long distances provided that the carrier has appropriate facilities.

- **FC Over ATM**. Mapping Fibre Channel over ATM was one of the first methods for providing long distance SANs. While ATM seems to be on the decline, it is still a

---

[81] This may require specialized SFPs and/or signal repeaters.

"tried and true" approach. It can be configured to be highly deterministic, tends to perform better than FCIP from a delay standpoint, and is highly reliable. However, ATM routers and services tend to be expensive.

- **FC Over IP**. FCIP is characterized by its ability to connect to ubiquitously available IP MAN/WAN services at relatively low cost. It is also the least reliable and lowest performing option. This is because IP WANs typically involve many hops across different carriers' equipment (so the environments are less controlled) and usually have high degrees of deliberately designed-in over subscription. This causes high congestion and packet loss rates compared to FC SANs. Theoretically, FCIP can use either switched IP/Ethernet services or dedicated point-to-point Gigabit Ethernet connections, but as a practical matter the latter are not used. If point-to-point connections are available, it is better to use native FC. For most applications, it is virtually mandatory to use some form of write acceleration technology in combination with FCIP.

Which MAN/WAN technology to use depends on a number of factors, such as:

- **Availability of Service**. Is there a provider that can deliver service at each site? For example, if dark fiber is not available between sites, then another technology will clearly need to be used no matter how well dark fiber otherwise would have met the network's requirements. FCIP tends to be the easiest fit in this category since IP services are almost universally available. It is somewhat harder to find IP services with appropriate bandwidth and service level agreements. (SLAs)

- **Application RAS Requirements**. For applications that require high reliability, availability, and serviceability, any of the technologies could be employed provided that appropriate SLAs are in place and only enterprise-class components are used. However, it is inherently easier to achieve RAS goals with native Fibre Channel solutions like dark fiber and xWDM since they involve fewer components from fewer vendors. No protocol translation for native FC means less complexity, which means lower potential for errors and simpler troubleshooting if there should be a problem. The fewer pieces of equipment involved in a connection, the less that can go wrong with it. FCIP tends to be the worst performer in the RAS category, with SONET/SDH and ATM in the middle.

- **Application Performance Requirements**. Many applications are sensitive to delay and error rates on their storage devices, while others are less so. Performance on hosts running synchronous mirrors over distance will be *severely* degraded unless WAN performance is best-in-class, whereas asynchronous mirroring applications can usually tolerate more delay and a higher error rate. Synchronous applications are better suited to SONET/SDH, ATM, xWDM, and dark fiber solutions; asynchronous applications could employ FCIP, but it is still critical to use a WAN with a top-notch service level agreement. Similarly, different applications require more or less throughput. An IP SAN connection over an ISDN 128k link will not be useful for most customers, because it does not support enough throughput. The best fit in the performance category is *always* native FC either running over dark fiber or xWDMs for medium distances, and FC over SONET/SDH or ATM for longer distances.

- **Distance Between Sites**. Some technologies are inherently limited to MAN and shorter WAN distances, such as dark fiber and xWDMs. Others, such as FCIP or iSCSI, can support long distances, but not without incurring delay and loss that may impact applications. SONET/SDH and ATM tend to be the best fits for very long distances.

- **Solution Cost**. How much does each service option and network infrastructure cost, both initially and on an ongoing basis? For example, if a customer has an application that would benefit from SONET/SDH, but only has half the budget necessary to deploy it, another solution will be needed or the project delayed. FCIP tends to cost less to implement than the alternatives due to volumes and availability of IP networks. However, its lower performance and reliability issues can make it rather more expensive in the long run.

In addition to choosing between protocols such as native FC, ATM, SONET/SDH, and IP, it is often necessary to select a lower-level protocol. Table 4 lists some MAN/WAN technologies and their speeds.

Table 4 - MAN/WAN Technologies and Speeds

Technology	Speed	Technology	Speed
ISDN BRI	128kbits	OC12	622Mbps
FracT1	≤1.5Mbps	STM4	622Mbps
ADSL [82]	≤1.5Mbps	Native GE (1)	1Gbps
ISDN PRI (NA)	1.5Mbps	Native FC (1)	1Gbps
DS1/T1	1.5Mbps	Native FC (2)	2Gbps
ISDN PRI (E)	2Mbps	OC48	2.5Gbps
E1	2Mbps	STM16	2.5Gbps
Ethernet	10Mbps	Native FC (4)	4Gbps
E3	34Mbps	Native FC (8)	8Gbps [83]
DS3/T3	45Mbps	OC192	10Gbps
Fast ENet	100Mbps	STM64	10Gbps
OC3	155Mbps	Native GE (10)	10Gbps
STM1	155Mbps	Native FC (10)	10Gbps

Note that speeds of less than 100Mbps may not be acceptable for *synchronous* SAN applications, and often multi-gigabit speeds are necessary for acceptable application performance to be maintained. OC3/STM1 are usually the baseline for this, and deployments using OC12/STM4 or be-

---

[82] Many providers now offer multi-megabit ADSL, but this is rarely used in SANs.

[83] Protocol is not widely available or cost effective at the time of this writing.

yond will probably have better results.[84] *Asynchronous* applications are often supportable with lower speeds and less reliable transports such as IP.

BC/DR "Bracketed" Routing Architecture

In most long distance SAN designs, it is desirable to isolate each site from the possibility of failures at each other site, and from instabilities in the MAN/WAN. It is also desirable to decouple the fabric services at each site from each other site in order to minimize the possibility that user error on the part of an administrator at one site could compromise a fabric configuration at another site. Because of this, most long distance SAN designs being deployed at the time of this writing involve using one or more routers at each side of the MAN/WAN, and then configuring selective connectivity between the sites using LSAN zones.

A detailed discussion of FC router architecture is beyond the scope of this work, and is discussed in depth in the book *Multiprotocol Routing for SANs* by Josh Judd. However, it is worth mentioning that it is almost always desirable to use EX_Port interfaces on the routers to *bracket* the MAN/WAN to achieve the best possible fault isolation. In other words, a conversation between a device at Site1 with a device at Site2 should look something like: Site1 Device → Fabric1 → Fabric1 E_Port → Router1 EX_Port → Router1 E_Port → MAN/WAN Transport (Backbone Fabric) → Router2 E_Port → Router2 EX_Port → Fabric2 E_Port → Fabric2 → Site2 Device.

The key element of this flow is that the EX_ports on the routers face *away* from the MAN/WAN on both sides. The routers at each site project EX_Ports towards their local fabrics, and E_Ports towards the MAN/WAN, i.e. towards each other. If the EX_Port faces into the MAN/WAN, then the

---

[84] It could take multiple FCIP portals on the gateway to fill these larger pipes.

E_Port on the other side is not as well-isolated from MAN/WAN instabilities.

Of course, there are occasionally reasons to use another approach, but the "default" behavior for a SAN designer should be to bracket the MAN/WAN in this manner.

FastWrite and Tape Pipelining

It turns out that latency can have a counter-intuitively high impact on application performance in some cases. Even if initiator-to-target latency is one or more orders of magnitude faster than disk seek times, it can still impact application performance because of the design of the SCSI protocol.[85]

The port-to-port latency of Brocade switches tends to be on the order of hundreds of nanoseconds or a few microseconds at most, which is more than fast enough to be application-transparent. Unfortunately, latency introduced between switches by the speed of light creates a problem in MAN/WAN configurations which cannot be mitigated by moving frames faster between switch ports. In this case, the latency isn't occurring inside the switch; it is occurring between switches on a piece of fiber optic cable. In high-speed DWDM solutions running 10Gbit FC links over 100km, it is possible to have many hundreds of frames simultaneously in flight over one single link.

This can cause a performance issue because the SCSI protocol will sometimes have to it idle during the round trip time. Whenever an initiator wants to send data to a target, it first asks permission, waits for a reply, then starts sending the data. On relatively high latency connections, this can create substantial "white space" where the initiator is waiting for its request and the target's reply to make a round trip, and is not

---

[85] Well, the FCP protocol to be more accurate, but the "offending" characteristics discussed in this section were inherited from SCSI.

transmitting any data in the interim. This can result in a dramatic underutilization of MAN/WAN bandwidth. This problem is illustrated in Figure 65 (p294).

The horizontal axis of this figure shows the distance between an initiator and a target, with the "conversation" crossing a WAN. The vertical axis represents time. Following the conversation along: first, a write request is sent. It takes essentially no time to get from the initiator to the local router. However, it does take some time to get to the remote target, and more time for the reply to get back. This interval is referred to as the "Round Trip Time" or RTT. This has to occur before the initiator is allowed to actually send data, so in the RTT interval, the initiator sits idle.

To solve this problem, it is possible to use intelligent SCSI-aware buffering inside SAN switches and routers to short-circuit the initial response to the "write permission" request command. Brocade offers several such products, each of which is tailored to different distance extension scenarios. For example, Brocade has FastWrite and Tape Pipelining features for its FCIP gateways, and a similar function for FC ISLs running across a MAN. The architecture of these services is discussed in the appendix under "FCIP FastWrite and Tape Pipelining" and "FC FastWrite" starting on page 379. The net result is a reduction in delay of one entire RTT interval, as shown in Figure 66.

From the standpoint of the SAN designer, the most important thing to know is that the FCIP acceleration services are implemented in a centralized manner on the FCIP ports themselves, but because of the substantially higher performance required for native FC solutions, FC FastWrite is implemented at the node port level. This requires the nodes which are to be accelerated to be directly connected to devices with the required hardware support, such as the FR4-18i blade. An example of an FC FastWrite deployment is provided in the next section.

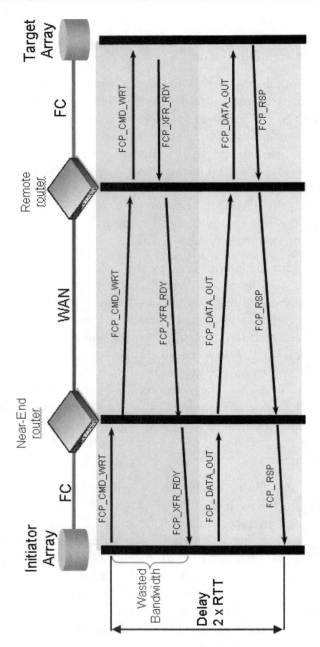

Figure 65 – SCSI Write Without FastWrite

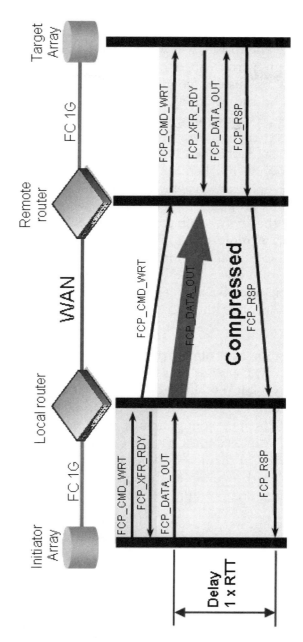

Figure 66 – SCSI Write With FastWrite

10Gbit Blades and DR/BC Solutions

In large-scale enterprises, it is sometimes necessary to create *extremely* high performance network infrastructures for disaster recovery or business continuance solutions. This requirement may be the result of a very high change rate of data, or a very large dataset, or a very short recover-point objective. In most such environments, the long distance connections are handled by *x*WDMs or dark fiber links, since this tends to provide the best throughput. This scenario is more or less the only case in which 10Gbit technology provides a better value proposition than trunked 4Gbit interfaces. This is because the higher initial acquisition cost of 10Gbit blades and media is more than offset by the lower recurring cost of using $1/3^{rd}$ as many inter-site dark fiber links or WDM lambdas for a given bandwidth requirement. The difference can sometimes be high enough that the savings on recurring costs can offset the incremental hardware cost in a single month.

For such customers, it often makes the most sense to use a combination of DWDMs with 10Gbit FC interfaces, Brocade directors with 10Gbit FC blades, FR4-18i blades for FC routing, and additional FR4-18i blades for write acceleration. Sometimes long distance configurations at this level can become complex. An example of this category of DR/BC solution is depicted in Figure 67. Note that this example is a bit more complex than most of the examples in this book, and that the diagram requires the text for intelligibility.

The diagram shows port-level connectivity details, since this can matter larger configurations, but it only shows a few of the ports as exemplars because it would otherwise be too cluttered to follow. For instance, it only shows a tiny subset of the inter-fabric links between one "edge fabric" chassis and the two "router" chassis at each site. The other connection patterns are structurally identical and are left to the reader's imagination. Here is what happens:

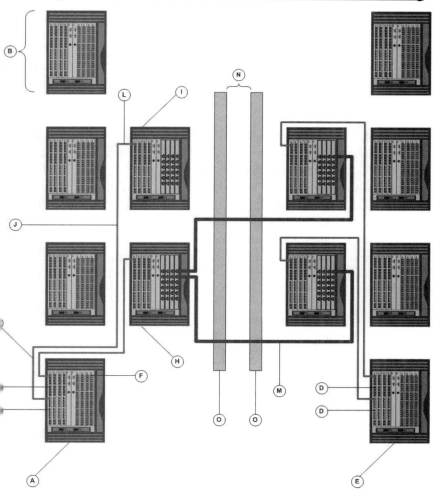

Figure 67 - Large-Scale 10Gbit Routed DR/BC Solution

This figure shows one half of a redundant SAN. I.e. it illustrates "Meta SAN A", and the "B" side would be identical. The design consists of eight single-domain edge fabrics (four at each site) and one backbone fabric per Meta SAN, resiliently connected, across a DWDM network. It delivers approximately 480Gbits of usable throughput between sites per Meta SAN. Assuming that active/active multipathing were used, this could result in a total of 960Gbits (1.9Tbits full-duplex) of replication or mirroring bandwidth between the two sites.

Each "edge" chassis -- such as the one indicated by label (A) on the lower left corner of the figure -- has four FR4-18i blades for write acceleration of storage-storage replication or mirroring ports, plus the E_Port side of IFLs (K), and four 48-port blades for hosts (F). Different edge chassis such as (B) are different edge fabrics, so that the maximum edge fabric size is 192 hosts and 64 storage ports. Eight storage ports for replication or mirroring[86] (C) are attached to FR4-18i blades within edge chassis such that four storage ports connect to one quad, then skip four ports an IFL trunk, then the next four storage ports are connected, followed by another IFL trunk. This connection patter is used to maximize the benefit of local switching on the director, and to maximize the use of expensive chassis blade slots.

The objective is to accelerate replication to symmetrically configured storage devices on the other end (D) attached to symmetrically configured chassis (E). The hosts in each fabric such as (F) might access the same storage ports being used for replication, or different storage ports on the same chassis, or ports on different chassis via LSANs.

This design looks quite a bit like a resilient Core/Edge architecture at each site, with the cores interconnected across long distance for DR/BC use. However, the "cores" at each site are actually resiliently-deployed chassis-based routers such as (H) and (I), rather than switches or "layer 2" style director configurations. Each edge chassis such as (A) or (B) connects to both cores via multiple 4-port IFL trunks (J). There would be a total of eight such trunks between each edge and the pair of cores: four 4-port IFL trunks between each edge and each core. These IFLs use FR4 ports on both ends, although the edge-side ports are configured as standard E_Ports (K)

---

[86] Hereafter just "replication" for short.

whereas the core-side ports (L) are configured as EX_Ports. One reason for using FR4 ports on the edge side is that they can locally switch from the replication ports, but this also improves reliability and makes optimal use of the non-over-subscribed bandwidth available on the FR4-18i blades. (It is generally not recommended to connect high performance storage ports to over-subscribed blades.) Traffic would be balanced across the IFL trunks via DPS, and within each path by frame-level trunking.

Each of the cores at each site are connected to each of the cores at the other site via a matrix of 10Gbit ISLs (M). The distance between the sites (N) is up to 120km or so, and the connection is provided by DWDMs (O) at each site. There are twelve (12) 10Gbit ISLs between each chassis-pair, and twenty-four (24) equal-cost paths from each core to each destination edge fabric. These links are balanced by a combination of DPS on the FR4-18i blades' Condor ASICs, a similar balancing scheme implemented by the router chips on the blades, and an internal frame-level backplane balancing mechanism within the chassis. In any case, this matrix forms a single balanced resilient BB fabric.

This is a fairly detailed example of a fairly complex solution. Many variations on this design are possible, but analyzing supportability can be tricky in such designs. As with all large-scale configurations, it is advisable to consult the appropriate support channel and/or Brocade Professional Services before deployment.

Fiber Optic Distance Limits

There are different distance limitations for each type of media and fiber optic cable. This is important when designing networks with native FC links. It is also necessary to understand that supported distance includes line rate as a variable: all other things being equal, faster signals have lower supported distance. Figure 68 shows how these variables interact.

Transceiver Type	Form Factor	Speed	Multi-Mode Media Maximum Distance			Single Mode Media Maximum Distance
			62.5um/200MHz (OM1)	50um/500MHz (OM2)	50um/2000MHz (OM3)	9um
SW	SFP	1Gbps	300m	500m	860m	N/A
	SFP/SFP+	2Gbps	150m	300m	500m	N/A
	SFP/SFP+	4Gbps	70m	150m	380m	N/A
	SFP+	8Gbps	21m	50m	150m	N/A
	XFP	10Gbps	33m	82m	300m	N/A
LW	SFP	2Gbps	N/A	N/A	N/A	30km
	SFP	4Gbps	N/A	N/A	N/A	30km
	SFP+	8Gbps	N/A	N/A	N/A	10km[5]
	XFP	10Gbps	N/A	N/A	N/A	80km

Figure 68 – Distance by Media, Speed, and Cable Type

This figure shows how transceiver types interact with link speeds and cable types to produce supportable distances. In general, as FC technology has improved in speed, the supported distance has dropped. For instance, in the late 1990s, 1Gbit FC using shortwave (SW) lasers could go 300 meters over the Multi-Mode Fiber (MMF) cabling used in most datacenters at the time: 62.5µm OM1. When devices moved to 2Gbit, the supported distance dropped to 150 meters.

However, at the same time, datacenters started to deploy more robust cables. With a cable plant based on the 50µm OM2 standard, 2Gbit FC was back up to 300 meters. A similar effect occurred with 4Gbit FC, except that the newer OM3 standard allows 4Gbit signals to run even farther: 380 meters. This is generally sufficient for most intra-datacenter applications, although there are exceptions at the top-end of the market place. The market will likely see another similar jump with 8Gbit and 10Gbit speeds.

In order to move native FC links over inter-datacenter distances, it is necessary to use fundamentally different cables and media. Instead of MMF cables, long distance connections use Single-Mode Fiber (SMF) with a 9µm size. In combination with longwave (LW) lasers, this allows an ISL to extend to tens of kilometers. In fact, some vendors produce extended long wavelength lasers (ELWL) which can push signals many times farther. If these media are also available in slightly different wavelengths, they may be used in combination with CWDM technology to carry multiple ISLs over a single physical piece of cable.

That said, for customers who need to push FC signals across tens of kilometers, it usually turns out to be more practical to deploy DWDMs. In this case, the media and cables in the FC fabric only needs to support the relatively short distance between the switches / routers and the local DWDM devices. It is the responsibility of the DWDMs to get the signal over to the remote data center.

See also "Optical Cables and Media" starting on p309.

12

12: Implementation Planning

Implementation planning in the context of SAN design relates to planning the SAN to facilitate ease of installation and maintenance. This chapter is *not* intended to provide a detailed tutorial on how to actually install and maintain SANs. It does not contain step-by-step rack mounting instructions, and is not intended to substitute for the product hardware and software manuals. In most large-scale installations, SAN design and SAN implementation are separate functions, usually performed by different personnel, and this book is intended for the designer. Therefore this chapter is focused on some of the items related to implementation that should be kept in mind while creating a SAN design, and may need to be included in the SAN project design and planning documentation.

Rack Locations and Mounting

Before committing to a specific design, make sure that suitable locations exist for all new SAN equipment. This means making sure that the right kinds of equipment racks are available, and that their locations are appropriate.

Different switches, routers, gateways, hosts, and storage devices have different rack heights, depths, structural integrity needs, weights, and even widths. In fact, one SAN vendor is selling a director chassis which exceeds the weight limits of most rack lifts, in which case it may be difficult or impossible to safely install their equipment. For fairly obvious reasons, it is important to ensure that the racks intended for mounting the SAN equipment have the same characteristics as the equipment to be mounted. This may require purchasing new racks, lifts, or cabinets specifically for the SAN.

It is also important to match the airflow of devices racked together in the same rack, or in adjacent racks. Some devices have front-to-back airflow; others have back-to-front designs. If the rack configuration requires putting both kinds near each other, then one or the other type should be rack mounted backwards, so that they all pull cold air from the same side of the rack, and vent hot air together as well. Otherwise, the exhaust fans from each set of equipment will blow hot hair into the intake ports on the other set, causing all of the equipment to overheat.

Fortunately, all Brocade products have been designed to match the OEM equipment it serves, and so it is rarely necessary to spend much time or effort on airflow with Brocade SANs. Not all vendors have planned this well, though, so it is critical that the designer at least look into the matter.

For example, one SAN infrastructure vendor actually has *side-to-side* airflow. This was standard practice in the early days of IP network equipment design, because there were several major differences in both equipment and data center design back then. Equipment was far lower in density and speed, resulting in a lower temperature per rack unit. In addition, data centers were much more sparsely populated, resulting in more free rack space. In these days of ultra-high-speed networks and data centers with "blade server" density, there is no "right" way to mount outdated side-to-side airflow equipment in most environments. If this equipment is placed next to another rack with identical equipment, the units will overheat each other, since one unit will blow hot air directly into the cold air intake of the other. The work around for this design defect is to leave half of each rack unoccupied: a disastrous waste of precious data center rack space. Figure 69 shows what happens when side-to-side airflow equipment is used, or when front-to-back / back-to-front equipment is mounted incorrectly.

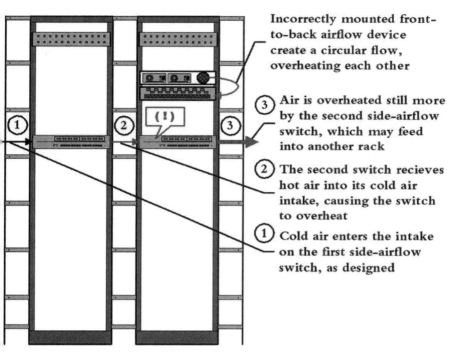

Incorrectly mounted front-to-back airflow device create a circular flow, overheating each other

③ Air is overheated still more by the second side-airflow switch, which may feed into another rack

② The second switch recieves hot air into its cold air intake, causing the switch to overheat

① Cold air enters the intake on the first side-airflow switch, as designed

Figure 69 - Bad Rack Design (Airflow)

It is also best to avoid creating single points of failure in the physical layout of the SAN, especially if redundant designs have been used (p245). The point of deploying redundant fabrics is to avoid single points of failure, and deploying two such fabrics within the same rack makes the rack itself into a failure point. The best-practice is to separate resilient cores and redundant fabrics into different racks, and to power the racks in such a way that a power failure does not cause either fabric to fail (see below). Ideally, resilient components should be at least one rack away from each other, and redundant fabrics should ideally be in different rooms. The degree of separation recommended depends on factors such as the size of each fabric, the difficulty of cabling to different areas, the impact to the organization of a failure to both fabrics at the same time, and so on. It comes down to balancing the risk of a simultaneous failure caused e.g. by a fire suppression system going off overhead, vs. the cost of distributing the components to different locations.

The bottom line is that the SAN designer should ensure that the racks targeted for equipment mounting will:

- Physically accommodate the equipment
- Support the HA architecture of the SAN
- Provide correct airflow to cool the equipment

Power and UPSs

When designing a SAN with availability in mind, it is important that duality be employed throughout the network design *and* the implementation. For HA SANs, ensure that the data center has separate power inputs, and that redundant components are connected to different UPSs and grids. Figure 70 through Figure 73 illustrate what can happen if the power design is improper, and the recommended solution.

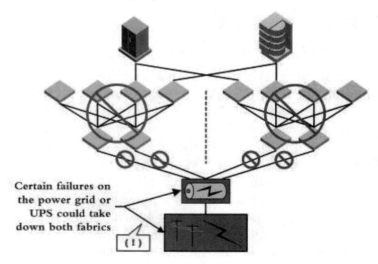

Figure 70 - Worst Power Design

Any failure in this system will take down both fabrics.

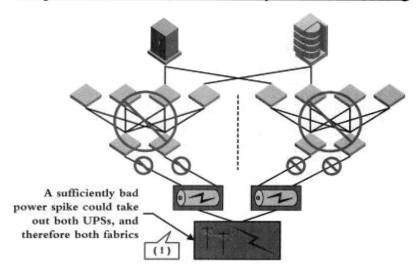

Figure 71 - Better, but still Flawed Power Design

This can withstand many failures, but a massive power spike could take out both UPS units, and thus both fabrics.

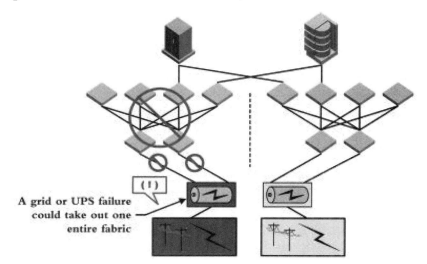

Figure 72 - Reasonable Power Design

Only one fabric can be taken out at a time. This could still cause a large-scale multipathing event.

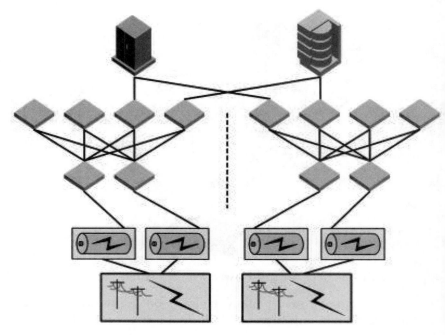

Figure 73 - Recommended Power Design

The best power design is similar in nature to the best HA network architecture: it is both resilient and redundant. The "A/B" fabrics share neither UPS units nor power grids, so massive surges – e.g. caused by a lightning strike – should usually only affect one fabric at worst. (Assuming that the separate grids truly are separate, and are not simply different circuits fed by the same infrastructure downstream.)

In addition to considering power redundancy, it is important for a SAN designer to think about total power consumption. For customers interested in "green" design best-practices, it is never desirable to use more energy than absolutely necessary. From a purely economic standpoint, this is still a sound stragegy: over the life of a SAN, it will probably cost more in electricity to power the SAN than the initial acquisition cost of the hardware and software. Thus, if increasing hardware cost by 10% results in a 50% energy savings, this tends to pay for itself in short order.

However, saving on power isn't always a matter of "power use vs. energy cost" or "money vs. the environment". It may simply be a matter of engineering necessity. In many data centers, there is a hard limit on how much total power can be supported, and on the power allowed per rack. Using a more power-efficient SAN design can make the difference between fitting the required equipment into an existing data center vs. constructing a new data center in a different building.

Whatever the cause, more and more SAN designers are using power consumption as a top-level decision point when selecting SAN switches and routers. For small SANs of fewer than 100 ports, this tends to indicate designs using the Brocade 4900 or 5000 switches. For SANs over 100 ports per fabric, or which are expected to grow to that level within one or two years, a collapsed design using Brocade 48000 directors is almost always the most efficient.

Cable and Media Selection and Management

This subsection discusses some of the necessary-yet-often-overlooked details associated with SAN implementation. This includes cable and media selection, and cable management guidelines.

Optical Cables and Media

Most storage networking devices use some form of optical connection to support longer distances and higher reliability levels than copper can provide. It is important to note that switches, routers, nodes, media, and cables cannot be arbitrarily mixed and matched. For example:

- It is not possible to use GBICs in a device designed to accept SFPs. The form factors are different, and a GBIC will simply not fit into an SFP socket. A SAN designer should make sure that the media ordered match the devices for which they have been ordered.

- If an MMF optical cable plant is installed, connecting devices designed for SMF cables will not work correctly. For example, connecting a 10Gbit device to a data center cable plant designed for 1Gbit, 2Gbit, or 4Gbit speeds is likely to fail. Be sure that the patch cables ordered match the rest of the infrastructure.

- SC cables cannot be connected to SFPs without an adapter. Similarly, LC cables cannot be directly connected to GBICs. If you have patch panels designed for one format, and media designed for another, be sure to order the correct patch cables.

- Switches, routers, and nodes only support specific makes / models of media. To support a given transceiver, [87] both software development and testing are required. Check with the support provider for a media support matrix prior to ordering SFPs or GBICs.

- The media must be designed to use the correct *mode* of optical cable. An SFP designed for single-mode fiber will not work correctly with multi-mode fiber.

SAN designers do not select a media type (SFP or GBIC) and then design the SAN around it. The media type will generally be dictated by the rest of the design. It is still important for a designer to be aware of which media will be provided with the equipment ordered. This will avoid compatibility problems during installation, make sure that required distances are supported, and ensure that the correct optical cables are also available.

The bottom line is that a SAN designer should work with equipment suppliers to ensure that all media and cables are appropriate *before* ordering equipment. Otherwise it may be impossible to install the system. It also helps to understand

---

[87] Transceivers convert copper signals used on the motherboard of a switch, router, or HBA into optical signals used in fiber optic cabling.

certain facts about cables and media related to distance extension. These are issues are discussed later.

SWL Media

Short Wavelength Laser (SWL) media are by far the most common. These media can be SFPs or GBICs. They are the least expensive of the optical media, and are used to connect Gigabit Ethernet or Fibre Channel switches, routers, and nodes over relatively short distances. They would typically be used within a data center, between different data centers in the same campus, or over longer distances if using an active distance extension device like a repeater or DWDM. SWL media are generally used with MMF cables. Designers will usually get SWL SFPs or GBICs unless they explicitly specify another option.

LWL and ELWL Media

Long Wavelength Laser (LWL) and Extended Long Wavelength Laser (ELWL) media are used to run native FC over dark fiber or xWDM for distance extension. Like SWL media, they can be either SFPs or GBICs, and can be used in either Fibre Channel or Gigabit Ethernet devices. As the name implies, they operate at longer wavelengths of light than SWL media, and can span longer distances as a result. They may be able to achieve distances in excess of 100km even without repeaters. SMF cables are required for LWL and ELWL media. Designers should work with their vendors to select and order these parts when extending FC lengths beyond the distances supported by SWL media. Be sure to determine whether or not the media is fully supported. Because of relatively low volumes, fewer LWL and ELWL options exist, and they may be qualified by OEMs and support providers using a different process than SWL media.

MMF Cables and Media

Multi-Mode Fiber (MMF) is used for short distances. It is much less expensive than SMF, and is the most common cable type for use inside a data center or campus. These use one of two diameters of fiber cores on the inside of the cladding.[88] The two formats are 50/125μm or 62.5/125μm. Brocade switches and routers work with either format. MMF cables are generally used with SWL GBICs and SFPs. All other things being equal, longer distances are supported with 50/125μm cables. Also, the more recent "OM3" standard should generally be used for larger data centers.

It is important to consider the format type (50/125μm or 62.5/125μm) when deploying MMF solutions. Be sure to check that the transceiver is designed to work with the particular cable diameter. Also, it is desirable to use the *same* format end-to-end in any connection. Using different formats between end devices can result in loss of signal strength, which can cause reliability issues or link failures.

SMF Cables and Media

Single-Mode Fiber can be used for short or long distances, but due to its greater cost it is almost exclusively used for long distance links in combination with LWL, ELWL or *x*WDM solutions. SMF cables use a smaller diameter fiber core inside the cladding: 9/125μm.

Cable Management

Poor cable management commonly causes issues within IT departments. For instance, it can reduce the supported distance of a link if the bend radius of the cable is violated. Proper cable management reduces the cost of SAN maintenance and helps cables and connectors last longer. It also facilitates easy cable identification, which is important for troubleshooting and accommodating the growth of the SAN.

---

[88] Cladding is the sheath around the outside of the fiber. The first number refers to the interior diameter, which is the relevant bit from the point of view of the laser. As a result, 50/125μm MMF will sometimes be written about as 50μm for short.

The strict uptime requirements of a SAN do not allow downtime for redeploying cables after the fact. To prevent additional cost and downtime, a reliable cable management strategy needs to be implemented when a SAN is first deployed. A complete layout and documentation plan needs to be created during the planning phase. By implementing a reliable cable management strategy, a SAN environment can gain the following benefits:

- Reduction in faults caused by operator error
- Improved overall supportability
- Improved fault identification
- Improved scalability
- Improved time to problem resolution

An effective cable management scheme should not only enable ease of maintenance, but should also be aesthetically pleasing. While aesthetics might not seem like a necessary design principal, it turns out that cable plants which "look nice" to most people also usually turn out to be the ones that are easiest to manage. In particular, the cables used for ISLs should be carefully labeled and bundled so that they cannot be mistaken for host or storage cables. Some data center managers even use different color cables for ISLs to make them easier to spot.

When the SAN designer is evaluating cable management solutions for racks, it is necessary for these solutions to have space to alleviate the bending of the fiber optic cable connector sheaths while they are plugged into the switch ports. For fiber optic cables, which are made of high quality glass, proper management reduces the risk of link failure by preventing the cable from curving tighter than the minimum bend radius. If bend radius is not managed, eventually there will be signal loss that could cause loss of frames and, potentially, data corruption. Even in the best cases, bending a fiber optic cable too tightly will reduce the strength of the signal, which will reduce the supported distance.

Next, cable layouts which obstruct the face of the switch make it more difficult and time consuming to replace Field Replaceable Units (FRUs). Good management prevents this. As a side benefit, cable management also makes it easier to identify the cables and to read each label. The use of cable guides will likely solve these problems.

The only way to safely route a large number of cables in a rack, or across a site, is to correctly use appropriate cable management products. There are a variety of cable management guides available. Horizontal guides can be used to route cables "cleanly" across a rack, and vertical guides provide for a large quantity of cables routed down the sides of or between racks.

A good rule of thumb is that it is always better to over-provision cable management systems. (That is the exact opposite of over-*subscription*.) For example, if you think that you will probably only need a two-inch wide cable management trench running down the right-hand side of a rack, consider deploying a four-inch trench down both sides. On the one hand, this does increase cost. On the other hand, the cost of a plastic cable management trench is less than the cost of a downtime incident resulting from e.g. having a technician pull out the wrong cable at the wrong time.

Switch Setup

Before switches are cabled together, certain parameters should be set. This includes IP information for management, and the switch name, which should be the same as the host name that maps to the switch's IP address. The specific method for setting these parameters is beyond the scope of this book, and is included in the product manuals in any case. However, there are areas of concern here for the designer.

The SAN designer should define a clear and intuitive naming convention for switches. This should enable easy identification of any physical switch in case a problem arises.

It should be possible to look at the switch name, and determine where is sits "logically" in the SAN (such as "Fabric A core" vs. "Fabric B edge") and where it sits physically, if more than one data center is involved.

The designer should also choose the correct Fabric OS version before implementing the SAN. This may or may not always be the latest release. The Fabric OS selection process might involve discussions with several SAN device OEMs and/or support providers, since Fabric OS support levels vary between vendors.

Each switch may have many different value-added and separately licensed features. (p364) The designer should ensure that switches are purchased will all necessary license keys, to avoid issues during installation.

Another thing to consider is Domain ID assignment. Brocade switches have been designed for maximum usability, and can generally automatically configure themselves where this and other parameters are concerned. However, it may be advantageous to override the default values for domain IDs in order to make management more intuitive. Using low domain IDs for core switches, and high and contiguous IDs for edge switches may allow administrators to identify switch locations in a fabric intuitively by domain ID, which can help when decoding analyzer output in more complex troubleshooting operations. It may also be desirable to manually avoid domain ID overlap between fabrics which might one day merge, and manually seek out domain ID overlap between fabrics configured as "A/B" pairs. (This also makes management more intuitive, since devices will have the same PIDs in both fabrics.)

Staging and Validation

Prior to transitioning a fabric to production, it is important to validate that the SAN is ready. The best way to do this is to build it in a separate "staging" configuration, and run tests over it to ensure that it satisfies performance and availability expectations.

Once the switches, routers, storage devices, and hosts are staged, the implementation team will need to inject faults into the fabric to verify that the fabric itself and all edge devices are capable of recovering. The next step involves generating an IO load in the SAN that approximates various application IO profiles. Finally, the team will want to run an IO load on the SAN while also injecting faults to approximate a worst-case scenario – a failure in the SAN while it is in production.

The designer will rarely be responsible for personally executing this process in a large scale environment. However, the designer will be in a good position to tell the implementation team how to design the IO profile that will run across the fabric(s), and what kinds of faults are expected to be recoverable.

Release to Production

Broadly, there are two categories of rollout for SANs: "green field" deployments where the storage network is being built from the ground up, and installed base upgrades, where existing fabrics are enhanced by adding new switches, routers, and other equipment.

Green Field Rollout

This is the easiest scenario to discuss, since there is no risk to production applications during the rollout phase. For most customers, the sequence for a green field rollout is as follows:

1. Create a SAN design and documentation set using the guidelines discussed in "Chapter 4: Design Overview" starting on page 95.
2. Create a high-level rollout plan, describing the phases below and giving schedule targets for each. This should include a schedule for the phases and a budget. Be sure to include professional services if a third party will be

assisting with the deployment, and budget for support contracts on all hardware and software.

3. Source and acquire equipment and software. This may be done all at once, or in a phased manner.

4. Begin to deploy and test the SAN. Build out the core infrastructure first, so that the overall structure of the network does not need to keep changing during the rollout. This means deploying all switches and routers first. Try using both localized and remote connections to test ISLs and IFLs. If IP SAN technology is to be used, this is the time to test that as well.

5. Once the network is structurally complete and stable, it can enter production even if the entire rollout is not yet complete. For example, if the network design calls for sixty edge fabrics, and only thirty have been deployed, it would be safe to release the solution to production and add the remaining fabrics as needed.

Installed Base Upgrade Rollout

Adding new network equipment to an existing environment can be as simple as plugging it in and turning it on, or as complex as building a dedicated test environment and running months of stress tests prior to production use. It depends on site-specific change control procedures, the degree of confidence the network administrators have in the new equipment, and the impact to the company that would result from a failure during the rollout.

For customers with extremely tightly controlled environments, release to production may resemble a green field deployment: the new solution could be built in an isolated environment and production applications migrated over to it only once it was proven to be stable.

Customers who have slightly less strictly controlled environments but still have robust change control procedures are likely to have A/B fabrics installed. If so, a reasonable precaution during rollout would be to install the new devices on one of the redundant fabrics at a time, and perform a suite of tests prior to using them for production traffic. Only once all "A" fabric connections are made and shown to be stable would devices be connected to the "B" fabrics. This process in combination with the redundant/resilient "A/B" approach (p245) can make rollouts into existing environments both easy and safe.

Finally, some customers may have many fabrics, each with different levels of business relevance. If this is the case, the new devices can be connected to lowest-tier fabrics first, so that any unanticipated problems will impact only non-critical applications.

Day-to-Day Management

There are a number of ways in which the designer can simplify ongoing management tasks. For example, using a redundant and resilient architecture simplifies upgrading to newer technologies which will inevitably be released over time. Also, as part of the design and implementation processes, the designer should create a document repository. If the design is well-documented, and maintenance procedures are created up front, management will be easier later on.

The designer should create a configuration log. This explains how the SAN is configured, and why it was configured that way. It should serve as a record for change management processes: if a change is made and something stops working, the SAN administrator will be able to refer back to this repository to find out what changed and why. The designer should ensure that procedures require that administrators update the repository whenever changes are made to existing configurations, or if switches are added or removed.

Brocade offers tools to simplify the creation and maintenance of such a repository. For example, Fabric Manager has change management features, and SAN Heath can be configured to automatically audit the environment periodically.

318

These tools will also simplify other ongoing operations, such as backing up switch and fabric-wide configurations, such as domain ID settings and the zoning database. Fabric Manager is also particularly well suited to performing operations such as firmware upgrades, and rolling firmware activations, in a consistent manner.

Planning for Troubleshooting

Like all other networking technologies, from time to time it will be necessary to troubleshoot a SAN, and like any other network, this process comes down to finding out which piece of hardware, software, or configuration is malfunctioning. The SAN designer is rarely responsible for performing troubleshooting, but there are ways in which the designer can simplify the process.

For example, it is generally easier to troubleshoot a small network than a large one. If the designer chooses a Meta SAN design, in which each fabric is a relatively small "subnet" in the larger connectivity model, then failures will be "scoped" to a smaller area. This makes it less likely that there will be trouble later on, as well as making it easier to figure out what went wrong if something does go awry.

Using locality is another good way to scope troubleshooting activities. When an administrator is trying to find out why a host and storage port cannot communicate, it is easier to do so if the traffic between them goes across fewer links. For business-critical applications, it is often possible to localize most IO within a single ASIC. In this case, the traffic will not even cross internal backplane links, which makes it very easy to identify the location of a problem.

Within each fabric, it is possible to use complex or simple design strategies. All other things being equal, simpler solutions tend to be better. This means using collapsed-core (director-based) designs for fabrics with a few hundred ports, and CE networks for larger requirements. Often, the CE design will use directors at both the core and the edge, to maximize scalability while minimizing the number of devices in the SAN which will be subject to troubleshooting.

Next, the designer can influence which tools are available to help administrators. Every Brocade product has built-in tools, and the first (and often the last) step in troubleshooting any Brocade networking product is to use them.[89] Brocade SAN Health should be high up on the list of tools, as should the Web Tools interface. The *portLogDump* CLI command can help when problems occur at the FC protocol level. (Which is fairly uncommon these days, but having the tool in your "pocket" never hurts.)

In some cases, it *might* also be desirable to have access to a Fibre Channel protocol analyzer. Brocade products are mature after many years of mission-critical production service, so problems rarely occur that require FC frame-level analysis. This was a relatively common event with first generation Brocade products, and still is today with other vendors new to Fibre Channel who have not finished debugging their products to that level. Most of the few protocol problems which occur in the field occur with experimental (non-production) devices, and/or can be found by using the *portLogDump* command. When an FC analyzer is needed outside of an engineering lab, it usually means that trained service personnel are on-site debugging a persistent problem and that all other debugging approaches have failed. But for customers with multi-thousand-port FC deployments, it might be beneficial to have one on hand, just in case.

---

[89] That is, it is the first step *after* making sure that everything is plugged in, powered on, and cabled properly. These three items create a larger number of support calls than you'd think.

Section Three

Reference Material

Section Topics

- Basic Reference
- Advanced Reference
- Study Guide
- FAQ
- Glossary

Appendix A: Basic Reference

This chapter provides reference material for readers who may be less familiar with either Fibre Channel or IP/Ethernet technology, or advanced readers who just occasionally need to look up certain details. Topics covered include an overview of some of the more notable items in the Brocade hardware and software product lines, and some of the external devices that might be connected to SAN infrastructure equipment.

Currently Shipping Brocade Platforms[90]

Brocade offers a full range of SAN infrastructure equipment, including switches and routers ranging from entry-level 8-port platforms up to 384-port enterprise-class fully-modular directors. The networking capabilities of the platforms allow solutions with up to about 10,000 ports in a single network today, with the potential to scale much higher in the future.[91] Brocade currently offers products with Fibre Channel, FICON, iSCSI, and FCIP. The Brocade Fabric Application Platforms deliver switching at all levels of the protocol stack up to and including the application layer.

---

[90] Shipping to OEMs for sale as of the date of first printing of this edition of this book. Check with the appropriate sales channel for product availability.

[91] Very large solutions generally require FC-FC routers as well as switches.

All currently shipping FC fabric switch platforms run a version of Brocade Fabric OS 5.x or higher.[92] The use of a common code base enables compatibility between switches and nodes, and consistent management between platforms. It also allows a common set of value-added software features. (See "Brocade Features" on p368.)

Brocade 200e FC Switch

The Brocade 200e (below) is the entry point into the Brocade FC product portfolio.

Figure 74 - Brocade 200e

This platform provides enterprise-class features, performance, and scalability, at an affordable price point for the entry market. Features include:

- Sixteen 4Gbit[93] non-blocking / uncongested interfaces to support the most performance-intensive applications: enterprise-class performance at an affordable price. It is the highest-performing 8-to-16-port SAN switch in the industry.
- Investment protection for existing SAN infrastructure to reduce deployment cost and complexity.

---

[92] Products brought into the Brocade family from the recent acquisition of McData are an exception to this rule. Brocade intends to converge these into a common director platform running Fabric OS in the future. Former McData customers are encouraged to discuss any concerns they may have regarding the roadmap with their local Brocade sales team.

[93] See also "4Gbit FC" on p446.

This means forward and backward compatibility with other Brocade switches, routers, and directors at 1Gbit, 2Gbit, and 4Gbit.[94]

- Enterprise-class features and high-availability characteristics such as hot-swappable FRUs and hot code load and activation. The switch is ideal for mission-critical SAN environments too small or cost-sensitive to allow director deployments.

- Ports on demand via optional software license keys allows the switch to be used in configurations starting at stand-alone 16-port solutions, but it can also be used as a core in small to medium CE fabrics, and as an edge in medium to large solutions.

The Brocade 200e was intended to replace the Brocade 3250 and 3850 (p361). In many respects, these switches similar. All have hot fixed fans and power supply(s). All support hot code load and activation. All are compatible with Fabric OS 5.0.1 and later. All three use SFP media.

However, the Brocade 200e also improves on the older switches in many ways. For example, the 200e uses more modern and highly integrated technology, resulting in a more reliable switch and lower power consumption. Most notably, the 200e is the first entry platform to use the forth-generation 4Gbit "Goldeneye" ASIC. (p424) In addition to the Brocade Fabric OS 5.x features available

---

[94] It is never possible for a technology company to perform regression testing for all firmware released on new products in all combinations with all firmware releases on all old products. This would result in a virtually infinite number of tests needing to be passed before any new products could be qualified for shipping. Since this is impractical, Brocade will periodically end support for very old platforms. For example, the SilkWorm 1000 series (which has not been shipping this century) has never been supported in combination with the Brocade 48000. Customers running products which have been at end of life for multiple years should explicitly check for compatibility before using them with newer platforms, and should consider upgrading in any case.

on other platforms, the Brocade 200e enables the next-generation features of the Goldeneye ASIC, including but not limited to:

- 4Gbit Fibre Channel interfaces
- Each port is an autosensing U_Port interface, supporting F_Port, FL_Port, and E_Port
- Auto-negotiates 4Gbit on ISLs and Trunks with other Goldeneye & Condor based switches.
- Capable of running all ports at 4Gbit line rate simultaneously. That is 128Gbits of cross-sectional bandwidth per switch.
- 4-way frame-based trunking, and DPS.
- Cut-through routing to minimize latency.
- Centralized pool of 288 buffer-to-buffer credits.
- Hardware offload support for node login. This improves control-plane scalability.
- Centralized hardware zone tables allow more flexible deployment scenarios. Up to 256 hardware zones are supported per ASIC.
- 8 VCs per E_Port to support non-blocking (HoLB) operations in larger networks. This can be used for advanced QoS features in the future.

Brocade 4100 Switch

The Brocade 4100 fabric switch is shown in Figure 75. This platform provides enterprise-class features, performance, and scalability.

Figure 75 – Brocade 4100

Some of its features include:

- 4Gbit non-blocking / uncongested interfaces to support the most performance-intensive applications, yielding enterprise-class performance at a midrange price. It is the highest-performing 16-to-32-port SAN switch in the industry.

- Investment protection for existing SAN infrastructure to reduce deployment cost and complexity. This means forward and backward compatibility with other Brocade switches, routers, and directors. All ports can operate at 1Gbit and 2Gbit, as well as 4Gbit, and that Fabric Services behaviors are consistent.

- Enterprise-class features and high-availability characteristics such as hot-swappable FRUs and hot code load and activation. The switch is ideal for mission-critical SAN environments too small or cost-sensitive to allow director deployments.

- Ports on demand via optional software license keys allows the switch to be used in configurations starting at stand-alone 16-port solutions, but it can also be used as a core in small to medium CE fabrics, and as an edge in medium to large solutions.

The Brocade 4100 replaced the Brocade 3900 (p361) in late 2004. In many respects, the two switches are very similar. Both provide up to 32 ports in high-density fixed configuration. Both have hot swappable fans and power supplies. Both support hot code load and activation. Both run Fabric OS. Both use SFP media.

However, the Brocade 4100 also improved on the 3900 in many ways. For example, the Brocade 3900 was 50% larger than the 4100, so the new platform supports higher density rack configurations. There were corner cases in which the Brocade 3900 could exhibit internal congestion; the 4100 is not subject to congestion in any traffic configuration.[95] (See "SilkWorm 12000 and 3900 "XY" " on p434 for more information about the 3900 internal architecture.) The 4100 uses more modern and highly integrated technology, resulting in a more reliable switch and lower power consumption.

Most notably, the Brocade 4100 is the first platform to use the forth-generation 4Gbit "Condor" ASIC. (See "Condor" on p428.) In addition to the Brocade Fabric OS features available on other platforms, the Brocade 4100 enables the next-generation features of the Condor ASIC, including but not limited to:

- 4Gbit Fibre Channel interfaces
- Each port is an autosensing U_Port interface, supporting F_Port, FL_Port, and E_Port
- Auto-negotiates 4Gbit on ISLs with 4Gbit switches.[96]
- Capable of running all ports at 4Gbit line rate simultaneously. That is 256Gbits of cross-sectional bandwidth per chip.
- 8-way frame-based trunking, and DPS.
- Cut-through routing to minimize latency
- Centralized pool of 1024 buffer-to-buffer credits
- Up to 255 buffers allocated to any given port
- Native FC connectivity up to 500 km

---

[95] Note that traffic patterns consisting of large percentages (e.g. 90%) of small (e.g. 64-byte) frames will have lower *throughput*. This is not caused by *congestion*. It is because the ratio of frame header and inter-frame gap to payload is less favorable with small frames. All networking technologies behave this way to some extent if they support variable frame sizes. Fortunately, there are no known bandwidth-sensitive applications that produce large percentages of small frames on all ports in a network simultaneously, which is the only scenario in which the switch would exhibit degraded performance. Typical SAN traffic patterns lean *much* more heavily towards 2k frames than towards 64-byte frames, and the average frame size is very close to 2k.

[96] At the time of this writing, there are few generally available 4Gbit nodes. The intent is for F_Ports also to auto-negotiate as the 4Gbit node market develops in much the same way that 1Gbit/2Gbit is auto-negotiated today.

- Hardware offload support for node login. This improves control-plane scalability.

- Centralized hardware zone tables allow more flexible deployment scenarios. Up to 256 hardware zones are supported per ASIC.

- 16 VCs per E_Port to support non-blocking (HoLB) operations in larger networks. This can be used for advanced QoS features in the future.

Brocade 5000 Switch

The Brocade 5000 fabric switch is shown in Figure 76. This platform provides enterprise-class features, performance, and scalability, delivering high value at an affordable price point. This product functionally replaces the Brocade 4100, and entirely replaces the M4700.

In many respects, these switches are very similar. All provide up to 32 ports in a high-density fixed configuration. All three have hot swappable fans and power supplies. Each can support hot code load and activation. Both the 4100 and 5000 run Fabric OS. Both use SFP media. One minor difference is that the 5000 has a combined FAN/Power Supply FRU, whereas the 4100 had separate FRUs for each of those parts. Since this has no impact whatsoever on availability, this is considered an academic difference.

Figure 76 – Brocade 5000

However, the 5000 is not simply a replacement for the 4100; it also improves on the 4100 in many ways. For example, the 4100 was twice as deep as the 5000. Because of the shallower "rack footprint", it is possible to mount the

5000 without a rail kit. In some configurations, the 5000 supports higher density rack configurations in that the it can be mounted back to back in a cabinet, provided that the overall airflow is appropriate. That is, it can be mounted on the direct opposite side of a cabinet vs. other equipment, or even behind another Brocade 5000. The 5000 uses more modern and highly integrated technology, resulting in a more reliable switch and lower power consumption: it is about 20% more efficient than the 4100.

From a software feature set viewpoint, the 5000 is identical to the 4100 with the exception that, at the time of this writing, the 4100 does not have a near-term roadmap to support native interoperability with McData fabrics whereas the Brocade 5000 does have this.

Brocade 4900 Switch

The Brocade 4900 fabric switch is shown in Figure 77. This platform is essentially identical to the Brocade 4100 (p326) and 5000 in terms of features supported. The difference is that it has twice as many ports, and takes up 2u instead of 1u. (I.e. the port *density* is identical.) The port on demand feature ranges from 32 to 48 to 64 ports. Like the Brocade 4100, the Brocade 4900 has sufficient internal bandwidth to support all ports at full-speed / full-duplex operation simultaneously in all traffic configurations. (I.e. is fully non-blocking and uncongested.)

Figure 77 - Brocade 4900

330

Brocade 48000 Director

The Brocade 48000 (below) is a fully-modular 10-slot enterprise-class director, and can be populated with up to eight port-blades and two Control Processors (CPs).

Figure 78 – Brocade 48000 Director

This platform first shipped in mid 2005. It can be configured from 32 to 384 ports in a single domain using 16-, 32-, and 48-port 4Gbit FC blades. Using the "Virtual Fabrics" feature, it can be carved up into multiple virtual chassis. The platform has industry-leading performance and high availability characteristics. Each blade is hot-pluggable, as are the fans, WWN card, and power supplies. The chassis has redundant control processors (CPs) with redundant active-active uncongested and non-blocking switching elements, which run Fabric OS 5.0.1 or higher and support HCL/A. To support 48-port blades,

Fabric OS 5.2.0 or higher is required and some advanced function blades may require higher OS releases.

The Brocade 48000 is an evolution of the Brocade 12000 and 24000 design. The blades can even use the same chassis as its predecessors in some cases: the power supplies, fans, backplane, and sheet metal enclosure are generally compatible. As a result, it is possible to upgrade an existing 12000 chassis all the way to the 48000 in the field by replacing just the CP and port blades.[97] Similar procedures can work with the 12000 to 24000, or 24000 to 48000. Look between Figure 78 and Figure 105 (p363) and the similarity will be apparent.

There are also differences between the directors. Some of the differences are minor. For example, the 24000 and 48000 chassis and blade set has an improved rail glide system that makes blade insertion / extraction easier compared to the 12000. Larger ejector levers help by providing greater mechanical advantage. The 48000 also has a redesigned cable management system to accommodate using the larger number of ports.

There are also much more important differences in the underlying technology. For example, the 24000 uses the 2Gbit "Bloom-II" ASIC, while the 48000 uses the 4Gbit "Condor" chipset. (See "Bloom and Bloom-II" p427 and "Condor" on p428.) The overall chassis power consumption and cooling requirements have been lowered drastically, with the result that ongoing operational costs are reduced and MTBF is increased substantially as well.

---

[97] As a practical matter, this is almost never done. It's virtually always easier, less risky, and even less expensive to deploy a new director vs. upgrading an existing chassis. Also, not all OEMs can support upgrading chassis for administrative reasons. For example, it may be that the chassis serial number is used to define the support contract for a platform, and it may not be administratively practical to change it from a 12000 to a 48000 in the support system, even if it is technologically possible from a hardware and software viewpoint. The bottom line is that field upgrades are rarely performed.

Further improvements in MTBF are achieved through component integration: fewer components means less frequent failures, and the Condor chipset is the most tightly integrated in the industry. Performance has been improved from the 12000 by changing the multistage chip layout from an "XY" topology to a "CE" arrangement. (See "Multistage Internal Architectures" on p432 for more information.) This allows the 48000 to present all of its ports in a single fully-internally-connected domain. The 12000, in contrast, presented two 64-port domains and required external ISLs if traffic was required to flow between the domains. In addition, the 48000 runs its internal links faster than the 12000 or 24000. Using the advanced trunking capabilities of Condor, the 48000 maintains an evenly balanced 1:1 relationship of front-end to back-end bandwidth on the 16-port 4Gbit blades. By taking advantage of local switching and high-port-count blades, it is not only possible, but actually *practical* to sustain 1.5Tbits (3Tbits cross-sectional) of throughput in the chassis.

When making design trade-offs, availability is usually considered the most important factor. This is especially true for customers of director-class products. Of course, the 48000 has the usual director-class feature set, but it also has a more subtle characteristic related reliability of port blades, which translates to availability of connections. The 48000 has the most efficient component integration of any FC director built to date.

Figure 79 – FC16 Port Blade for Brocade 48000

Note the highlighted section of the figure in the middle of the blade. This is the blade's "Condor" ASIC. It is the "brain" of the blade, containing the FC protocol logic, the serdes[98] functions, buffer memory, zoning enforcement memory and logic, performance counters, and so on. Having all of these functions in a single chip drastically reduces the complexity of the blade vs. competing approaches, which improves MTBF and lowers power and cooling requirements. Compare the single-ASIC approach of the FC16 to any other director in the industry, and the difference will be immediately apparent. It is certainly apparent when comparing the refinement of this blade to the port blade designs from its predecessors.

Perhaps the most important difference between the 48000 and it's predecessors is that the Brocade 48000 is the "go forward" platform for the Brocade Enterprise roadmap. This means that purchasing a Brocade 48000 today is a strategic investment that will still have value for years to come. Brocade shipped the FR4-18i blade for FC routing and FCIP some time ago, and recently shipped several additional blades such as:

- iSCSI port blade
- 10Gbit FC blade
- Application Processor (AP) blade

The advanced feature blades are discussed in more detail later in this section.

---

[98] A "Serializer / Deserializer" function, or serdes for short, is required by all FC switches to convert frames from a parallel mode (such as being held in a buffer) to a serial format suitable for transmission. In non-Brocade switches, serdes functions are generally on separate chips, which increases power draw, and lowers reliability.

The intention is to be able to populate the chassis with many different combinations of port blades.[99] For example, the system should support a configuration with a combination of e.g. 128 4Gbit fabric ports plus two LSAN router blades plus two iSCSI blades.

The Brocade 48000 Fibre Channel Director provides the following features today:

- 384 ports per chassis configured in 16-, 32-, or 48-port increments
- Curent port blades support 1Gbit, 2Gbit, and 4Gbit Fibre Channel on a per-port basis
- FR4-18i router blade supports LSANs and FCIP
- FC4-16IP blade with FC and iSCSI support
- FA4-18 Application Blade with 16 virtualization ports
- FC10-6 10Gbit Fibre Channel blade
- Management access via 10/100Base-T RJ45 Ethernet ports and DB9 serial ports
- 14U rack mountable enclosure <30 inches deep. This allows up to 768 ports in a single rack.[100]
- High-availability features include hot-swappable FRUs for port blades, redundant power supplies and fans, and redundant CP blades
- Extensive diagnostics and monitoring for high Reliability, Availability, and Serviceability (RAS)
- Non-disruptive software upgrades (HCL/A)
- Non-blocking architecture enables 128 ports to operate at full 4Gbit line rate in full-duplex mode

---

[99] It is possible that some combinational restrictions could apply, and support may vary between OEMs.

[100] Not all racks can support high-density configurations. The rack must be at least 42u high. There may need to be space between chassis for cable management. Power and cooling infrastructure, cable management, and structure of the floor must be sufficient. The organization supporting the SAN must often approve the installation of extremely high density deployments.

- Forward and backward compatibility within fabrics with all Brocade 3000-series and later switches
- Brocade 12000s are upgradeable to 48000s
- Small Form-Factor Pluggable (SFP) optical transceivers allow any combination of supported Short and Long Wavelength Laser media (SWL, LWL, ELWL), as well as CWDM "colored laser" media
- Cables, blades, and PS are serviced from the cable side and fans from the non-cable side
- Air is pulled into the non-cable-side of the chassis and exits cable-side above the port and CP blades and through the power supplies to the right

Brocade AP7420 Multiprotocol Router

Routers are used to connect different networks together, as opposed to bridging segments of the same network. In this context, "multiprotocol" means connecting networks using different protocols, generally at the lower levels of the stack.

For example, one network could use SCSI over Fibre Channel (i.e. FCP) and another could use SCSI over IP (e.g. iSCSI). In general usage, a router that can merely handle multiple Upper Layer Protocols (ULPs) but *not* different lower layer protocols is *not* considered multiprotocol.[101] For example, the ability to handle both SCSI/FC and FICON/FC would not qualify a product as a multiprotocol router, whereas handling both SCSI/FC and SCSI/IP might qualify for the term.

---

[101] For differing ULPs, a router may not need any special capabilities. For example, an IP/Ethernet router can handle both HTTP/IP/Ethernet and Telnet/IP/Ethernet without being "multiprotocol" per se: the ULP is transparent to the router. In some cases, a switch may need special "upper layer services" support for a ULP, such as CUP support on a FICON/FC switch. Even this does not qualify the switch as a multiprotocol router; it is simply an FC switch with enhanced FICON support.

In the context of SANs, a multiprotocol router must connect Fibre Channel fabrics to each other and/or to some other networking protocols. Fibre Channel is mandatory since it is by far the leading protocol for use in SANs. Other protocols that a router may connect to include IP storage protocols such as FCIP and the emerging iSCSI standard.

 Side Note

To learn more about SAN routing in general and the Brocade routers in particular, read the book Multiprotocol Routing for SANs, *by Josh Judd.*

Brocade has created a multiprotocol SAN router provides which three functions critical to modern enterprise SAN deployments, and is designed to provide more in the future. At the time of this writing, the multiprotocol router software provides:

- FC-FC Routing Service for greater connectivity than traditional Fibre Channel SANs provide
- FCIP Tunneling Service for extending FC fabrics over distance using IP wide area networks
- iSCSI Gateway Service for sharing Fibre Channel storage resources with iSCSI initiators

In addition to running these three services, the Brocade router is also a high-performance FC fabric switch.

The first platform the multiprotocol router software was delivered on was the Brocade AP7420 Multiprotocol Router (Figure 80). This platform first became generally available in early 2004. Multiprotocol router capabilities were added to the Brocade 48000 director in early 2006 via the FR4-18i blade, and the 4Gbit Brocade 7500 router shipped in the same timeframe. For most routing deployments, these two platforms have supplanted the 7420. For most application-layer deployments, the Brocade 7600 and FA-18 blade have replaced the 7420. However, this device is still useful in some cases.

Figure 80 – Brocade AP7420

Multiprotocol routing is a subset of the AP7420s capabilities: as well as performing its role as a multiprotocol router, it was designed to handle storage application processing requirements (a.k.a. "virtualization") for the full range of environments from small business to large-scale enterprises.

At only two RETMA units (2U) in height, the AP7420 allows deployment of fabric-based applications and multiprotocol routing using very little space. With "ports on demand" licensing, a single platform can be purchased with as few as eight ports and is scalable to sixteen ports with only the addition of a license key. Furthermore, its advanced networking capabilities allow scalability far beyond that level.

The AP7420 can make switching decisions using any protocol layers up to the very top of the protocol stack. This means that the platform hardware is able to function as a standard Fibre Channel fabric switch, an FC-FC router, or a virtualizer. Similarly, it could theoretically function as an Ethernet or IP switch from layer 2 to layer 4.[102] The platform has considerable flexibility, since every

---

[102] Of course, as a practical matter, not *all* features and combinations of features will be supported in *software* just because the platform *hardware* is capable of

338

port has its own ASIC with multiple embedded CPUs and both Ethernet and Fibre Channel protocol support.

The Brocade AP7420 Fabric Application Platform provides the following features:

- 16 ports with software selectable modes, including auto-sensing 1Gbit/2Gbit FC, and 1Gbit Ethernet
- 2U rack mountable enclosure ~25 inches deep
- HA features including redundant hot-swappable power supply and fan FRUs
- Compatibility with all Brocade 2000-series and later Brocade switches within fabrics
- Management access via dual 10/100Base-T RJ45 Ethernet ports and one RJ45 serial port
- When in Fibre Channel mode:
- Auto-sensing ports negotiate to the highest speed supported by attached devices
- FC ports auto-negotiate as E_ or F_Ports. Any port may be configured as an FL_Port to permit an NL_Port device to be attached, or as an EX_Port for FC-FC routing
- Exchange-based ISL and IFL routing
- When in Gigabit Ethernet mode:
- Hardware acceleration through offloading TCP to port ASICs' ARM processors
- FCIP for deliver TCP/IP distance extension
- iSCSI initiator to FC target protocol mediation
- Per-port XPath ASICs for rapid data manipulation
- The XPath Fabric ASIC provides non-blocking connectivity between port ASICs
- SFP optical transceivers allow any combination of supported SWL, LWL, and ELWL media

---

delivering them. For combinations not explicitly called out in this book, discuss them with support and sales personnel.

Basic Reference

- Latency is minimized through the use of storage application processors inside each port ASIC.
- Each port has LEDs to indicate behavior and status
- Air is pulled into the non-cable-side of the chassis, and exits cable-side above the SFPs

Brocade 7500 Multiprotocol Router

The Brocade 7500 (Figure 81) is a fixed-configuration 16-port 4Gbit FC router/switch with two additional ports for FCIP connectivity. The FCIP ports have the same capabilities as in the FC4-18i (p341). In addition to being able to perform all standard FC switching functions, it has the ability to route FC (i.e. to form IFLs) on all sixteen FC ports, and to route tunneled FC IFLs across the FCIP ports. This is a multiprotocol routing switch running Fabric OS 5.1 or above. In almost all cases, this is considered to be a replacement for the AP7420.

Figure 81 – Brocade 7500 Multiprotocol Router

Like the FC4-18i, the sixteen Fibre Channel ports will negotiate 1Gbit, 2Gbit, or 4Gbit speeds. The internal switching architecture is fully non-blocking and uncongested at full-speed / full-duplex. The internal switching fabric supports up to 256Gbits of bandwidth: more than enough to handle all ports at full speed.

Brocade 7600 Application Platform

The Brocade 7600 is a fixed-configuration 16-port Application Platform / Virtualization Switch. In addition to the 16 FC ports it has two additional 1000baseT ports for application management connectivity. This platform requires Fabric OS 5.3 or above.

340

Figure 82 - Brocade 7600

The sixteen Fibre Channel ports that will negotiate 1Gbit, 2Gbit, or 4Gbit speeds. The internal architecture is fully non-blocking and uncongested at full-speed / full-duplex. The internal switching fabric supports all ports at full speed. In addition to the switching bandwidth it also has 128Gbit of virtualization bandwidth and the ability to support more than 1 million IOPS.

FR4-18i Multiprotocol Routing Blade

The FR4-18i (Figure 83) is a multiprotocol routing blade for the Brocade 48000 director (p331). There are sixteen FC ports on the blade, and two FCIP ports.

Figure 83 - FR4-18i Routing Blade

Each of the FC ports may be used for attachment of 1Gbit, 2Gbit, or 4Gbit FC devices such as hosts or storage, connection of FC Inter Switch Links (ISLs), or for FC to FC routing via Inter Fabric Links (IFLs). It is also possible to use this blade to enable FC write-acceleration features generally applicable to DWDM or FCIP deployments in enterprise DR or BC solutions.

The FCIP ports may tunnel IFLs or ISLs. They support advanced distance extension features such as compression, encryption, and FastWrite acceleration, as well as having hardware acceleration for TCP headers to ensure top performance and standards compliance.

FA4-18 Application Blade

The FA4-18 (Figure 84) is an Application / Virtualization blade for the Brocade 48000 director. There are sixteen (16) FC ports on the blade, and two (2) GE ports.

Figure 84 - FA18 Application Blade

Each of the FC ports may be used for attachment of 1Gbit, 2Gbit, or 4Gbit FC devices such as hosts or storage, or for FC ISLs. The internal architecture of the blade is fully non-blocking and uncongested at full-speed / full-duplex. The internal switching fabric supports up to 128Gbits of bandwidth: more than enough to handle all ports at full speed. In addition to the switching bandwidth it also has 128Gbit of virtualization bandwidth and the ability to support more than 1 million IOPS. The two 1000baseT ports are used to connect to external application management servers.

FC10-6 10Gbit Fibre Channel Blade

The FC10-6 (Figure 85) is a 10Gbit FC blade for the Brocade 48000 director. There are six (6) 10Gbit FC ports on the blade. Each of the ports may be used for attachment of 10Gbit FC ISLs. The internal architecture of the blade is fully non-blocking. There are two Condor ASICs to handle backplane connectivity, and six Egret ASICs (p431) to operate the 10Gbit ports. Each Egret has 720 buffer-to-buffer credits, which is sufficient to support a full-speed connection at 120km.

Figure 85 - FC10-6 10Gbit FC Blade

The 10Gbit FC ports are only supported for ISL connectivity at this time, as no 10Gbit Fibre Channel devices (hosts or storage) are widely available. Brocade does not expect 10Gbit devices to become widely available because 10Gbit is not cost efficient for nodes, and less expensive 8Gbit FC will be available before nodes could take full advantage of higher speeds in any case. 10Gbit Fibre Channel is targeted for MAN/WAN deployments over *x*WDM or dark fiber networks.

FC4-16IP iSCSI to Fibre Channel Blade

The FC4-16IP (Figure 86) has a combination of 8 x 1Gbit iSCSI/Ethernet ports (GE) and 8 x 4Gbit Fibre Channel (FC) ports. It is designed for use in the Brocade 48000 director (p331).

The GE ports are used to connect to external iSCSI initiators directly, or (more typically) via external Ethernet switches for fan-in. The blade can support up to 64 iSCSI initiators per port (512 per blade).

Figure 86 – FC4-16IP iSCSI Blade

At the time of this writing, iSCSI initiators for Microsoft Windows, HP-UX, Solaris, Linux (RedHat and SuSE), and AIX are supported. The iSCSI initiators can take advantage of advanced features such as LUN masking and re-mapping. Additional features include Error Level Recover 0, 1 and 2, iSCSI load balancing, CHAP support, and many other iSCSI protocol-specific features.

Each of the FC ports may be used for attachment of standard 1Gbit, 2Gbit, or 4Gbit FC devices such as hosts or storage, or connection of FC Inter Switch Links (ISLs). The internal architecture of the blade is fully non-blocking and uncongested at full-speed / full-duplex.

Embedded Platforms

In addition to stand-alone platforms, Brocade ASIC and software technology is used *within* products from a number of partners and OEMs. For example, Brocade FC switch ASICs are embedded into blade server products offered by some of the industry's top OEMs. This allows the connection of high density server blades into either existing fabrics or directly to storage. Brocade technology is also embedded within storage array controllers, providing a server fan-in capability integrated into the array. In effect, the OEM host or storage product contains some or all of the SAN internally, which tends to improve manageability and reliability, and also lowers power, cooling, and rack space requirements.

Historically, connecting a large number of platforms with embedded switches to a larger SAN created scalability and manageability problems. If each storage device or blade-chassis also had one or more switch domains inside it, the size of the FC fabric could get out of hand quickly. Brocade developed the Access Gateway feature (p376) to eliminate this effect. Now, most embedded switches are capable of connecting to Brocade fabrics as F_Ports instead of E_Ports, so that they do not "show up" as switches in the fabric. Instead, they are projected as one or more nodes... which is actually what they really are, so that tends to work out well. To support Access Gateway, it is necessary to run appropriate code levels in the fabric as well as on the embedded switch, and OEM support is also required. Consult your local support organization to see if you can benefit from this feature.

Brocade 4020 Embedded FC Switch

The Brocade 4020 was designed for the IBM eServer BladeCenter & the Intel Blade Server. It is powered by the "Goldeneye" ASIC (p424). The product is a single-stage central memory switch. It has a cross-sectional bandwidth sufficient to support all ports full-speed full-duplex at once in any traffic configuration. Fabric OS 5.0.2 or later is required.

The Brocade 4020 (Figure 87) has six outbound (to the SAN) and 14 inbound ports (one to each blade server), all are non-blocking and uncongested 4Gbit (8Gbit full-duplex) Fibre Channel fabric U_Ports. This platform was introduced in 2006 by Brocade and IBM. The 4020 is available with software packages ranging from entry level (10-ports enabled) package up to the full enterprise-class

Fabric OS 5.x feature set (as well as all 20-ports enabled). This allows the platform to be purchased with the right balance of cost vs. features for a wide range of customers, from small businesses to major enterprises. Regardless of licensed options, the 4020 has enterprise features such as HCL/A and the Fabric OS CLI.

Figure 87 – Brocade 4020 Embedded Switch

Brocade 4016 Embedded FC Switch

The Brocade 4016 was designed for the Dell Power-Edge blade server and for Fujitsu-Siemens PRIMERGY Server Blade. It is powered by the "Goldeneye" ASIC (p424). The product is a single-stage central memory switch. It has a cross-sectional bandwidth sufficient to support all ports full-speed full-duplex at once in any traffic configuration. Fabric OS 5.0.4 or later is required.

The Brocade 4016 (Figure 88) has six outbound ports (to the SAN), which are 4Gbit, and 10 inbound ports (one to each blade server), which are 2Gbit non-blocking and uncongested Fibre Channel fabric U_Ports. This platform was introduced in 2006 by Brocade and Dell. The 4016 is available with software packages ranging from entry level ("12-ports enabled") package up to the full enterprise-class Fabric OS 5.x feature set and all 16-ports enabled via Port-On-Demand. (See "Brocade Software" on p354.)

Figure 88 - Brocade 4016 Embedded Switch

Brocade 4018 Embedded FC Switch

The Brocade 4018 (Figure 89) was designed for the Huawei Blade Server Chassis, and was introduced in 2006 by Brocade and Huawei. It is powered by the "Goldeneye" ASIC (p424). The product is a single-stage central memory switch. It has bandwidth sufficient to support all ports full-speed full-duplex at once in any traffic configuration. Fabric OS 5.0.5 or later is required.

Figure 89 - Brocade 4018 Embedded Switch

The 4018 has four outbound ports (to the SAN) and 14 inbound ports (one to each blade server). All ports are non-blocking and uncongested 4Gbit (8Gbit full-duplex) Fibre Channel fabric U_Ports. This board is typically factory installed, since - unlike other blade switches - it is a daughter board for an already existing controller module.

Brocade 4024 Embedded FC Switch

The Brocade 4024 was designed for the HP **c**-class BladeSystem. The Brocade 4024 is powered by the "Goldeneye" ASIC (p424) and is a single-stage central memory switch. It has a cross-sectional bandwidth sufficient to support all ports full-speed full-duplex at once. Fabric OS 5.0.5 or later is required.

The Brocade 4024 (Figure 90) has eight outbound ports (to the SAN) and 16 inbound ports (one to each blade server), all ports are non-blocking and uncongested 4Gbit (8Gbit full-duplex) Fibre Channel fabric U_Ports. This platform was introduced in 2006 by Brocade and HP. The 4024 is available with software packages ranging from entry level ("12-port configuration") up to the full enterprise-class Fabric OS 5.x feature set with all 24-ports enabled via Ports-On-Demand.

Figure 90 - Brocade 4024 Embedded Switch

Brocade 4012 Embedded FC Switch

The Brocade 4012 was introduced in 2005 by Brocade and HP. It represented the industry's ever first 4Gbit switch for embedded Blade Server market. The Brocade 4012 was specifically designed for the HP p-class BladeSystem. It is powered by the "Goldeneye" ASIC. It has a cross-sectional bandwidth sufficient to support all ports full-speed full-duplex at once. Fabric OS 5.0.1 or later is required. The Brocade 4012 (Figure 91) has four outbound (to the SAN) and 8 inbound ports (one to each blade server), all outbound ports are non-blocking and uncongested 4Gbit (8Gbit full-duplex) and the inbound are all non-blocking and uncongested 2Gbit (4Gbit full-duplex) FC fabric U_Ports.

Figure 91 - Brocade 4012 Embedded Switch

Brocade iSCSI Gateway

The Brocade iSCSI Gateway is an iSCSI-optimized product, designed to connect enterprise FC fabrics to low-cost "edge" servers. (Figure 92)

Figure 92 - Brocade iSCSI Gateway

Because this platform is smaller and offers fewer features than the FC4-16IP (p344), it can be less expensive, and may be adequate for users who desire an entry point into the iSCSI bridging market. However, there are a differences between the platforms besides cost and port count which must be considered when making a selection.

The iSCSI Gateway product is not capable of providing FC fabric switching. It has fewer features and lower performance than the bladed version. The Gigabit Ethernet interfaces on the iSCSI product are low-end copper, whereas the FC4-16IP uses more reliable optical ports capable of spanning greater distances. Because the iSCSI Gateway has RJ45 copper GE interfaces on the gateway itself, rather than just on the iSCSI hosts, users need to make sure that their IT networking group provides the correct interface.

This solution should be considered for customers who need a low cost entry point into the iSCSI bridging market above all else. Otherwise, a native Fibre Channel solution or the FC4-16IP will likely provide better results.

Classic McData Platforms

In 2007, Brocade purchased McData: one of its long-time rivals. However, this was not the first time that the two companies had enjoyed a partnership-style relationship. In fact, McData was one of Brocade's first customers, having purchased intellectual property from Brocade with which to implement its line of FC directors. Many McData installed-base platforms still run Brocade ASICs and code-chunks to this day. In addition, some of the companies that McData acquired prior to being purchased by Brocade had equivalently long-term partnerships with Brocade. For example, Brocade had a long-standing relationship with CNT in which CNT resold Brocade switches, and Brocade supported CNT for DR and BC solutions requiring certain distance extension methods.

Upon the close of the acquisition, Brocade announced end of sale for a subset of McData products in cases where they directly overlapped with Brocade offerings. For example, the McData "pizzabox" edge switches were superseded by the Brocade 5000. They had no value-added features beyond those available on the Brocade switches, so it was not necessary to continue to ship them for much longer after the close of the acquisition. Brocade announced that it intended to stop shipping these platforms at the end of 2007.

However, Brocade has a firm commitment to McData customers, and has not stopped shipping products such as the 140- or 256-port directors. It is expected that these platforms will converge with the Brocade director strategy at some point, but even when that happens they will be supported in Brocade networks via routed connections and compatible software releases for the foreseeable future. Also, Brocade intends to honor the support lifecycle commitments made by McData, which means that even products which Brocade no longer intends to actively sell are still being supported. Typically, support continues for five years after end of sale is announced.

This section discusses a few of the more notable classic McData products, and indicates how they may be integrated into a Brocade environment.

Brocade Mi10k Director

The Brocade Mi10K offers up to 256 1-, 2-, and 4Gbit FC ports in a 14 U chassis. 10Gbit FC interfaces are also available for DR and BC solutions. It offers exceptional performance and availability. In some cases, it can even outperform the Brocade 48000, although in most deployments the 48000 has 50% more usable bandwidth[103] as well as 50% greater rack density, and much lower power and cooling requirements. Brocade is actively selling the Mi10k platform and has no immediate plans to stop doing so.

While this director is built using somewhat limited technology compared to the Brocade 48000, costs quite a bit more, and requires considerably more power and cooling resources, for Classic McData customers who already

---

[103] The cases in which the Mi10k can outperform the 48000 are those in which little or no flow locality is achievable, *and* the host-to-storage port ratio is near 1:1. If either of those statements are false, then the 48000 will outperform the Mi10k by a considerable margin.

have extensive Mi10k deployments, this is still the best option for transparently growing those environments. It is expected that Brocade will converge the applicable portions of the Mi10k feature-set with Brocade "native" director technology at some point in the future. In the mean time, the Mi10k is still being sold and supported, and can co-exist with Brocade-classic platforms using a number of strategies such as compatible firmware, routers, and storage-centric network topologies.

Brocade M6140 Director

The 140-port Brocade M6140 provides a high availability, high-performance, flexible building block for large SAN deployments. It is a single-stage, 140-port director designed supporting 1Gbit to 10Gbit FC interfaces. It can meet the connectivity demands of both open systems and mainframe FICON environments. Brocade is actively selling this platform and has no immediate plans to stop doing so.

While this director is built using somewhat outdated technology compared to the Brocade 48000, for Classic McData customers who already have extensive M6140 or 6064 deployments, the M6140 is still the best option for transparently growing those environments.

Brocade M4400 and M4700 Edge Switches

The M4400 has 16x 4Gbit FC ports in a 1u / ½ rack-width form factor. The M4700 has 32x 4Gbit FC ports in 1u, and takes a full rack-width. These two platforms are still shipping at the time of this writing. Since the Brocade 5000 offers a superset of their capabilities, Brocade will stop selling the M4400 and M4700 at the end of 2007. Support is expected to continue for five years after the final shipment date.

Brocade M1620 and M2640 Routers

The M1620 has two GE ports for SAN extension, and two FC ports for local E_Port connectivity. The platform can be deployed to support lower-end DR and BC environments. The M2640 has a similar architecture and use case, but with 12x FC ports and 4x GE ports.

These platforms used the now-defunct iFCP protocol for SAN extension. Since no other vendors ever implemented iFCP besides McData, and even McData had an FCIP roadmap, the iFCP protocol has actually been considered a dead end by the industry at large for several years. As a result, Brocade intends to stop selling these two platforms at the end of 2007 in favor of extension solutions using the Brocade 7500 router and FR4-18i blade, which support the FCIP protocol.

Brocade Edge M3000 Gateway

The Edge M3000 interconnects Fibre Channel SAN islands over an IP, ATM or SONET/SDH infrastructure. Brocade is actively selling this platform and has no immediate plans to stop doing so.

The M3000 enables many cost-effective, enterprise-strength data replication solutions, including both disk mirroring and remote tape backup/restore to maximize data availability and business continuity. Its any-to-any connectivity and multi-point SAN routing capability provide a flexible storage infrastructure for remote storage applications.

In most cases, the Edge M3000 has been superseded by the Brocade 7500 router and FR4-18i blade. However, in some cases the M3000 provides a superior fit. For example, depending upon the nature of the payload, the M3000 can compress data by up to 20:1, dramatically reducing bandwidth costs. With this compression technology, customers can achieve gigabit per second throughput using

Basic Reference

existing 100Mb Ethernet infrastructure – but at a fraction of the cost. It also implements tape pipelining which can provide a considerable performance benefit for remote tape vaulting solutions.

Of course, not all customers have such highly compressible data, and equivalent features enabled or planned for the Brocade 7500 and FR4-18i may provide equivalent benefits, so the market for the M3000 is considered to be limited where compression and tape pipelining in particular and concerned. But the M3000 does have ATM and SONET/SDH connectivity advantages which are likely to keep it in the product portfolio for quite some time to come.

Brocade USD-X Gateway

The USD-X is a high-performance platform that connects and extends mainframe and open-systems storage-related data replication applications for both disk and tape, along with remote channel networking for a wide range of device types. Brocade is actively selling this platform and has no immediate plans to stop doing so.

While it is possible to use this platform in pure open-systems environments, the primary current use cases for this product are mixed and pure mainframe environments as other products solve the extension problem more cost-effectively for most open-systems customers.

This multi-protocol gateway and extension platform interconnects host-to-storage and storage-to-storage systems across the enterprise – regardless of distance – to create a high capacity, high performance storage network using the latest high speed interfaces. It supports Fibre Channel, FICON™, ESCON, Bus and Tag, or mixed environment systems. The intermediate WAN may be ATM, IP, DS3, or many other technologies.

Installed Base Brocade Platforms

One of the advantages that Brocade has in the SAN marketplace is its large installed base. Brocade has millions of ports running in mission-critical production environments around the world, representing literally billions of hours of production operation to date. Brocade has a policy of prioritizing backwards compatibility with the installed base for new products.[104] This allows customers buying Brocade products to get a long useful life out of them, to achieve high ROI before needing to upgrade.

This subsection describes many of the platforms in the Brocade installed base. SAN designers may encounter any of these products, and must know their capabilities when designing solutions that involve them.

SilkWorm 1xx0 FC Switches

The first platform-group that Brocade shipped was the Brocade 1xx0 series (Figure 93 and Figure 94). Shipped first in early 1997, this design was simply called the "SilkWorm switch" as there were no other Brocade platforms to differentiate between. Over time, other platforms were added. The first 16-port switch became known as the "SilkWorm I," with its successor being the "SilkWorm II." In early 1998, a lower cost 8-port "SilkWorm Express" platform was shipped based on the same architecture, but with half of the ports removed. By the time that the SilkWorm 2000 series shipped, Brocade had enough platforms that the first generation switches became known as the "SilkWorm 1xx0 series."

---

[104] Some restrictions apply, of course. For example, it may be necessary to run certain firmware versions and design solutions within scalability constraints to fit within a vendor support matrix. Also, it is not possible to continue support for an installed-base platform literally forever. The typical case is to continue support for five years after the last sale date of a product line.

Figure 93 – SilkWorm II (1600) FC Fabric Switch

Figure 94 – SilkWorm Express (800) FC Fabric Switch

These switches could be configured at the time of manufacture to support either FC-AL or FC fabric devices (Flannel or Stitch ASICs respectively, p425) using combinations of 2-port daughter cards (Figure 95).

Figure 95 – SilkWorm 1xx0 Daughter Card

All SilkWorm 1xx0 switches ran Fabric OS 1.x. The product line consisted of 8- and 16-port FC fabric switches, with all ports running at 1Gbit. (8-port = SilkWorm Express and SilkWorm 800; 16-port = SilkWorm II and SilkWorm 1600.) Ports could accept either optical or copper GBICs. Management tasks could be performed using buttons on the front panel on most models. All models had RJ45 IP/Ethernet and DB9 serial interfaces.

This Brocade platform group is considered to be entirely obsolete. The 1xx0 switches are simply not compatible with many of the new features released from Brocade over the past few years, and the hardware predated some of the FC standards. Brocade recommends that SilkWorm 1xx0 series switches be upgraded to newer Brocade products and technologies in all cases.

SilkWorm 2xx0 FC Switches

The SilkWorm 2xx0 series consisted of several platforms all using the Loom ASIC (p426) and running Fabric OS 2.x. The first platforms in this group – the SilkWorm 2400 and 2800 – shipped in the middle of 1999. At the time of this writing, the SilkWorm 2xx0 platform group has reached the end of its supportable life. Most OEMs have declared these switches to be unsupported, and the rest are expected to do so by the end of the year. Users should consider 2xx0 switches to be obsolete, and should plan for upgrading in the near future.

Figure 96 through Figure 99 show the most popular 2xx0 series platforms. All of these products operated at 1Gbit Fibre Channel, and had a single-stage central memory architecture for non-blocking and uncongested operation. All of the switches in this series had an IP/Ethernet management port. Most had a DB9 serial port for initial configuration, emergency access, and out-of-band management, with the 2800 being the exception to that rule. (It had a push-button control panel and screen for initial configuration.)

The 2xx0 series has been superseded by other Brocade products. However, these switches are still widely deployed. Brocade has found that the number of SilkWorm 2800 platforms still in production is close to the number that originally shipped: something on the order of a million ports in production. As a result, Brocade anticipates that many customers will need to perform 1Gbit to 4Gbit migrations over the next year, now that these switches have reached the end of their lifecycle.

SilkWorm 20x0

The entry-level SilkWorm 20x0 (Figure 96) was a 1u 8-port switch, with seven fixed ports (GLMs) and one port with removable media (GBIC).

The platform could be purchased in three varieties, depending on the software keys that were loaded at the factory. The third digit in the platform product ID (20x0) indicated these software options, not any difference in hardware. The 2010 came with support only for Quick-Loop, so only FL_Ports could be attached, not F_Port fabric devices or E_Ports. The 2040 supported fabric nodes but only one E_Port, and the 2050 had unlimited fabric support. Both the 2010 and 2040 provided customers with complete investment protection, as either could be upgraded to the full-fabric 2050 with license keys available through all channel partners. Power input was provided by a single fixed supply, and fans were fixed as well, so the entire platform was considered a FRU.

Figure 96 – SilkWorm 2010/2040/2050

SilkWorm 22x0

The 1.5u 16-port SilkWorm 22x0 (Figure 97) brought higher rack density to the entry-level switch market.

Figure 97 - SilkWorm 2210/2240/2250

It had a single fixed power supply, like the 20x0, and could be purchased with the same three software license variations. Also like the 20x0, the entire platform was considered a single FRU. However, all 16 media on the 22x0 were removable GBICs.

This platform was also used as the basic building block for the SilkWorm 6400, which consisted of a sheet metal enclosure containing six SilkWorm 2250 switches, configured and wired together at the factory to form a Core/Edge fabric, manageable as a single platform. That arrangement yielded sixty-four usable ports.

SilkWorm 2400

The SilkWorm 2400 (Figure 98) was targeted at the midrange segment. Like the 20x0, it was an 8-port switch, but had redundant hot-swappable power supplies and fans.

Figure 98 - SilkWorm 2400

SilkWorm 2800

The SilkWorm 2800 (Figure 99) was a 16-port switch like the 22x0, but had enterprise-class RAS features like the 2400. This was by far the most popular of the 2xx0 series. In many environments, the number of 2800 switches installed today still rivals the number of later platforms. This was the only platform in the series that did *not* have an externally-accessible serial port. Instead, the initial switch configuration could be performed using buttons and a screen built into the cable-side panel.

Figure 99 – SilkWorm 2800

SilkWorm 3200 / 3800 Switch

In 2001, the SilkWorm 2xx0 product family was superseded by the SilkWorm 3200 and 3800 switches. They were both powered by the Bloom ASIC (p427), which increased the port speed to 2Gbit and added a range of new features including trunking, advanced performance monitoring, and more advanced zoning. Both platforms had IP/Ethernet and DB9 serial management interfaces, and both ran Fabric OS 3.x. Another major difference between these and prior Brocade platforms was that the SilkWorm 3200 and 3800 used SFPs, whereas all prior platforms had used GBICs.

At the time of this writing, the SilkWorm 3200 has been superceded by the SilkWorm 3250 (p361), and the SilkWorm 3800 has been largely superceded by the Silk-Worm 3850. (The SilkWorm 3800 is still shipping, but most users are expected to transition to the 3850 in the near future because of its many improvements.)

SilkWorm 3200

This platform had eight 2Gbit FC ports in a 1u enclosure. It was targeted at the entry market. Like its predecessor, the SilkWorm 20x0, this switch had a single fixed power supply and fixed fans: the entire platform was considered a FRU.

Figure 100 - SilkWorm 3200

SilkWorm 3800

The SilkWorm 3800 was targeted at the midrange and enterprise markets. It had RAS features equivalent to the SilkWorm 2800.

Figure 101 - SilkWorm 3800

SilkWorm 3250 / 3850 FC Switches

These platforms represented the entry level of the Fibre Channel fabric switching market. They each had non-removable power supplies. Both were powered by the "Bloom-II" ASIC (p425). The ASIC arrangement in both platforms yielded a single-stage central memory switch. They both had a cross-sectional bandwidth sufficient to support all ports full-speed full-duplex at once. Fabric OS 4.2 or later was required. The SilkWorm 3250 (Figure 102) had eight non-blocking and uncongested[105] 2Gbit (4Gbit full-duplex) Fibre Channel fabric U_Ports.[106] The SilkWorm 3850 (Figure 103) had sixteen ports.

---

[105] There has been debate in the industry about the definition of "blocking." When Brocade uses the word, it refers to Head of Line Blocking (HoLB). For example, the SilkWorm 24000 is not subject to HoLB because it uses virtual channels on the backplane. It is therefore "non-blocking." All ports can run full-speed full-duplex at the same time, which is "uncongested operation."

[106] U_Port interfaces automatically detect FC topology to become F_Port, FL_Port, or E_Port as needed.

Basic Reference

These two platforms were introduced in 2004 to replace the popular SilkWorm 3200 and 3800 switches. Both were available with software packages ranging from the lowest entry level ("Value Line") package up to the full enterprise-class Fabric OS 4.x feature set. (See "Brocade Software" on p368.) This allowed the platforms to be purchased with the right balance of cost vs. features for a wide range of customers, from small businesses to major enterprises. Regardless of licensed options, both switches had enterprise features such as hot (non-disruptive) code load and activation (HCL/A) and the Fabric OS CLI.

Figure 102 - SilkWorm 3250

Figure 103 - SilkWorm 3850

SilkWorm 3900 and 12000

The SilkWorm 3900 (Figure 104) delivered 32 ports of 2Gbit Fibre Channel in a 1.5u rack-mountable enclosure.

Figure 104 - SilkWorm 3900

First shipped in 2002, this platform was targeted at the midrange SAN market, but had many features appropriate for the enterprise market as well. In many ways, the Silk-Worm 3900 was more like a small director than like a switch. Like the SilkWorm 12000, this platform had an "XY" topology CCMA multistage architecture. (See "Multistage Internal Architectures" on p432.) Like the 12000, it supported FICON (a mainframe protocol), had redundant and hot swappable power and cooling FRUs, and ran Fabric OS 4.x with hot code load and activation.

Typical usage cases for the 3900 included stand-alone applications for small fabrics, edge deployments in small to large Core/Edge (CE) fabrics, and core deployments in small to medium CE fabrics.

The SilkWorm 12000 (Figure 105) was Brocade's first fully-modular 10-slot enterprise-class director. This system first shipped in 2002.

Figure 105 - SilkWorm 12000 Director

The chassis was rack-mountable in 14u, and could be populated with up to eight port-blades and two CPs. Overall, the chassis could be configured starting with 32 and going up to 128 2Gbit Fibre Channel ports. Each blade was hot-pluggable, as were the fans and power supplies. The redundant CPs ran Fabric OS 4.x and supported

HCL/A. Typical usage cases for the 12000 included stand-alone applications, edge deployments in large CE fabrics, and core deployments in medium to large CE fabrics.

The backplane interconnected the port blades with each other to form two separate 64-port domains. The interconnection employed an "XY" topology CCMA multistage architecture, much like the SilkWorm 3900. The two 64-port domains were both controlled by the same redundant CP blades, and resided in the same chassis, but had no internal data path between them. They could be used separately in redundant fabrics, or could be used together in the same fabric by connecting them with ISLs.

At the time of this writing, the SilkWorm 3900 has been superseded by the SilkWorm 4100 (p326), and the SilkWorm 12000 has been superseded, first by the Silk-Worm 24000 (p329), and then the 48000 (p329). For the foreseeable future, the older platforms will continue to be supported in networks with more advanced platforms. In addition, the SilkWorm 12000 chassis can be upgraded in the field to become a SilkWorm 24000 or 48000.[107]

SilkWorm 24000 Director

The SilkWorm 24000 (Figure 106) was a fully-modular 10-slot enterprise-class director, and could be populated with up to eight port-blades and two Control Processors (CPs). This platform first shipped in early 2004. It could be configured from 32 to 128 ports in a single domain using 16-port 2Gbit Fibre Channel blades. The platform had industry-leading performance and high availability characteristics. Each blade was hot-pluggable, as were the fans and power supplies. The chassis had redundant control processors (CPs) with redundant active-active

---

[107] Of course, not all OEMs support this procedure.

uncongested and non-blocking switching elements, which ran Fabric OS 4.2 or higher and supported HCL/A.

Figure 106 – SilkWorm 24000 Director

The SilkWorm 24000 was an evolution of the Silk-Worm 12000 design. It could use the same chassis as the 12000: the power supplies, fans, backplane, and sheet metal enclosure were all compatible. As a result, it was possible to upgrade an existing 12000 chassis to the 24000 in the field by replacing just the CP and port blades. Look between Figure 106 and Figure 105 (p363) and the similarity will be apparent. It can also support 16-port 4Gbit FC Brocade 48000 blades in some combinations with existing SilkWorm 24000 blades.

Even though the chassis were mechanically compatible, there were differences between the SilkWorm 24000 and the SilkWorm 12000.

Some of the differences were minor. For example, the 24000 chassis and blade set had an improved rail glide system that makes blade insertion / extraction easier. Larger ejector levers helped by providing greater mechanical advantage. The 24000 CP blades had a blue LED to indicate which CP was active.

There were also more important differences in the underlying technology. For example, the 24000 used the "Bloom-II" ASIC, while the 12000 used the original "Bloom" chipset. (See "Bloom and Bloom-II" p427.) The overall chassis power consumption and cooling requirements were lowered by more than 60%, with the result that ongoing operational costs were reduced and MTBF increased by more than 25%. Further improvements in MTBF were achieved through component integration: fewer components means less frequent failures. Performance was improved by changing the multistage chip layout from an "XY" topology to a "CE" arrangement. (See "Multistage Internal Architectures" on p432 for more information.) This allowed the 24000 to present all of its ports in a single internally-connected domain. The 12000, in contrast, presented two 64-port domains and needed external ISLs if traffic was required to flow between the domains.

The SilkWorm 24000 Fibre Channel Director provided the following features:

- 128 ports per chassis in 16-port increments
- Port blades are 1Gbit/2Gbit Fibre Channel
- Management access via Ethernet and serial ports
- High-availability features include hot-swappable FRUs for port blades, redundant power supplies and fans, and redundant CP blades
- Extensive diagnostics and monitoring for high Reliability, Availability, and Serviceability (RAS)
- Non-disruptive software upgrades (HCL/A)
- 14U rack mountable enclosure allows up to 384 ports in a single rack.
- Non-blocking architecture allows all 128 ports to operate at line rate in full-duplex mode

- Forward and backward compatibility within fabrics with all Brocade 2000-series and later switches
- SilkWorm 12000s are upgradeable to 24000s
- Small Form-Factor Pluggable (SFP) optical transceivers allow any combination of supported Short and Long Wavelength Laser media (SWL, LWL, ELWL), as well as CWDM media
- Cables, blades, and PS are serviced from the cable side and fans from the non-cable side
- Air is pulled into the non-cable-side of the chassis and exits cable-side above the port and CP blades and through the power supplies to the right

Embedded Products

SilkWorm 3016 Embedded FC Switch

The SilkWorm 3016 was specifically designed for the IBM eServer BladeCenter. It was powered by the "Bloom-II" ASIC. It had a cross-sectional bandwidth sufficient to support all ports full-speed full-duplex at once. The SilkWorm 3016 (Figure 107) has two outbound ports (i.e. facing to the SAN) and 14 inbound ports (one to each blade server), all are non-blocking and uncongested 2Gbit (4Gbit full-duplex) Fibre Channel fabric U_Ports. This platform was introduced in 2004 by Brocade and IBM. The 3016 was available with software packages ranging from entry level ("Value Line") package up to the full enterprise-class Fabric OS 4.x feature set.

Figure 107 - SilkWorm 3016 Embedded Switch

SilkWorm 3014 Embedded FC Switch

The SilkWorm 3014 was specifically designed for the Dell PowerEdge blade server. It was powered by the "Bloom-II" ASIC. It had a cross-sectional bandwidth sufficient to support all ports full-speed full-duplex at once. The SilkWorm 3014 (Figure 108) had four outbound (to the SAN) and 10 inbound ports (one to each blade server), all were non-blocking and uncongested 2Gbit (4Gbit full-duplex) Fibre Channel fabric U_Ports.

Figure 108 – SilkWorm 3014 Embedded Switch

This platform was introduced in late 2004 by Brocade and Dell. The 3014 was available with software packages ranging from entry level ("Value Line") package up to the full enterprise-class Fabric OS 4.x feature set.

Brocade Features

Brocade adds value in its products with both hardware (i.e. ASICs) and software. This subsection describes some of the most popular software features Brocade offers. It only covers features developed internally by Brocade Engineering; it does not, for example, discuss third-party management tools which use one of the supported APIs.

Brocade Licensing Model

Some features are basic components of the operating system and platform ASICs, such as support for nodes using N_Port. (I.e. support for F_Port on a switch.) These generally do not require purchasing a license key, but do add value. Some Brocade competitors (i.e. loop-switch vendors) do not offer products that support F_Port, so even though it seems like this should be a basic building block of all switches, it is worth calling it out explicitly to show its value.

Other features, such as the FC-FC Routing Service, require much higher value enhancements to both ASIC and OS support. Routing features and more advanced fabric service options require the purchase and installation of license keys to enable them. On all platforms, the CLI[108] command *licenseShow* can be used to determine which keys are installed. If a desired feature is missing, work with the appropriate sales channel to purchase the key, and then use the *licenseAdd* command to install it on the switch or router.

Fabric Node Attachment (F_Port)

At the time of this writing, most Fibre Channel nodes (e.g. host and storage devices) use the N_Port topology. "Node Port" is a set of standards-defined behaviors that allow a node to access a fabric and its services most cleanly. In order to connect an N_Port to a switch, the switch must support the corresponding "Fabric Port," or F_Port topology as defined in the standards. Every Brocade platform ever shipped supports F_Port, although in a few of the older platforms (e.g. the SilkWorm 2010) this feature required purchasing a separate license key. This is the preferred method for connecting nodes into fabrics.

Loop Node Attachment (FL_Port) (QL/FA)

Early in the evolution of Fibre Channel, there was debate about whether or not fabrics were necessary. Some vendors believed that FC-AL hubs and "loop switches"

---

[108] There are also equivalent GUI commands in WEBTOOLS and Fabric Manager. CLI commands are generally used for examples because all platforms include the CLI as part of the base OS, while some do not include the GUI tools.

provided sufficient connectivity. The argument went something like, "How many people will ever need more that a dozen or so devices in a SAN? Nobody!" It turned out that the real answer was, "Just about everybody," so the vastly more scalable and flexible fabric switches rapidly eroded the hub market.

To accomplish this market transition gracefully, it was necessary for nodes designed for FC-AL hubs to attach to fabric switches. The Fibre Channel standards defined a switch port type to accomplish this: the FL_Port. ("Fabric Loop" port.) This allowed, for example, HBA drivers written for hubs to present NL_Ports ("Node Loop" ports) and plug into switch FL_Ports. Brocade developed the Flannel ASIC (p425) to address this need. Platforms using Flannel needed to be configured with loop ports at the factory, but in subsequent products with more advanced ASICs, any port could support loop nodes.[109]

There are some important variables that affect how loop devices connect to a fabric:

- Does the loop device know how to talk to the name server, and does it know how to address devices using all three bytes of the fabric "PID" address? (Public vs. private loop.)
- If the device uses private loop, is it an initiator or a target? Private loop initiators need more help to use fabric services, i.e. the name server.
- Is there just one loop device directly attached to a switch port (like an NL_Port HBA) or are there many loop devices on that port (like a JBOD)?

---

[109] Throughout the remainder of this subsection, the obsolete SilkWorm 1xx0 series will not be considered. E.g. statements about "all platforms" may actually refer to "all platforms except the SilkWorm 1xx0."

Public loop support for a directly attached NL_Port is the easiest case for a switch to handle. The switch ASIC needs to be able to support FC-AL "loop primitives," which is the protocol used for loop initialization and control. All ports on all Brocade platforms today have the hardware and software to support this mode of operation as part of the base OS.

Public loop support for multiple nodes on a single switch port is slightly more complex. At the time of this writing, all platforms except the AP7420 Multiprotocol Router support this mode as part of the base OS. The major application for this is JBODs: it is not currently possible to attach a JBOD directly to the AP7420, but JBODs can coexist in a fabric or Meta SAN with that platform.

Private loop *storage* devices require still more advanced ASIC functionality known as "phantom logic," and corresponding software enhancements. This allows Network Address Translation (NAT) between the one-byte private loop and three-byte fabric address spaces. This needs ASIC hardware support because every frame needs to be rewritten without performance penalty. Trying to implement multi-gigabit NAT in software would not be practical. Brocade began to provide support for private loops with the Flannel ASIC.

Private loop technology has been declining rapidly, so Brocade had not prioritized phantom logic for future platforms. All ASICs through Bloom-II (p427) support this, but subsequent ASICs like FiGeRo (p431) and Condor (p428) do not. Platforms like the Multiprotocol Router and the Brocade 4100 cannot accept direct private storage attachment, but can co-exist seamlessly in networks with private storage attached to Loom, Bloom, and Bloom-II switches. Switches with private *storage* support include it as part of the base OS.

Private loop *initiators* (hosts) are the hardest case to solve. Not only do they require loop primitives and phantom logic, but they also require much more advanced fabric services enhancements.

An initiator normally queries the fabric name server for targets, and then sends IO to them. With *public initiators* talking to *private targets*, a switch can "notice" the IO from the initiator and automatically set up phantom logic NAT entries as needed. *Private initiators* do not know how to talk to the name server; they learn about available targets by probing their loop. They cannot send IO to a target until after NAT has been set up, so the automatic learning mechanism does not work.

The "Quick Loop / Fabric Assist" optionally licensed feature set is designed to address this need. Users explicitly define which devices a private host needs to access using zoning, and the switch creates the required NAT entries on that basis. QL/FA is supported as an optionally licensed feature on the SilkWorm 2xx0 series, and the SilkWorm 3200/3800 switches, i.e. all Fabric OS 2.x and 3.x platforms. QL/FA only applies to private initiators, not to any other usage case, and private initiators are the most rapidly declining segment of the SAN market. As a result, Brocade has not prioritized porting the feature to 4.x or beyond, except to support QL/FA on 2.x/3.x switches in the same fabric as 4.x switches. At the time of this writing, even that level of QL/FA support is essentially obsolete.

Multi-Switch Fabrics (E_Port)

The E_Port (Expansion Port) protocol allows switches to be interconnected to form a larger fabric: a single region of connectivity built from multiple discreet switching components.[110] This feature allows SAN solutions to be built using a "pay as you grow" approach, adding switches to a fabric as needed. It also allows much more flexible network designs, including support for geographical separation of components. Without this feature, the maximum scalability of a connectivity model would be limited to the number of ports on a single switch, and the maximum geographical radius of a network would be the distance supported by a node connected to that switch.

Today, the ability to network switches together to form a fabric seems commonplace, but when Brocade started selling switches for production use in 1997, it was a key differentiator. Most competitors could not do this at all, and the few that had the feature had many configuration constraints. Brocade was not just *a* pioneer in this space; Brocade was *the* pioneer. This is reflected in the fact that FSPF[111] was authored and given to the standards bodies by Brocade. Without this and other Brocade-authored protocols, it would not be possible much less commonplace to form multi-switch fabrics today.

Virtual Channels

A unique feature available in every Brocade 2Gbit and 4Gbit fabric switch, Brocade Virtual Channel (VC) technology represents an important breakthrough in the design of large SANs.[112] To ensure reliable ISL communications, VC technology logically partitions bandwidth within each ISL into many different virtual channels as shown in

---

[110] This also requires the interaction of other fabric services, such as the name server and zoning database processes, but Brocade keys the feature off of E_Port.

[111] The protocol used by all vendors to determine topology and path selection.

[112] Actually, even the SilkWorm 1xxx series of switches had a form of VC support, but it was quite different and not particularly relevant to SAN design today. But it is interesting to note that Brocade has already gone through four generations of VC development: it's a "well-baked" feature.

Figure 109, and prioritizes traffic to optimize performance and prevent head of line blocking.

Fabric Operating System automatically manages VC configuration, eliminating the need to manually tune links for performance. This technology also works in conjunction with trunking to improve the efficiency of switch-to-switch communications, and simplify fabric design.

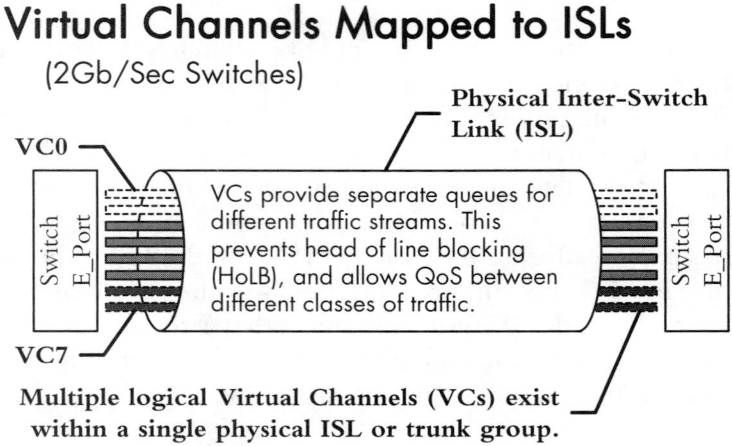

Virtual Channels Mapped to ISLs

(2Gb/Sec Switches)

Physical Inter-Switch Link (ISL)

VC0

Switch E_Port

VCs provide separate queues for different traffic streams. This prevents head of line blocking (HoLB), and allows QoS between different classes of traffic.

Switch E_Port

VC7

Multiple logical Virtual Channels (VCs) exist within a single physical ISL or trunk group.

Figure 109 - VCs Partition ISLs into Logical Sub-Channels

In 2Gbit Brocade products, there were a total of 8 VCs (0-7) assigned to any link. This could be internal links, ISLs, or trunk groups. Each VC had its own independent flow control mechanisms and buffering scheme.

In Brocades 4Gbit products, the Virtual Channel infrastructure has been greatly enhanced, and some of the automatic assignment mechanisms have been improved. There are now 17 VCs assigned to any given internal link: one for class F traffic and sixteen for data. Each data VC now has 8 sub-lists or sub-Virtual Channels; each of *those* has its own credit mechanism and independent flow control. SID/DID pairs are assigned in a round-robin fashion across all the VCs, but with these new enhancements, a better distribution is made. Of course, when connecting 4Gbit switches together with 2Gbit switches, the ISLs and trunk groups still use 8 VCs. This is done to avoid potential backwards compatibility issues.

In the near future, Brocade will be releasing a QoS feature which allows 4Gbit switches to use the increased VC capabilities to prioritize some flows above others in congested networks. As a practical matter, this feature is expected to apply almost exclusively to long distance connections in DR or BC solutions, since, for local-distance ISLs and IFLs, it is generally better to avoid congestion in the first place than it is to manage which devices are most harmed by congestion.

Buffer to Buffer Credits

Buffer-to-buffer (BB) credits are used by switch ports to determine how many frames can be sent to the recipient port, thus preventing a source device from sending more frames than can be received. The BB credit model is the standard method of controlling the flow of traffic within a Fibre Channel fabric.

Like VCs, BB credits are handled automatically by the Fabric Operating System in most cases. For extremely long distance links, it may be desirable to manually increase the number of credits on a port to maximize performance. (This may require an Extended Fabrics license.)

In the context of host or storage connections to a switch, the number of BB credits on a link will be negotiated between the device and the switch at initialization time. For ISL connections, each Virtual Channel will receive its own share of BB credits. In this case, credits are handled the same way whether the port is part of a trunk group or operating independently.

This topic is discussed in more detail under "FC Buffer-to-Buffer Credits" on page 281.

Access Gateway

Access Gateway uses the N_Port ID Virtualization (NPIV) standard to present blade server FC connections as logical nodes to fabrics. This eliminates entire categories of traditional heterogeneous switch-to-switch interoperability challenges. Attaching through NPIV-enabled switches and directors, Access Gateway seamlessly connects server blades to Brocade, classic-McDATA, or even to other vendors' SAN fabrics.

Traditionally, when blade server chassis have been connected to SANs, each enclosure would add one or two more switch domains to the fabric, which had a potentially disastrous effect on scalability. Increasing the number of blade enclosures also meant additional switch domains to manage, increasing day-to-day SAN management burden. These additional domains created complexity and could sometimes disrupt fabric operations during the deployment process. Finally, fabrics with large numbers of switch domains created firmware version compatibility management challenges: sometimes it was impossible to find a firmware version which was supported by all devices in the fabric.

To address these challenges, Access Gateway presents blade server NPIV connections rather than switch domains to the fabric. This means that Access Gateway can support a much larger fabric, and that switch firmware on the Access Gateway does not interact with the other switches in the fabric *as* a switch. Rather, it interacts as a node, which greatly reduces firmware dependencies. Unlike FC pass-through solutions, it can do all of this without substantially increasing the number of switch ports required.

To enhance availability, Access Gateway can automatically and dynamically fail over the preferred I/O connectivity path in case one or more fabric connections fails. This approach helps ensure that I/O operations finish to completion, even during link failures. Moreover, Access

Gateway can automatically fail back to the preferred fabric link after the connection is restored, helping to maximize bandwidth utilization.

Value Line Software

The Value Line software license packages reduce the cost of acquiring and deploying an entry-level SAN, while allowing software-key upgrades to full enterprise-class functionality. Designed for small and medium sized organizations, the Value Line integrates innovative hardware and software features that make it easy to deploy, manage, and integrate into a wide range of IT environments. These powerful yet flexible capabilities enable organizations to start small and grow their storage networks in a scalable, non-disruptive, and efficient manner. This is especially beneficial for organizations that need to upgrade their existing SAN environment with minimal disruption. In addition, they simplify administration through embedded Brocade WEBTOOLS software.

The main thing that SAN designers need to be aware of is that a Value Line switch might not have full fabric capabilities. In exchange for substantially reduced acquisition cost, the buyer of a Value Line switch would give up features such as fabric scalability (number of domains supported) or number of E_Ports allowed. When deploying a Value Line switch into a larger solution, it might therefore be necessary to upgrade its license key to a full fabric key.

Virtual Fabrics / Admin Domains

Virtual Fabrics allows the partitioning of one physical fabric into multiple logical fabrics that can be managed by separate Admin Domain administrators. Virtual Fabrics are characterized by hierarchical management, granular and flexible security, and fast and easy reconfiguration to adapt to new infrastructure requirements. They allow IT administrators to manage separate corporate functions separately, use different permission levels for SAN administrators, provide storage for teams in remote offices without compromising local SAN security, and increase levels of data and fault isolation without increasing SAN cost and complexity. Once Fabric OS 5.2.0 or later is installed in the SAN, Virtual Fabrics can be implemented on the fly with no physical topology changes and no disruption.

The Administrative Domains feature is the key enabler for Virtual Fabrics technology. Admin Domains create partitions in the fabric. Admin Domain membership allows device resources in a fabric to be grouped together into separately managed logical groups. For example, a SAN administrator might have the Admin role within one or more Admin Domains, but be restricted to the Zone Admin role for other Admin Domains.

Although they are part of the same physical fabric, Virtual Fabrics are separate logical entities because they are isolated from each other via several mechanisms such as:

Data isolation: Although data can pass from one Virtual Fabric to another using device sharing, and links can be shared among multiple Virtual Fabrics, no data can be unintentionally transferred even when Virtual Fabrics are not zoned.

Control isolation: Within Virtual Fabrics, fabric services are independent and are secured from unwanted interaction with other Virtual Fabric services. This includes zoning, RSCNs, and so on.

Management isolation: Switches in a Virtual Fabric provide independent management partitions. If a switch is a member of more than one Virtual Fabric, it has multiple, independent management entities. Administrators are authenticated to manage one or more Virtual Fabrics, but they cannot access management objects in other, unauthorized Virtual Fabrics.

Fault isolation: Data control or management failures in one Virtual Fabric will not impact any other Virtual Fabric services.

Admin Domain administrators can manage one or more Admin Domains while Virtual Fabric administrators have administrative permissions on all Admin Domains. Separate Admin Domains can be created for different operating systems (FICON®, Z-Series, and open systems FCP, for example).

Devices can easily be shared among different Admin Domains without any special routing requirements. Admin Domain administrators can configure and manage their own zones; they can configure all rights and devices as long as they have the Admin role for that particular Admin Domain. The Admin Domain feature is backwards compatible with the millions of Brocade SAN ports already deployed, and no new hardware is required.

Implementing Virtual Fabrics is straight-forward, and fits into existing SAN management models. The management and best practices used today in a pre-Fabric OS 5.2.0 physical fabric with zoning can be implemented in the same way in a Fabric OS 5.2.0 fabric with Admin Domains and zoning.

FCIP FastWrite and Tape Pipelining

FCIP is a method of transparently tunneling FC ISLs between two geographically distant locations using IP as a transport. Storage is often sensitive to latency, and throughput is a great concern as well. Unfortunately, IP networks tend to have high latency and low throughput compared to native FC solutions. Tape Pipelining and FastWrite are features available on the Brocade 7500 router and FR4-18i blade that improve throughput and mitigate the negative affects of IP-related delay.

Tape Pipelining refers to writing to tape over a Wide Area Network (WAN) connection. FastWrite refers to Remote Data Replication (RDR) between two storage subsystems. Tape is serial in nature, meaning that data is steadily streamed byte by byte, one file at a time onto the tape from the perspective of the host writing the file. Disk data tends to be bursty and random in nature. Disk data can be written anywhere on the disk at any time. Because of these differences, tape and disk are handled differently by extension acceleration technologies.

Tape Pipelining accelerates the transport of streaming data by maintaining optimal utilization of the IP WAN. Tape traffic without an accelerator mechanism can result in periods of idle link time, becoming more inefficient as link delay increases.

When a host sends a write command, a Brocade 7500/FR4-18i sitting in the data path intercepts the command, and responds with a "transfer ready". The router buffers the incoming data and starts sending that data over the WAN. The data is sent as fast as it can, limited only by the bandwidth of the link or the committed rate limit. On the heels of the write command is the write data that was enabled by the proxy target's transfer-ready reply. After the remote target receives the command, it responds with a transfer ready. The remote router intercepts that transfer ready, acts as a proxy initiator, and starts forwarding the data arriving over the WAN.

The host is on a high-speed FC network, and most often will have completed sending the data to the local router by this time. The local router returns an affirmative response. While the buffers are still transmitting data over the link, the host sends the next write command and the process is repeated on the host side until the host is ready to write a filemark. This process maintains a balance of data in the remote router's buffers, permitting a constant stream of data to arrive at the tape device.

On the target side, the transfer ready indicates the allowable amount of data that can be received, which is generally less than what the host sent. The transfer ready on the host side, from the proxy target, is for the entire quantity of data advertised in the write command. The transfer ready the proxy target responds with for the entire amount of data does not have to be the same as the transfer ready the tape device responds with, which may be for a smaller amount of data, that is, the amount that it was capable of accepting at that time. The proxy initiator parses out the data in sizes acceptable to the target per the transfer ready from the tape device. This may result in additional write commands and transfer readies on the tape side compared to the host side. Buffering on the remote side helps to facilitate this process.

The command to write the filemark is not intercepted by the routers and passes unfettered from end to end. When the filemark is complete, the target responds with the status. A status of OK indicates to the host that it can move on.

FastWrite works in a somewhat different manner. FastWrite is an algorithm that reduces the number of round trips required to complete a SCSI write operation. FastWrite can maintain throughput levels over links that have significant latency. The Remote Data Replication (RDR) application still experiences latency; but reduced *throughput* due to that latency is minimized.

There are two steps to a SCSI write:

1. The write command is sent across the WAN to the target. This is essentially asking permission of the storage array to send data. The target responds with an acceptance (FCP_XFR_RDY).

2. The initiator waits until it receives that response from the target before starting the second step, which is sending the actual data (FCP_DATA_OUT).

With the FastWrite algorithm, the local SAN router intercepts the originating write command and responds immediately requesting the initiator to send the entire data set. This happens in a couple of microseconds. The initiator starts to send the data, which is then buffered by the router. The buffer space in the router includes enough to keep the "pipe" full plus additional memory to compensate for links with up to 1% packet loss.[113] The Brocade 7500/FR4-18i has a continuous supply of data in its buffers that it can use to completely fill the WAN, driving optimized throughput.

The Brocade 7500/FR4-18i sends data across the link until the committed bandwidth has been consumed. The receiving router acts on behalf of the initiator and opens a write exchange with the target over the local fabric or direct connection. Often, this technology allows a write to complete in a single round trip, speeding up the process considerably and mitigating link latency by 50%.

There is no possibility of undetected data corruption with FastWrite because the final response (FCP_RSP) is never spoofed, intercepted, or altered in any way. It is this final response that the receiving device sends to indicate that the entire data set has been successfully received and committed. The local router does not generate the final response in an effort to expedite the process, nor does it need to. If any single FC frame were to be corrupted or lost along the way, the target would detect the condition and not send the final response. If the final response is not received within a certain amount of time, the write sequence times out (REC_TOV) and is retransmitted. In any case, the host initiator knows that the write was unsuccessful and recovers accordingly.

---

[113] If a link has more than 1% packet loss or more, it means that there are serious network issues that must be resolved prior to a successful implementation of FastWrite.

FC FastWrite

For native FC links or FC over xWDM, delay and congestion are typically one or more orders of magnitude better than with FCIP. However, the speed of light through glass still creates noticeable latency over long distance connections. As a result, it is possible for FC links over MAN/WAN distances to benefit from the same algorithms used in FCIP FastWrite. Brocade has added support for this feature to its 4Gbit router portfolio.

For example, it is possible to deploy FR4-18i blades into chassis at each side of a DR or BC solution, and attach storage ports directly to these blades. (This is illustrated in "10Gbit Blades and DR/BC Solutions" starting on page 296.) After configuring appropriate zoning policies, any replication or mirroring traffic between the storage ports will be accelerated using a similar mechanism to the one described in the previous section. This can sometimes result in massive increases in throughput, with the exact improvement depending on the distance, congestion of the network, block size, and the number of devices sharing the inter-site links.

Hot Code Load and Activation

Hot code load and activation supports the stringent availability requirements of mission-critical environments by enabling firmware upgrades to be downloaded and activated without disrupting other operations or disruption to data traffic in the SAN. The switch continues to route frames and provide full fabric services while new firmware is loaded onto its non-volatile storage. Once the download is complete, the new image is activated. During the activation process, the switch still continues to route frames, without losing even a single bit of data traffic.

Advanced ISL Trunking (Frame-Level)

Brocade ISL Trunking is ideal for optimizing perform-ance and simplifying the management of a multi-switch SAN fabric containing Brocade switches. When two, three, or four adjacent ISLs are used to connect two Bro-cade 2Gbit FC switches, the switches automatically group the ISLs into a single logical ISL, or "trunk." With 4Gbit switches, it is possible to trunk up to eight adjacent links. Traffic will be balanced across these links, while still guar-anteeing in-order and on-time delivery.

ISL Trunking is designed to significantly reduce traffic congestion in storage networks. When up to eight 4Gbit ISLs are combined into a single logical ISL, the aggregated link has a total bandwidth of 32 Gbit/sec which can sup-port a large number of simultaneous full-speed "conversations" between devices.

To balance workload across all of the ISLs in the trunk, each incoming frame is sent across the first available physical ISL in the trunk. As a result, transient workload peaks for one system or application are much less likely to impact the performance of other parts of the SAN fabric. Because the full bandwidth of each physical link is avail-able, bandwidth is not wasted by inefficient traffic routing. As a result, the entire fabric is utilized more efficiently.

Dynamic Path Selection (Exchange-Level)

Dynamic Path Selection (DPS) may also be referred to as exchange-level trunking. Like Advance ISL Trunking, DPS balances traffic across multiple ISLs. Unlike trunking, DPS does not require that the ISLs be adjacent. It uses the industry standard Fabric Shortest Path First (FSPF) algo-rithm to select the most efficient route for transferring data in multi-switch environments. Any paths which are deemed by FSPF to have equal cost will be evenly bal-anced by the DPS software and hardware. This is a particular advantage in core/edge networks with multiple core switches, since DPS can distribute load between different cores while Advanced ISL Trunking cannot do so.

DPS matches or outperforms all similar features from any vendor *except* for Brocade Advanced ISL Trunking. However, because DPS can be combined with frame-level trunking, organizations can achieve both maximum performance and availability.

Zoning

Brocade Zoning is a feature of all switch models. Using zoning, organizations can automatically or dynamically arrange fabric-connected devices into logical groups (zones) across the physical configuration of the fabric. It is functionally similar to VLANs from the IP networking world, though considerably more advanced in many ways. In fact, zones could be thought of as being a combination of VLAN controls plus firewall-like ACLs.

Providing secure access control over fabric resources, Zoning prevents unauthorized data access, simplifies heterogeneous storage management, segregates storage traffic, maximizes storage capacity, and reduces provisioning time.

The need for this kind of access control relates to the "roots" of SAN technology: the SCSI DAS model. Storage devices directly attached to hosts (DAS) have no need for network-based access control features: access by other hosts is precluded by the limitations of the DAS architecture. In contrast, SANs allow a potentially large number of hosts to access all storage in the network, not just the systems that they are *intended* to access. If each host is allowed to access every storage array, the potential impact of user error, virus infection, or hacker attacks could be immense. To prevent unintended access, it is necessary to provide access control in the network and/or the storage devices themselves.

There are many mechanisms for solving the SAN-based access control problem. All of them have some form of management interface that allows the creation of an access control policy, and some mechanism for enforcing that policy. Brocade switches and routers use a set of methods collectively referred to as "Brocade Advanced Zoning." Brocade Advanced Zoning requires a license key on all platforms, but all currently shipping platforms bundle this key with the base OS.

Using this key allows the creation of many zones within a fabric, each of which may be comprised of many "zone objects," which are storage or host PIDs or WWNs. These objects can belong to zero, one, or many zones. This allows the creation of overlapping zones. Every switch in the fabric then enforces access control for its attached nodes. Zone objects are grouped into zones, and zones are grouped into zone configurations. A fabric can have any number of zone configurations. This provides a comprehensive and secure method for defining exactly which devices should or should not be allowed to communicate.

Fabric OS CLI

All Brocade switches provide a comprehensive Command Line Interface (CLI) which enables manual "lowest common denominator" control, as well as task automation through scripting mechanisms via the switch serial port or telnet interfaces.

WEBTOOLS

Brocade WEBTOOLS is web-browser-based Graphical User Interface (GUI) for element and network management of Brocade switches. WEBTOOLS uses a set of processes (e.g. httpd) and web pages that run on all Fabric OS switches in a fabric. Once a switch or router has an IP address configured, it is possible to manage most functions simply by pointing a Java-enabled web browser at that address.

This product simplifies management by enabling administrators to configure, monitor, and manage switch and fabric parameters from a single online access point. Organizations may configure and administer individual ports or switches as well as small SAN fabrics. User name and password login procedures protect against unauthorized actions by limiting access to configuration features. WEB-TOOLS provides administrative control point for Brocade Advanced Fabric Services, including Advanced Zoning, ISL Trunking, Advanced Performance Monitoring, Fabric Watch, and Fabric Manager integration. For instance, administrators can utilize timesaving zoning wizards to step them through the zoning process.

While this is technically a licensed feature, like zoning, WEBTOOLS is included with all currently shipping Brocade platforms.

Fabric Manager

Fabric Manager is a flexible and powerful tool that provides rapid access to critical SAN information and configuration functions. It allows administrators to efficiently configure, monitor, provision, and other perform daily management tasks for multiple fabrics or Meta SANs from a single location. Through this single-point SAN management architecture, Fabric Manager lowers the overall cost of SAN ownership. It is tightly integrated with other Brocade SAN management products, such as Web Tools and Fabric Watch, and enables third-party product integration through built-in menu functions and the Brocade SMI Agent. Organizations can use Fabric Manager in conjunction with other leading SAN and storage resource management applications as the drill-down element manager for a single or multiple Brocade fabrics, or use Fabric Manager as the primary SAN management interface.

SAN Health

SAN Health is a powerful tool that helps optimize a SAN and track its components in an automated fashion. The tool greatly increases SAN manager productivity, since it automates many mandatory recurring SAN management tasks. It simplifies the process of data collection for audits and change tracking, uses a client/server "expert systems" approach to identify potential issues, and can be run regularly to monitor fabrics over time. This is especially useful to SAN designers in three ways:

- When designing changes to existing environments, the tool can help to audit the target environment before finalizing a design
- In any design context, it can help to document a SAN after implementation
- It can be specified in the SAN project plan as an ongoing proactive maintenance and change-control tool to satisfy manageability requirements

The tool has two software components: a data capture application and a back-end report processing engine. SAN managers may run the data capture application as often as needed. After SAN Health finishes capturing diagnostic data, the back-end reporting process automatically generates a point-in-time snapshot of the SAN, including a Visio topology diagram and a detailed report on the SAN configuration. This report contains summary information about the entire SAN as well as specific details about fabrics, switches, and individual ports. Other useful items in the report include alerts, historical performance graphs, and any recommended changes based on continually updated best practices.

The SAN Health program is powerful and flexible. For example, it is possible to configure many different fabrics in a single audit set, and schedule them to run automatically on a recurring basis. These audits can run in "unattended mode", with automatic e-mailing of captured data to a designated recipient.

The tool also has enhanced change-tracking features to show how a fabric has evolved over time, or to facilitate troubleshooting if something goes wrong. This can be an invaluable addition to the change-tracking process, both for most-mortem analysis *and* for proactive management. For instance, SAN Health can track traffic pattern changes in weekly or monthly increments. This can help to identify looming performance problems proactively, and take corrective action before end-users are affected.

SAN Health is currently available to SAN end-users and Brocade OEM and reseller channel partners. It can be used with Brocade install-base fabrics, and fabrics using equipment from selected other infrastructure vendors as well. The tool is available for download on the public Brocade web site (www.brocade.com/sanhealth). For partners, Brocade also provides a co-branded version.

Fabric Watch

Brocade Fabric Watch provides advanced monitoring capabilities for Brocade products. Fabric Watch enables real-time proactive awareness of the health, performance and security of each switch, and automatically alerts network managers to problems in order to avoid costly failures. Monitoring fabric-wide events, ports, and environmental parameters permits early fault detection and isolation as well as performance measurement.

With Fabric Watch, SAN administrators can select custom fabric elements and alert thresholds or they can choose from a selection of preconfigured settings for gathering valuable health, performance and security metrics. In addition, it is easy to integrate Fabric Watch with enterprise systems management solutions.

By implementing Fabric Watch, storage and network managers can rapidly improve SAN availability and performance without installing new software or system administration tools.

Advanced Performance Monitoring

Brocade Advanced Performance Monitoring is a comprehensive tool for monitoring the performance of networked storage resources. It enables administrators to monitor both "transmit" and "receive" traffic from source devices to destination devices, enabling end-to-end visibility into the fabric. Using this tool, administrators can quickly identify bottlenecks and optimize fabric configuration resources to compensate.

Extended Fabrics

Extended Fabrics software enables native Fibre Channel ISLs to span extremely long distances. Extended Fabrics optimizes switch buffering (BB credits) to ensure the highest possible performance on these long-distance ISLs. When Extended Fabrics is installed on gateway switches, the ISLs (E_Ports) are configured with a large pool of buffer credits. The enhanced switch buffers help ensure that data transfer can occur at full or near-full bandwidth to efficiently utilize the connection over the extended links. As a result, organizations can use Extended Fabrics to implement strategic applications such as wide area data replication, high-speed remote backup, cost-effective remote storage centralization, and business continuance strategies.

Remote Switch

Remote Switch is a now largely obsolete feature which enabled fabric connectivity of two switches over long distances by supporting external gateways to encapsulate Fibre Channel over ATM. Connecting SAN islands over Fibre Channel-to-ATM device enabled organizations to extend their solutions over a WAN. This type of configuration could be used for solutions such as remote disk mirroring and remote tape backup. While ATM extension may still be used, this method has largely been superseded by FC over SONET/SDH and native FC links using Extended Fabrics. For all such configurations, Brocade now supports an "Open E_Port" mode to support for Gateway/Bridge devices. Customers may simply use *portCfgISLMode* CLI command which is now part of the base OS: there is no need for a license anymore.

FICON / CUP

The Brocade directors and selected switches support the FICON protocol for mainframe environments, enabling organizations to utilize a single platform for both open systems and mainframe storage networks. FICON-certified Brocade platforms support the ability to run both open systems Fibre Channel and FICON traffic on a port-by-port basis within a single platform. The Brocade FICON implementation also supports cascaded FICON fabrics at 1 and 2 Gbit/sec FICON speeds.

With Fabric OS version 4.4, Brocade fully supports CUP in-band management functions, which enable mainframe applications to perform configuration, management, monitoring, and error handling for Brocade directors and switches. CUP support also enables advanced fabric statistics reporting to facilitate more efficient network performance tuning.

Fibre Channel Routing

The Brocade FC-FC Routing Service provides connectivity between two or more fabrics without merging them. Any platform it is running on can be referred to as an FC router, or FCR for short. At the time of this writing, the feature is available on the Brocade AP7420, the Brocade 7500, and the FR4-18i blade.

Basic Reference

The service allows the creation of Logical Storage Area Networks, or LSANs, which provide connectivity that can span fabrics. It is most useful to think of an LSAN in terms of zoning: an LSAN is a zone that spans fabrics. The fact that an FCR can connect autonomous fabrics without merging them has advantages in terms of change management, network management, scalability, reliability, availability, and serviceability to name just a few areas.

The customer needs for this product are similar to those that brought first routers and then Layer 3 switches to the data networking world. An FC router is to an FC fabric as an IP router is to an Ethernet subnet. Early efforts were made to create large, flat Ethernet LANs without routers. These efforts hit a ceiling beyond which they could not grow effectively. In many cases, Ethernet broadcast storms would create reliability issues, or it would become impossible to resolve dependencies for change control. Perhaps merging Ethernet networks that grew independently would involve too much effort and risk. An analogous situation exists today with flat Fibre Channel fabrics. Using an FCR with LSANs solves that problem, while other proposed solutions – such as VSANs – just move the problem around in a shell-game effort to confuse users.

For more information about this feature, see the book *Multiprotocol Routing for SANs* by Josh Judd.

FCIP

Fibre Channel over IP (Internet standard RFC 3821) is one of several mechanisms available to extend FC SANs across long distances. FCIP transparently tunnels FC ISLs across an intermediate IP network, making the entire IP MAN or WAN appear to be an ISL from the viewpoint of the fabric. This is available as a fully-integrated feature on the Brocade AP7420 Multiprotocol Router, the Brocade 7500 router, and the FR4-18i blade.

It is important to note that FCIP is neither the only nor always the best approach to distance extension. The major advantages of FCIP are cost and ubiquitous availability of IP MAN and WAN services. However, for users interested in reliability and performance, it is theoretically impossible for FCIP – or any other IP SAN technology for that matter – to match native FC solutions. Generally speaking, SAN designers prefer distance extension solutions in the following order:

1. Native FC over dark fiber or xWDM
2. FC over SONET/SDH
3. FC over ATM
4. FC over IP

Many of the shortcomings of FCIP can be mitigated – though not eliminated – by using FastWrite and/or Tape Pipelining. (p379) In fact, before the advent of FC Fast-Write, it was sometimes even possible to achieve better performance on a 1Gbit FCIP link than a 4Gbit FC link. FCIP should therefore almost always be used in combination with some form of write acceleration technology.

For more information about this feature, see the book *Multiprotocol Routing for SANs* by Josh Judd.

Secure Fabric OS

As organizations interconnect larger and larger SANs over longer distances and through existing networks, they have an ever greater need to effectively manage their security and policy requirements. To help these organizations improve security, Secure Fabric OS™, a comprehensive security solution for Brocade-based SAN fabrics, provided policy-based security protection for more predictable change management, assured configuration integrity, and reduced risk of downtime. Secure Fabric OS protected the network by using the strongest, enterprise-class security methods available. With its flexible design, Secure Fabric OS allowed organizations to customize SAN security in order to meet specific policy requirements. All Secure Fabric OS features have now been made available in the base OS for free as of Fabric OS 5.3.0. It is recommended that customers migrate to that solution as it provides additional features such as DH-CHAP to end devices (HBAs) and is also more scalable.

Return on Investment Calculation

This section provides guidance on ways to calculate the Return on Investment (ROI) for the SAN project. For a more comprehensive evaluation of the benefits of a SAN, it is better to perform a Total Cost of Ownership (TCO) analysis. However, TCO is harder to calculate, and ROI analysis may be sufficient in many cases, so this is usually where a designer would start.

In fact, even doing a detailed ROI analysis is not needed in most cases. This should be done only if the stakeholders responsible for signing off on the SAN budget have asked for it. For example, if the SAN is being deployed in order to meet a legal requirement for a disaster recovery solution, the implementation is mandatory, so analyzing the financial ROI could be meaningless. After all, if the legal requirement is not met, it could cause an organization-wide disaster, so most stakeholders would agree that the deployment is needed regardless of the financial ROI analysis. Many organizations also put in a SAN based on a total cost of ownership justification, which may not require ROI justification.

For installations which *do* require it, the ROI analysis method below will provide a useful guideline for how to approach the project. It is not intended to be viewed as a hard and fast procedure set, indicating the only "right" way of calculating ROI, but simply as a starting point. In many organizations, there is already an established methodology for ROI calculations, in which case the following guidelines can be mapped into the existing processes.

394

Some of the sources of SAN ROI include:

- Additional revenue or productivity gains generated during backups that - prior to the SAN - required taking systems off line.
- Similar gains generated through higher average system or application uptime
- Lower IT management costs and increased productivity generated through the centralization of resources.
- Significantly shorter process time for adding and re-configuring storage.
- Reduced capital spending through improved utilization of space on shared storage.

To perform an ROI analysis for a SAN, the following steps can be used:

- Identify the servers and applications which will participate in the SAN. (This should already have been done previously in the planning process. Refer to "Chapter 5: Project Planning" starting on page 119.)
- Select ROI scenarios. These are the primary functions that the SAN is expected to serve, such as storage consolidation or backups.
- Determine the gross business-oriented benefits of this scenario. E.g. how much money will the company save by purchasing fewer storage arrays?
- Determine costs to achieve this benefit. (Again, this should already have been done in a previous step in the planning process.)
- Calculate the net benefits. Essentially, this means subtracting the costs from the benefits.

ROI Analysis Objectives

An ROI analysis can focus on specific themes which generally have business relevance. This will help IT organizations demonstrate the financial value of the SAN. The Brocade ROI model clarifies in non-technical terms the benefits of SANs, quantifying the financial benefits to demonstrate real-world ROI. Five key SAN benefit themes which are often used for ROI analysis are:

- **Improved storage utilization**: SAN-enabled access to enterprise storage will result in economies of scale
- **Improved availability of information**: Enterprises are increasingly relying on information to control costs and improve their competitive advantage. SAN-enabling access to storage (where the information resides) will make that information more available by keeping the systems processing the information running longer. Backups (and restores) will finish quicker in SAN-enabled environments. The result is that mission critical information is at the disposal of the enterprise more of the time.
- **Improved availability of applications**: SAN solutions dramatically reduce application downtime – both scheduled and unscheduled. Global enterprises can profit from the extra availability.
- **More effective storage management**: SAN-based solutions are easier to manage because they tend to be centralized. Centralization translates to increased operational control and management efficiencies. These are directly related to cost reductions.
- **Foundation for disaster tolerance**: Certain elements of SAN-enabled solutions create the opportunity for improved disaster tolerance as a by-product of the architecture. Examples include remote backups, disk-to-disk-to-tape backups, data mirroring or replication, and inter-site applications failovers.

Analysis Step 1: Identifying Nodes and Apps

The first step is to define important servers, their applications, and their associated storage. This should have been done during the requirements gathering phase of the SAN planning process. Then group them according to the *role* they play. For example, an organization might have back-end database servers, front-end application servers, email servers, web servers, and servers hosting network file systems such as NFS or CIFS.

Using data from the inventory of existing equipment, define groups of servers performing similar tasks. For each server-group, define the average amount of direct-attached storage they currently have configured. Also define for each server-group how fast their storage capacity is growing and how much space they need to leave unoccupied on storage arrays to grow into for a given year. (I.e. how much headroom each requires.) Also define the availability requirements for each server group, if you have not already done so.

Analysis Step 2: Selecting Scenarios

In the beginning of this chapter we discussed the business requirements of the SAN. The requirements define a set of ROI scenarios. This next section illustrates how to process three common scenarios: Storage consolidation, backup and restore, and high availability clustering. (These and other scenarios are discussed in "Chapter 2: SAN Solutions" starting on page 49.) In your own analysis, include *all* business-oriented benefits which the SAN will provide.

Storage Consolidation

The goal of this scenario is to migrate from traditional Directly Attached Storage (DAS) to SAN-based storage. Two benefits to consider are (1) reduced need for storage headroom (a.k.a. "white space"), and (2) reduced downtime associated with storage adds, moves, and changes. See "Storage Consolidation" starting on page 49 for a description of this scenario.

Backup and Restore

This scenario addresses backup and restore savings opportunities based on performance. It is assumed that an existing enterprise network-based distributed backup/restore facility is already in place, e.g. sending backup data to a tape server via a LAN. If that is *not* true, then the ROI will be greater. See "Tape Consolidation / LAN-free Backup" starting on page 58 for a description of this scenario.

High Availability Clustering

High Availability (HA) clustering is a method of improving of the availability of applications. Normally in HA configurations, a standby server stands at the ready to "step in" for a failing production server. If the production server fails, the applications are transferred to the standby server through partially or totally automated means. In addition to protecting against failures, HA clusters can be used to reduce planned downtime for upgrades or changes to a server hardware platform. In this case, an administrator would manually trigger an application failover (usually called a "switchover" in this context) to the standby server, perform maintenance on the primary, and then manually move the application back once the maintenance was complete and verified.

Most HA configurations have a dedicated standby server for every production server they are protecting. One reason for is the inability to attach more than two computers to external SCSI disk arrays. The resulting 1:1 ratio of primary to hot standby servers means a very costly HA facility, which – in practice – means that most applications are not included in HA clusters, and are therefore exposed to outages during failures or planned hardware maintenance operations. See "High Availability Clustering" starting on page 53 for a more comprehensive discussion of this topic.

Analysis Step 3: Determine Benefits by Scenario

Once you have decided which scenarios apply to your SAN by looking at the business problems which it will address, it is time to calculate the benefits of those scenarios. When calculating ROI, benefits are commonly divided into two types: hard benefits, and soft benefits.

"Hard" benefits include any benefits for which a specific monetary savings or revenue increase can be identified with a high degree of confidence. For example, it is often relatively easy to assign specific values to reduced capital expenditures, operational budget savings, and gains through some kinds of staff productivity increases.

"Soft" benefits include items for which specific monetary savings are more difficult to define. One typical example is opportunity costs. It may be difficult to assign an exact value to the opportunity cost of degraded performance, system downtime for repairs, lengthy backup windows, or lengthy data restoration times. The characterization of a benefit as "soft" does not imply that it is less important; just that it is harder to prove exactly how much money it is worth.

Remember while reading the remainder of this section that each of the benefits listed below can be classified as either hard or soft. Also remember that *costs* will be calculated in a subsequent step; this section is only about *benefits*.

Storage Consolidation

Benefits of storage consolidation can be calculated by evaluating the savings of eliminating unused white space on storage (a.k.a. excess headroom), which is a "hard" benefit, and the savings obtained by the elimination of some of the downtime associated with upgrading server-attached storage, which is usually a "soft" benefit.

Headroom savings are *deferred* savings, which means that the organization will get benefits in the future, and will continue to get the benefits perpetually instead of merely having a one-time savings. If the overall storage capacity keeps expanding in an organization, so will the requirement for storage headroom. Of course, this is true of both SAN and DAS environments. The difference is that the demand for storage headroom will always be proportionally lower in a SAN. So as long as the need for storage grows over time, the benefits of the SAN will keep growing, too.

The benefit of reduced downtime includes the savings obtained by eliminating much of the downtime associated with upgrading storage. If an administrator adds a new storage array to a SAN, configuring servers to access it can be completely non-disruptive, and much of the configuration can be performed by management software. Adding storage in a DAS environment usually requires rebooting or even disassembling servers, which is costly in administrative time as well as causing an application outage.

 Side Note

It is possible to achieve ROI through improved management of storage, or through economies of scale in purchasing power achieved by using few large arrays instead of many small units.

Here is an example of how storage consolidation ROI might be discussed in the SAN project planning document:

Notes on ROI of Storage Consolidation

In our current environment, we have 60% unused space on our storage arrays, on average. This ranges from 1% free space on some arrays, to over 95% free space on others. I estimate that we will need to spend $x to purchase new arrays over the next year, if we continue to use directly attached storage. This is be-

cause the servers currently at the "1% free" end of the spectrum will need to grow their storage pool, but cannot access the arrays attached to the servers at the "95% free" end. I.e. we have plenty of free space, but no way to get the servers which need it to the arrays which have it. By putting in a SAN, we should be able to avoid all of the new array purchases this year, and for most of next year as well. This means that we will directly save more than $x through implementing a SAN.

In addition, the SAN will increase the uptime of each server. Today, each time a server runs out of space, we need to schedule an outage to add another disk, controller, or array. In some cases, this is no problem, but in others, it is extremely disruptive to our business. For example, the manufacturing line relies on several of the servers which are currently almost out of space. It may be necessary to shut down the line to add more disk. Shutting down the line costs $y per hour. Last year, we had to take four hours of manufacturing line outages for storage upgrades, and next year is projected to be even higher. Therefore we will save in excess of $4y per year in downtime by putting in the SAN.

Total First Year Benefit: *$x due to reduced array purchases because of white space optimization, plus $4y from reduced downtime on the manufacturing line.*

An ROI benefit expressed as a dialogue such as the one above will often be translated into another form to satisfy an accountant. This is often just a spreadsheet, with little or no supporting text. However, it is usually not the responsibility of the SAN designer to do this translation. Rather, the technical team would normally provide this kind of dialogue to an accounting department member.

Backup and Restore

The backup scenario contracts the backup window, thus reducing amount of time the servers are unavailable or have degraded performance because their data is being backed up. Shrinking the backup window creates savings for the organization through increased productivity, whether or not the applications need to be taken off line. Even if they are still online during the operation, performance is often degraded quite a bit. This is often a "soft" benefit, though it might be quantifiable for mission-critical applications.

In addition to speeding up backups, a SAN will speed up restore operations. A restore will occur when data is lost or corrupted, and in most cases, operations at the organization will be disrupted while waiting for this to complete. The ROI to an organization for improved restore time is the reduced opportunity cost of being unable to operate between the time of a data loss and the final restoration of data. Typically, the metrics for quantifying this will involve productivity decreases and lost revenue during the outage.

In many cases, it is easy to determine the cost of an outage to a system. The previous scenario gave the example of a manufacturing line, which had a defined cost of downtime. However, in that example, the SAN project manager had a good idea of how many outages could be avoided. By looking at historical growth for storage array data, it is possible to make defensible projections about future growth. This told the SAN project manager which arrays were likely to run out of space. It is harder to predict which systems will have corrupted filesystems, or in which cases user error will require a restoration. Avoidance of unplanned downtime has to be calculated based on statistical probabilities: what is the percentage chance that a restoration will need to happen on any given server? How long is that likely to take without a SAN? How long will it take *with* a SAN? Once you know how much time a SAN would save in restoring from a *hypothetical* downtime event, and how much per hour uptime of the system is worth, you multiply the savings times the probability of the event occurring to get the benefit of the shorter restore time.

This example calculates the savings realized through improved backup and restore performance alone. Another possibility is consolidating many small tape drives onto fewer larger libraries. This can create a significant economy of scale when buying new tape libraries, and can reduce management costs as well. Yet another way to achieve backup savings via a SAN is to consolidate white space on tapes, in much the same way that the previous scenario consolidated space on disk drives. Each tape in a backup set is only partially used. Depending on the backup software used, it may be possible to put backups from multiple servers onto a single tape, thus filling it more completely. This is generally *not* possible with DAS tape solutions. Over time, the savings achieved by using up fewer tapes could be significant.

For example, take the manufacturing line SAN again. That SAN might be performing backups as well as consolidating storage arrays. The SAN project manager might make an entry in the planning document like this:

Notes on ROI of SAN-Enabled Backups

The manufacturing line has to run backups once a day. When we do this, the server response time drops by 50%, and as a result, the line runs 50% slower. That window currently lasts one hour. 50% performance degradation for one hour on the line costs at least $x in lost revenue. The SAN will reduce that window to six minutes, or 90% of the window. In addition, the SAN-enabled software is more efficient, and will lower the performance impact to the application during the remaining window, though it will not be possible to quantify that until implementation time. This means that we will directly save more than **0.9 times $x** *through implementing a SAN.*

In addition, using centralized tape libraries will allow us to compress white space out of backup tapes. Currently, our average tape utilization is 50%. With the SAN, our utilization will reach increase enough to use 10% fewer tapes. We cur-

rently spend $y per month on tapes, so the SAN will save **0.1 times $y** *each month. Since our storage needs increase over time, this benefit will increase as the SAN ages.*

Finally, the SAN will reduce downtime during data restorations. Last year, the manufacturing line had two hours of downtime for restores. If we assume that the same things will happen next year, the higher performance of SAN-enabled restorations will reduce the restoration time by 25% or more. Total downtime for the line costs $z per hour, so the SAN will save an estimated **0.75 times 2 times $z**. *Another way to estimate the potential for needing to restore data is to look at the overall odds of a failure occurring. By taking the mean time between failures (MTBF) and mean time to repair (MTTR) of all components in the manufacturing systems into account, I estimate the probability being 50% that we will have four hours of downtime due to component failures. A 50/50 chance of four hours of downtime means that avoidance of the risk is worth 50% of the cost of the outage. This is* **0.5 times 0.75 times 4 times $z***, which reduces down to the same equation as the two hour estimate above.*

Total First Year Benefits: *0.9 times $x due to increased productivity on the manufacturing line from backup window reduction, plus 0.1 times 12 times $y from reduced monthly tape consumption, plus an estimated 0.75 times 2 times $z from hypothetical reduced restoration times.*

In general, the cost of downtime will vary by server class. The example above showed only one class of server: the platforms running applications critical to the manufacturing line. In most large-scale SANs, there will be more than one class of server attached. For example, the SAN might connect both the manufacturing servers above, and also the corporation's email servers and fileservers. Each class of server should have its own separate valuation for uptime. Even servers for which "hard" uptime numbers are unavailable should be included in the ROI analysis as a "soft" benefit, with an indication that the exact financial value is unknown.

High Availability Clustering

SANs and complementary software products eliminate many of the restrictions traditionally associated with HA solutions, and allow solutions based on clusters of more than two servers. Larger clusters allow for a single platform to serve as a standby for more than one primary server. (I.e. SANs allow an n:1 ratio of primary to hot standby servers.) This dramatically reduces the cost of protecting applications. This is illustrated in Figure 17 and Figure 18 starting on page 54.

In addition to achieving ROI through lowered cost of protecting mission-critical applications, SANs also expands the number of applications which can be cost-justified to participate in an HA solution. That means that an organization can achieve ROI through increased uptime and associated productivity / revenue gains for the services which would otherwise not have been protected.

The benefits of HA clustering can be found by calculating the savings on both planned and unplanned downtime for all protected server classes, and the savings on equipment obtained by implementing n:1 HA cluster instead of using a 1:1 primary/standby design. Additional savings can be calculated by accounting for the reduced the maintenance cost for all protected server classes over a year. I.e. having fewer total platforms in the solution means buying maintenance contracts on fewer machines, and – statistically – reducing the number of repairs needed.

Once again, take the manufacturing line SAN as an example. There could be four critical applications required to support the line, one of which (application number "a4") spans two platforms. An outage to either platform causes an outage to a4. The project manager might make an entry in the planning document like this:

Notes on ROI of SAN-Enabled HA Cluster

The manufacturing line has four critical applications: a1, a2, a3, and a4. The value of protecting these applications via an HA solution is increased uptime for the manufacturing operation. Previously, the value of uptime for the line was show to be $x per hour. Last year, we had two outages to the line caused by failures of these applications, which could have been avoided by clustering them. The total avoidable downtime to repair them was four hours. Assuming that the same events occurred over the next year, the avoided cost would be **4 times $x**. *Using the MTBF and MTTR of all related components to calculate the statistical probability of a failure in the line shows that there is a 25% chance of eight hours of avoidable downtime.* **0.25 times 8 times $x** *reduces to* **2 times $x**, *which is lower than the previous estimate. We will use midpoint for this analysis, and say that HA protection will likely save the company more than* **3 times $x** *in downtime for each year of operation. This is a conservative estimate, particularly since our business is growing. This means that the number of servers requiring protection will increase, which will increase the likelihood of an avoidable failure and the cost of failures not avoided, so the benefit of clustering will increase substantially in subsequent years. In addition to unplanned failures, we had to take four hours of planned downtime last year, and expect the same for next year. Half of that would be avoidable with a cluster, so the total downtime reduction is* **5 times $x** *for both planned and unplanned downtime.*

There are two approaches to building this HA solution: we can dedicate a hot standby server for each application platform, or we can use a SAN to allow one standby platform to protect all of the production servers.

The a4 application spans two hosts, so there are a total of five servers which need to be protected. This will require five standby servers in the first method, or just one in the second. The difference is four extra platforms, vs. installing a SAN. Accounting for software package and operating system licenses, maintenance *contracts, and projected staff time for performing maintenance, each extra server costs $y, so the SAN will save* **4 times $y** *on hardware, software, and maintenance.*

This benefit will accelerate with time. The clustering package we propose to use allows up to z platforms to be protected by a single hot standby server, so we will include several lower-tier applications in the cluster as well. This will still leave room for projected increases in the number of manufacturing line servers required for the next year, so we can add to the cluster without increasing its cost.

Total First Year Benefits: 5 times $x *due to increased productivity on the manufacturing line from downtime reduction, plus* 4 times $y *from reduced hardware, software, and maintenance cost. We would also receive "soft" benefits from having lower-tier applications protected by the cluster.*

It is also worth mentioning that one SAN can support many clusters. The benefits of protecting the manufacturing line might easily justify the cost of the SAN by themselves, but whether they do or not, it would often be possible to connect other mission-critical hosts to the same SAN even if they are in a different cluster or even if they use a completely different *kind* of clustering software. While evaluating SAN ROI, look at all of the applications which could benefit from SAN attachment, whether or not they are the immediate focus of the project.

Combined Solutions

This brings up the topic of combined SAN solutions. Historically, almost all SANs were built as application-specific islands. However, today's SANs are increasingly heterogeneous, with one SAN supporting not just different applications, but indeed supporting hardware and software from different vendors. The SAN used in the preceding examples could support a storage consolidation solution, a tape backup / restore solution, and an HA clustering solution. The benefits of the SAN would come from all three use cases, but the cost of the infrastructure would only need to be paid once. Always look for other applications which could benefit from SAN attachment even if one particular application is "driving" the project. To the extent that any can be identified, see if they can be quantified as "hard" benefits. In most cases, even if the SAN is initially envisioned only to host one application, over time more and more uses will inevitably come to light. Even if there are no initial plans to include other uses, it is appropriate to include some discussion of this principle in the ROI analysis as a "soft" benefit.

Analysis Step 4: Determine Associated Costs

The next step is to determine the costs required to achieve the benefits. As this cost determination is being done in the early stages the cost used will be preliminary estimates. If you are following the overall SAN project plan discussed in this chapter, you will already have a good idea about the costs of the project at this stage. If this is the case, utilize this information and proceed to the step five on page 409.

If you do *not* already have a cost estimate, you will need to make one. To create an estimate, the top-level SAN architecture must be defined. The architecture need not be correct in every detail: for a SAN of any complexity, it will have to be refined as the project progresses. It only needs to be sufficient for budgetary purposes, which means knowing more or less how many ports you will need to buy, and their HA characteristics.

Create an estimate of costs for each scenario. Treat each scenario independently and create discreet ROI calculations for each. This will allow you to determine the most effective strategy for justifying the SAN infrastructure. However, this means that the analysis will contain duplicated elements. For example, one switch port used for an ISL will support traffic from a backup solution, a storage consolidation solution, and an HA cluster solution. Therefore you should present an aggregate ROI as opposed to the sum of the individual ROI analysis numbers to show the real cost savings.

Analysis Step 5: Calculate the ROI

In step three, you showed the *gross* benefits of a SAN. I.e. you showed how much money the SAN would save or help to produce, but did not take into account the costs to achieve those benefits. In this step, you will produce an estimate of the *net* benefit that the SAN will deliver: the benefits minus the costs.

There are a number of ways to calculate ROI. Two of the most common methods are Internal Rate of Return (IRR) and Net Present Value (NPV). Here are commonly used "accountant" definitions of the two methods:

IRR: The discount rate to equate the project's present value of inflows to present value of investment costs.

NPV: The sum of a project's discounted net cash flows (present values including inflow and outflows, discounted at the project's cost of capital).

What do you actually *do* to calculate either of those? One answer is, "get an accountant to do it." In fact, most organizations have a preferred method for performing an ROI calculation, and have accounting departments which would insist on being the ones to perform the analysis in any case, so this is the answer that most SAN designers will use.

However, it is sometimes useful for the SAN project team to estimate the ROI of the project before discussing it with accounting. To do a rough ROI estimate, simply subtract any identified costs from any quantified benefits. In the example used throughout the previous sections, the manufacturing line would receive benefits from three dif-

ferent sources. Add all three up to get a total first-year figure. Then add up the costs of the project as estimated in
previous steps. Subtract the second number from the first,
and that is how much "hard" benefit the SAN will provide in the first year of operations. An accountant would
also need to take equipment depreciation into account,
and might look at ROI over a longer timeframe, but this
should at least give the SAN design team an idea of how
the ROI analysis will come out.

The key to ROI is to be sure you have identified and
accounted for all of the benefits. Many things in life tend
to have hidden costs – such as the maintenance problems
associated with buying a used car. However, some things
also have hidden benefits – such as the reduction in administrative   overhead   inherently   associated   with
implementing a SAN. As long as the ROI analysis includes
all costs and all benefits – both hard and soft – it will give
you a good idea about whether or not a SAN is right for
your organization.

Ethernet and IP Network Equipment

This section does not provide a comprehensive tutorial
on Ethernet or IP equipment. Nor is it intended to sup-
plement the manuals for those products. It is simply a
high-level discussion of how such equipment relates to the
Brocade AP7420 Multiprotocol Router, and other Brocade platforms.

Ethernet L2 Edge Switches and Hubs

It is possible to use commodity 10/100baseT hubs
and/or switches to attach to the Ethernet management
ports of an FC switch or router. It is *not* recommended to
use hubs for data links to iSCSI hosts or for FCIP connections, since performance on hubs is rarely sufficient for
even minimal SAN functionality.

410

When connecting to iSCSI hosts, it is *possible* to use accelerated Gigabit Ethernet NICs with optical transceivers to connect hosts directly to the router. However, this is not *recommended*: this approach has much higher cost and much lower performance than attaching the host to a Fibre Channel switch using a Fibre Channel HBA. The value proposition of iSCSI vs. Fibre Channel only works if the low-end hosts are attached via already existing software-driven NICs to a low-cost Ethernet edge switch. Many iSCSI hosts then share the same router interface. There are many vendors who supply Ethernet edge switches. Figure 110 shows an example from Foundry Networks. (http://www.foundrynetworks.com)

Figure 110 - Foundry EdgeIron 24 GigE Edge Switch

IP WAN Routers

When connecting to a WAN in an FCIP solution, it is usually necessary to use one or more IP WAN routers. These devices generally have one or more Gigabit Ethernet LAN ports and one or more WAN interfaces, running protocols such as SONET/SDH, frame relay, or ATM. They almost always support one or more IP routing protocols like OSPF and RIP. Packet-by-packet path selection decisions are made at layer 3 (IP).

Figure 111 (p412) shows an IP WAN router from Tasman Networks. (http://www.tasmannetworks.com) There are many other vendors who supply IP WAN routers, such as Foundry Networks (Figure 112).

Make sure that the WAN router and service are both appropriate for the application. Two considerations to keep in mind when selecting a WAN router for SAN extension are performance and reliability. Most WAN technologies were not intended for either the performance or reliability needs of SANs.

Figure 111 - Tasman Networks WAN Router

Figure 112 - Foundry Modular Router

Finally, for redundant deployments it is strongly desirable for a WAN router to support a method such as the IEEE standard VRRP. Such methods can allow redundantly deployed routers to fail over to each other and load balance WAN links while both are online. Figure 113 shows one way that an IP WAN router might be used in combination with the Multiprotocol Router.

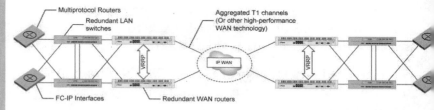

Figure 113 - WAN Router Usage Example

In this example, there are two sites connected across a WAN using FCIP. The Multiprotocol Routers each have two FCIP interfaces attached to enterprise–class Ethernet switches. These are connected redundantly to a pair of WAN routers, which are running VRRP.

Copper to Fiber Gigabit Ethernet Converter

Some IT organizations supply Gigabit Ethernet connections using copper 1000baseT instead of 1000baseSX or LX. To connect copper Ethernet ports directly to optical FCIP or iSCSI ports - e.g. on a Brocade AP7420 - is not possible. One solution is to use a Gigabit Ethernet switch with both copper and optical ports, attaching the router to the optical ports and the IT network to the copper ports. A product such as the Foundry switch shown in Figure 110 (p411) could be used in this manner. Alternately, a media converter (sometimes called a "MIA") can be used. There are a number of vendors who supply such converters. TC Communications is one example. (www.tccomm.com)

Figure 114 - Copper to Optical Converter

Appendix B: Advanced Ref.

This chapter provides advanced material for readers who need the greatest possible in-depth understanding of Brocade products and the underlying technology. It is not necessary for the vast majority of Brocade users to have this information. It is provided for advanced users who are curious, for systems engineers who occasionally need to troubleshoot very complex problems, and for OEM personnel who need to work with Brocade on new product development.

Routing Protocols

This subsection is intended to clarify the uses for the different routing protocols associated with the multiprotocol router, and how each works at a high level. Broadly, there are three categories of routing protocol used: intra-fabric routing, inter-fabric routing, and IP routing. The router uses different protocols for each of those functions.

To get from one end of a Meta SAN to another may require all three protocol groups acting in concert. For example, in a disaster tolerance solution, the router may connect to a production fabric with FSPF, use OSPF to connect to a WAN running other IP routing protocols, and run FCRP within the IP tunnel.

FSPF: Intra-Fabric Routing

Fabric Shortest Path First (FSPF) is a routing protocol designed to select paths between different switches within the same fabric. It was authored by Brocade and subsequently became the FC standard intra-fabric routing mechanism. [114] [115]

FSPF Version 1 was released in March of 1997. In May of 1998 Version 2 was released, and has completely replaced Version 1 in the installed base. It is a link–state path selection protocol. FSPF represents an evolution of the principles used in IP and other link-state protocols (such as PNNI for ATM), providing much faster convergence times and optimizations specific to the stringent requirements of storage networks.

The protocol tracks link states on all switches in a fabric. It associates a cost with each link and computes paths from each port on each switch to all the other switches in the fabric. Path selection involves adding the cost of all links traversed and choosing lowest cost path. The collection of link states (including cost) of all the switches in a fabric constitutes the topology database.

FSPF has four major components:

- The FSPF hello protocol, used to identify and to establish connectivity with neighbor switches. This also exchanges parameters and capabilities.
- The distributed fabric topology database and the protocols and mechanisms to keep the databases synchronized between switches throughout a fabric
- The path computation algorithm
- The routing table update mechanisms

The first two items must be implemented in a specific manner for interoperability between switches. The last two are allowed to be vendor-unique.

---

[114] Much of the content in this subsection was adapted from "Fabric Shortest Path First (FSPF) v0.2" by Ezio Valdevit.

[115] This and other Fibre Channel standards can be found on the ANSI T11 web site, http://www.t11.org.

The Brocade implementation of FSPF allows user-settable static routes in addition to automatic configuration. Other options include Dynamic Load Sharing (DLS) and In-Order Delivery (IOD). These affect the behavior of a switch during route recalculation, as, for example, during a fabric reconfiguration.

This feature works in concert with Brocade frame-by-frame trunking mechanisms. Each trunk group balances traffic evenly on a frame-by-frame basis, while FSPF balances routes between different equal-cost trunk groups.

The Brocade Multiprotocol Router further enhances FSPF by providing an optionally licensed exchange-based dynamic routing method that balances traffic between equal cost routes on an OX_ID basis. (OX_ID is the field within a Fibre Channel frame that uniquely defines the exchange between a source and destination node.) While this method does not provide as even a balance as frame-by frame trunking, it is more even than DLS.

FCRP: Inter-Fabric Routing

The Fibre Channel Router Protocol (FCRP) is used for routing between different fabrics. It was designed to select paths between different FC Routers on a backbone fabric, to coordinate the use of xlate domains and LSAN zoning information, and to ensure that exported devices are presented consistently by all routers with EX_Ports into a given edge fabric. Like FSPF, this protocol was authored by Brocade. At the time of this writing it is in the process of being offered to the appropriate standards bodies. (T11)

Within FCRP, there are two sub-protocols: FCRP Edge and FCRP Backbone.

The FCRP Edge protocol first searches the edge fabric for other EX_Ports. If it finds one or more, it communicates with them to determine what other fabrics (FIDs) their routers have access to, and to determine the overall Meta

SAN topology. It checks the Meta SAN topology, looking for duplicate FIDs and other invalid configurations. Assuming that the topology is valid, the routers hold an election to determine ownership of xlate phantom domains for FIDs that they have in common.

For example, if several routers with EX_Ports into the FID 1 fabric each have access to FID 5, one and only one of them will "own" the definition of network address translation to FID 1 from FID 5. This router will request a domain ID from the fabric controller for the xlate domain intended to represent FID 5, and will assign PIDs under that domain for any devices in LSANs going from FID 5 to FID 1. All of the other routers with FID 5 to FID 1 paths will coordinate with the owner router and will present the xlate domain in exactly the same way. If the owner router goes down or loses its path to FID 5, another election will be held, but the new owner must continue to present the translation in the same way as the previous owner. (In fact, all routers save all translation mappings to non-volatile memory and even export the mappings if their configurations are saved to a host.)

Note that the owner of the FID 5 to FID 1 mapping does *not* need to be the same as the owner of e.g. the FID 4 to FID 1 mapping. Each xlate domain could potentially have a different owner.

It is important to stress that the Fibre Channel standard FSPF protocol works in conjunction with FCRP. Existing Fibre Channel switches can use FSPF to coordinate with and determine paths to the phantom domains projected by the router, but only because FCRP makes the phantom domain presentation consistent.

On the backbone fabric, FCRP operates using ILS 0x44. It has a similar but subtly different set of tasks. It still discovers all other FC Routers on the backbone fabric, but instead of operating between EX_Ports it operates between domain controllers. For each other FCR found, a router will discover all of its NR_Ports and the FIDs that they represent, each of which yields a path to a remote fabric. It will determine the FCRP cost of each path. Finally, it will transfer LSAN zoning and device state information to each other router.

When the initial inter-fabric route database creation is complete, routers will be consistently presenting EX_Ports with xlate domains into all edge fabrics, each with phantom devices for the appropriate LSAN members. Into the backbone fabrics, routers will present one NR_Port for each EX_Port. This is another situation in which FCRP and FSPF work together: FCRP allows the NR_Ports to be set up and their activities coordinated. Once traffic starts to flow across the backbone, it will flow between NR_Ports. FSPF controls the path selection on the standard switches that make up the backbone.

Side Note

Not only FSPF and FCRP are complementary. On an FCIP connection in a Meta SAN, all routing protocol types plus layer 2 protocols like trunking and STP can apply to a single connection. STP works outside the tunnel on LANs between FCIP gateways and WAN routers, IP protocols like OSPF work through the WAN outside the tunnel, FSPF operates at the standard FC level inside the tunneled backbone fabric, and FCRP operates above FSPF but still within the tunnel.

FCR Frame Header Formats

The FC-FC Routing Service defines two new frame headers: an encapsulation header and an Inter-Fabric Addressing (IFA) header. These are used to pass frames between NR_Ports of routers on a backbone fabric. These extra headers are inserted by the ingress EX_Port and interpreted and removed by the egress EX_Port.

The format for these headers going to be submitted for review in the T11 FC Expansion Study Group and is subject to change. Since frame handling is performed by a programmable portion of the port ASIC on router platforms, header format changes can be accommodated without hardware changes.

The Inter-Fabric Addressing Header (IFA) provides routers with information used for routing and address translation. The encapsulation header is used to wrap the IFA header and data frame while it traverses a backbone fabric. This header is formatted exactly like a normal FC-FS standard header, so an encapsulated frame is indistinguishable from a standard frame to switches on the backbone. This ensures that the router is compatible with existing switches, unlike proprietary tagging schemes proposed by other vendors.

Zoning Enforcement Mechanisms

This subsection discusses three different *enforcement* mechanisms used in zoning, including when each is used, and what the significance is in each case. For a high level discussion of zoning, see "Zoning" on p385.

"Software Zoning" – SNS Enforcement

When an HBA logs into a Fibre Channel fabric, it queries the name server to determine the fabric addresses all storage devices. The most basic form of zoning is to limit what the name server tells a host in response to this inquiry. Hosts cannot access storage devices without knowing their addresses, and the SNS[116] inquiry is the only way they should have of obtaining that information. If the name server simply does not tell a host about any storage devices other than the ones it

---

[116] Both Fibre Channel and iSCSI support automatic device discovery through a name server. In Fibre Channel, the service is known as the "Storage Name Server," or SNS. In iSCSI, it is known as the iSNS. This subsection discusses FC SNS zoning, but a similar mechanism works with the iSNS.

is allowed to access, then it will never try to violate the access control policy.

SNS zoning works well unless the HBA driver is defective in a significant and specific way and/or the host is under control of a *very* skilled attacker. It does rely on each host to be a "good citizen" of the network, but in most cases this is a safe assumption.

SNS zoning is always used in Brocade SANs if zoning is enabled at all, but it is *always* supplemented by one or both of the two "hardware" methods below.[117]

"Full Hardware Zoning" – Filtering Every Frame

In the per-frame hardware zoning method, switches program a table in destination ASIC ports with all devices allowed to send traffic to that port. This is in addition to SNS zoning, not instead of it.

For example, if the access control policy for a fabric allows a host to "talk" to a storage device, then the ASIC to which the storage is attached will be programmed with a table entry for that host. It will drop any frame that does not match an address in the table.[118] This method is very secure. Even if a host tries to access a device that the SNS does not tell it about (extremely rare but theoretically possible) hardware zoning will prevent frames from that host from reaching the storage port.

---

[117] The exceptions are the SilkWorm 1xx0 or 2xx0 series switches. The SilkWorm 1xx0 switches did not support hardware zoning at all, and the SilkWorm 2xx0 switches only supported hardware zoning for policies defined by PID, not by WWN.[117] All 200, 3xx0, 4xx0, 12000, 24000, and 48000 products support one or both hardware zoning methods in all usage cases. In other words, all Brocade switches shipped in this century.

[118] Note that there is no performance penalty for hard zoning with Brocade ASICs.

However, in very large configurations it is possible to exceed the table size for a destination port.[119] If this happens on a particular storage port, the per-frame hardware zoning method will usually still be in force on the host port, which is sufficient to prevent access. Even if all ports in a fabric were to exceed zoning table size limitations (*highly* unlikely) all now-shipping Brocade switches can fall back to the "Session Hardware Zoning" method.

Another limitation on hardware zoning is related to WWN zoning vs. "Domain, Port", or *PID* zoning. In the older "Loom" switches, WWN zones were software enforced, and only PID zones would be enforced by hardware. With all currently shipping switches, full hardware enforcements is available whether using WWN or PID zoning definitions, but only for zones that contain WWNs *or* PIDs. If a single zone uses both WWNs *and* PIDs, that zone will use session hardware zoning.

"Session Hardware Zoning" – Command Traps

If the fabric access control policy results in a zoning table larger than a destination ASIC can support, or if a zone contains both WWNs and PIDs, then some ports on the affected chip(s) will use the second hardware zoning method. In addition to SNS enforcement, certain command frames (e.g. PLOGI) will be trapped by the port hardware and filtered by the platform control processor.

This is effectively like the previous method, except that hardware filtering is not done on *all data frames*, which is why it is called *session* hardware zoning. This works because Fibre Channel nodes require command frames to allow communication: data frames sent without command frames will be ignored by destination devices. For example, if a host cannot

---

[119] Each generation of Brocade ASIC has improved the zoning subsystem, but it is never possible to support "infinitely large" tables within an ASIC.

PLOGI into a storage device, the storage should not accept data from the host since PLOGI is needed to setup a session context in the storage controller.[120] Any frames that managed to get past both SNS zoning and hardware-based session command filtering should be dropped by the destination node.

Since this is based on a category of frame rather than a device address, there is no theoretical limit to the number of devices supportable with this method, short of the main system memory and CPU resources on the platform CP. Since the trap is implemented in hardware, it is still secure and efficient.

FC Protocols and Standards

All Brocade products adhere to applicable standards wherever possible. In some cases, there may not be a ratified standard. For example, there is no standard for upper-level FC-FC routing protocols at this time, so Brocade created FCRP in much the same way that Brocade created FSPF when there was a vacuum in the standards for switch to switch routing. Brocade has in fact either authored or co-authored essentially every standard used in the Fibre Channel marketplace. While Brocade tends to offer such protocols to the standards bodies, there is no guarantee that they will be adopted by competitors.

Some of the applicable standards include FC-SW-x, FC-FLA, FC-AL-x, FC-GS-4, FC-MI-2, FC-DA, FCP-x, FC-FS, and FC-PI-x.

---

[120] This is effective unless the storage device has a serious driver defect. That small chance is the main reason why Brocade implements "full" hardware zoning whenever possible, but as a practical matter the "command" version works fine. There has never been a reported case of an initiator accessing a storage device protected by "command" zoning, even in a lab environment in which experts were trying to achieve that effect.

For more information on these and other Fibre Channel standards, visit the ANSI T11 website, www.t11.org.

 Side Note

Gigabit Ethernet was created by "bolting on" some of the existing Ethernet standards on top of 1Gbit FC layers. Few IP network engineers realize it, but all optical Gigabit Ethernet devices still use Fibre Channel technology today.

Brocade ASICs

Brocade adds value as a SAN infrastructure manufacturer by developing custom software and hardware. Much of the hardware value-add comes from the development of Application-Specific Integrated Circuits (ASICs) optimized for the stringent performance and reliability requirements of the SAN market.[121] Brocade has been building best-in-class custom silicon for SAN infrastructure equipment since 1995. This also enables greater software value-add, since custom silicon is required to enable many software features like hardware zoning, frame-filtering, performance monitoring, QoS, and trunking. This subsection discusses several[122] Brocade ASICs, and shows how their feature sets evolved over the years.

ASIC Evolution

Brocade takes an "evolution, not revolution" approach to ASIC engineering. This balances the need to add as much

---

[121] ASICs are customized microchips designed to perform a particular function very well. Brocade uses ASICs developed in-house as opposed to using generic "off the shelf" technology designed to perform different tasks such as IP switching. Most other FC vendors use off the shelf technology.

[122] Brocade has developed a number of ASICs that are not yet being shipped, and thus are not included in this work. Register on the *SAN Administrator's Bookshelf* website to receive updated content as additional chips become generally available.

value as possible with the need to protect customer investments and de-risk new deployments. Each generation of Brocade ASICs builds upon the lessons learned and features developed in the previous generation, adding features and refinements while maintaining consistent low-level behaviors to ensure backward and forward compatibility with other Brocade products, as well as hosts and storage. Brocade has been developing ASICs for a decade now, with each generation becoming more feature-rich and reliable than the last.

Side Note

The ASIC names used in this subsection are the internal-use Brocade project codenames for the chips. Brocade codenames generally follow a theme for a group of products. There have been three different themes for ASICs to date: fabric-related, bird-related, and music-related. Platforms and software packages also have codenames, but their external "marketing" names are used throughout this book. This is not done with ASICs because Brocade does not have external-use names for ASICs.

Stitch and Flannel

The first ASIC that Brocade developed was called Stitch. Development on Stitch began in 1995. It was initially introduced to the market in the SilkWorm 1xx0 series of Fibre Channel switches in 1997. (See "SilkWorm 1xx0 FC Switches" on p355.)

Stitch had a dual personality: it could act as either a 2-port front-end Fibre Channel fabric chip, or a back-end central memory switch. The SilkWorm 1xx0 motherboards had a set of back-end Stitch chips, and accepted 2-port daughter cards that each had one front-end Stitch. The ASIC could support F_Port and E_Port operations on those cards. However, it could not support FL_Port.

Advanced Reference

To address that gap, Brocade developed the Flannel ASIC. Flannel could act as a front-end loop chip on a daughter board, but could only act as an FL_Port. It was therefore necessary to configure a SilkWorm 1xx0 switch as the factory for some number of fabric ports and some number of loop ports. Once deployed, the customer would need to live with the choices made at the time the switch was ordered. Furthermore, there was no way to make device attachment entirely "auto-magic;" it could matter which port a user plugged a device into.

Loom

The second-generation Brocade ASIC, Loom, was designed to replace both Stitch and Flannel. The new ASIC lowered cost, improved reliability, and added key features. The first Loom-based products were introduced in 1999.

The port density of the chip was increased from 2-port to 4-port, and each Loom had the personalities of both Stitch and Flannel. Four Looms could be combined to form a single non-blocking and uncongested 16-port central memory switch. This substantially lowered the component count in the SilkWorm 2xx0 series platforms, improving reliability as well as lowering cost. (See "SilkWorm 2xx0 FC Switches" on p357.)

Feature improvements were made in many areas, including PID-based hardware zoning, larger routing tables, and improved buffer management. Updated "phantom logic" was introduced to support private loop hosts. (The QL/FA feature.) Virtual channels were added to eliminate blocking on inter-switch links.

One of the most important features that Loom introduced was the U_Port. All three port types (F, FL, and E) could exist on any interface, depending on what kind of device was attached to the other end of the link. Switches using Loom could auto-detect the port type of the remote device: a substantial advance in "plug and play" usability. Auto-detecting switch ports came to be known as a Universal Ports (U_Ports) and the SilkWorm 2800 running the Loom ASIC was the first in the industry to support this feature.

Loom enjoyed remarkable success and longevity. Brocade shipped well over a million Loom ports, and still has a very high percentage of them active in the field, despite the length of time for which the chip has been shipping. Brocade has therefore continued to support backwards compatibility with Loom-based products in all subsequent ASICs and platforms.

Bloom and Bloom-II

Bloom was designed to replace Loom, again lowering cost, improving reliability, and adding features.

Bloom first appeared in 2001 in the SilkWorm 3800 switch. It had eight ports per ASIC, and two Blooms could be combined to form a single non-blocking and uncongested 16-port central memory switch called a "Bloom ASIC-pair." (One ASIC-pair is what powered the SilkWorm 3800, for example.) Because this ASIC had more ports than its predecessor, Brocade named the chip by adding a "B" in front of "Loom" to indicate that it was Bigger than Loom.

Bloom also increased the port speed to 2Gbit, doubling performance vs. Loom. In addition, the new ASIC added better hardware enforced zoning (both PID- and WWN-based), frame-level trunking to load-balance groups of up to four ports, frame filtering, end-to-end performance monitoring, and enhanced buffer management to support longer distances on extended E_Ports. The chip also had routing table support allowing many chips to be combined to form a 128-port single-domain director (SilkWorm 24000).

The Bloom-II ASIC has such minor changes to Bloom that it is considered a simple refinement, not a new generation. A new process was used in its design to shrink the size of each chip, lowering power and cooling requirements. Additional test interfaces were added to improve manufacturing

Advanced Reference

yield and reliability. Buffer management was improved to allow longer distance links at full 2Gbit speed.

At the time of this writing, Bloom is still shipping in the SilkWorm 12000 port blade and the SilkWorm 3800 switch. It was also used in the SilkWorm 3200 and 3900 switches, and in a number of OEM embedded products. Bloom-II is still shipping in the SilkWorm 3250 and 3850 switches, and in the SilkWorm 24000 blade set. (See both "Currently Shipping Brocade Platforms" on p323 and "Installed Base Brocade Platforms" on p355.)

Condor

The fourth generation ASICs from Brocade have code-names related to birds. Condor is the fourth-generation Fibre Channel fabric ASIC, and the first of its generation to become generally available. It builds upon the previous three ASIC generations, adding significant features and improving reliability to an unprecedented degree. At the time of this writing, Condor is shipping in the Brocade 4100 and 4900 switches, and Brocade 48000 director.

Like previous Brocade ASICs, Condor is a high-performance central memory switch, is non-blocking, and does not congest. It builds on top of the advanced features that Brocade added to Bloom-II.[123] However, Condor has many major enhancements as well, and is not simply a "Bloom-III." It is truly a fourth-generation technology.

Condor has thirty-two ports on a single chip, with each port able to sustain up to 4Gbits per second (8Gbits full-duplex) in all traffic configurations. Each chip has 256Gbits of cross-sectional bandwidth. It was designed to support single-

---

[123] Except for private loop support. This is near end of life based on declining customer demand, so priority was given to other features. Private loop devices are almost entirely out of circulation already, and the little remaining demand can be met by using Bloom-based switches in the same network as Condor platforms.

domain director configurations much larger than the Bloom-II-based SilkWorm 24000, in which case the platform cross-sectional bandwidth will be *massively* higher. For example, if the Brocade 48000 is configured with 128 4Gbit Condor ports, its internal cross-sectional bandwidth is 1Tbit. The number of virtual channels per port has also been increased to allow non-blocking operation in larger products and networks.

The doubling in port speed is only the beginning of Condor's performance enhancements. Frame-based trunking has been expanded to support 8-way trunks, yielding 32Gbits (64Gbits full-duplex) per trunk. Exchange-based load balancing (DPS) is possible between either trunked or non-trunked links. (See "Link Balancing" starting on page 220.) Two Condor ASICs networked together with half of their ports could sustain 64Gbits (128Gbits full-duplex) between them, and far more bandwidth could be sustained between Condor-based blades in directors. In fact, combining multiple Condor ASICs running 4Gbit links with frame and exchange trunking can yield 256Gbit evenly balanced paths.

Condor also improves control-plane performance. Each ASIC can offload the platform CP from many node login tasks. When a Fibre Channel device attempts to initialize its connection to the fabric, previous ASICs would forward all login-related frames to the CP. Condor is capable of performing much of this without involving the CP, which improves switch and fabric scalability as well as response time for nodes.

The ASIC memory systems have also been improved. Buffer management and hardware zoning tables are the primary beneficiaries of this. A centralized buffer pool allows better long distance support.: any port can receive over 200 buffers out of the pool. Centralized zoning memory allows more flexible and scalable deployments using "full" hardware zoning. (See "Zoning Enforcement Mechanisms" on p420 for more information about the different zoning enforcement mechanisms.)

Goldeneye

Goldeneye, like Condor, is part of the fourth-generation Fibre Channel fabric ASIC set from Brocade, and the second of its generation to become generally available. It builds upon the previous three ASIC generations, adding significant features and improving reliability to an unprecedented degree. At the time of this writing, Goldeneye is shipping in the embedded switches and Brocade 200e switch.

Like previous Brocade ASICs, Goldeneye is a high performance central memory switch, is non-blocking, and does not congest. It builds on top of the advanced features that Brocade added to Bloom-II. However, Goldeneye has many major enhancements as well, and is not simply a "Bloom-III." It is truly a fourth-generation technology.

Goldeneye has 24 ports on a single chip, with each port able to sustain up to 4Gbits per second (8Gbits full duplex) in all traffic configurations. Each chip has 192Gbits of cross-sectional bandwidth. It was designed to support highly dense products such as the embedded blade server switches.

The doubling in port speed is only the beginning of Goldeneye's performance enhancements: Frame-based trunking can support up to 4-way trunks, yielding 16Gbits (32Gbits full-duplex) per trunk. Exchange-based load balancing (DPS) is possible between either trunked or non-trunked links.

Goldeneye also improves control-plane performance. Each ASIC can offload the platform CP from many node login tasks. When a Fibre Channel device attempts to initialize its connection to the fabric, previous ASICs would forward all login-related frames to the CP. Goldeneye is capable of performing much of this without involving the CP, which improves switch and fabric scalability as well as response time for nodes.

The ASIC memory systems have also been improved. Buffer management and hardware zoning tables are the primary beneficiaries of this. A centralized buffer pool allows better long distance support: any port can receive over 200 buffers out of the pool. Centralized zoning memory allows more flexible and scalable deployments using "full" hardware zoning.

Egret

Egret is a bridge chip which takes three internal 4Gbit FC ports on a blade, and converts them into a single external 10Gbit FC interface. At the time of this writing, it is used only on the FC10-6 blade (p343), which has six Egret chips connected to two Condor ASICs. From a performance standpoint, an Egret-Egret ISL can be thought of as functionally identical to a three-port by 4Gbit frame-level trunk.

The are differences, however. The Egret approach uses $1/3^{rd}$ of the number of fiber optic strands or DWDM wavelengths, which can produce substantial cost-savings in some long distance solutions. On the other hand, 10Gbit FC requires more expensive XFP media, more complex and thus more expensive blades, and single-mode cables, which can increase cost massively for shorter-distance ISLs. As a result, it is expected that Egret will only be used for DR and BC solutions. In addition to aggregating three interfaces into one, the Egret chip also contains its own buffer-to-buffer credit memory, allowing each and every 10Gbit port to support a full-speed connection over dark fiber or xWDM of up to 120km.

FiGeRo / Cello

The FiGeRo and Cello chips power the Brocade Multiprotocol Router (AP7420). Both ASICs were acquired when Brocade bought Rhapsody Networks. The platform consists of sixteen FiGeRo chips (one per port) interconnected via one Cello that acts as a cell switching fabric.

FiGeRo was codenamed to follow a music theme. (As in, "The Marriage of Figaro.") The "Fi" and "Ge" components of the name refer to the fact that a FiGeRo ASIC can act as either a Fibre Channel port or a Gigabit Ethernet port. Cello got its name by being a cell switching ASIC.

Each FiGeRo ASIC has fixed gates to perform frame-level functions efficiently, and three embedded RISC processors plus external RAM to give each port exceptional flexibility for higher-level routing and application processing functions. Currently, the Multiprotocol Router running FiGeRo supports FC fabric switching, FC-to-FC routing, FCIP tunneling, and iSCSI bridging. More advanced fabric applications are being developed by Brocade and its partners. In fact, at the time of this writing, several ILM and UC applications for this architecture are just beginning to ship.

Similar functionality is expected to be available throughout the Brocade product line by the end of 2005.

Multistage Internal Architectures

Modular switches like SAN directors always require internal connectivity between discrete components over a midplane or backplane. It is not possible or even desirable to have, for example, a single-ASIC director. Some of the major benefits of a bladed architecture are that customers can select different blade types for different applications, swap out old blades one at a time during upgrades, and have the overall system continue to operate even in the face of failures on some component. A single-chip solution would prevent all of these features and more from working. As a result, all such products from all vendors have some chips on port blades, some other chips on control processor blades, and (typically) some chips on back-end data-plane switching blades. The Brocade directors are no exception.

There are many different approaches that can provide the required chip-to-chip connectivity. It is possible to use shared memory, a crossbar, a cell switch, or a bus, to name just a few approaches that have been used in the networking industry. A director might have connectivity between front-end protocol blades via a crossbar using "off the shelf" commodity chips, or it might use native Fibre Channel connections between blades using SAN-optimized ASICs. High-speed packet switches for both Ethernet and Fibre Channel use shared memory designs for highest performance. Commodity Ethernet switches often use crossbars to lower research and development costs, thus increasing short-term profits for investors at the expense of long-term viability and customer satisfaction. It is also possible for more than one option to be combined within the same chassis, which is often known as a *multistage* architecture.

Most Brocade products are single-stage central memory switches, often consisting of just one fully-integrated chip. However, some of the larger products use multistage designs to support the required scalability and modularity. All of internal-connectivity approaches from all vendors have an *internal topology*, a set of *performance characteristics*, and a set of *protocols*, much like a network.[124] The arrangement of the chips and traces on the backplane or midplane create the topology, and the chips connected to this topology have link speed and protocol properties. Indeed, it is possible to make many analogies between networks and internal director designs, no matter what connectivity method is used.

Brocade multistage switches use central memory ASICs with back-end connections based on the same protocol as the front-end ports. This avoids the performance overhead associated with protocol conversions that affect other designs like

----

[124] While the internal connectivity in a chassis does not work exactly the same way that an external network works, they do have enough in common that this provides a useful analogy.

crossbars. The back-end connectivity is an enhanced Fibre Channel variant called the "Channeled Central Memory Architecture." (CCMA) The connections between ASICs are therefore called CCMA Links. While these are enhanced beyond standard FC links in a number of ways, the payload and headers of frames carried by the CCMA Links use an <u>un</u>modified, native Fibre Channel frame format. This allows the director to operate efficiently and reliably.

The use of CCMA links defines protocol characteristics, but there are variations in terms of other performance characteristics and topology depending on *how* CCMA connections are made. (I.e. the back-end topology of a director is the geometrical arrangement of the back-end ASIC-to-ASIC links, much the same way as the topology of a SAN is the arrangement of ISL connection.) The remainder of this subsection discusses two variations on the Brocade CCMA multistage architecture in detail.

SilkWorm 12000 and 3900 "XY" Architecture

The Brocade SilkWorm 12000 is a highly available Fibre Channel Director with two domains of 64 ports each, and the SilkWorm 3900 is a high-performance 32-port midrange switch. Both platforms can deliver full-duplex line-rate switching on all ports simultaneously using a non-blocking CCMA multistage internal architecture. This section discusses the details of how ASICs are interconnected inside the two products, and provides some analysis of how that structure performs.

SilkWorm 12000 Blade Interconnections

The SilkWorm 12000 chassis (Figure 105 p363) is comprised of up to two 64-port domains, each of which may contain up to four 16-port cards. Each card is divided into four 4-port groups known as quads. Viewed from the front and the side, a blade is constructed as depicted in Figure 115.

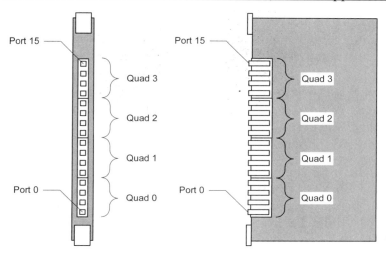

Figure 115 - SilkWorm 12000 Port Blades

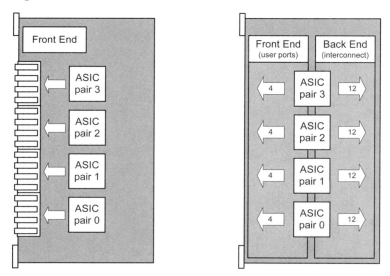

Figure 116 - SilkWorm 12000 ASIC-to-Quad Relationships

The SilkWorm 12000 uses a distributed switching archi-tecture. Each quad is a self-contained 16-port central memory switching element, comprised of two ASICs. Four ports of each quad are exposed outside the chassis, and may be used to attach FC devices such as hosts and storage arrays, or for Inter-Switch Links (ISLs) to other domains in the fabric. The remaining twelve ports are used internally, to interconnect the quads together, both within and between blades. This means that the SilkWorm 12000 actually has three ports of internal bandwidth for each port of external bandwidth: a 1:3 undersubscribed design. Viewed logically from the side, the ASIC-to-quad relationship on a blade can be viewed in either of the ways shown in Figure 116.

The interconnection mechanism used to tie the quads together involves connecting each quad directly to every other quad in the same row and column with one internal 4Gbit CCMA link. Each link uses two internal ports plus frame-level trunking to achieve 4Gbit full-duplex bandwidth on its path. Three of the six links are vertical (within a blade) and three are horizontal (between blades). Within a blade, the connection pattern is as shown in Figure 117.

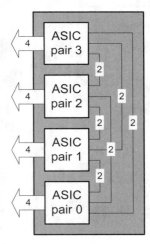

Figure 117 - SilkWorm 12000 Intra-Blade CCMA Links

Each of the four quads has four ports for front-end connections, and six ports (three 4Gbit VC links) going to the other quads within that blade. (Each of the lines with a "2" in the figure represents 2x2Gbits balanced with frame trunking.) Figure 118 provides a more abstract depiction of this.

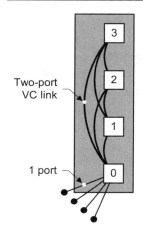

Two-port
VC link

1 port

Figure 118 - SilkWorm 12000 CCMA Abstraction

Each <u>one</u> curved vertical line represents a <u>4Gbit</u> internal trunk. Each numbered box is a quad, which has four external connections, represented by the four "pins" attached to quad 0. The diagram represents one SilkWorm 12000 port blade.

In addition to the three vertical back-end 4Gbit CCMA links within the blade, each quad has three horizontal back-end 4Gbit links to the other three blades in the domain. The overall interconnection within a SilkWorm 12000 64-port domain can be viewed like Figure 119.

This matrix connection method is known as the "XY" method, since the internal CCMA links follow a grid. The name comes from mathematics. The horizontal connections are called "X" connections, since that is the variable traditional used to represent the horizontal axis on a graph. The vertical connections are called "Y" links.

If the source and destination quads are in the same row, the director will use one X-axis internal CCMA "hop" to get between them, since there is a direct connection available. This adds just 700 or so nanoseconds of latency. If they are in the same column, it will use one Y-axis hop. Look back at the figure. See how any two quads in the same row or column are directly connected? This shortest path" will always

Advanced Reference

be used if it is available. If the source and destination are in different rows and columns, there is no direct connection. In that case, in the default shipping configuration, the platform will route traffic between any two quads using an X-then-Y formula: first the frame will traverse a horizontal CCMA link to an intermediate ASIC, then it will take the vertical link to the destination ASIC.

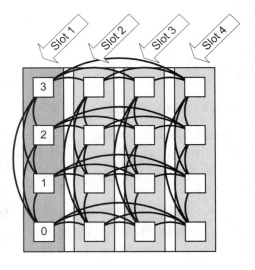

Figure 119 – SilkWorm 12000 64–Port CCMA Matrix

SilkWorm 3900 Port Interconnections

SilkWorm 3900 internal connections are similar to those in the SilkWorm 12000 port blade. The platform consists of four ASIC-pairs wired together in an XY topology. Since there are no other blades to connect to, all of the links are used to connect the ASIC-pairs into a square. Each quad has eight external ports, and eight internal ports. Like the 12000, traffic will take a direct path if it is available, and will take an X-then-Y path if moving diagonally.

"XY" Performance Analysis

There are three ways to evaluate performance of a network product: theoretical analysis, empirical stress-testing, and real-world performance testing.

From a theoretical standpoint, both XY products have more than adequate performance. There is more bandwidth used to interconnect the quads together on a 12000 than there is input bandwidth on the front-end of the switch. This is referred to as an *under-subscribed* architecture: for each quad, there are fewer ports subscribed to the backend than there is bandwidth on the backend by a ratio of one-to-three, usually written 1:3. (Four front-end connections to twelve back-end ports reduces to a ratio of 1:3.) This is 8Gbits of front-end bandwidth feeding into 24Gbits of total back-end bandwidth per quad. The SilkWorm 3900 has a 1:1 subscription relationship: 16Gbits of input feeding into 16Gbits of back-end CCMA link capacity.

 Side Note

For almost all users, all Brocade multistage platforms have "plug and play" performance, and the information in this section is only provided to satisfy curiosity. However, for advanced users who need to tune their applications for ultimate performance, the topology information below can be relevant. The rule of thumb is this: It is worth taking the time to understand the internal topology of a multistage product only if it is necessary to run all ports on the platform full-speed, full-duplex, for sustained periods, and there will be a business impact if even a few of the ports run slower than the theoretical maximum possible line rate.

While the front-end ports cannot generally flood all of the back-end bandwidth on the SilkWorm 12000, it is theoretically possible for certain traffic patterns to exhibit congestion due to an *imbalanced usage* of this bandwidth. To determine if theoretical limits of a platform can be exhibited in the real world, empirical testing can be performed. This has been done extensively by Brocade, by third parties such as networking magazines, major customers, and independent laboratories, and – of course – by other switch vendors. In every case, the conclusion was the same: the XY products produce uncongested operation in any real-world and most purely contrived traffic patterns. Even incredibly stressful traffic configurations such as a full mesh test will produce no congestion.

For example, it is possible to connect all 32 ports of a SilkWorm 3900 to a SmartBits™ traffic generator. Using their management tool, the SmartBits can be configured to send traffic flows from every port on the switch to every other port. This is known as a full mesh traffic pattern, and is generally acknowledged as one of the most stressful traffic configurations possible. Figure 120 illustrates an eight node full mesh and a sixteen node full mesh. Each box represents a port on the switch, and each line a pair of flows.

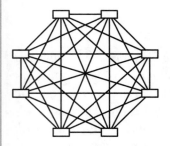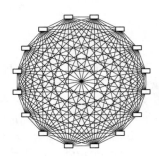

Figure 120 – Full-Mesh Traffic Patterns

Clearly, there are quite a few simultaneous traffic flows in these configurations. When testing the SilkWorm 3900 with a 32-port full mesh, far more connections are in play, and yet all 32 ports show full-speed, full-duplex performance. Similarly, the SilkWorm 12000 will perform at peak with a 64-port full mesh.

It seems unlikely based on this that any given environment would experience any internal performance bottlenecks related to the XY CCMA architecture. If that ever did happen, there are a number of options for tuning XY performance. For example, following Brocade's tradition of supporting localized switching, each group of four ports on the 12000 (quad) and eight ports (octet) on the 3900 can switch locally without even using the XY traces. This provides users who take advantage of known locality the opportunity to optimize performance still further.

Brocade 24000 and 48000 "CE" Architecture

The Brocade 24000 and 48000 chassis (Figure 106 p365 and Figure 78 p331 respectively) are functionally equivalent to that of the SilkWorm 12000. Both are CCMA multistage directors, though the products use different backplane traces. Both of the newer directors can exhibit uncongested operation both in theory *and* in empirical testing.

In the Brocade 24000, each port blade has two Bloom-II (p427) ASIC-pairs which expose eight ports to the user, and have equivalent bandwidth used for backplane CCMA links: any given octet has 16Gigabits (32G full-duplex) of possible external input, and the same bandwidth available to connect to any other octet. Local switching can be done within an 8-port group.

The Condor-based (p428) Brocade 48000 has 16-, 32-, and 48-port blades. Local switching is possible within a 16-port group on the first two, and a 24-port group on the 48-port blade. In each case, the director has 64Gbits of internal bandwidth per slot (128Gbits full-duplex) *in addition* to the local switching bandwidth. This means that the 16-port blade has a 1:1 subscription ratio even if all external ports are all connected to 4Gbit devices and no traffic is localized. The larger blades also have 4Gbit interfaces, and are uncongested in most real-world scenarios. However, it is important to realize that the larger blades *can* exhibit internal congestion if (a)

Advanced Reference

traffic on enough ports is sustained at or near full speed, and (b) none of the flows are localized. Most environments have some degree of "burstyness" and/or some degree of locality, so the oversubscription of the two high-port-count blades is largely academic.

The characteristics of the two newer directors are similar to the SilkWorm 12000 in some respects, but radically different in others. This is because the two newer platforms use a Core/Edge (CE) ASIC layout instead of the XY layout. The CE layout is more symmetrical: all ports have equal access to all other ports. In addition, local switching is allowed within an octet rather than a quad on the 24000, which doubles the opportunity to tune connection patterns for absolute maximum performance if locality is known. The 48000 doubles that again for two blades, and triples it for the 48-port blade.

Figure 121 shows how the blade positions in the Brocade 24000 director are connected to each other. On the left is a somewhat abstract cable-side view of the director, showing the ten blade slots. Each of the port cards has four quads depicted. Quad boundaries are still relevant for things like ISL trunking. The top two and bottom two quads on each blade each form an octet for local switching.

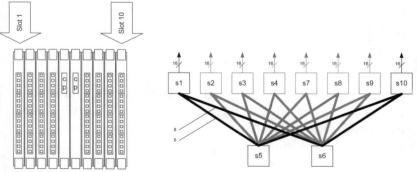

Figure 121 – Top-Level "CE" CCMA Blade Interconnect

On the right is a high-level diagram of how the slots interact with each other over the backplane. Each thick line represents a set of eight 2Gbit CCMA links connecting the port blades with the CP blades. The CP blades contain the ASICs that switch between octets. Every port blade is connected to every CP blade, and the aggregate bandwidth of these CCMA links is equal to the aggregate bandwidth available on external ports. Each port blade has 16 2Gbit FC ports going outside the box, and 2x8=16 2Gbit CCMA Links going to the backplane.

As this diagram illustrates, the internal connectivity looks similar to a resilient core/edge fabric design. This is no accident: the geometry of the core/edge design has been universally accepted as *the* best-practice for high-performance, highly scalable, high availability SAN designs, and is currently recommended by all vendors. By using the same geometry for the internal layout of its directors, Brocade has achieved the same benefits within the chassis that users have adopted for external connections. The "every port blade to every CP blade mesh" is what makes it a "CE" layout, and the 1:1 internal-to-external bandwidth ratio makes it a "fat-tree" or non-over-subscribed layout.

The Brocade 48000 has the same top-level connectivity diagram when populated with 16-port blades. The difference is that each "unit" represents a 2Gbit connection in the 24000 and a 4Gbit connection in the 48000. So, for example, the "8 unit" link between s1 and s5 represents 16Gbits of aggregate bandwidth in the Brocade 24000, and 32Gbits in the Brocade 48000.

Of course, the two directors are not *really* Core/Edge networks of discrete switches, but thinking of them that way does provide a useful visualization. Because they are fully-integrated single-domain FC directors and not merely "networks in a can", the two platforms also:

- Are easier to manage than the analogous network of individual switches.
- Take up less rack space than a network would use.
- Are easier to deploy and manage.

Advanced Reference

- Simplify the cable plant by eliminating the large number of ISLs and media required for a network.
- Are far more scalable, as they do not consist of a large number of independent domains.
- Are much less expensive, both in terms of its initial and ongoing costs.
- Have higher reliability due to having far fewer active components.
- Do not run switch-to-switch protocols internally.
- Are capable of achieving even greater performance due to internal routing optimizations.

When frames enter a port blade on either director, under normal working conditions it can select between either of the two CP blades to switch the traffic. This provides redundancy in case one CP blade should fail, and also allows full performance. For example, the Brocade 48000 uses frame-level and exchange-level trunking to balance IO between the two CPs in much the same was Condor-based switches can balance traffic in a core/edge fabric. The net result is that no empirical test has ever shown congestion within either director: testing from Brocade, independent laboratories, networking magazines, and other vendors alike have confirmed that these two platforms are simply the highest performing SAN products in the world today.

Link Speeds

Storage networks may operate at a variety of speeds. Fibre Channel standards define speeds including 1Gbit, 2Gbit, 4Gbit, 8Gbit, and 10Gbit.[125] Ethernet defines 10Mbit,

---

[125] FC-PH also defines 250Mbit "1/4 speed" and 500Mbit "1/2 speed" Fibre Channel interfaces. However, 1/4 speed has been obsolete for about a decade, and 1/2 speed was never implemented. It is also possible to run Fibre Channel at other speeds on intra-platform links. For example, the Condor ASIC is capable of forming 3Gbit FC connections to other Brocade ASICs, even though there is no standard defined for this.

100Mbit, 1Gbit, and 10Gbit, though only 1Gbit and 10Gbit are relevant to storage networking.

This subsection discusses each link speed. More detail is provided for 4Gbit FC than for the other speeds, since it is the newest of the link rates from an implementation perspective. (Although it predates 10Gbit from a standards point of view.)

Encoding Formats

Each of the link speeds discussed in this section has an *encoding format*. Encoding is used on the signal to make it transition from zero to one more often, thus allowing the high vs. low signals to be distinguished from each other. If long periods were allowed to elapse between transitions, a link might not be able to tell the difference between minor signal variations (i.e. noise) and real 0/1 transition. It could begin treating noise as if it were data, which could cause link failures and even data corruption in extreme cases. Encoding formats ensure that this will not occur. As a side benefit, encoding provides an error detection method, somewhat like parity bits in a modem protocol.

There are many formulas that can be used to encode a signal. Some encoding formats are referred to by the number of bits on the link required to represent a certain number of data bits, such as "8b/10b." The ratio indicates the amount of user data in a given data unit.

8b/10b requires that ten bits be sent down the line to represent eight data bits. This affects throughput. 8b/10b is 20% "encoding overhead."

In contrast, the "64b/66b" encoding format is only about 3% overhead, which means more payload can be moved for a given link speed. However, it also means that the link can be less effective at detecting errors, and could be subject to more frequent failures.

Advanced Reference

The bottom line is that encoding is necessary and present on all technologies discussed below. It is also necessary that devices on both ends of a connection use the same encoding format, i.e. 8b/10b *or* 64b/66b. It is not possible to have an 8b/10b device talk to an 64b/66b device natively; one or the other would need to be converted before communication would be possible. This caveat only applies to 10Gbit, since *all* other speeds use 8b/10b encoding.

1Gbit FC

1Gbit Fibre Channel was defined in the FC-PH standard in 1994. All Brocade platforms ever shipped support this speed. It was considered the "sweet spot" in the industry for many years, and is still viable today for many customers. Links running at this speed use 8b/10b encoding, and can achieve a user-data throughput of just over 100Mbytes/sec. (200Mbytes full duplex.) Both copper and optical media are defined by the standard. 1Gbit interfaces most often use GBICs, although 2Gbit Fibre Channel SFPs also support this rate to maintain backwards compatibility.

2Gbit FC

2Gbit Fibre Channel was defined in the FC-PH-2 standard in 1996, though no vendor implemented it for some time after that. All Brocade platforms more recent than the SilkWorm 2xx0 series support auto-negotiation between 1Gbit and 2Gbit FC. This is considered to be the "sweet spot" in the industry today, although 4Gbit is expected to re-place 2Gbit in 2005. Links running at this speed use 8b/10b encoding, and can achieve a user-data throughput of just over 200Mbytes/sec. (400Mbytes full duplex.) Both copper and optical media are defined by the standard. 2Gbit interfaces most often use SFPs.

4Gbit FC (Frame Trunked or Native)

For several years now, Brocade has offered frame-level trunking (p384) on all 2Gbit products. This can be used to combine two 2Gbit interfaces into one evenly balanced 4Gbit channel.

Recently, Brocade introduced a *native* 4Gbit interface, in which each individual port can run at that speed. These ports still may be trunked to form even higher rate pipes. This allows node connections at 4Gbit as well as higher speeds and lower costs for ISL connections. Native 4Gbit is expected to become the "sweet spot" in the SAN industry for 2005 and beyond.

Like 2Gbit Fibre Channel, native 4Gbit was defined in the FC-PH-2 standard in 1996. The first Brocade platform to support this standard is the Brocade 4100. (p326) It can support auto-negotiation between 1Gbit and 2Gbit FC on all ports for backwards-compatibility. While other 4Gbit vendors may not support trunking, on *Brocade* platforms up to eight 4Gbit links can be trunked to form a single 32Gbit channel (p456), and multiple trunks can be balanced into a single 256Gbit pipe.

Links running at 4Gbit use the same 8b/10b encoding as existing 1Gbit/2Gbit infrastructure, and can achieve real-world payload throughput of over 400Mbytes/sec. (Over 800Mbytes in full-duplex mode.) 4Gbit interfaces use the same SFP standard and optical cabling as 1Gbit and 2Gbit interfaces, which allows 4Gbit products to be backwards compatible with installed base switches, routers, nodes, and data center cable plants.

Despite the fact that the 4Gbit standard was ratified at the same time as the 2Gbit standard, no 4Gbit products were built until 2004. There was a debate in the FC industry about whether or not to build 4Gbit products at all, or to go straight to 10Gbit. The debate ended when the Fibre Channel Industry Association voted to adopt 4Gbit, and all major FC vendors began to add 4Gbit products to their roadmaps. The factors that motivated the industry in this direction included both economic and technological trends.

Advanced Reference

Technical Drivers for Native 4Gbit FC

Two of the most critical questions in the 4Gbit vs. 10Gbit debate were whether or not higher than 2Gbit speeds were needed at all, and if so which of the candidates could be widely deployed in the most practical way.

Higher speeds were deemed desirable for several reasons. For example, some hosts and storage devices – e.g. large tape libraries – were running fast enough to saturate their 2Gbit interfaces. In some cases, this was causing a business impact for customers: if a backup device could stream data faster, then backup windows could be reduced and/or fewer tape devices could be purchased. Furthermore, running faster ISLs would mean needing fewer of them, thus saving cost on switches and cabling. For long distance applications running over xWDM or dark fiber, the reduction in number of links could have a substantial ongoing cost savings.

For these and many other reasons, the industry acknowledged that 2Gbit speeds were no longer sufficient for storage networks. The choice was to use 4Gbit or 10Gbit. It turned out that 4Gbit had substantial technical advantages related to deployment, and provided at least the same performance benefits as 10Gbit.

Hosts and storage devices that were exceeding their 2Gbit interface capacity were not doing so by a large amount. Some tape drives were designed to stream at between 3Gbit and 4Gbit, and some hosts could match these speeds, but only a handful of the highest-end systems in the world could exceed 4Gbit, and even these could not generally sustain 10Gbit streams. 4Gbit interfaces could be marketed at cost parity with 2Gbit, but 10Gbit interfaces demanded a massive price premium due to architectural differences in the interfaces, so there was no point in using the more expensive 10Gbit interface in a node that could not even saturate a 4Gbit interface. Actual performance on nodes would be identical whether using 4Gbit or 10Gbit, and 10Gbit cost more across the board.

448

The biggest barrier to wide deployment of 10Gbit was its innate incompatibility with existing infrastructure. It required different optical cables, used different media, and was not backwards compatible with 1Gbit or 2Gbit. Needing to rip and replace all HBAs and storage controllers at once, not to mention an entire data center cable plant would not only be prohibitively expensive, but operationally impossible in the "always on" data centers that power today's global businesses.

It became clear because of these factors that the optimal speed for nodes would be 4Gbit. However, there was still a case to be made for *ISLs* at 10Gbit.

Replacing the optical infrastructure would be less of a technical issue with backbone connections, because there are typically far fewer of them than there are node connections. Additionally, some high-end installations really do require their switch-to-switch connections to run faster than 4Gbit. Indeed, some networks require backbones to run at far higher than 10Gbit speeds. No matter how fast an individual interface can be made, there always seems to be an application that needs more bandwidth. Brocade decided to solve this with trunking for 4Gbit interfaces, giving 4Gbit networks performance parity with 10Gbit (and indeed beyond) while still lowering costs and simplifying deployments.

Another technical factor to consider is network redundancy. Most users configure links in pairs, so that there will be no outage if one link should fail. With a single 10Gbit link, any component failure will result in an outage, which means that the minimum realistic configuration between two switches is 20Gbits (2x 10Gbit links). Relatively few applications require so much bandwidth between each pair of switches, and given the cost of 10Gbit interfaces, redundancy would be harder to justify to management when purchasing a SAN.

To fully appreciate this, consider the performance parity case. If three 4Gbit links are configured, and one fails, the channel is 33% degraded. For a network with the exact same performance requirement, a single 10Gbit link is needed, which is more expensive than the three 4Gbit interfaces and requires more expensive single-mode optical infrastructure. If that link fails, the network has an outage because 100% of bandwidth is lost, thus requiring a second expensive 10Gbit link to be provisioned, even though the additional performance is not required. If a 10Gbit proponent were to argue that two times the performance were really needed, the 4Gbit proponent could configure six 4Gbit links, which would still cost less, have higher availability, and perform identically.

All of this adds up to substantial technical advantages for 4Gbit above 10Gbit. Until mainstream nodes can saturate 4Gbit channels, this is likely to remain the mainstream interface speed for storage networks.

Economic Drivers for Native 4Gbit FC

In the final years of the 20th century, companies were buying technology for its own sake, regardless of proven value proposition. In the early 21st century, however, the overall global economic downturn caused the high-tech industry to adapt: any new technology had to provide end-users with a proven Return on Investment (ROI) in order to be adopted, so technology companies began to reevaluate their value propositions before going to market with new products. Since 4Gbit interfaces could provide more real technical benefit than 10Gbit in most cases, it became a question of which technology could lower the total cost of ownership the most, thus providing the highest ROI.

When using 10Gbit interfaces, the lowest speed possible is on a link is, obviously, 10Gbit. If a network designer feels that less performance is needed, and that less cost would be appropriate, there is no way to install *part* of a 10Gbit pipe. With 4Gbit trunked interfaces, the granularity of configuration is much finer: a designer can start with one 4Gbit link and add more links as needed if real performance data justifies the added cost.

4Gbit interfaces use the same low-level technology and standards as 1Gbit and 2Gbit across the board: the encoding format is just one example. One way to think of a 4Gbit switch is that it is *like* running a 2Gbit switch with a higher clock rate. The net result is that 4Gbit products can be marketed at about the same price as the existing 2Gbit products. 10Gbit, on the other hand, is fundamentally different: it uses technology that requires different components, which are all much lower volume. This is true to such an extent that current price projections indicate that three 4Gbit links will cost quite a bit less than one 10Gbit link, so even deploying equal bandwidth is more economical with 4Gbit.

With 4Gbit, redundancy and performance can be decoupled to a greater extent than with 10Gbit: redundant configurations can start at 8Gbit (2x 4Gbit) at a fraction the cost of a *non*-redundant 10Gbit link, and can scale up to trunked configurations supporting far more bandwidth than 10Gbit: Brocade 4Gbit ASICs support up to 256Gbit configurations using frame-based plus exchange-based trunking algorithms.

Not only were 10Gbit interfaces more expensive, but the optical infrastructure users already installed for 1Gbit and 2Gbit would not work with 10Gbit devices. 10Gbit interfaces require expensive single-mode fiber, and the vast majority of data centers today are wired with multi-mode fiber. 4Gbit, on the other hand, could use the existing cable plant, and could support the same SFP interface used for 1Gbit and 2Gbit. This meant that media and cable plants could be designed to run at all three speeds, providing backwards compatibility, whereas 10Gbit installations would require forklift upgrades.

Since 4Gbit products cost less than 10Gbit even at performance parity, and installation would be less expensive as

Advanced Reference

well, the economic debate came out firmly on the side of 4Gbit, just as had the technical discussion.

Native 4Gbit Adoption Timeline

At every point in the price / performance / redundancy / reliability map, 4Gbit is more desirable than 10Gbit. All major Fibre Channel vendors have 4Gbit on their roadmaps, including switch, router, HBA, and storage manufacturers. The Fibre Channel Industry Association has officially backed this movement, and it is expected that most FC equipment shipping by the end of 2005 will run at this speed. Indeed, at the time of this writing, Brocade has already been shipping 4Gbit products since late 2004.

Even though the benefits are clear and numerous, 4Gbit will not fully penetrate the Fibre Channel market immediately. Like any new technology, 4Gbit FC is expected to follow a curve of adoption, with different market penetration extents and different end-user benefits at different points on the timeline.

During the early-adoption time, 2Gbit native switches will still be in high volume production. First, the 4Gbit technology will be available only in selected pizzabox switches like the SilkWorm 4100. It is usual for director-class products to follow behind switches by at least several months, since modular platforms are by nature harder to engineer, test, and market. This is why the Brocade 48000 shipped later than the 4100. During the interim period, 4Gbit switches will be deployed in stand-alone configurations, as the cores and/or edges of small to medium CE networks, and as edge switches in larger SANs.

Once 4Gbit blades begin to ship in higher volume, Silk-Worm 24000 2Gbit directors at the edge of fabrics will simply have all net-new blades purchased with SilkWorm 48000 4Gbit chips. There is probably no real incentive for most users to throw out their existing 2Gbit blades, so it is likely that 4Gbit ports will simply sit along side the existing

2Gbit interfaces within existing chassis.[126] The new 4Gbit blades will replace 2Gbit ISLs going to the core. Directors at the core of large SANs will either have their blades upgraded (4Gbit blades purchased and old blades transferred to edge chassis) or in some cases the entire core chassis may be migrated to the edges of a fabric.

The time lag between edge switches and directors is not considered to be a problem: the industry does not believe that 2Gbit is by any means obsolete. Most customers do not immediately require 4Gbit interfaces, and many customers will be able to use their 2Gbit switches for years to come. In fact, it is likely that 2Gbit switches will still be shipping for all of 2005 and even into 2006: they will simply decline in volume over that time.

Some time after the first 4Gbit switches ship, node vendors will start to come out with 4Gbit interfaces. Most users will not have an immediate need for e.g. 4Gbit HBAs, so it is likely that only net-new installations will use this speed. (This is why backwards compatibility with 1Gbit and 2Gbit was so important: it will take years for the installed base to become purely 4Gbit.)

By the end of 2005, it is expected that all major vendors will ship 4Gbit interfaces by default on products in every segment, and that the vast majority of green field deployments will use this speed almost exclusively.

8Gbit FC (Frame Trunked or Native)

Brocade offers 8Gbit FC trunks on all of its 2Gbit platforms today. 8Gbit trunks are created by striping data across four 2Gbit channels to form one 8Gbit pipe. It is also possible

---

[126] Brocade will offer 4Gbit blades that can co-exist with SilkWorm 24000 2Gbit blades in the same chassis, but at least two other vendors require forklift chassis upgrades. Be sure to ask if a 2Gbit chassis purchased today will support 4Gbit and 10Gbit blades in the future, and if these can co-exist with existing blades in an existing chassis.

to trunk two native 4Gbit interfaces on products which support that link rate; this has the same effect. Trunking can be used to resolve or proactively prevent performance bottlenecks in the network, which is where high-speed links are most needed.

In the future, it is expected that storage controllers and some hosts will need higher speeds on their network interfaces as well, and trunking cannot easily be used to solve this challenge. Unfortunately, the theory that 10Gbit would be the next logical step for node interconnects has run into cost and technology problems, as discussed under "10Gbit FC" later. As a result, the FCIA announced that its members have ratified the extension of the Fibre Channel roadmap to include native 8Gbit speeds on a single interface.

This should allow each interface on a node or switch to support 1Gbit, 2Gbit, 4Gbit, or 8Gbit, all using the same media and cable types. The intent is to allow customers to preserve their existing infrastructure investments and avoid costly "forklift" upgrades, which would be needed to support 10Gbit technology.

In fact, at the time of this writing, 8Gbit products are already in late stages of development, and so some additional details are now available about this technology. It is expected that 8Gbit products will sell for a premium above 4Gbit, and that they will of course require new SFP media to operate at that speed. In general, 8Gbit can operate over the same optical infrastructure as 4Gbit, but it is advisable to run some tests – e.g. for DB loss – to make sure that the cable plant is sufficiently reliable. For a given cable quality, 8Gbit may support a shorter distance than 4Gbit, in the same way that 2Gbit supported shorter distances than 1Gbit. Finally, it seems almost certain that 8Gbit capable media will *not* auto-negotiate all the way down to 1Gbit; they will support 2Gbit, 4Gbit, and 8Gbit negotiation. The SFP industry realized that it would be costly and complex to add 1Gbit support, and did not expect customers to pay a premium for 8Gbit media only to connect it to 1Gbit devices. There is a simple work around for this: if you intend to connect 1Gbit devices to an 8Gbit switch, use 1Gbit, 2Gbit, or 4Gbit SFPs to do so.

10Gbit FC

10Gbit FC uses a different low-level encoding format (p445) than any of the other port speeds – 64b/66b instead of 8b/10b – so a 10Gbit FC link has the throughput of three 4Gbit links. 10Gbit can be thought of as equivalent to 12Gbit from a payload carrying standpoint. On the other hand, at the time of this writing, three 4Gbit links cost *much* less than one 10Gbit link, and have higher availability: if a 10Gbit link fails, the connection is 100% down, whereas if a 4Gbit link fails in a 3-port trunk, the link is just degraded.

Perhaps more to the point, 10Gbit has fundamentally different requirements vs. any of the other link speeds across the board. 1Gbit, 2Gbit, 4Gbit, and 8Gbit can all use SFPs and multi-mode fiber, but 10Gbit uses XFPs and more expensive single-mode fiber. Most existing data center infrastructure is designed with multi-mode fiber, and virtually all existing SAN components are designed to receive 8b/10b format; substantial reengineering is required for 64b/66b both at the product and data center levels. This adds total cost of ownership burden far beyond the massive price premium that 10Gbit interfaces are currently demanding.

This has kept 10Gbit adoption slow. In fact, there is widespread speculation that 10Gbit FC will simply never be implemented in hosts or storage devices, and that the industry will bypass it by adopting 8Gbit and then 16Gbit or faster link speeds based on the 8b/10b encoding method. However, there is a case to be made in favor of 10Gbit links for DWDM extension, since these products already have 10Gbit interfaces today. Brocade has therefore developed a 10Gbit FC blade for the Brocade 48000 director to support these distance extension applications. See the sections "Brocade 48000 Director" on page 331 and "FC10-6 10Gbit Fibre Channel

Blade" on page 343 for more information. The section "10Gbit Blades and DR/BC Solutions" starting on page 296 has an extended example of this use case.

32Gbit FC (Frame Trunked)

All of the Condor-based platforms support 32Gbit FC trunks. These are evenly balanced paths, so that one 32Gbit trunk is truly equivalent to a single link operating at that speed. The major difference is that trunks are comprised of multiple physical interfaces, and therefore have an inherent element of redundancy built in: if one link fails in a 32Gbit trunk, the remaining seven links will still deliver 28Gbits of bandwidth: more than 87% of the original capacity will remain. A single physical 32Gbit link would have failed down to 0% in a similar scenario.

256Gbit FC (Frame and Exchange Trunked)

Up to eight 8-port frame-level trunks can be balanced at the exchange level by DPS to form a single 256Gbit path. In this case, a single link failure will still leave in excess of 98% of the aggregate capacity. This is most likely only applicable to large-scale CE networks formed from Brocade 48000 directors at both the core and edge layers.

1Gbit iSCSI and FCIP

In theory, it should be possible to achieve about $1/4^{th}$ the performance of a Fibre Channel link by using commodity Ethernet equipment instead of purpose-built storage network gear. If this were true, it might allow organizations to deploy their SANs at a lower cost, if performance were not a factor. As it turns out, neither iSCSI nor FCIP can achieve nearly 1Gbit of real throughput on a 1Gbit interface. See "iSCSI" on page 41 for some of the reasons behind this.

10Gbit iSCSI and FCIP

Some industry commentators make an argument which goes something like this:

1Gbit iSCSI cannot meet requirements for performance in today's SANs, much less meet requirements for future datacenter architectures involving ILM or UC. However, deploying 10Gbit interfaces with hardware iSCSI and TCP engines will allow 10Gbit iSCSI to almost match 4Gbit Fibre Channel performance. Therefore 10Gbit iSCSI shall have a market.

On the one hand, Brocade does carry numerous iSCSI and FCIP products, and is investing substantial R&D money in improving them. There are use cases for SAN technologies which do not require the performance of Fibre Channel, and Brocade intends to support them.

On the other hand, just as with 10Gbit FC, this is *not* expected to form a substantial percentage of the overall SAN market, because arguments like the one above are unlikely to convince many users. It is currently possible to implement 3x 4Gbit FC ports for about the same price as a single *non-*accelerated optical 10Gbit Ethernet link, and iSCSI protocol acceleration typically adds up to an order of magnitude to the cost of an interface. With Fibre Channel maintaining that kind of lead in price/performance, and also having about a decade lead in maturity and market adoption, IP SAN interfaces are likely to remain a fringe market for the future.

Appendix C: Study Guide

This study guide is divided into two sections: a set of questions, and a corresponding set of answers. After reading the main body of the book, go through the questions below, and on a separate sheet of paper, write your answers. If you cannot think of an answer, first try looking it up in the preceding chapters. If you cannot find the answer there, also try looking in "Appendix D: FAQ" starting on page 471.

Once you have completed the questions, double-check your answers by looking at the section "Study Guide Answers" on page 468. You can also use that section as a last resort if you cannot think of an answer and cannot find it by looking it up in the main body of the book or in the FAQ.

Study Guide Questions

1. Storage Area Networks (SANs) are primarily intended to provide _____ level connectivity between hosts and storage devices.

2. _____ is by far the most common technology used for SANs today.

3. The traditional _____ architecture failed to meet increasing storage performance and asset utilization requirements, which paved the way for SANs.

4. Existing network technologies like _____ were too slow and unreliable to support SANs, which prompted the SAN industry to invent the _____ protocol.

5. _____ is a SAN solution category which allows improved asset utilization through reduced white space on storage arrays.

6. _____ is the industry leader in SAN infrastructure, carrying FC, iSCSI, FCIP, virtualization, and SAN Management products.

7. _____ is a set of processes and procedures related to managing the way the business value of information changes over time.

8. Switches are distinguished from hubs in that switches do not have a _____ architecture.

9. When deploying a SAN to support mission-critical systems, industry best-practices mandate a _____ SAN architecture with redundant HBAs and multi-pathing software.

10. When communication between port-pairs in a switch or network of switches *impair* communication between other ports it is known as _____. This distinguished from *blocking* which actually *prevents* communication, and is a typical characteristic of crossbar switches.

11. In order to optimize compute resources such as CPU cycles, a _____ solution should be considered.

12. The last step in the SAN planning process is to create a more detailed _____ document and _____ plan.

13. The ILM and UC trends intersect in the _____.

14. To justify the cost of a SAN, the design team should compare the hard and soft benefits of the SAN to the costs as part of a _____ analysis.

15. When considering which protocol to use for a SAN, it is important to understand that the _____ protocol is vastly more efficient and mature than _____.

16. The first step in designing a SAN is to _____.

17. The _____ has the responsibility of coordinating the entire SAN effort and usually has the SAN project plan as a deliverable.

18. In order to optimize _____, it is best to move tape systems onto the SAN.

19. SAN-enabled _____ are a good way to increase application uptime by allowing a standby node to take over if a production node fails.

20. The mapping of SCSI over Fibre Channel is called ____, whereas the mapping of SCSI over IP is called _____.

21. Looking at Gigabit Ethernet and Fibre Channel from a maturity standpoint, one factor to consider is that _____ came first, and _____ was actually on top of the _____ protocol layers.

22. Originally invented by Brocade, _____ is now the industry-standard protocol for routing between FC switches in a fabric.

23. The time during which the backup runs is called the _____ and its maximum size is determined by the length of time that the business can tolerate the associated performance degradation or application outage.

24. _____ is the fundamental storage protocol that lies under both FC and IP SAN technologies.

25. To connect a host to a Fibre Channel fabric, a card called a _____ is required.

26. To achieve even a fraction of FC performance, iSCSI hosts require an expensive _____.

27. _____ are sets of processes and overall design and management philosophies, not specific products.

28. Currently shipping Fibre Channel products support the following link rates: _____.

29. The FC standards also provide for the following <u>link</u> rates: _____, some of which are obsolete and some of which are expected to ship in the future.

30. Two important concepts for SAN designers moving forward are _____, both of which are related to virtualizing resources, and neither of which are currently available in "feature complete" solutions.

31. In order for devices on a SAN to discover each other, they need to register with and inquire from the _____, which is built in to FC switches but generally requires external hardware in an iSCSI network.

32. _____ is a solution category related to moving data between storage subsystems e.g. when old systems are coming off of lease.

33. The Fibre Channel equivalent of an Ethernet hub uses the rather limited _____ protocol.

34. In order to achieve faster performance between switches than a single ISL can support, Brocade supports two link aggregation methods: _____ and _____.

35. Almost all companies use _____ or _____ instead of iSCSI when they want to support storage over IP.

36. Regulatory requirements and fiduciary duty to investors are increasingly driving IT departments to implement _____ solutions, which are facilitated by SANs mapped over a MAN or WAN.

37. _____ is a category of SAN solution used in most other SAN solutions, which results in more efficient utilization of storage assets.

38. _____ is the concept that resources such as CPU power, RAM, and storage capacity could be provided in a manner similar to an electric power grid.

39. In an HA cluster or UC solution, compute nodes need access to each other's data sets to enable application mobility. This means building the cluster onto a _____.

40. JBODs and SBODs are almost never used as primary storage in mission-critical applications. Such needs are usually better met by _____ arrays.

41. _____ in the context of SANs are behaviors that devices must follow in order to communicate.

42. SANs have been used to connect multiple processing nodes to scale _____, either through parallel operations or sequential workflow optimization.

43. Running backups over _____ robs hosts of needed CPU power, whereas running them over _____ is even more efficient than DAS.

44. Using the FC protocol guarantees _____ and timely frame delivery with negligible error rates.

45. _____ pose the greatest challenge for compatibility testing within storage networks, regardless of protocol.

46. In a "formulaic" resilient CE fabric, _____ core switches interconnect many edge switches.

47. Fibre Channel SANs almost always outperform DAS, but _____ most often does not.

48. FC links can be extended across up to a hundred kilometers or so of dark fiber using long-wavelength _____.

49. _____ allows an organization to determine where data belongs at any point in time.

50. UC is being driven primarily by three factors: _____.

51. There are five phases to the SAN planning process for green field deployments: _____.

52. There are five layers to the UC and ILM data center architectures: _____.

53. The place where ILM and UC intersect is the _____.

54. Specific _____ requirements must be gathered to determine what the SAN is supposed to accomplish for the organization.

Study Guide

55. "Compatible" devices are capable of being _____.

56. If devices are not compatible, further analysis is _____ because the network will simply not function.

57. Designers should try to support *initial* performance requirements, and also _____.

58. _____ is a measure of how often service personnel need to "touch" a system.

59. _____ is a measure of how much time a system is able to perform its higher-level functions.

60. _____ is a somewhat subjective measure of, among other things, how easy it is to fix problems in a SAN.

61. _____ allows multiple fabrics to be controlled from a single management point.

62. _____ automatically checks the SAN against evolving best-practices and has automated "housekeeping" features such as looking for unused zones.

63. _____ refers to how large a network can become without needing to be fundamentally restructured.

64. The most common SAN topology is _____.

65. _____ allows native FC ISLs to cross very long distances while maintaining full performance.

66. The rule of thumb is that it takes one _____ per kilometer of distance for full-speed 2Gbit operation.

67. Performance in a network will _____ over time.

68. _____ are the most common performance limiting factor in a SAN.

69. The mechanism which carries traffic across a SAN between edge devices is known as the SAN _____. FC and iSCSI are two examples.

70. _____ is a condition in which more devices *might* need a resource than that resource can serve.

71. _____ is a condition in which devices actually *are* trying to use a path beyond its capacity, so some of the traffic destined for that path must be delayed.

72. _____ refers to a queuing problem, not merely to contention for bandwidth on a link.

73. _____ is how long it takes to forward a frame.

74. _____ is often matched to the ratio of storage to hosts.

75. Using the _____ product will help to automate UC and other advanced solutions by managing the complex relationships between hosts, storage, operating systems, and applications.

76. _____ is the practice of optimizing traffic by putting ports that communicate "close" together.

77. _____ is the practice of connecting hosts to one group of switches, and storage to a different group.

78. _____ are two features which allow traffic to be balanced across ISLs while preserving in order delivery.

79. The process of taking a design from paper all the way through release to production is _____.

80. Avoid single points of failure when selecting racks for switches by _____.

81. The most effective access control mechanism for a SAN is _____, because it is enforced by both the Name Server and the ASIC.

82. It is important to _____ a SAN before releasing it to production to verify that all switches, routers, devices and applications are capable of recovering from faults.

83. Maintaining a _____ can help with tasks such as switch and fabric maintenance, troubleshooting, and recovery.

84. Users interested in clean, stable fabric environments should run _____ regularly.

85. It is possible to use the _____ product to optimize storage performance at branch offices.

86. When evaluating candidate SAN designs, it is appropriate to consider which of the following factors:

    a. Compatibility
    b. RAS
    c. Scalability
    d. Performance
    e. Manageability
    f. Total solution cost
    g. All of the above

87. Any SAN design should meet or exceed all requirements, but most designers consider _____ to be the most important consideration when making trade-offs.

88. If a fabric has a single point of failure, and the SAN has only one fabric in it, then the overall architecture is considered to be _____.

89. Connecting a host to the same switch as its primary storage is an example of the use of _____.

90. ILM and UC are two trends which are likely to increase the use of _____ fabric topologies, in which hosts are connected to one group of switches and storage to a different group.

91. To maximize fabric scalability, compatibility, and reliability, when planning zoning for a fabric it is best to zone HBAs so that:

    a. All HBAs accessing a given storage port are in the same zone.
    b. Hosts with a common OS type are all zoned together, and separated from all other OSs.
    c. Each HBA is in its own dedicated zone.
    d. All devices in the fabric are in one zone.
    e. If possible, zoning should be avoided, since it is hard to manage.

92. If every switch in a fabric is directly connected to every other switch, this is an example of a _____ topology.

93. The most reliable way to connect fabrics across MAN or moderate WAN distances is by using _____ connections, either over dark fiber or xWDM equipment.

94. The FCIA has approved the _____ line rate, which has now replaced 2Gbit as the basic rate for FC fabrics.

95. Dividing a director into two or more partitions - using zoning, VSANs, or a similar scheme such as the dual-domain capability of a Brocade director - will make it into a highly available system. (True/False)

96. Some of the options available for increasing the performance of a fabric include _____.

97. It is necessary for a SAN designer or project manager to prepare and maintain proper _____ to ensure that future administrators will know what has been done and why various decisions were made.

98. The simplest fabric design is the _____ topology, but this is only suitable for very small deployments, due to its limited scalability, performance, and reliability.

99. Proper use of zoning will improve fabric services scalability and reliability through Brocade's automatic use of _____ scoping.

100. The maximum number of ports currently supported by Brocade inside a single-domain director is _____. The smallest switch offered by Brocade has _____ ports.

101. The single biggest factor in determining how vulnerable a SAN is to DoS attacks or failures is whether or not the SAN uses a _____ design.

Study Guide

Study Guide Answers

1. block
2. Fibre Channel (FC)
3. Directly Attached Storage (DAS)
4. Ethernet and IP ; Fibre Channel
5. storage consolidation
6. Brocade
7. Information Lifecycle Management (ILM)
8. shared bandwidth
9. Redundant (A/B) fabrics
10. congestion
11. Utility Computing (UC)
12. SAN design ; implementation plan
13. Storage Area Network (SAN)
14. Return on Investment (ROI)
15. Fibre Channel ; iSCSI
16. gather business-oriented requirements
17. SAN Project Manager
18. Backup, restore, and LAN performance
19. HA clusters
20. FCP ; iSCSI
21. Fibre Channel ; Gigabit Ethernet ; FC-0 and FC-1
22. Fabric Shortest Path First (FSPF)
23. backup window
24. SCSI
25. Host Bus Adapter (HBA)
26. iSCSI hardware accelerated HBA
27. Utility Computing (UC) and Information Lifecycle Management (ILM)
28. 1Gbit, 2Gbit, 4Gbit
29. 133Mbaud, 266Mbaud, 531Mbaud, 8Gbit, 10Gbit
30. ILM and UC
31. Name Server
32. data igration
33. Fibre Channel Arbitrated Loop (FC-AL)
34. frame-level trunking ; Dynamic Path Selection (DPS)

35. NFS ; CIFS
36. Disaster Tolerance (DT), Disaster Recovery (DR), or Business Continuity and Availability (BC&A)
37. storage consolidation
38. UC
39. SAN
40. Redundant Array of Independent Disks (RAID)
41. Protocols
42. compute power
43. TCP/IP
44. On-time and in-order
45. Storage-related services, such as FC fabric services
46. two or more
47. iSCSI
48. SFPs, GBICs, or other similar laser media
49. ILM
50. Lowering capital costs, increasing management efficiency, and improving application performance
51. gathering requirements, developing technical specifications, estimating cost, performing an ROI analysis, and creating a detailed design and rollout plan
52. clients, LAN, compute nodes, SAN, storage
53. SAN
54. business-oriented
55. connected to each other directly or across a network
56. irrelevant
57. all anticipated future increases in performance demand
58. Reliability
59. Availability
60. Serviceability
61. Fabric Manager
62. SAN Health
63. Scalability
64. Core/Edge (CE)
65. Extended Fabrics
66. BB credit
67. increase
68. Hosts and storage devices

69. protocol
70. Over-subscription
71. Congestion
72. Blocking, or "Head of Line Blocking" (HoLB)
73. Latency
74. ISL over-subscription
75. Tapestry Application Resource Manager (ARM)
76. Locality
77. Tiering
78. Frame-level trunking and exchange-level Dynamic Path Selection (DPS)
79. SAN implementation
80. separating redundant fabrics into different rack and providing separate power grids and UPSs
81. hard zoning
82. stage and validate
83. configuration log
84. SAN Health
85. Tapestry Wide Area File Services (WAFS)
86. "G"; all of the above
87. Application availability
88. Non-resilient and non-redundant
89. Locality
90. Tiered
91. "C"; each HBA should have its own zone
92. full mesh
93. Native FC
94. 4Gbit
95. False – One of anything is not HA
96. adding ISLs or IFLs, increasing line rates, using trunking and/or DPS, localizing flows
97. SAN documentation
98. cascade
99. Registered State Change Notification,(RSCN)
100. 256; 8
101. redundant (A/B) fabric

Appendix D: FAQ

Q: What SAN planning process does Brocade use?

A: There are five phases in the recommended SAN planning process: gather the requirements of the SAN through interviews, develop preliminary technical specifications, estimate the project cost, calculate ROI, and finally create a detailed SAN design and rollout plan.

Q: What is a SAN project plan?

A: The SAN Project Plan may be very similar to other IT project planning tools used within your company. The key items it should include are: notes and documents to support collected data such as interviews and device surveys; interpretations of the data; the design which emerges from the data; a list of required equipment and associated costs; a plan for implementing, testing, releasing to production, and managing the SAN.

Q: Generally, who is included on the project team?

A: The SAN Project Manager and SAN Designer are arguably the two most important roles. The project manager will coordinate the effort and the designer will translate business needs into technical requirements. It is not uncommon for both roles to be accomplished by the same person. The technical team will consist of SAN Administrators, System Administrators, Storage Administrators, IP Network Administrators, Database Administrators and Application Specialists. The members of the team should have a strong interest in, or have decision making authority related to the project.

Q: What is the difference between a business requirement and a business problem?

A: A business *problem* is a statement about what needs to be "fixed" or at least improved to help the organization accomplish its mission. For example, "Backups are interfering with customer service." A business *requirement* will state a direction for the solution to one or more business problems, and can be used as a guideline for choosing the appropriate solution. For example, "The SAN must complete the backup in no more that x hours, and remain online during the process. This will save $\$y$ by increasing productivity."

Q: What should be included in business requirements?

A: Be sure to gather *specific* business requirements, with each requirement statement including *what* needs to happen, *when* it needs to happen, and how much *money* or *mission impact* is involved if the requirement is not met. This answers what, when, and why. "How" is answered by a subsequent step. "Where" is generally self-evident.

Q: How do I develop technical specifications for a SAN?

A: The specification document will be created in the planning phase. A number of factors must be taken into consideration in addition to the business requirements statement. The locations of SAN equipment, the mechanisms for connecting the locations together, estimated bandwidth, uptime, and the number of attached devices must all be analyzed when creating the specifications document.

Q: How do I justify my project?

A: As part of the ROI analysis you will have to produce an estimated net benefit. This is done by subtracting the estimated cost of equipment from the projected gross benefits. The projected benefits may include things like increased productivity, lower management costs, reduced capital spending, and revenue gains. This task may be best suited for your accounting department, or at least should be taken on in partnership with them.

Q: What is the most commonly used SAN technology?
A: Fibre Channel. Period.

Q: iSCSI is supposed to be cheaper, but there do not seem to be many real-world deployments. Why is it not being used extensively?
A: Although many vendors, including Brocade, offer iSCSI solutions, it is an immature and unreliable protocol with marginal ROI and many hidden costs. FC products have had price reductions which eroded the iSCSI value proposition, and serial ATA is available in the low end market. This is "squeezing" out iSCSI from both ends of the market, and its long-term viability is now in question.

Q: What is the difference between an ISL and an IFL?
A: An Inter-Switch Link, or ISL, is the connection between two FC switches in a fabric. An Inter-Fabric Link, or IFL, is the connection between an FC switch and an FC-FC router. LSANs cross IFLs. An IFL allows traffic to flow between different fabrics in a Meta SAN, whereas an ISL allows traffic and services to flow between switches within a single fabric.

Q: How can SANs be extended over long distances?
A: There are many options to extend a FC network over long distances including SONET/SDH, xWDM, ATM, and native FC over dark fiber. With limited solutions, IP may also be an option. Both ATM and SONET/SDH solutions have very high performance and reliability compared to IP SAN solutions, but also tend to cost more.

Q: What services do Fibre Channel switches provide?
A: Unlike IP SAN switches, all Brocade FC switches have a robust group of built-in services. Fabric services include a name services, management services, high-speed routing services, auto-discovery and configuration, and so on.

FAQ

Q: What is driving the increased Fibre Channel speeds?

A: There are always increasing demands for performance in networking. One example is the need to reduce backup windows. Another is the increasing need for high-speed long-distance connections to support disaster recovery. ILM and UC architectures are also drivers.

Q: Will my SAN support HA clustering?

A: All modern clustering methods have one thing in common: in order for one node to be able to take over an application if another node fails, it needs to have access to the data set that the failed node was using just before the crash. As long as your SAN provides that connectivity, it should be a good basis for building HA clusters.

Q: What is SAN implementation?

A: This is the process of taking your "paper" design to physical setup, through staging and testing, all the way through release to production.

Q: I am designing dual fabrics, what are the implementation considerations?

A: The concept of dual fabrics is to avoid any single point of failure. For high-availability fabrics, ensure that you have separate power circuits available, and mount redundant devices into different racks.

Q: What is the difference between hard and soft zoning?

A: Hard zoning is enforced by ASICs, while soft zoning is enforced by the name server. All Brocade platforms shipped since about the turn of the century support some form of hard zoning in all usage cases. Older switches supported hardware zoning only when zones were defined by PID.

Q: How do I prepare my SAN to go into production after it has been cabled and configured?

A: Prior to transitioning your fabric to production, it is important to validate the SAN by establishing a profile and injecting faults into the fabric to verify that the fabric and the edge devices are capable of recovering.

Q: Will keeping a change management log be helpful?

A: A diligently maintained configuration log can help you with many tasks such as switch and fabric maintenance as well as troubleshooting and recovery.

Q: Zoning is backed up to every switch, but what about the rest of the configuration parameters?

A: The best-practice is to create a backup of each switch configuration on a host when implementing a new SAN, changing a switch configuration, or adding or replacing a switch in the SAN.

Q: With so many protocols available, which should be used in my SAN?

A: Fibre Channel is the dominant SAN transport because of the importance for even lower-tier storage networks to have high performance and reliability. Brocade supports other options, but FC should be the default choice unless there is a comprehensive business case showing why another option should be used, and proving that it will actually work properly.

Q: What are common performance limitations in a SAN?

A: SAN attached devices, the SAN protocol, and link speeds are usually the bottlenecks.

Q: What is the impact of protocol selection on the SAN?

A: It affects performance, reliability, scalability, manageability, cost, and indeed most other aspects of SAN design. The best approach is to use a protocol with a long and proven track record of production deployment.

Q: My SAN will initially be used as a low-end SAN but I would like to scale in the future, is Fibre Channel an appropriate choice?

A: Fibre Channel networks can be configured to meet any performance requirement. Also, Brocade SANs can be designed to scale and for investment protection.

Q: What are some of the cost issues should think about when designing ISLs and IFLs?

A: The cost to performance ratio is probably the most obvious, but some designers may forget to consider the total cost of a connection. This means the cost of cables and connectors. It also means the cost of downtime if redundant links are *not* used, and the cost of productivity of links are allowed to congest massively.

Q: What is over-subscription?

A: Over-subscription refers to a condition in which more devices might need to access a resource than that resource could fully support. In many instances, oversubscription is deliberately engineered into a SAN to reduce cost.

Q: Does over-subscription cause congestion?

A: No. However, it does create the potential for congestion. Congestion is a condition in which devices are actually trying to use a path beyond its capacity, so some of the traffic destined for that path must be queued and transmitted after a delay.

Q: What can I do to avoid congestion in my SAN?

A: The most common approaches for dealing with congestion include using locality, faster links such as 4Gbit or 10Gbit interfaces, or using hardware trunking to broaden link speeds into higher path rates.

Q: Do Brocade switches have Head of Line Blocking?

A: No. Head of Line Blocking occurs on poorly designed switches. Brocade does not ship products which are capable of exhibiting this misbehavior. However, other SAN infrastructure vendors do.

Q: How do Brocade switches have such low latency?

A: Brocade uses "cut-through routing" which allows a frame to be transmitted out the destination switch port while it is still being received into the source port.

Q: How do I determine the amount of bandwidth will be required for any given path?

A: Analyze how much data each application will need to move over that path, and then apply one of several calculation methods. For example, it is possible to all up all application peak loads, or to take their average loads, or simply to apply a rule of thumb such as using the ratio of hosts to storage ports.

Q: In addition to increasing SAN performance what other benefits does locality provide?

A: Locality improves RAS as there are fewer links and therefore fewer total components in the network, thus reducing cost and improving reliability numbers like MTBF.

Q: Do Brocade switches offer load balancing?

A: Brocade switches have an option that allows FSPF to reallocate routes whenever a fabric event occurs. This feature is called Dynamic Load Sharing (DLS) because it allows routes to be reset dynamically under conditions that can still guarantee in order delivery. Also, Brocade platforms support one or more forms of hardware trunking.

Q: Does trunking work well over long distances?

A: Yes, although different trunking methods work over different distances, or work best in different ways.

Q: What factors affect compatibility?

A: Protocols, frame formats, node-to-node compatibility, node-to-switch storage services behaviors, switch-to-switch services exchange.

Q: How important is it to plan for future expansion?

A: Always consider performance and scalability requirements of the initial deployment, *and* all anticipated future

FAQ

increases in demand. Network requirements tend to increase rather than decrease over time, and so all SAN protocol and topology choices should be able to accommodate a wide range of scenarios.

Q: What can impact SAN performance?

A: Areas to consider when thinking about SAN performance include protocols, link rates, congestion, blocking, and latency.

Q: Should I be more concerned with congestion or blocking?

A: Congestion does not stop communication between endpoints entirely; it just slows it down somewhat for a period of time. Blocking, more properly called Head of Line Blocking (HoLB), can actually stop communication for an extended period of time and is therefore an area of concern. Brocade does not sell any product which exhibits HoLB and any such product should be avoided.

Q: How should I prioritize RAS?

A: Application availability is the most important consideration in SAN designs overall because an availability issue can have an impact at the end-user level. Reliability should be considered second because of the potential impact of a failed component to the SAN. Serviceability is usually of least concern; however it should be considered.

Q: What SAN management tasks should be expect on a day to day basis?

A: Day-to-day management tasks generally include monitoring the health of the network, and performing adds, moves, and changes to the SAN itself and to the attached hosts and storage devices. Using Fabric Manager will simplify tasks associated with coordinating day-to-day management of multiple fabrics. SAN Health will vastly simplify proactive management, since it automatically checks the SAN against evolving best-practices and has automated "housekeeping" features such as looking for unused zones.

Q: When planning my SAN for scalability, what is the best approach?

A: To maximize the scalability of a SAN, it is always best to break it down into smaller fabrics. Use an A/B redundant model first, then split off other fabrics by function, geographical location, administrative groups, or by spreading storage ports.

Q: When planning for scalability, what limitations should be considered in the SAN design?

A: Limitations can be classified into five categories: manageability, fault containment, vendor support matrices, storage networking services, and the protocol itself.

Q: Which topologies are the most commonly used?

A: Just a few topologies are typically used as the basis for SANs, and these are combined or varied to fit the needs of specific deployments. The most common topologies for SANs include cascades, rings, meshes, and various core/edge designs.

Q: What is the best way to prevent denial of service attacks against a SAN?

A: It is never possible to make a system completely proof against deliberate or accidental DoS attacks. However, it is possible to make such events far less likely. Following security best-practices is a good start. Implementing sound management procedures helps, too. However, the single biggest factor in determining vulnerability to this form of attack is whether or not the SAN uses physically isolated redundant fabrics, with redundant HBA connections.

Q: What is the best long-distance method in a SAN?

A: Extended native Fibre Channel ISLs or IFLs over long distances are generally the easiest extension solutions to manage and have the highest performance. Long distance

ISLs require that the SAN designer have an understanding of buffer to buffer credits (BB credits).

Q: What are buffer to buffer credits (BB credits)?

A: In order to prevent frames from dropping, no port can transmit frames unless the port to which it is directly communicating has the ability to receive them. It is possible that the receiving port will not be able to forward the frame immediately, in which case it will need to have a memory area reserved to hold the frame until it can be sent on its way. This memory area is called a buffer. All devices in a SAN have a limited number of buffers, and so they need a mechanism for telling other devices if they have free buffers before a frame is transmitted to them. This mechanism is the exchange of BB credits.

Q: How do BB credits impact long distance links?

A: When using FC over long distance links, BB credits become important. The rule of thumb is that it takes one credit per kilometer for full-speed 2Gbit operation. Given a fixed number of BB credits, a link can go twice as far at 1Gbit as with 2Gbit. With 4Gbit links, twice as many buffers per kilometer are required as with 2Gbit links. However, it is important to note that all currently shipping Brocade platforms support more BB credits than are needed to go the maximum distance supported by today's optical components. Realistically, it is necessary to move to an DWDM architecture to go beyond a hundred kilometers or so, regardless of how many credits a switch can supply, and the leading DWDM vendors also provide a credit mechanism which supersedes that of the switches. Note that BB credits to not apply to FCIP or other protocol tunneled links in any significant way.

Glossary

Access Gateway Uses NPIV to connect an embedded switch in a bladed server chassis into a fabric with an N_Port rather than E_Port method

AL_PA Arbitrated Loop Physical Address is used to identify a device in an arbitrated loop.

American National Standards Institute See ANSI

ANSI American National Standards Institute is the governing body for standards in the United States. The ANSI T11 committee sets standards for FC.

AP Application Platforms enable fabric-based storage applications such as mirroring, data migration, snapshots, virtual tape, etc..

API Application Programming Interfaces provide a layer of abstraction between complex lower-level processes and upper level applications development. They facilitate building complex applications by providing building blocks for programmers to work with.

Application Platform See AP

Application Programming Interface See API

Application-Specific Integrated Circuit See ASIC

Application Resource Manager Management framework including both software and hardware which enables certain Utility Computing functions for Brocade SAN environments. Also known as the "Tapestry Application Resource Manager" or "Tapestry ARM".

Arbitrated Loop Shared Fibre Channel transport supporting a theoretical maximum of 126 devices

ARM See Application Resource Manager

ASIC Application-Specific Integrated Circuits are fixed-gate microchips designed to perform specific functions very well

Asynchronous Transfer Mode See ATM

ATM Asynchronous Transfer Mode is a cell-switching transport used for transmitting data over CANs, MANs, and WANs. ATM transmits short fixed-length units of data. Characterized by relatively high performance and reliability vs. switched IP solutions.

Backbone Fabric See BB Fabric

Bandwidth Transmission capacity of a link or system.

BB_Credit Buffer-to-buffer credits are a flow control mechanism used to determine how many frames can be sent to a recipient from any given port

BB Fabric The FCR allows an optional Backbone Fabric to interconnect routers for more scalable and flexible Meta SANs. Routers connect to the BB Fabric via E_Ports.

Bloom Third-generation Brocade FC switch ASIC. Based on a 2-chip 16-port central memory design. Used in the SilkWorm 3000 and 12000 series. Also used in embedded products (such as RAID controllers) from Brocade OEMs. All ports can run at 1Gbit or 2Gbit FC.

Bloom-II Enhanced version of Bloom. Uses less power, produces less heat, and has minor enhancements to buffer management features for long distance support. Used in the SilkWorm 3250, 3850, 24000, and embedded products from Brocade OEMs.

Broadcast Transmitting to all nodes on a fabric.

Bridge Connects segments of a single network

Brocade Founded in 1995, Brocade rapidly became the leading provider of Fibre Channel switches. At the time of this writing, the company carries switches, directors, and multiprotocol routers.

Buffer-to-Buffer Credits See BB_Credit

CAN Campus Area Networks tend to be under a kilometer or so in size. They are distinguished from LANs in that those tend to be in the ~100 meter range, but more importantly CANs cross between buildings. This characteristic tends to imply thinner cabling, potentially higher speeds running over that cabling, and higher locality.

Carrier Sense Multiple Access with Collision Detection See CSMA/CD

Class Of Service See COS

CLI Command Line Interfaces are text-oriented methods of managing devices. The FCR uses a CLI based on the Brocade Fabric OS CLI to make administrator training easier.

Coarse Wave Division Multiplexer See CWDM

Command Line Interface See CLI

Condor Fourth-generation Brocade FC fabric ASIC. Based on a 1-chip 32-port central memory design. Used in the Brocade 4100 switch; targeted for use throughout the product lineup by the end of 2005. All ports can run at 1Gbit, 2Gbit, or 4Gbit FC. May be used in conjunction with Egret for 10Gbit FC.

COS Class Of Service represents connection quality: a profile for attributes such as latency and data-rate.

CRC Cyclic Redundancy Check is a self-test for error detection and correction. All Brocade ASICs perform CRC checks on all frames to ensure data integrity

Credit Numeric value that represents the maximum number of receive buffers provided by an F/FL_Port to its attached N/NL_Port such that the N/NL_Port may transmit frames without overrunning the F/FL_Port.

CSMA/CD Carrier Sense Multiple Access with Collision Detection defines how Ethernet NICs behave when two or more attempt to use a shared segment at the same time

CWDM Coarse Wave Division Multiplexer. See also WDM and CWDM.

Cyclic Redundancy Check See CRC

Dark Fiber A leased fiber optic cable running between sites characterized by *not* having a service provided on the wire by the leasing company. All services are provided by the customer.

DAS Direct Attached Storage is the method of connecting a single storage device directly to one and only one host. In the enterprise data center, DAS is obsolete and has been replaced by storage networking. DAS is still used in desktops and laptops, and in lowest-tier hosts, although low-cost Fibre Channel HBAs seem likely to eliminate that last application.

Denial of Service See DoS

Dense Wave Digital Multiplexer See DWDM

Destination Fabric ID See DFID

Destination Identifier See DID

DID Destination Identifiers are three-byte Fibre Channel addresses that used to specify the physical location - switch domain, port on the switch, and position if applicable on the loop - of the receiver of a frame. A DID represented as 010100 would designate domain 1, port 1, no loop. Typically written in hex.

Direct Attached Storage See DAS

DLS Dynamic Load Sharing allows for recomputing of routes when ports go up or down

Domain ID Unique number between 1 and 239 that identifies an FC switch, router port, or translation address to a fabric

DoS Denial of Service attacks may be launched deliberately by a hacker or virus, or may happen accidentally. Either way, the result is downtime. The best approach for preventing DoS attacks in a SAN is to follow security best-practices, and to use redundant (A/B) fabrics.

DWDM Dense Wave Digital Multiplexer.   See also WDM and CWDM.   Allows more wavelengths than a CWDM.

Dynamic Load Sharing See DLS

E_D_TOV Error-Detect Time Out Value is the maximum round trip time an operation is allowed before declaring an error condition

E_Port Expansion port connecting two switches to form a fabric. Connected E_Ports form ISLs. E_Ports may also now connect to EX_Ports to form IFLs.

Edge Fabric Fibre Channel fabric connected to an FCR via an EX_Port. This is largely the same as any standard Fibre Channel fabric. This is where the hosts and storage are attached in a Meta SAN

FAQ

Egret Brocade ASIC which balances three internal 4Gbit links and converts them into a single external 10Gbit link.

ELWL Extended Long Wavelength Laser transceivers may be based on 1550nm lasers. They are used to run native Fibre Channel connections over even greater distances than LWL media can support. Generally these media types use SMF cables.

Error-Detect Time Out Value See ED_TOV

Ethernet The basis for the widely implemented IEEE 802.3 standard. Ethernet is a LAN protocol that supports data transfer rates of 10Mbps. It uses the CSMA/CD to handle simultaneous access to shared media. Fast Ethernet supports data transfer rates of 100 Mbps, and Gigabit Ethernet supports 1 Gbps and there is also an emerging 10Gbps standard.

EX_Port Enhanced E_Port used to connect a router to an edge fabric. From the point of view of a switch in an edge fabric, an EX_Port is virtually indistinguishable from an E_Port. It follows applicable Fibre Channel standards other Brocade E_Ports. However, the router terminates EX_Ports rather than allowing different fabrics to merge as would happen on a switch with regular E_Ports. Each EX_Port presents a set of translation phantom domains representing remote fabrics, each with "attached" proxy devices representing devices on those fabrics.

Exchange The highest-level FC mechanism used for communication between N_Ports. Exchanges are composed of one or more related sequences.

Expansion Port See E_Port

Exported Device Nodes in one fabric can be exported to other fabrics through an FC Router by using LSAN zoning. A node exported from one fabric must be imported into another, as in, "The host was exported from Fabric 1 and imported into Fabric 2."

Extended Long Wavelength Laser See ELWL

F_Port Fabric port on a switch to which an N_Port such as an HBA can attach

Fabric (1) The Fibre Channel topology that occurs when N_Ports are connected to F_Ports on a switch. (2) One or more Fibre Channel switches in an ISL networked topology. (3) A collection of ISL connected Fibre Channel switches and their devices such as hosts and storage. (4) The software known as Fabric Services, which consists of the Storage Name Server, Management Server, FSPF routing, etc., etc..

Fabric Identifier See FID

Fabric Loop Port See FL_Port

Fabric Operating System See FOS

Fabric Port See F_Port

Fabric Shortest Path First See FSPF

FC Fibre Channel is the protocol of choice for building SANs. Unlike IP and Ethernet, FC was designed from the ground up to support storage devices of all types.

FC–0 Physical layer in Fibre Channel

FC–1 Fibre Channel encoding layer. This means 8b/10b with 1G, 2G, or 4G; 64b/66b is used with 10G.

FC–2 Handles framing, protocol, sequence/exchange management, and ordered sets for Fibre Channel

FC–3 Common services for Fibre Channel

FC–4 Mapping of ULPs such as SCSI or IP onto FC

FC–FC Routing Service A.k.a. FCR service. Brings hierarchical networking capabilities to Fibre Channel fabrics, allowing creation of LSANs so that devices located on

FAQ

separate fabrics can communicate without merging the fabrics. See also FCR.

FCIP Tunneling Service FCIP is a TCP/IP-based tunneling protocol that allows a transparent interconnection of geographically distributed fabrics through an IP-based network. This allows SANs to span longer distances than could be supported with native FC links. The service allows mapping an E_Port through an FCIP transparent tunnel to another FCIP gateway and switch on the other end. The port itself is both an E_Port and an FCIP port at the same time.

FC-NAT Fibre Channel Network Address Translation allows devices in fabrics to communicate even if the name spaces of those fabrics should overlap. This is similar to "hide behind" NAT in data networks.

FCP Fibre Channel Protocol is the mapping of SCSI over Fibre Channel. Probably the most popular ULP used in storage networks at the time of this writing.

FCR Fibre Channel Routers are platforms running the FC-FC Routing Service. Note that an FCR may also be running other software, so one platform could theoretically be an FCR at the same time as an FCIP tunnel or iSCSI gateway.

FCRP Fibre Channel Router Protocol is a Brocade-authored protocol that allows FCRs to perform routing between different edge fabrics, optionally across a backbone fabric.

Fibre Channel See FC

Fibre Channel Router See FCR

Fibre Channel Router Protocol See FCRP

FID Fabric IDs uniquely identify a fabric in a Meta SAN. See also Global Header, SFID, and DFID.

Field Programmable Gate Array See FPGA

Field Replaceable Unit See FRU

Flannel First generation Brocade ASIC for FC-AL to FC fabric conversion. Used in SilkWorm 1000 series in conjunction with the Stitch ASIC.

FL_Port Fabric loop port to which a loop or loop device attaches. It is the gateway to the fabric for NL_Ports on a loop.

FOS Brocade's Fabric Operating System is the software architecture that runs on most Brocade platforms. At the time of this writing, the most current Fabric OS version is 4.x. See also XPath.

FPGA Field Programmable Gate Arrays are similar to ASICs, except that their hardware logic is not fixed. It is possible to reprogram an FPGA in the field. Generally more expensive and possibly slower than an ASIC, but more flexible.

Frame Data unit containing a Start-of-Frame (SoF) delimiter, header, payload, CRC and an End-of-Frame (EoF) delimiter. The payload can be from 0 to 2112 bytes, and the CRC is 4 bytes. When operating across EX_Ports, the maximum payload is 2048 bytes.

FRU Field Replaceable Units are components that can be swapped out by users or service personnel

FSPF Fabric Shortest Path First was created by Brocade, and has since been adopted as the industry standard for routing between Fibre Channel switches within a fabric

Full Duplex Concurrent transmission and reception of data on a single link

G_Port Generic port that auto negotiates to support E_, F_, or FL_Port functionality

GBIC Gigabit Interface Controller (or Converter) is a removable optical-to-copper transceiver module that has been largely superceded by SFP media.

Generic Port See G_Port

Gigabit Interface Controller See GBIC

Global Header Information on a BB fabric that identifies devices in full Meta SAN context. It consists of the inter-fabric addressing header (IFA header) and a normal FC-FS frame header containing an SID and DID that correspond to the actual PIDs of the source and destination devices. This is transparent to switches in the BB fabric.

HBA Host Bus Adapter is an interface between a server or workstation bus and the Fibre Channel SAN

Host Bus Adapter See HBA

Hot Swappable Component that can be replaced while the system is under power

IEEE Institute of Electrical and Electronics Engineers defines standards used in the computer industry

IETF Internet Engineering Task Force is the group that develops protocols for the Internet

iFCP Internet Fibre Channel Protocol was a standard proposed to compete with FCIP for extending Fibre Channel over IP WANs. At the time of this writing, only one vendor has implemented it, while many have implemented FCIP.

IFL Inter-Fabric Links are connections between routers and edge fabrics. Similar to ISLs. Architecturally, these can be EX_Port to E_Port or EX_Port to EX_Port, though only the former is implemented at the time of this writing. See also EX-IFL and EX^2-IFL.

490

ILM Information Lifecycle Management is the concept that information can be matched to resources most appropriate for its value at any point in its lifetime

In Order Delivery See IOD

In-Band Transmission of management or service protocol over the Fibre Channel transport. FSPF and FCRP are both in-band.

Initiator Node on a Fibre Channel network that initiates transactions to tapes or disks. See also HBA.

Information Lifecycle Management See ILM

Institute of Electrical & Electronics Engineers See IEEE

Inter-Fabric Link See IFL

Internet Engineering Task Force See IETF

Internet Fibre Channel Protocol See iFCP

Internet Protocol See IP

Internet Storage Name Server See iSNS

Inter-Switch Link See ISL

IOD In Order Delivery is a parameter than when set guarantees that all frames will be delivered in order or not at all. If they cannot be delivered in order, they will be dropped by the fabric.

IP Internet Protocol is the addressing part of TCP/IP

IPsec Internet Protocol Security is a set of protocols that provide network layer security. This is often used to create VPNs. It may be used to authenticate nodes, encrypt data, or both.

iSCSI Gateway Service iSCSI is a mapping of the SCSI protocol to the IP transport. The gateway service

FAQ

projects iSCSI hosts onto the backbone fabric of a gateway switch.

ISL Inter–Switch Link is a connection between two switches using E_Ports

iSNS Internet Storage Name Server is the iSCSI equivalent of the Fibre Channel SNS.

JBOD Just a Bunch Of Disks; disks typically configured as an Arbitrated Loop within a chassis

Just a Bunch Of Disks See JBOD

L_Port Node Loop port supporting the FC_AL protocol

LAN Local Area Network; a network where transmissions are typically under 5km.

Latency The period of time that a frame is held by a network device before it is forwarded, ant the time that it sits on a cable between devices. (The latter is usually only significant on long distance links.)

LED Light Emitting Diodes. Used as status indicators.

Light Emitting Diode See LED

Logical Storage Area Network See LSAN

Loom Second-generation FC fabric ASIC. Based on a 4-chip 16-port central memory design. Used in the Silk-Worm 2000 series. All ports operate at 1Gbit FC.

LSAN Logical Storage Area Networks span between fabrics. The path between devices in an LSAN may be local to a fabric, or may cross one or more FC Routers and up to one BB fabric. Administered using zones.

LSAN Zone The mechanism by which LSANs are administered. An FC Router attached to two fabrics will "listen" for the creation of matching LSAN zones on both fabrics. If this occurs, it will create phantom domains and

FC-NAT entries as appropriate, and insert entries for them into the name servers on the fabrics. LSAN zones are compatible with standard zoning mechanisms. Their only distinguishing features are that they can only contain WWNs or WWN aliases, and that they must start with "LSAN_".

Local Area Network See LAN

Long Wavelength Laser See LWL

LUN Logical Unit Numbers are used to identify different SCSI devices or volumes that all have the same SCSI ID. In Fibre Channel, LUNs differentiate devices or volumes that share a WWN/PID address.

LWL Long Wavelength Laser transceivers may be based on 1310nm lasers. They are used for long distance native FC links. Generally these media types use SMF cables.

MAC Media Access Control is one of the sublayers in the OSI Data Link layer. It is responsible for moving packets between NICs using a shared media.

MAN Metropolitan Area Networks typically cover longer distances than LANs, but shorter distances than WANs. MANs may connect different campuses within a city, or between cities in a closely linked group. The size tends to be that of a metropolitan region: they can be tens of miles in radius, but cannot generally be more than a hundred miles or so. They tend to be provided by a single carrier from end-to-end, whereas WANs may involve different carriers.

Mean Time Between Failures See MTBF

Mean Time To Repair See MTTR

Media Access Control See MAC

Meta SAN The collection of all devices, switches, edge and BB fabrics, LSANs, and FC routers that makes

FAQ

up a physically connected but router-partitioned storage network. LSANs span between edge fabrics in a Meta SAN using FCRs, which provide both isolation and connectivity between the edges. In a data network, this might be called an "internetwork," or sometimes just "the net."

Metropolitan Area Network See MAN

MMF Multimode Fiber is a fiber-optic cabling specification that allows up to 500-meter distances between devices. MMF cables can have either 50 or 62.5 micron optical cores. Generally used with SWL media.

MTBF Mean Time Between Failures is the average time between the failure of any component in a system. This equates to how often service needs to be performed, and does not necessarily refer to how often availability is impacted.

MTTR Mean Time To Repair is the average amount of time it takes to repair a failed component.

Multicast Transmitting to a set of nodes on a fabric. More than one (which would be unicast) and less than all (which would be broadcast). This is often used in video applications.

Multimode Fiber See MMF.

Multiprotocol A device capable of using more than one protocol. For example, a router that has both Ethernet and Fibre Channel interfaces would be a multiprotocol router.

N_Port Fibre Channel host or storage port in a fabric or point-to-point connection. Stands for "Node Port."

Name Server/Service See SNS

NAS Network Attached Storage is a common name for network filesystem (usually CIFS and/or NFS) servers that are specially optimized for that task. Often the only difference between a NAS filer and e.g. a UNIX NFS server is packaging.

Network Attached Storage See NAS

Network Interface Card See NIC

NIC Network Interface Cards connect a host's bus to a network. Similar to an HBA.

NL_Port Node Loop port supporting FC_AL protocol

Node Loop Port See L_Port and NL_Port

NPIV N_Port Id Virtualization is used to aggregate multiple operating system instances behind a single N_Port connection into a fabric, e.g. with Access Gateway

OEM Original Equipment Manufacturers buy Brocade products, integrate them with other storage products such as disk drives, tape libraries, and hosts, and resell them under their own brand names.

Open Shortest Path First See OSPF

Original Equipment Manufacturer See OEM

OSPF Open Shortest Path First is a link-state router-to-router protocol for IP networks. By IP routing protocol standards, it is fairly robust.

PID Port IDs are three-byte addresses that describe the physical location of a Fibre Channel node within a fabric. PIDs are divided into a three-level hierarchy: Domain_ID, Area_ID, and Port_ID, which Brocade uses to represent switch domain, switch port, and FC-AL AL_PA respectively. A typical PID might look like this: 010f00.

Point-to-Point Dedicated Fibre Channel connection between two devices, usually a host and storage port

Port Identifier See PID

FAQ

Proxy Device Also known as an "xlate device," this is how a device looks to a fabric to which it has been exported. The PID of a proxy device will start with the xlate phantom domain that represents its fabric.

QoS Quality of Service is a somewhat generic term that can refer to a mechanism that can guarantee priority, bandwidth, latency, error rate, and similar characteristics for the network path between nodes.

Quality of Service See QoS

R_A_TOV Resource Allocation Time Out Value; maximum time a frame can be delayed in a fabric and still be delivered

RAID Redundant Array of Independent (formerly Inexpensive) Disks. A set of disks that looks like a single volume. There are several RAID levels used to solve different storage performance, scalability, and availability problems. Most are fault-tolerant and/or high performance.

RAS Reliability Availability and Serviceability collectively refers to the overall quality of a component, device, or network. Factors that influence RAS include things like the MTBF and MTTR of components, software architecture, and redundant deployment strategies.

Redundancy Having multiple occurrences of a component to maintain high availability

Redundant Array of Independent Disks See RAID

Registered State Change Notification See RSCN

Reliability Availability and Serviceability See RAS

Resource Allocation Time Out Value See RA_TOV

RETMA Radio Electronics Television Manufacturers Association in the context of storage networks is a standard specification for data center racks. A typical rackmountable network device is designed to fit into a standard 19 inch RETMA rack, and its height is usually referred to in terms of RETMA "rack units." (Each unit is about 1.75 inches for obscure historical reasons.)

Route (1) The path between two switches in a fabric in the context of FSPF. (2) The path between different fabrics in a Meta SAN in the context of FCRP.

Router Device for interconnecting at least two different networks into an internetwork.

RSCN Registered State Change Notifications allow notification to nodes if a change occurs within a fabric

SAN Storage Area Networks link computing devices to disk or tape arrays. Almost all SANs at the time of this writing are Fibre Channel fabrics.

SAN Island When a SAN has no connectivity to other SANs in an organization, it is called an island to indicate its isolation. Islands can be merged into large fabrics or interconnected via FC-FC routers.

SCR State Change Registrations are used by devices to register to receive RSCNs

SCSI Small Computer Systems Interface as originally defined was a family of protocols for transmitting large blocks up to of 15-25 meters. SCSI-2 and SCSI-3 are updated versions of this. As the direct attachment of storage moved to a network model, SCSI has been mapped to protocols such as FC and IP.

SCSI Inquiry SCSI command that generally causes a target to respond with a string telling the requester information such as its make, model, and firmware version. Used by the SNS to further identify Fibre Channel devices. The iSCSI Gateway Service inserts IP and IQN

FAQ

strings using this SNS field.

SDH See SONET/SDH

Sequence Group of related frames transmitted from one N_Port to another

Serial The transmission of data bits in sequential order over a single line

SFP Small Form-Factor Pluggable media have supplanted the GBIC as the optical-to-copper transceiver module of choice for Fibre Channel and Gigabit Ethernet equipment, though some Gigabit Ethernet devices still use GBICs.

SID Source Identifiers are three-byte Fibre Channel addresses that are used to specify the physical location – switch domain, port on the switch, and position if applicable on the loop – of the sender of a frame. A SID represented as 010100 would designate domain 1, port 1, no loop. Typically written in hex.

SilkWorm Registered trademark for the Brocade family of switches, directors, and routers. Subsequent to the acquisition of McData and the associated rebranding, this term is no longer used for currently-shipping Brocade platforms.

Simple Name Server See SNS

Single Mode Fiber See SMF

SMF Single Mode Fiber is a cabling specification that allows 10km or even greater distances. SMF cables have nine micron optical cores. Generally used with either LWL or ELWL media.

Small Computer Systems Interface See SCSI

SNS Simple (or Storage) Name Server (or Service); the service provided by a switch that stores names, addresses and attributes related to Fibre Channel objects. Also known as the directory service.

SONET/SDH Synchronous Optical Networks are used in MANs and WANs. FC can be mapped to SONET/SDH. Characterized by high performance and reliability. The analogous service is called SDH in other countries.

Source Identifier See SID

State Change Registration See SCR

Stitch First generation Brocade FC fabric ASIC. Used in the SilkWorm 1000 series in conjunction with Flannel.

Storage Device used to store data like disk or tape

Storage Area Network See SAN

Storage Subsystem See Subsystem

Storage Virtualization See Virtualization

Subsystem Synonym for storage device. Often external. On a SAN, may be shared between many compute nodes.

SWL Short Wavelength Laser transceivers based on 850nm lasers are designed to transmit short distances. This is the most common type of media.

Synchronous Digital Hierarchy See SDH

Synchronous Optical Networks See SONET/SDH

T11 ANSI committee chartered with creating standards for data movement to/from central computers

Tapestry Trademark briefly used for a Brocade family of upper-layer products, such as virtualizers.

Target Disk array or a tape port on a SAN

TCP/IP Transmission Control Protocol over Internet

Protocol is the communication method for the Internet

TCP Transmission Control Protocol is a connection-oriented protocol responsible dividing a message into packets, passing them to IP, and reassembling them into the original message at the other end. Detect errors / lost data and triggers retransmission if needed.

TCP Offload Engine See TOE

TCP Port Addresses component that allow nodes to access a *specific service* for a given address. There are many well-known ports that allow standard upper-layer protocols like HTTP to work: web servers know to listen on the same port, and web clients know to attach to that port.

TOE TCP Offload Engines are used on iSCSI NICs to accelerate performance an prevent the host's CPU from being overloaded. Even the fastest TOE NICs can achieve at best half of Fibre Channel HBA speeds, and tend to cost as much as or more than HBAs.

Topology The physical, logical, or phantom arrangement of devices in a networked configuration

Transceiver Device that converts one form of signaling to another for transmission and reception. Fiber-optic transceivers convert from optical to electrical.

Transmission Control Protocol See TCP

Tunneling Technique for making networks interact where the source and destination are on the same type of network, but there is a different network in between

UC Utility Computing is the concept that compute resources can be treated like an electric power grid

U_Port Universal Ports can operate as G/E/F/FL_Ports. All Silkworm 2xxx and higher switches use Universal Ports to allow any device to connect to any port. Selection of actual port type is automatic.

ULP Upper Level Protocols run on top of FC through the FC-4 layer. Examples include SCSI, IP, and VI.

Unicast Sending a frame between just two endpoints. Distinguished from broadcast and multicast where one transmitter has multiple receivers.

Universal Port See U_Port

Upper Level Protocol See ULP

Utility Computing See UC

Virtual Local Area Network See VLAN

Virtual Private Network See VPN

Virtual Router Redundancy Protocol See VRRP

Virtual Storage Area Network See VSAN

Virtualization The manipulation and abstraction of storage devices such as disks and tapes. Generally performs functions above and beyond those performed by traditional RAID applications. Examples include LUNs that span multiple subsystems, LUN over-provisioning where the size of a presented LUN is larger than the underlying storage capacity, and application-invisible data replication and migration.

VLAN Virtual Local Area Networks allow physical network devices to be carved into smaller logical segments. This is done in IP/Ethernet networks to prevent broadcast storms from creating instability. The analogous feature in Fibre Channel has been provided for years by zoning.

VPN Virtual Private Networks use encryption to create tunnels through public networks, so devices on one either end appear to be located on a physically isolated network.

VRRP Virtual Router Redundancy Protocol allows one router to take over the duties of another in the event of a failure. It can be thought of as a router clustering

FAQ

method. This prevents IP network nodes (like ports on the Multiprotocol Router in iSCSI or FCIP mode) from needing to support routing protocols like OSPF or RIP.

VSAN Virtual SANs are a vendor-proprietary implementation of a feature similar to zoning, though more limited. This should not be confused with LSANs. VSANs partition a network that previously allowed connectivity, whereas LSANs selectively allow connectivity where it was previously absent.

WAN Wide Area Networks span cities, states, countries, and even continents. They tend to have higher delays due to their longer distances. WANs are often used by storage networks in disaster tolerance or recovery solutions.

WAFS Tapestry Wide Area File Services is a product designed to optimize cost, manageability, reliability, and performance of storage volumes in branch offices.

Wavelength Division Multiplexer See WDM

WDM Wavelength Division Multiplexers allow multiple wavelengths to be combined on a single optical cable

Wide Area Network See WAN

World-Wide Name See WWN

WWN World-Wide Names are registered 64-bit unique identifier for nodes and ports in a fabric. A typical WWN might look like this: 10:00:00:60:69:51:0e:8b.

XPath Similar to Fabric OS, XPath is an OS architecture that runs on Brocade platforms. At the time of this writing, it is used on the AP7420 Multiprotocol Router.

xWDM See DWDM and CWDM

Zoning Standard access control mechanism for fabrics. May be defined by PID or WWN.